A GUIDE TO SECRETARIAL PRACTICE AND OFFICE PROCEDURE

B. K. Debnath

CENTRAL

A GUIDE TO
SECRETARIAL PRACTICE
AND
OFFICE PROCEDURE

[For B.Com. (Hons. & Pass) Courses of the Indian Universities and Intermediate Examinations of the Institutes of Company Secretaries / Cost & Works Accountants / Chartered Accountants of India]

B. K. Debnath

M.Com., B.A., LL.B., FICWA, FCS, CAIIB, FASM

Company Secretary, Discount and Finance House of India Ltd., Mumbai;
Chief Examiner / Papersetter & Hony. Lecturer; Project Guide / Co-author
for the Indian Institute of Bankers' Publications
'Basic Accountancy' / 'Bank Financial Management';
Formerly : Company Secretary & Asst. General Manager,
SBI Factors & Commercial Services Ltd., Mumbai;
Faculty, State Bank Training Centre, Calcutta.

NEW CENTRAL BOOK AGENCY (P) LTD.

8/1 Chintamoni Das Lane, Calcutta 700 009 (India)

A Guide to
Secretarial Practice
And
Office Procedure

First Published in India : January 1976
Second Edition in India [Thoroughly revised & enlarged] : May 1979
Third Edition [Thoroughly revised & substantially enlarged] : January 1987
Fourth Edition : July 1991
Fifth Edition : March 1994
With Additions : 1997
Sixth Edition (Revised & Enlarged) : February 2001

Published and Typesetted by	:	New Central Book Agency (P) Ltd 8/1 Chintamoni Das Lane, Calcutta 700 009
Printed by	:	New Central Book Agency (P) Ltd. [Web Offset Division] Dhulagori, Sankrail, Howrah
Cover Designer	:	Ankit 6A Atalbehari Bose Lane, Calcutta 700 011
Cover Printer	:	Biswanath Studio 3 Garanhatta Street, Calcutta 700 006
Project Manager	:	Usha Ranjan Bhowmik
Project Team	:	Prabir Ghosh, Sukumar Patra, Prabhat Jas and Subas Maitra

ISBN 81-7381-315-9

Price : Rs. 115.00 [Rupees One hundred and fifteen] only

Dedicated to

My Parents

Dr. H. K. Saharay

M.A. (Triple), M.Com., LL.B., Ph.D. (LONDON), BAR-AT-LAW
Lecturer in Commerce & Political Science
Calcutta University

FOREWORD

I have read the manuscript of "**A Guide to Secretarial Practice**" by Shri B. K. Debnath, M.Com., B.A., LL.B., AICWA, ACS, CAIIB, Instructor, Staff Training Centre, State Bank of India, Calcutta, and Examiner of various professional Institutes as well as Honorary Lecturer. Though this is his maiden venture as an author, he has made the best use of his expertise both as a qualified Secretary and a teacher in this pursuit. Despite the fact that this book is in the form of question-answer, it covers the entire syllabi of the Three Year Degree Course (B.Com.) of the Indian Universities and the Intermediate Examination of the Institute of Company Secretaries of India. The questions under each of the Chapters have been so arranged as would render the image of a good text book and help the readers a lot who propose to take up the Examination of the Institute / University. The author has dealt with the past questions of the different Examination Bodies and this, meseems, is an asset of the book. The book is really well-planned and the style in which the whole idea has been presented is very clear and lucid. I am quite sure that it will prove to be a useful book to those who desire to study "Secretarial Practice."

Sd / H. K. Saharay

Ashutosh Building
University College of Commerce
Calcutta University
Calcutta 700 012
Dated the 24th December 1975

PREFACE TO THE SIXTH EDITION

At the very outset, I sincerely and gratefully thank my readers—teachers and students alike—for their continued patronage extended to this publication over a period of two decades so much so that a thoroughly revised and substantially enlarged edition is in your hands. While revising the book, I have carefully considered the suggestions received from the readers and incorporated them at the appropriate places. In the current edition, I have tried my level best to make use of my decade-long experience as a Company Secretary in two public sector companies based in Mumbai so as to make the answers more practical. As a sequel to passing/promulgation of the Companies (Amendment) Act, 1996, the Companies (Amendment) Ordinance, 1998, as well as 1999, and the Companies (Amendment) Act, 1999, necessary changes have been made in the answers at the appropriate places. The guidelines of the Securities Exchange Board of India, wherever applicable, have also been incorporated. Twenty-six Short Questions with answers on local self-government (Panchayati Raj) have been included. Model Answers to the Calcutta University Questions have been provided up to 2000.

I would deem my labour amply rewarded if the book proves to be more reader-friendly.

I record my profound appreciation for the keen interest and strenuous efforts put in by Sarvashri Jogendranath Sen and Amitabha Sen, Directors of the publishing house, in bringing out this edition as expeditiously as possible. I am also thankful to my wife, Smt. Bani Debnath, and my son, Shri Debasish, for rendering auxiliary services.

A creative feedback and healthy criticism from the readers for further improvement of the book in the forthcoming editions will be gratefully acknowledged.

B. K. Debnath

162 Juhu Trishul
Gulmohar Cross Road No. 6
JVPD Scheme
Mumbai 400 049
Phone : 022 623-5586
Dated : 25.12.2000

PREFACE TO THE FIRST EDITION

Consequent upon passing of the Companies (Amendment) Act, 1974, and the various rules framed thereunder, the profession of the Companies Secretaries has gained a new fillip and the education and training, therefore, have achieved a paramount importance in the present era. The examination of the Institute of Company Secretaries of India and the paper on Secretarial Practice of the Indian Universities are, of late, showing more bent towards professional approach. Although there appears to have umpteen books on the subject in the market but my long and valued association with the students and a number of professional Institutes prompts me to pronounce that majority of the students need such a book as would both be comprehensive and in the form of Question-Answer to guide them in dealing with the problems set out to them, would also indicate the trend of questions set by different examination bodies and should inculcate in the students the basic knowledge a Company Secretary should possess. I was, of course, a bit hesitant in adding yet another book on the subject to the inflating number already reigning in the market but I had to eschew the initial hesitation on my present pursuit —which, incidentally, is my first venture—under the persistent pressure from Shri Provat Kumar Chatterjee, Lecturer, Bidhan Chandra College, as well as from my students and colleagues.

2. For the convenience of the examinees and to make the book more useful, questions during the period from April 1969 to April 1975 of the Institute of Company Secretaries of India (Intermediate Examination) and 1965 to 1975 of the Calcutta University (Three Year Degree Course B.Com. Examination) have been incorporated and discussed. I am grateful to the Institute and the Universities for their kind permission to use their past questions. Free and frequent reference to a number of books on 'Company Law' and 'Secretarial Practice' has been made and I am very much grateful and indebted to the respective authors. In writing this book, care has been taken to incorporate the provisions of the Companies (Amendment) Act, 1974, in proper places.

3. I feel very much indebted to Dr. H. K. Saharay, M.Com., M.A., Bar-at-Law (London), Ph.D., Lecturer in Commerce and Political Science, Calcutta University, for his kindly forewording the book. I am extremely thankful to Shri Saroj Kumar Chatterjee, M.Com., LL.B., A.C.S., an experienced Company Secretary and Advocate, for his valuable suggestions to make the book useful especially to those who propose to take up the Intermediate Examination of the Institute. I am indebted to Sarvashri Arun Ghose of Messrs. Caxton & Co., Salil Kumar Banerjee, Lecturer, Bidhan Chandra College, Ashim Pal, Aniruddha Ghosh, Dipak Sarkar, Ajoy Kumar Nath, Prabir Mukherjee, C. S. Mazumder, Amitava Mukherjee, R. Karmakar and Ranjit Kumar Chakraborty for their kind help and cooperation.

I would fail in my duty if I do not mention Shrimati Bani Debnath, my wife, but for whose affectionate toleration of the oppressive irregularities of the writer, the venture would have remained incomplete.

In fine, the manuscript could not see the light of the day if Messrs New Central Book Agency—the Publishers, and Messrs Tiger Lily Press—the printers, did not come forward with their helping hands and whole-hearted cooperation. Let my debts to both the Publishers and the Printers remain long outstanding.

Any suggestion for improvement of the book in the subsequent editions is welcome by the author.

B. K. Debnath

10 Chandra Mandal Lane
Calcutta 700 026
Dated the 17th December 1975

SYLLABI

THE UNIVERSITY OF CALCUTTA (NEW SYLLABUS)

SECRETARIAL PRACTICE AND OFFICE PROCEDURE (PASS)

GROUP I : PAPER 3

Full Marks : 100

1. **Secretarial Function :** Definition of Secretary—Importance—Essential qualifications—Secretary's functions—different classes of secretaries—their status and functions—Private Secretary—Secretary of Association or Club—Company Secretary—Secretary of Local Bodies—Secretary of Zilla Parishad, Panchayat Samity and Gram Panchayat, Municipality—educational institution—Secretary of Co-operative Society—Profession of Secretaryship : Definition—characteristics—Secretaryship as a profession in India.

2. **Company Secretary :** Definition—Statutory and other qualifications—Legal and Actual Status—Appointment—Dissmissal—Rights and Liabilities—Functions and Duties—Company Secretary's Office.

3. **Office Procedure :** (a) Secretary's Office : Definition—Functions of the Office—Routine work of the office—Importance—Secretary as Office Manager, (b) Office organisation; Importance of organisation—Steps in organising the office—Departmentation—Office and other departments—Centralisation of office services—Office systems and procedures. (c) Office accommodation : Location of Office—Office Lay-out—Open and Private offices. (d) Office environment : Lighting—Ventilation—Temperature and humidity—Interior decoration and Colour conditioning—Freedom from noise and dust—Safety—Sanitary requirements—Secrecy and security. (e) Office operations : Office correspondence—Organisation of correspondence work—Handling of correspondence—Organisation of Mail handling work. (f) Maintenance of Records : Importance—Filing and Indexing—Centralised and Departmental Filing—classification of files—Methods of filing—Methods of Indexing. (g) Office communication (internal and external)—forms, control and design—Office stationery and supplies. (h) Office machines and labour-saving devices : Objective and importance—Advantages of office mechanisation—Uses of modern office machines of various types.

4. **General Principles of Meetings :** Definition and classification—Requisites of valid meeting—Lawful and Unlawful meeting—Notice, Agenda, Quorum of meetings—Preparation for meetings—Conduct of meetings—Chairman (qualifications, powers and duties)—Motions, Resolutions and Amendments—Discussion and order of debate—Formal motions—Privilege in speeches—Voting procedure and methods—Minutes and proceedings—Reports of meetings—Press in meeting.

5. **Meetings of Local Bodies and Panchayats :** Meetings of Municipal Corporations and Municipalities—Meetings of Zilla Parishad, Panchayat Samity and Gram Panchayat—duties of Secretary.

6. **Company Meetings :** Kinds of meetings—Requisites of Notice, Agenda and Quorum—Chairman—Motions and Resolutions—Minutes—Procedure and methods of voting—Privilege—Secretary's duties regarding different kinds of company meetings.

7. **Secretarial Practice :** (a) Drafting of Notices and Circulars. (b) Drafting of Minutes and Resolutions. (c) Drafting of Reports—Types, Styles and Presentation—Routine and Special Reports. (d) Drafting of Business Letters : Functions and importance of business letters—Style of business letters—Essentials—Form and arrangement—Kinds of business letters—Drafting of business letters (singly or in a series) in matters like : (i) Offers, Quotations, and Orders. (ii) Confirmation, Execution, Refusal and Cancellation of Orders. (iii) Claims, Complaints and Adjustments. (iv) Collection. (v) Agency. (vi) Status Enquiries. (vii) Recommendations & Credit. (viii) Banking and Insurance. (ix) Company matters. (x) Letters and Representations to Government.

N. B. : To be answered in **English**. Questions are to be set in such a way as to ensure that all parts of the syllabus have to be studied. There should be one or two compulsory questions on Drafting.

C.U. B.COM. SYLLABUS (HONS.)

COMMERCE GROUP I : PAPER I

BUSINESS ORGANISATION AND SECRETARIAL PRACTICE

Full Marks : 100

A. BUSINESS ORGANISATION **(50 Marks)**

1. **Nature and Scope of Business :** Characteristics and Functions—Differences from other social organisations—interconnection—Industry, Trade and Commerce—Role of business in economic and social development—Growing complexities of business—Objectives and social responsibilities of business—relationship between Government and Business—Role of Government as Promoter, Regulator and Arbitrator of a Business.

2. **Environment of Business :** Elements of environment—Need for identifying environmental facilities and constraints—Features of business environment in India.

3. **Forms of Business**

(A) Private Sector : (i) Ownership, features, status, control and management of sole-proprietorship and partnership business (ii) Company : features—Promotion and formation of a company—Regulatory measures relating to formation—Company law administration—Private Limited, Public Limited and Government Companies—Board of Directors, Managing Director/Manager : Functions—Co-operative ventures and their characteristics.

(B) Public Sector : Objectives—Forms—Government policies and control—Performance and prospect of public enterprises in India.

(C) Joint Sector : Features—Roles—Problems—Government Policy.

4. **Business Combination :** Definition—Causes—Types and forms—combination in India—Government Policy.

5. **Small Business :** Features—Roles—Problems—Government Policy.

6. **Organised Market :** Capital Market, Money Market and Commodity Market—Nature and importance—Objectives and functions.

B. SECRETARIAL PRACTICE **(50 Marks)**

GROUP A **(30 Marks)**

1. **Secretarial Functions :** Definition and importance of secretary—Essential qualifications of secretary—Secreataries' function—Different classes of secretaries, their status, qualifications and functions (Private/Company/Co-operative Society)—Secretaryship as a profession.

2. **Secretary's Office Organisation and Operation :** Routine work of the office—Departmentation—Centralisation and decentralisation of office service—Office layout—

Office environment—Handling of Office correspondence (incoming and outgoing)—maintenance of office records—Filing and indexing—Office machines and labour-saving devices including computer.

3. **Meetings** :

(A) Principles of Meetings : Lawful and unlawful meeting—Notice, Agenda, Quorum of Meetings—Conduct of meetings—Chairman (qualifications, powers and duties)—Motions, Resolutions and Amendments—Voting Procedure—Minutes and Proceedings.

(B) Company Meetings : Kinds of meetings—Essential requisites—secretary's duties regarding different kinds of company meetings.

GROUP B **(20 Marks)**

1. **Drafting** : Notice—Circulars—Minutes and Resolutions—Reports—Business letters (matters like offers, quotations, orders—confirmation, execution, refusal and cancellation of orders, status inquiries, recommendations and credit, banking and insurance, company matters).

N. B. : Secretarial Practice portion is to be answered in ENGLISH.

THE UNIVERSITY OF BURDWAN

SECRETARIAL PRACTICE (50 Marks)—(TO BE ANSWERED IN ENGLISH)

1. **Secretarial Functions**—Definition of secretary, different types of secretary, Need for a secretary in a business firm. Status, role and functions of a company secretary; company secretary—the statutory requirements, qualifications, status, statutory and non-statutory functions.

2. **Office Organisations and Operation**—Factors to be considered for office organisations, centralised and decentralised office services, departments. Office operations, Organisation of Mail-handling work, inward and outward correspondence, Maintenance of records, Filing and Indexing, Classification of files, Methods of Indexing, office machines and labour-saving devices.

3. **Company Meetings**—Kinds of meetings, Requisites for the Notice, Agenda, Quorum, Chairman's functions and powers, Secretary's duties and responsibilities, Motions, Resolutions and Minutes, Procedures and methods of voting.

4. **Secretarial Practice**—Drafting of notices and circulars, Drafting of minutes and resolutions. Drafting of reports : types, styles and presentation—Routine and special reports. Drafting of business letters, functions. Importance of business letters, styles of business letters, essential forms and arrangement, Kinds of business letters, Drafting of business letters (singly or in a series) in letters like (i) Offers, Quotations and Ordering; (ii) Confirmation, Execution and Cancellation etc.

VIDYASAGAR UNIVERSITY

MIDNAPORE 721101

SECRETARIAL PRACTICE AND OFFICE PROCEDURE

Secretarial Function : Definition of Secretary & Importance of Secretary—Essential Qualifications—Common features of Secretary's functions—Different classes of secretaries & their functions : Private secretary, secretary of an Association, of Club, company secretary, secretary of Local Bodies—Zilla Parishad, Panchayat Samity and Gram Panchayat, secretary of Co-operative Society—Profession of secretaryship—scopes & facilities of training.

Company Secretary : Definition—Statutory & Other Qualifications—Appointment—Rights, Duties and Liabilities (Statutory and non-statutory duties—Statutory & Contractual Liabilities)—Legal & Actual Status.

Office Procedure : (i) Secretary's Office—functions of the Office—routine work of the office—importance of business enterprises—secretary as Office Manager.

(ii) Office organisation—How to organise an office—Departmentation—Relationship of the office with other departments of the enterprise, viz.—Purchasing, Sales, Accounting etc.—centralisation of office services—office systems & procedures.

(iii) Office Accommodation and environment—Location and Arrangement of office accommodation—Planning & Layout of accommodation—Furniture & Fixture, Lighting & Ventilation—temperature and humidity—freedom from noise and dust—safety and sanitary arrangements—colour conditioning.

(iv) Office operations—Handling of mail (inward and outward)—Maintenance of Records—Filing and Departmental Filing—Office communication (internal and external)—Forms—Design and Control—continuous stationery—Office stationery and supplies—control of stationery.

(v) Office machines and Labour-saving devices—Objective & Importance, Advantages of Mechanisation—uses of modern office machines for Typing, Duplicating, Accounting, Calculating, Mailing etc.

Meetings : General principles of meeting with special reference to different types of company meetings—Requisites of valid meeting—Lawful & Unlawful meetings, Notice, Agenda, and Quorum—Preparation for holding meeting—Conduct of meeting—Chairman—his powers and duties, Motions, Resolutions and Amendments—Discussion and order of debate—Privilege in speeches—Voting Procedures—Minutes and Proceedings—Recording, Circulation, Confirmation—reports and summaries.

Secretarial Practice : (a) Preparation of precis of business correspondence, reports, memoranda, etc. (b) Drafting and issue of Notices and Circulars, (c) Drafting of Minutes and reports of meetings, (d) Drafting of Reports : types, style and presentation—Routine and

Special Reports, (e) Drafting of business letters and circulars (single or in series) in matters like : (i) order, quotations and orders, (ii) confirmation, execution, refusal and cancellation of orders, (iii) Claims, Complaints and Adjustments, (iv) Collection, (v) Agency, (vi) Status Enquiries, (vii) Recommendation and Credit, (viii) Banking and Insurance, (ix) Company matters, (x) Representation to Government.

(Questions are to be set in such a way as to ensure that all parts of the syllabus have to be studied. There should be one or two compulsory questions on Drafting.)

NORTH BENGAL UNIVERSITY

SECRETARIAL PRACTICE AND OFFICE PROCEDURE (GENERAL)—100 Marks

1. **Secretary**—Definition—Importance. Types of Secretaries. Secretary of a Local Body like Municipality, Corporation, Panchayat Samiti, Zilla Parishad—Secretary of a Co-operative Society, Company Secretary—Position of a Secretary—Qualities of a successful Secretary.

2. **Secretary's Office**—Function and Importance.

3. **Office Correspondence and Records**—Organisation of correspondence department—Handling of correspondence—handling of incoming and outgoing letters.

4. **Filing and Indexing**—Filing—Object—Importance and Organisation—Classification of files. Methods of Filing—Indexing.

5. **Office Accommodation, Layout and Equipment**—Office accommodation, Office layout—Labour-savings devices.

6. **Company Secretary—Classes of Companies—Position.**

Position and status (legal & otherwise) of a Company Secretary—rights & liabilities—Incorporation of Companies. Mode of formation—Memorandum and Articles of Association and other papers to be filed—Forms to be used and Fees—Certificate of Incorporation—Registered office—Formal Appointment of the Secretary—Prospectus and Statement in lieu thereof.

Issue of Shares and Debentures : Types of Shares and Debentures—application and allotment procedure—Calls and forfeiture—Methods of Flotation of shares and debentures—Control of Capital issues—Stock Exchange Listing conditions of commencement of business—issue of Share Certificate.

(**N. B.** :—Regulations relating to the above matters and the Forms to be used in practice should be studied.)

Registers and Books to be maintained by a Company—Purpose and forms.

Meetings and Resolutions : Statutory Meeting and Report—Annual General Meeting—Extraordinary General Requisition Meeting—Ordinary and Special Resolutions and Resolutions requiring special notice—Filing of Resolution—Board Meetings. Minutes of Meetings, Statements, Returns and Documents to be filled with the Registrar of Joint Stock Companies—Annual Account and Balance Sheet—Audit and Auditor's Report. Directors' Report.

Payment of Dividends and Interest : Legal requirement—Issue of Warrants—Deduction of Income-tax—Payment of interest out of Capitals Tax—free payments to officers and others.

7. **Drafting of Reports and Commercial Correspondence** : Features—Preparation of reports. Drafting of correspondence—Advertising & Application for Employment—Letters of Recommendation, Letters of Credit, Status Enquiries, Quotations and office orders, Circulars and Circular letters, Claims, Agency, Banking letter, Insurance, Export and Import—Correspondence with Government—Correspondence of a Company Secretary—letters to editors.

BERHAMPORE UNIVERSITY (ORISSA)

Company Secretary : His duties, powers and functions.

Floating a Company : Different types of companies, Memorandum and Articles of Association, Prospectus, Certificate of Commencement.

Share Capital and Debenture

Applications, Allotment, Call and Forfeiture of shares, Different types of shares and debentures, Register of Members and Debentureholders. Share Certificate and Share Warrant; Transfer and Transmission of Shares and Debentures, Borrowing Powers.

Company Management

(i) Directors, Managing Agents, Managers, Secretaries and Treasurers, their appointment, powers and remuneration.

(ii) Meetings—Classes of Company Meetings—Constituents Meetings, Procedure at Meetings, Agenda, Voting, Poll, Proxies, Resolution and Minutes, Prevention of oppression and Mismanagement.

Accounts and Audit : Maintenance of Books and Records and Preparation and Audit of Final Accounts.

Office Procedure and Filings in Company Office—Winding-up of Companies.

INSTITUTE OF COMPANY SECRETARIES OF INDIA

(Intermediate Examination)

Company Administration : Hierarchy of Company Administration; Shareholders, Board, Managerial Personnel and Company Secretary.

Who is a Secretary?—Importance, Position, Qualities of a successful Secretary.

Secretary of a Co-operative Society, Statutory Body and Corporation.

Who may be a Company Secretary?—Statutory position; Appointment and Dismissal; Scope of Work; Powers; Rights, Duties and Responsibilities; Liabilities—Statutory and Contractual.

Role of the Company Secretary

As Statutory Officer; compliance of requirements of Companies Act, MRTP Act and other Economic and social Legislations applicable to a Company.

As Co-ordinator : Relation with the Board, Chairman, Managing Director, Line and Staff Functionaries, Shareholders, Auditors, Government and the General Public, Management—Union relations.

As Chief Administrative Officer : Administrative Duties relating to Personnel, Office Management, Service, Property, Transport Services, Security of Company's Personnel and Property, Insurance of Company Assets.

Meetings

Definition of Meeting, Kinds of Meetings, general Principles governing Meetings, Constitution and Conduct of Meetings, Rights, Restrictions and Preservation of Order at Meetings, Law of Defamation relating to Meetings, Admission of Press to Meetings, Appointment, Duties and Powers of Chairman.

Requisites of a Valid Meeting : Notice, Agenda, Quorum, Proxy, Motion, Amendment, Voting, Polling, Resolutions, Minutes, Adjournment and Postponement.

Law and Practice relating to Company Meetings

Kinds of Company Meetings : Meetings of Shareholders; Statutory, Annual General, Class, requisitioned and other General Meetings; Meetings of Debentureholders; Meetings of the Creditors; Meetings of the Board of Directors and its Committees.

Notice; Agenda; Explanatory Statement; Quorum; Chairman; Motions and Resolutions; Amendment; Resolutions requiring Special Notice; Resolution by Circulation; Proxy; Sense of the Meeting; Adjournment and Postponement; Record of the Business of the Meetings.

Work of the Company Secretary before, during and after a meeting including Directors' Report and Chairman's Speech.

UNIVERSITY OF CHENNAI

COMPANY LAW AND SECRETARIAL PRACTICE (CORE)

1. Concept of Company—Definition of Companies—Kinds of Companies—Public and Private—Holding and Subsidiaries—One-man companies—The features of various types of Companies—Differences between Private Companies and Public Companies—Conversion of Private Companies into Public Companies and vice versa.

2. Incorporation of Companies—Promotions, Pre-incorporation contracts, Role of Pro-tem Secretary—Memorandum of Association and Articles of Association—their significance and the differences between the two—Alteration—Secretary's duties pertaining to alteration—Doctrine of ultra vires—Doctrine of Indoor Management—Constructive notice—Recent amendments—Certificate of Incorporation—Prospectus—Commencement of Business—Matters relating to issue of prospectus—Liability for mis-statement in the Prospectus.

3. Members of Companies and their rights.

4. Secretary—Methods of Appointment of Rights and Liabilities of a Company Secretary—Secretary's role in the working of the Company.

5. Methods of raising finance—Shares and Debentures—Kinds of Shares—Rights attached thereto—Application and Allotment Procedure—Issue to Public of different kinds of shares—Rights attached thereto—Procedure of Allotment—Issue of allotment letters—Partial allotment—Letter of Regret—Statutory and other books of the Company—Issue of Share Certificate—the procedure for the issue of bonus shares—splitting allotment letters.

6. Calls and forfeiture—Meaning and the Procedure to be followed—Re-issue of forfeited shares.

7. Transfer and transmission—Legal effect of transfer—Certification of transfer—Formalities of transfer of shares—Forged transfer—closing the transfer books—Issue of duplicate share certificates.

8. Divisible Profits—payment of dividends—Procedures to be followed.

9. Borrowing powers—Debentures—Kinds—fixed charge and floating charge.

10. Secretary's duties connected with meeting—sending the Notice—Preparation of Agenda—Statutory Meeting and the Statutory Report—Convening the annual meeting—Annual Report—Proxy—Polling Preparation—Extraordinary meeting—Meeting of the Directors—Chairman—Duties and Rights.

11. Resolution—kinds—Ordinary and Special—Drafting—Filing of Resolutions with the Registrar.

12. Minutes—Compilation—Its essentials—Indexing of Minutes—Alteration of Minutes—Inspection of Minutes Book.

13. Management—Directors—Managing Directors—Powers and Restrictions—Managerial Remuneration—Prevention and Oppression and Mismanagement by undesirable persons—Rule in FOSS vs. HARBOTTLE—Investigation of Company's affairs—maintenance of Books of Account—Company Auditor : Appointment, qualifications, rights, duties and liability.

14. Winding-up of Companies—Meaning—different modes.

UTKAL UNIVERSITY

SECRETARIAL PRACTICE (B.Com.)

Company Secretary

His Duties, Powers and Functions.

Floating a Company : Different types of companies, memorandum and articles of association, prospectus, certificate of commencement, share capital and debenture—applications, allotment, call and forfeiture of shares—different types of shares and debentures—register of members and debentureholders—share certificate and share warrant—transfer and transmission of shares and debentures, borrowing powers.

Company Management

(i) Directors, Managing Agents, Managers, Secretaries and Treasurers : their appointment, powers and remuneration.

(ii) Meetings, classes of company, meetings, constituents of meetings, procedure at meetings, agenda, voting, poll, resolutions and minutes—prevention of oppression and mismanagement.

Accounts and Audit

Legal provisions regarding accounts and audit—Office procedure and filing in Company office—Winding-up of companies.

UTKAL UNIVERSITY

SECRETARIAL PRACTICE (I.Com.)

1. **Office Procedure :** Maintenance of different kinds of registers prescribed for use in the Secretariat—Difference between guard files and precedent register—Log Book, Diarying of Daks—Opening files—File indexing.

2. **Noting and Drafting in different forms :** Resolutions, notifications, official and semi-official letters, telegrams, memorandum, press communiques, preparation of reports and returns.

3. **Business Communications :** Parts of business letters—kinds of business letters—Letters regarding goods—General Circular, enquiries and their replies, orders and their execution and complaints and claims, Agency and consignment letters, Insurance letters, Bank letters and Joint Stock Company letters.

CONTENTS

ABBREVIATIONS USED

I. C. S. I.	—	Institute of Company Secretaries of India
C. A.	—	Institute of Chartered Accountants of India
I. C. W. A.	—	Institute of Cost & Works Accountants of India
C. U.	—	Calcutta University
B. U.	—	Burdwan University
N. B. U.	—	North Bengal University
V. U.	—	Vidyasagar University

1

INTRODUCTION— SECRETARIAL FUNCTION

Contents : Definition of Secretary—Importance—Essential qualifications—Secretary's functions—Different classes of secretaries—their status and functions—Private Secretary—Secretary of Association or Club—Company Secretary—Secretary of Local Bodies—Secretary of a Zilla Parishad, Panchayat Samiti and Gram Panchayat, Municipality—Educational institution—Secretary of Co-operative Society—Profession of Secretaryship : Definition—Characteristics—Secretaryship as a profession in India.

Q. 1. Explain the term "Secretary". Name four classes of Secretaries and enumerate their respective functions. (C.U. 1998, 1990, 1984, 1966, 1964)

Ans. : The term "Secretary" is derived from the Latin word *secretarius* which implies a confidential writer or officer. In earlier days, the Secretary's principal function was restricted to handling correspondence of the king. But, with the passage of time, the Secretary has gained in importance and, consequently, he is now deemed to be an officer who is entrusted with confidential matters and he handles *correspondence, keeps records* and *transacts other business*.

The concept of secretary is a very old one and it has been very aptly said that a busy executive or a man of action needs the services of such a helping hand. In ancient Rome, the Secretary (*scribae*) occupied a key position and was responsible for the functions of the State. More often than not, he was required to handle secret matters of the State.

With the growing constitutional and functional changes in the various organisations and institutions, the position of the Secretary also has undergone changes. But these changes have not, in any way, brought about any positional change to his detriment. Till now he holds a very honourable position as his counterpart in the older days. With the passage of time, he is shouldering enormous responsibility and he has proved his stay in any organisation as indispensable. In the spheres of trade, commerce and industry, he plays a very important role. His role is like that of a playback singer and, as such, he mostly stays behind the screen.

Types of Secretaries

There are various types of secretaries in the modern complex society and the position and functions of each of these types are discussed next.

1. **Private Secretary** : Busy men in the society do have very little time to spare for the routine and unimportant work. For example, top executives, ministers, legislators, authors, advocates, doctors, artists, filmstars, etc. have to employ private secretaries. A private secretary looks after the personal and day-to-day routine work of his employer and thus keeps him free from the pressure of routine work and enables him to devote his time to such work which demands his personal attention and can be done by him alone.

2. **Secretary of a Government Department** : In the USA and England, the minister presiding over a government department is officially designated as Secretary. In India, the heads of Government Departments are known as Secretaries. The functions of such a Secretary can be summed up as under :

(a) the policies formulated by the minister relating to his department are translated into practice;

(b) to liaise between the concerned minister and the machinery of the Government;

(c) to keep the minister posted with the general feelings of the public.

3. **Secretary of an Embassy** : Most of the civilized countries have their embassies, missions or legations in other countries whose functions are both complex and varied in nature. The head of such an office is known to be the ambassador or envoy who looks after the political interest of his country. In the proper and efficient discharge of his duties, he is assisted by a person who is called the Secretary. During the period of absence of the ambassador or envoy, the Secretary is called upon and empowered to act on behalf of the ambassador or envoy. His functions can be summed up as under :

(a) obtaining instructions from his country and conveying them to the ambassador;

(b) keeping records of day-to-day work of the ambassador;

(c) preparation of reports, communiques, etc. to be issued by the ambassador or envoy to different authorities;

(d) to liaise between the Government Departments of the country where he is posted and his own government;

(e) to look after the interest of the people of the country where he is posted.

4. **Secretary of a Trade Union, Association or Club** : The Secretary of a Trade Union is to look after the interests of his members. He is the spokesman of the members and negotiates with the management with regard to the various grievances of the members. He is the man who keeps liaison between the members and the management. His duties are administrative, advisory and negotiatory in nature. Social and cultural organisations, sports clubs, chambers of commerce, etc. often have secretaries for the purpose of promoting some common cause. These organisations may appoint a paid Secretary or a honorary Secretary. The Secretary is to implement the decisions taken by the Executive or Managing Committee at the meetings.

5. **Secretary of Local Bodies** : Municipalities, Corporations, Panchayats, etc. are required to appoint a Secretary either because of necessity or for the purpose of complying with

the provisions of any enactment. The duties of such a Secretary may be laid down by the relevant statute. Otherwise, his primary functions would be :

(a) to implement the decisions of the authorities;

(b) to liaise between the staff and the authorities;

(c) to co-ordinate, control and supervise the activities of the office;

(d) to maintain various records;

(e) to issue notices of different meetings, help the chairman in the conduct of meetings and prepare minutes of various meetings;

(f) to prepare accounts and forecasts or estimates/budgets.

His functions are partly executive and partly administrative in nature.

The terms Gram Panchayat Secretary, Panchayat Samiti Secretary, Zilla Parishad Secretary and Municipal Secretary have been defined in Chapter 8.

6. **Secretary of a Co-operative Society** : A co-operative society may be formed by voluntary membership for the purpose of production, distribution or finance. Management of the society is vested in a small group of elected honorary members collectively known as the Managing Committee. According to the provisions of the Bengal Co-operative Societies Rules, a Secretary has been defined as "a person who, subject to the control of the Managing Committee, has the management of affairs of a co-operative society and includes a member of the managing committee or any other person discharging the duties of a secretary by whatever name called and whether under a contract of service or not." It can be deduced from the definition that a Secretary may be elected by the Managing Committee from amongst the members to work on an honorary basis or he may be selected from outside to work as a salaried employee. Besides supervision of the routine activities, he conducts meetings of the Managing Committee and general members of the society and endeavours to give the decisions of the meetings a concrete shape.

7. **Company Secretary** : Amongst the various types of Secretaries, this class holds by far the most important position. In Joint Stock Companies, though the shareholders are the real owners of the company, yet it is not possible on their part to manage the affairs of the company inasmuch as they remain scattered all over the country. They, therefore, elect a number of directors and the management of the company is vested in the Board of Directors. The aloofness of the Board of Directors—who are the real managers of the company—from the affairs of day-to-day management of the company has perhaps resulted in the creation of the Company Secretary. It may, therefore, be said that this class of secretaries is the creation of necessity and law.

Gone are the days when M. R. Esher opined in 1887—in the case of Barnett Hoares & Co. vs. the South London Tramways Co.—that "a Secretary is a mere servant; his position is that he has to do what he is told to do, and no person can assume that he has any authority to represent anything at all." The existence of Company Secretary got recognition for the first time in India as a sequel to passing of the Companies Act, 1956. Now a Company Secretary is a principal officer of the Company and he has "ostensible authority to sign contracts on behalf of the Company." According to the provision of Section 2(45) of the Companies (Amendment) Act of 1988 : "Secretary means a Company Secretary within the meaning of Section 2(1) (c) of the Company Secretaries Act, 1980, and includes any other individual possessing the prescribed qualifications, appointed to perform the duties which may be performed by a Secretary under the Act and any other purely ministerial or administrative duties." It may, therefore, be deduced from the above definition that he is a principal officer of the company who acts under the control of the Board of Directors. Able assistance is rendered by him to the Board in various matters. The decisions taken by the Board of Directors are implemented by the Secretary. He is the connecting link between the employees of the company and the Board of Directors.

Q. 2. Discuss the usefulness and functions of a Private Secretary to the Chief Executive of a large company. (V. U. 1988; C. U. 1974)

Or, What is the role of a Private Secretary? Enumerate the principal functions performed by him. (C. U. 1998, 1996, 1994, 1990, 1982, 1968; B. U. 1964)

Ans. : A Private Secretary is a person employed by the busy men of society to look after their personal and day-to-day routine work. The employers are, therefore, relieved from the burden of stereotyped and unimportant as well as complicated matters. For example, top executives, ministers, legislators, authors, advocates, filmstars, etc. employ Private Secretary. The Secretary will have to deal with confidential matters very secretly and he should endeavour his best to win the confidence of his employer.

A Private Secretary should have the following qualifications :

(a) **Personality** : He should be a man of personality and of amiable nature.

(b) **Academic attainment** : The level of educational attainment required of him largely depends on the work to be performed by him. He should possess a good knowledge of English, elementary accounts and commercial correspondence.

(c) **Loyalty** : He must be fully loyal to his employer. Diffusion of his own interest in the employer is expected of him.

(d) **Understanding** : He should be able portray a clear picture of the liking for and the aversion to various things of his employer.

(e) **Regularity and Punctuality** : He should be very regular and punctual with regard to his work.

(f) **Tactfulness** : He must be shrewdly tactful in handling matters and dealing with the parties of his employer. In the absence of his employer, he is required to tackle his employer's work. He must be of strong common sense and should exercise his discretion as the circumstances warrant.

(g) **Knowledge of Shorthand and Typewriting etc.** : Though this is not a 'must' for a Private Secretary, yet this counts much. He should have knowledge of e-mail, Internet, Personal Computer, Office Computer, Office equipments and machines etc.

Functions of a Private Secretary

The functions of a Private Secretary largely depend on his employer. For example, a Private Secretary of a top business executive will have work different from that of the Private Secretary of a filmstar. While the duties and functions of other types of secretaries are determined by the respective statutes, the functions of a Private Secretary are fully dependent on the desire and requirements of his employer. His functions, in general, include the following :

(a) **Handling routine correspondence :** Daily incoming mail is opened by him and letters which are important and need the attention of his employer are placed before him. The other routine letters, such as supplying any information, replying to an invitation, extending congratulation, etc. are handled by him. He also sends suitable reminders on behalf of his employer.

(b) **Maintaining books and records :** He may be required to maintain various books of account and registers according to the need of his employer. He looks after filing and indexing also.

(c) **According reception :** He welcomes the persons wishing an interview with his employer. After discussions with the visitors, he disposes some of the callers whose queries are satisfactorily replied to by him. He arranges interviews with his employer for the remaining visitors. In this connection, he places the relevant papers before his boss so as to enable him to take quick decisions. Telephone calls, both incoming and outgoing, are initially attended by him. The calls which require consideration of his employer are transferred to him.

(d) **Arranging daily programme of employer :** A Private Secretary is required to remind his employer of his daily programme. He prepares the notes for various meetings to be attended to or presided over by his employer and hands over these notes for ready reference. Sometimes he is required to accompany his master to the meetings and he has to make notes of the proceedings of the meetings. He has to keep or maintain a diary for his master or employer.

(e) **Acting as a Stenographer :** As said earlier, a Private Secretary should preferably be a good shorthand-typist. While giving dictation to the Private Secretary, the employer may miss or overlook a few points or, in a hurry, he may even commit some mistakes. The Private Secretary may bring these facts to the notice of his employer. Alternatively, while typing out the dictation, he makes the necessary corrections and places the final letters for the signature of his employer. He is authorised to make these changes and, in extreme cases, he may even re-write the dictation of his employer. He should be very tactful and handle these cases in such a way that his boss is not offended. That is why a "Private Secretary" is more than a good shorthand-typist. A shorthand-typist is required to transcribe the dictation as it is given by his employer. He has no authority to effect any changes in the dictation given by his boss even though there are mistakes in this dictation.

(f) **Miscellaneous functions**

(i) to maintain the employer's personal accounts;

(ii) to arrange for filing of the tax returns of the employer at the appropriate time;

(iii) to maintain records of various investments and incomes or dividends to be derived therefrom;

(iv) to arrange for payment of subscriptions to various associations, clubs, etc.;

(v) to arrange for payment of bills in respect of telephone, gas, electric, etc.;

(vi) to arrange for entertainments.

Q. 3. Enumerate the routine functions of a private secretary to a top executive or a renowned industrialist.

Ans. : A private secretary to a top executive or a renowned industrialist has to perform varieties of work which includes daily routine work. He remains so busy with other work of his employer that it is quite likely that he may forget to attend to one or a few items of the routine work. An efficient private secretary, therefore, prepares a routine of his own to tackle such a situation. To perform the duties efficiently and tactfully, the private secretary should take the help of memory aids like diaries, note-books etc. In such cases, a personal computer is of immense help to him. His principal routine duties may be enumerated below :

(i) He should be punctual in attendance and reach office before his employer.

(ii) He must see to it that the chamber of his employer is ready in all respects so that his boss can start working as soon as he enters his chamber.

(iii) He should check up his own diary as well as his employer's and remind him about the day's appointments.

(iv) He should open the incoming mail and place the papers on the table of his boss, with remarks, if necessary.

(v) He should maintain various books/registers and books of account on behalf of his boss.

(vi) He should properly maintain the filing and indexing systems.

(vii) He has to take dictations from his boss for transcription. After the letters or notes are typed, he has to place them before his employer for his perusal and signature.

(viii) He has to look after the outgoing mail also.

(ix) He must know how to operate the various office machines and equipment.

(x) He should arrange for deposit of cash/cheque or withdrawal of cash and maintain the bank account on behalf of his boss.

(xi) He should attend the telephone calls and pass on those to his boss which need his attention.

(xii) He has to welcome the visitors/callers and arrange interview with his employer in deserving cases only.

(xiii) He should leave office after his boss and see that all the files, papers, books, etc. have been kept back in the almirahs/cabinets—properly locked.

(xiv) He must go through the diaries of his boss as well as his and note the next day's appointments and, if necessary, prepare himself and his boss for them.

Q. 4. What is the difference between the status of a Private Secretary and a Personal Assistant? **(C. U. 1999, 1996, 1989, 1981)**

Ans. : The status of a private secretary is high as compared to the personal assistant. A personal assistant is ordinarily a stenographer attached to a particular executive. His functions are purely of a routine nature and he takes down the dictation of his boss for transcription. He has no authority to work on behalf of his boss. A private secretary is a personal assistant plus something much more. He looks after the personal and day-to-day routine work of his employer and, when his boss is away, he has to tackle the situation.

Q. 5. Distinguish between the status/position of a Private Secretary and a Shorthand Typist.

Ans. : A busy person of the society employs a private secretary to look after his personal and day-to-day routine work. The Secretary has to represent his boss as and when needed. He fixes up the appointments of his boss. He takes down dictations from his boss and places the typed out letters and notes for signature of his boss. In case there is a mistake or some points are missing in the dictations, he can make the necessary corrections or incorporate the missing points at the time of typing. However, he should be intelligent and tactful to tackle such a situation.

A shorthand-typist, on the other hand, is a routine worker whose duty is confined to taking dictations from his boss and typing out the dictated matters without any change—even though there are some mistakes or some points left out.

It will be observed from the above that a private secretary has to perform a number of duties, one of which is taking down dictations and transcribing them. Here lies the similarity between the work of a private secretary and a stenographer. But a private secretary is not a mere routine worker inasmuch as he has to perform many other duties. As such, the status/position of a private secretary is high as compared to the shorthand-typist.

Q. 6. What is the difference in status of a Personal Assistant, Confidential Assistant and Private Secretary?

Ans. : Though each of the three persons mentioned in the question renders his services to a particular person, there is difference in their respective status. A Personal Assistant, popularly known as P.A., is practically a routine steno-typist/clerk attached to a particular officer. A Confidential Assistant, popularly known as C.A., handles some confidential files and papers of his 'boss' besides doing his routine work of clerk/steno-typist. So he holds a better position as compared to the Personal Assistant. A Private Secretary has to represent his 'boss' very often and he performs the private and confidential work of his employer. Ordinarily, some authority is delegated to him by his boss. So, among the three, the Private Secretary enjoys the highest status.

Q. 7. Distinguish between Private Secretary and Company Secretary.

Private Secretary	Company Secretary
(i) A Private Secretary is a person appointed by men of eminence like senior office executives, businessmen, filmstars etc. to perform their personal and confidential work.	(i) A Company Secretary is appointed by a company to perform the duties which are required to be performed by him under the provisions of the Companies Act and any other enactments.
(ii) Appointment of a Private Secretary is not compulsory.	(ii) Appointment of a Company Secretary is compulsory for companies having paid-up capital of not less than Rs. 50 lakhs.
(iii) No statutory qualification is necessary for the appointment of a Private Secretary.	(iii) He has to be a member of the Institute of Company Secretaries of India in case he is appointed in a company having paid-up capital of not less than Rs. 50 lakhs. In case of other companies, he may have any one or more of the qualifications—A.C.A., A.I.C.W.A., M.B.A., M.Com., LL.B, Pass in Intermediate Examination of the I.C.S.I.
(iv) He is responsible to his master only.	(iv) He is responsible for proper discharge of his statutory duties and duties to shareholders.
(v) He is an agent of his principal (i.e., the boss or master).	(v) He is one of the principal officers of the company.

Q. 8. State the main functions of the Secretary of a Co-operative Society. Does he take part in the management of the Society?

(C. U. 1998, 1996, 1994, 1989, 1987, 1976, 1973, 1970, 1965)

Ans. : According to the provisions of the Bengal Co-operative Societies Rules, a Secretary is "a person who, subject to the control of the managing committee, has the management of the affairs of a Co-operative Society and includes a member of a managing committee or any other person discharging the duties of a Secretary by whatever name called and whether under a contract of service or not." He is the principal executive officer of the Society. Though his main function is to manage the affairs of the Society, he is to work under the advice, direction and control of the managing committee.

The functions of the Secretary of a Co-operative Society may be summed up as under :

(a) **Routine activities :** He is to conduct and supervise the routine activities which include correspondence, maintenance of records, registers and accounts, receipts and payments of cash, preparation and submission of statements and returns to the Registrar of Co-operative Societies.

(b) **Relating to meetings :** He is to look after all the activities before, at, and after the meetings, e.g., issuance of notices and agenda, keeping records of attendance, recording resolutions and proceedings of the meetings, preparation and circulation of the minutes of the meetings and helping the chairman to successfully conduct the meetings.

(c) **Agent of the Managing Committee :** He plays the role of an agent of the managing committee in so far as his dealings with the members, employees and public are concerned. He is the spokesman of the managing committee.

(d) **Advisory function :** He renders very useful service to the managing committee with regard to legal and other affairs of the Society.

The model bye-laws annexed to the Act contain a number of powers and duties of a Secretary and these indicate the functions and responsibilities of a Secretary.

These are

(i) to control the staff of the Society;

(ii) to institute, defend and conduct legal proceedings in Law Courts and other places;

(iii) to call the general meetings and the meetings of the managing committee, prepare agenda, issue notices, draft circulars, etc. of the society and attend meetings;

(iv) to prepare and place before the managing committee the budget estimates for the next year;

(v) to receive all moneys on behalf of the Society, issue receipts therefor and deposit all moneys and other properties in such a bank as the managing committee may direct;

(vi) to pay all expenses of the Society for which the Secretary is authorised;

(vii) to maintain proper books of account to show the working of the Society.

(viii) to prepare annual accounts for placing before the Auditors of the Society.

(ix) to advise the Managing Committee in legal and other matters.

(x) to act as the mouthpiece of the Managing Committee with the members, public and staff.

The Secretary of a Co-operative Society is the chief executive officer and he takes part in the management of the Society. He acts under the direction and control of the managing committee and he is liable to the committee for proper and systematic management of the Society.

Thus, the Secretary of a Co-operative Society has mainly to act in the following capacities—as an executive, as an adviser to the management and as an agent or a liaison officer.

Q. 9. Give an outline of the steps that the Secretary should take for holding the annual general meeting of a Co-operative Credit Society. (C. U. 1977)

Ans. : The Secretary should take the following steps for holding the annual general meeting of a Co-operative Credit Society :

(a) Meeting of the Managing Committee has to be convened.

(b) Report of the Managing Committee in respect of the activities of the Society during the last year has to be prepared.

(c) Audit of the last year's accounts of the Society has to be completed.

(d) Preparation of the budget/estimate for the next year and placement thereof to the Managing Committee for consideration.

(e) Amendments of the bye-laws of the Society, if so required, have to be processed.

(f) Preparation of the agenda for the meeting in consultation with the Chairman.

(g) Serving notice on those who are entitled to attend the meeting.

(h) Arrangements for accommodation, reception and entertainment of the members have to be made.

(i) Minutes of the last annual general meeting should be kept ready for signature of the Chairman in the meeting.

Q. 10. Is there any distinction between an elected Secretary and appointed Secretary in a Co-operative Society? (C. U. 1987)

Ans. : The Secretary of a Co-operative Society may be either elected by its general members or appointed by its Board of Directors. An elected Secretary is a member of the society and, usually, the post is honorary. An appointed Secretary, on the other hand, is an outsider and he is a salaried employee of the society.

2

JOINT STOCK COMPANIES, DIRECTORS AND COMPANY SECRETARY

[**Contents** : Company—Definition—Types—Distinction between Private & Public Companies—Steps for conversion of a Private Company to a Public Company & vice versa—Memorandum of Association—Definition, Contents, Alteration—Articles of Association—Definition, Contents, Alteration—Prospectus—Appointment, Role, Rights, Duties, Liabilities—Definition, Qualifications, Appointment, Role, Rights, Duties, Liabilities—Difference between Occupation & Profession—Company Formation & Secretary—Stock Exchange Enlistment—Procedure for Public Issue—Reduction of Share Capital—Legal Position of Secretary—Allotment of Shares—Share Certificate—Calls—Forfeiture of Shares—Re-issue of Forfeited Shares—Transfer & Transmission of Shares—Bonus Shares—Rights Shares—Dividend—Share, Stock, Share Scrip, Share Warrant, Share Certificate, Debenture, Common Seal, Sweat Equity shares, Dividend Warrant—Member of a Company.]

Q. 1. Define a Company, describe its characteristics and explain the different kinds of companies which are found in India.

Ans. : According to Sec. 3(1) (i) of the Companies Act, 1956, "Company" means a company formed and registered under this Act or an existing company. A company is an association of persons formed for some common purpose and registered according to law relating to the companies. It is an artificial person. Though it is invisible and intangible, it has got existence in the eyes of law. A company signifies its assent by means of a common seal.

The principal characteristics of a company are

(i) it is a voluntary association of persons;

(ii) it is a creation of law and it has perpetual succession;

(iii) it is incorporated (i.e., registered) for some specific object(s);

(iv) it is a legal entity;

(v) it acts through its common seal;

(vi) its management is separate from its ownership.

Various Types of Companies

1. **Statutory Company :** A statutory company, as the name suggests, is formed by a special statute or act passed by the Central or State Legislature. A statutory company is a

limited liability company but it is exempted from using the word limited at the end of its name. Examples of statutory companies are Reserve Bank of India, State Bank of India, Life Insurance Corporation of India, Unit Trust of India, etc.

2. **Registered Company :** A registered company is formed under the provisions of the Companies Act, 1956, or any of the earlier enactments. A registered company may be subdivided into the following classes :

(a) **Company limited by shares :** In this type, the liability of the members, who subscribe to the share capital of the company, is restricted to the face value of the shares. Most of the Indian companies belong to this category.

(b) **Company limited by guarantee :** In this type, the Memorandum of Association may provide that, in the event of winding-up of the company, members have to pay a fixed amount. This amount is known as guarantee. This type of company may be with or without share capital. The liability of the members is restricted to the face value of the share (where there is share capital) and the guarantee.

(c) **Unlimited Company :** Each of the members of this type of company is liable proportionately to his interest for the debts of the company. The members of the company cannot be sued individually. The liability of the members ceases on expiry of one year from the date of cessation of their membership.

3. **Chartered Company :** A company incorporated under a special charter by the King or Sovereign is known as a chartered company.

In the seventeenth century, a number of companies were incorporated in the UK by the Royal Charter in England. Examples are : East India Company, Bank of England, etc. In India, after independence, this type of company is treated as foreign company.

4. **Government Company :** Sec. 617 of the Companies Act states that "A Government Company is one in which not less than 51% of the paid-up share capital is held by the Central Government and/or any State Government or Governments or by any two or more of them together. The subsidiary of such a company is also a Government Company." Examples are : Hindusthan Machine Tools Limited, Heavy Engineering Corporation Ltd., Fertilizer Corporation of India Ltd., etc.

5. **Foreign Company :** The provisions of Sections 591 to 608 of the Companies Act govern foreign companies. Companies falling under the following two classes are called foreign companies :

(a) Companies incorporated outside India which, after the commencement of the Companies Act of 1956, established a place of business within India.

(b) Companies incorporated outside India which, after the commencement of the Companies Act of 1956, established a place of business within India and continue to have the same at the commencement of the Act.

Public Limited and Private Limited Companies

Registered companies (i.e., companies limited by shares, companies limited by guarantee and unlimited companies and foreign companies may again be either public limited or private limited.

According to Sec.3(1)(iii), a "Private Company" means a company which, by its articles

(a) restricts the right to transfer its shares, if any;

(b) limits the number of its members (excluding its employees) to fifty, and

(c) prohibits any invitation to the public to subscribe for any shares in, or debentures of, the company.

Sec. 3(1)(iv) states that "Public Company" means a company which is not a private company.

Q. 2. Write a short note on the deemed public limited companies, under Section 43A of the Companies Act, 1956, as amended by the Amendment Act of 1988.

Ans. : Under Section 43A of the Companies Act, 1956, as amended in 1988, a private company will become a deemed public company in the following cases :

1. When not less than 25% of the paid-up share capital of the private company is held by one or more bodies corporate (i.e., Private and/or Public Company). [Section 43-A(1)]

2. When the annual average turnover (inclusive of sales tax and excise duty) is not less than Rs. 25 crores, vide GSR No. 130(E) dated 23.2.99. [Section 43A(1-A)]

3. When a Private Company holds not less than 25% of the paid-up share capital of a Public Company. [Section 43-A(1B)]

4. When a Private Company accepts, after an invitation is made by an advertisement, or renews deposits from the public. [Section 43A(1C)]

Within a period of three months from the date on which a private company becomes a deemed public company, the company shall inform the Registrar that it has become a public company and the Registrar will thereupon delete the word "Private" before the word "Limited" in the name of the company upon the register and shall also make necessary alterations in the Certificate of Incorporation issued to the company and in its Memorandum of Association. A Private Company which has become a deemed public company shall continue to be public company until it has, with the approval of the Central Government and in accordance with the provisions of this Act, again become a private company. Every private company having share capital shall file with the Registrar along with the annual return a certificate signed by both the signatories of the return stating that since the date of Annual General Meeting/date of incorporation, it did not hold 25% or more of the paid-up share capital of one or more public companies.

A deemed public company is not a public company for all purposes. Its Articles of Association must continue to include provisions relating to restrictions on transfer of shares, limitation on the number of its members to 50, and invitation to the public to subscribe for its shares. It is, therefore, obvious that the expression 'Public Company' in Section 3(1)(iv) cannot be equated with a 'Private Company' which has become a deemed public company. It may be mentioned in this context that a deemed public company cannot be incorporated and registered under the Companies Act as such but it becomes so by operation of law. Sections 174 and 252 —which deal with quorum for meetings and minimum number of directors — respectively recognise expressly the separate existence of public companies which have become such under Section 43A. Such companies are required to comply with all the provisions of the Companies Act except those expressly excluded.

The provisions of Section 44 as regards filing of a statement in lieu of prospectus do not apply to a deemed public company. A deemed public company is required to submit along with its annual return the following certificates to the Registrar of Companies :

(i) As regards any body corporate holding 25% of its paid-up share capital;

(ii) As to its average annual turnover, and;

(iii) That it did not accept or renew deposits from public.

Q. 3. Define the terms (i) Holding Company and Subsidiary Company and (ii) Closely-owned and Widely-owned company.

Ans. : (i) Section 4 of the Companies Act, 1956, has defined the terms 'Holding Company' and 'Subsidiary Company'. A holding company is one which directly or indirectly holds more than 50% of the equity share capital or controls the composition of the Board of Directors of the other company. It is the holding company which controls the affairs of its subsidiary company or companies. The company whose shares are so held by another company or whose composition of the Board of Directors is so controlled by a holding company is known as subsidiary company. The subsidiary of a subsidiary company is automatically a subsidiary of the holding company.

(ii) A closely-owned company is one which offers its shares to a limited number of persons mostly known to each other and are friends and relatives. There is no distinct separation of ownership and control. A widely-owned company, as the name suggests, offers its shares to the people at large scattered all over the country. In such a company, there is wide (i.e., distinct) separation between management and control.

Q. 4. Distinguish between a public limited and a private limited company. What are the privileges enjoyed by a private limited company?

Ans. : Prior to the enactment of the Companies Act, 1913, there was no difference between a public limited and a private limited company. The points of difference between the two are summed up as follows under suitable headings :

1. **Number of Members :** The minimum and maximum numbers of members in case of a private company are two and fifty whereas, in case of a public company, the numbers are seven and unlimited, respectively.

2. **Transfer of Shares :** There is restriction on the transfer of shares of a private company but no such restriction applies to a public company.

3. **Public Subscription :** A private company cannot offer its shares for public subscription whereas a public company is authorised to do so.

4. **Using the word 'Limited'** : A public company must use the word 'Limited' as a part of its name and a private company is to add the words 'Private Limited' at the end of its name.

5. **Privileges** : A private company enjoys certain special privileges which a public company cannot.

Privileges and Exemptions of Private Companies

The privileges and exemptions of the private companies are, briefly, the following :

1. The minimum number of persons which is required to form a private company is two only.

2. A private company need not file a prospectus or a statement in lieu of prospectus. [Section 70(3)]

3. A private company can commence business and exercise borrowing powers just after its incorporation. [Section 149(7)]

4. Restrictions with regard to further issue of share capital are not applicable to a private company. [Section 81(3)(1)]

5. A private company need not hold the statutory meeting or file the statutory report. [Section 165(10)].

6. As sequel to passing of the Act of 1956, a private company must have two directors whereas a public company must have at least three directors. [Section 252(2)]

7. The rules regarding "minimum subscription" do not apply to a private company.

8. Unless the Articles of Association provide for a larger number, two members personally present form the quorum of a meeting of a private company.

9. The filing of consent in writing is not necessary from the directors of a private company.

10. A separate resolution for appointment of each director is not required individually.

11. Rules as to qualification shares for directors are not applicable to a private company. [Section 265(5)]

12. While ascertaining the number of directorship of public companies (maximum being twenty), directorship of private company is not taken into account.

13. An interested director can be present, take part in the discussion and vote at the meeting of the Board of Directors of a private company.

14. A director of a private company holding office for life before 1st April 1952, cannot be removed as required under Section 284 of the Companies Act.

15. Restrictions with regard to managerial remuneration do not apply to a private company.

Q. 5. How can a private company be converted into a public company? Enumerate the steps to be taken in this regard. Draft a suitable resolution to be passed in connection with the conversion.

Ans. : The following steps are required to be taken to convert a private company into a public company :

(a) A Board meeting shall be convened to finalise the plan of conversion and pass the necessary resolution.

(b) A new set of Articles of Association has to be prepared.

(c) An Extraordinary General Meeting has to be convened and due notice therefor issued to members together with explanatory statement.

(d) An announcement regarding meeting has to be made through the press.

(e) Necessary resolutions (*ordinary* or *special*) have to be passed at the meeting.

(f) A prospectus or a statement in lieu of prospectus has to be filed with the Registrar of Companies.

(g) Copies of special resolutions have to be filed with the Registrar within 30 days from the date of passing of the resolutions.

A Specimen Resolution

"Resolved that Messrs. O' Neil & Co. Pvt. Ltd. (Private Company) be and is hereby converted into Messrs. O' Neil & Co. Ltd. (Public Company) and accordingly Memorandum and Articles of Association of the Company be and are suitably altered."

Q. 6. Enumerate the steps to be taken to convert a public limited company to a private company and the resolution to be passed in this regard.

Ans. : The following steps are required to be taken for converting a public company into a private company :

(a) A Board meeting has to be convened for consideration and approval of the proposed plan of conversion.

(b) A resolution to this effect is to be passed at the Board meeting.

(c) Notice of Extraordinary General Meeting together with the relative explanatory statement is to be sent well in advance.

(d) Special resolutions are to be passed at the Extraordinary General Meeting for conversion of the company and altering the Articles of Association.

(e) Approval of the Central Government has to be obtained for alteration of the Articles. [Section 31(1)]

(f) Copies of special resolutions have to be filed with the Registrar within 30 days from the date of the meeting.

(g) Approval of the Central Government for conversion has to be obtained.

(h) A printed copy of the new/altered Articles of Association of the company together with a copy of the Government's letter of approval is to be filed with the Registrar of Companies within 30 days. [Section 31(2A)]

A Specimen Resolution

"Resolved that Messrs. Bani & Co. Ltd. (Public Company) be and is hereby converted

into Mesrs. Bani & Co. Private Ltd. (Private Company) and the necessary steps be taken to alter the Memorandum and Articles of Association accordingly."

Q. 7. Define a Memorandum of Association and state what are its contents. Can the Memorandum be altered?

Ans. : Section 2(28) of the Companies Act states that a "memorandum means the Memorandum of Association of a Company as originally framed or as altered from time to time in pursuance of any previous Company law or of this Act". The Memorandum of Association is a formal and essential document of a registered company which contains the fundamental rules regarding the constitution and activities of a company.

Contents of Memorandum : Sec. 13 provides that a memorandum should contain the following particulars :

1. The name of the company with the word 'Limited', if it is a public company, and with the words 'Private Limited', if it is a private company.

2. The name of the State wherein the registered office of the company is situated.

3. The object of the company stating separately

(i) The main objects and objects incidental and ancillary to the main objects, and

(ii) other objects.

4. The State or States where the objects of the company extend (other than a trading corporation).

5. In the case of a company limited by shares or guarantee, it should contain a statement which indicates that the liability of the members is limited.

6. The amount of capital and division thereof into shares of a fixed amount (in the case of a company having a share capital).

7. The Association clause and subscription : In this declaration, the subscribers sign their names and their respective addresses, occupations, number of shares agreed to be taken by them, etc.

Alteration of the Memorandum : Sec. 16 provides that a company shall not alter the conditions contained in its memorandum except in the cases, in the manner and to the extent provided by the Act. The rules regarding alteration of the different clauses of the memorandum are different. The alterations require special resolutions and confirmation by the Company Law Board.

Q. 8. What is an Articles of Association and what are its contents? Can the Articles of a company be altered?

Ans. : Sec. (2)2 of the Companies Act defines the term Articles of Association. The "Articles" is a document which contains regulations for internal management of a company.

Contents : Sec. 30 provides that the "Articles" must be printed and be divided into paragraphs numbered consecutively and be signed by each subscriber of the Memorandum in the presence of at least one witness who must attest the signature.

According to the provisions of Sections 26 and 28 of the Companies Act, if no Articles are registered or filed, Table A applies. Table A is a set of model Articles contained in Schedule I to the Companies Act. Even if the Articles are registered, Table A applies in so far as the regulations contained are not excluded or modified by the Articles.

The Articles of a private limited company must state the number of members with which the company is to be registered.

The Articles of the unlimited company should state the number of members with which the company is to be registered and, in case the company has a share capital, the amount of share capital needs mention.

Other Contents

The Articles, inter alia, contain provisions regarding

(a) share capital together with its division into different classes of shares with face values of each category :

(b) calls on shares;

(c) transfer and transmission of shares;

(d) forfeiture and surrender of shares;

(e) share certificates and share warrants;

(f) custody of the common seal of the company;

(g) holding of different types of meeting;

(h) alteration and reduction of share capital;

(i) borrowing powers of the company;

(j) maintenance of books of account and distribution of dividends;

(k) appointment of managing director, director, secretary, etc., of the company.

(l) winding-up of the company.

Alteration of the Articles

Sec. 31 of the Act states the rules regarding alteration of the Articles. Subject to the provisions of the Act and the conditions contained in its memorandum, a company may, by special resolution, alter its Articles.

Alteration of Articles is, however, subject to the following restrictions :

1. No change is permitted which violates any provision of the Companies Act.

2. Any alteration contrary to the provision of the Memorandum is void.

3. Alteration must not contain anything illegal.

4. Alteration must not in any way increase the liability of members without their prior consent.

5. Certain alterations need prior consent of the Central Government.

Q. 9. What is a prospectus? What is its implication? What are its contents?

Ans. : Section 2(36) of the Companies Act, 1956, defines a prospectus as "any document described or issued as a prospectus and includes any notice, circular, advertisement or other document inviting deposits from the public for the subscription or the purchase of any shares in, or debentures of, a body corporate." The following characteristic features may be said to constitute a prospectus :

(i) there must be an invitation to the public;

(ii) the invitation must be made by or on behalf of the company or in relation to an intended company;

(iii) the invitation must be to subscribe or purchase;

(iv) the invitation must relate to shares, debentures or such other instruments.

Prospectus is a document through which the promoters of the company appeal to the public for raising necessary capital. It highlights—with supporting facts and figures—the soundness of the business and tries to convince the public so that they come forward for the subscription or purchase of shares in or debentures of the company. It must make true and proper disclosures to enable the public to form their opinion and take proper decisions. From the viewpoint of the company, the implication of the prospectus is to raise maximum possible capital from the market by convincing the public at large with as much disclosure as possible.

Section 56 of the Companies Act, 1956, requires every prospectus to disclose the matter as specified in Schedule II to the Act. The Schedule has been amended on October 3, 1991, and the matters to be stated under the revised Schedule II are divided into three parts which are as under :

Part I contains

(a) General information like name and address of registered office, consent of Central Government, Name(s) of Stock Exchange(s) where application has been made for listing of present issue, date of opening/closing of the issue etc.

(b) Details of the capital structure of the company.

(c) Details of the terms of the present issue.

(d) Particulars of the issue viz., objects, project cost and means of financing.

(e) Particulars of the company, management and project.

(f) Disclosure of particulars of outstanding litigation, criminal prosecution and default etc. launched against the company and its directors.

(g) Disclosures of particulars of outstanding litigation, criminal prosecution and defaults etc. launched against the company and its directors.

(h) Disclosure of management perception of risk factors.

Part II contains

(a) General information like consent of directors, auditors, solicitors/advocates, expert opinion, authority for the issue, procedure and time schedule for allotment and issue of certificates etc.

(b) Financial information;

(c) Statutory and other information like minimum subscription, fees payable to advisors/registrars/managers, underwriting commission etc.

Part III requires that any report of the accounts under Part II must be made by a qualified chartered accountant who should not be an officer of the company or its holding/subsidiary company.

The prospectus must end with a declaration by the directors that all the relevant provisions of the Companies Act, 1956, and the guidelines issued by the Government (now Securities Exchange Board of India—SEBI) have been complied with and that no statement made in the prospectus is contrary to the provisions of the Act.

After repeal of the Capital Issues Control Act, in 1992, the Securities and Exchange Board of India has issued a set of guidelines to regularise the capital market in the country. These guidelines—which have been amended/clarified several times—mainly aim at investor protection through disclosures in the prospectus.

Liabilities for Omission and Misstatement in the Prospectus

The facts, figures and various information given in the prospectus must be true. However, if there is any omission, misstatement or concealment of any material fact, the company and its directors may be held responsible and liable. The liabilities may be civil or criminal, or both. The aggrieved investor will have remedies against the company as well as its directors.

Q. 10. What steps should be taken by the Company to change its 'Name Clause'? Draft a specimen resolution to be passed in this context.

Ans. : The steps to be taken to change the 'Name Clause' of the company are enumerated below :

(a) *An application has to be made to the Central Government and its approval in writing has to be obtained by the company.* [Section 21]

(b) An Extraordinary General Meeting is to be convened and proper notice thereof together with the relative explanatory statement is to be sent to the members as per the provisions of the Act.

(c) *A special resolution has to be passed to this effect at the meeting.* [Section 21]

(d) A copy of the resolution is to be filed with the concerned Registrar of Companies within 30 days from the date of the meeting.

(e) *The Registrar of Companies will incorporate the new name in the register in place of the former name and shall issue a fresh certificate of incorporation with the necessary alterations embodied therein.* [Section 23(1)]

(f) The Registrar shall also make the necessary alterations in the Memorandum of Association of the company. [Section 23(2)]

(g) Necessary alterations in the Articles have to be made by the company.

(h) Copies of Memorandum and Articles duly altered shall be filed with the Registrar within 3 months.

A Specimen Resolution (to be passed as a Special Resolution) :

"Resolved that consequent upon obtaining the written approval of the Central Government, the name of the company be and is hereby changed to The Unique Engineering Co. Ltd. and necessary alterations be made in the company's Memorandum and Articles of Association."

Q. 11. What steps should be taken by the company to change 'the Domicile Clause' (or Registered Office) of the Company? Draft a resolution to be passed in this regard.

Ans. : There may be either of the following three possibilities in regard to change of the 'Domicile Clause' : (1) within the local limits of any city, town or village; (2) outside the local limits of any city, town or village but within the same State and (3) from one State to another.

The company may change its registered office within the local limits of any city, town or village by passing a resolution to this effect at the Board Meeting. A notice is to be given to the concerned Registrar of Companies of the new address of the company.

The company may change its registered office outside the local limits of any city, town or village but within the same State by taking the following steps :

(a) A special resolution authorising the change is to be passed by the company.

(b) A copy of the resolution is to be filed with the Registrar within 30 days.

(c) A notice advising the change in address of the registered office is to be given to the Registrar within 30 days from the date of change. [Section 146(2)]

In the case of an inter-State change of the registered office of the company, the steps to be taken are :

(a) A special resolution is to be passed at the Extraordinary General Meeting of the company.

(b) A copy of the special resolution is to be filed with the Registrar of Companies within 30 days from the date of passing such resolution.

(c) The sanction of the Company Law Board is to be obtained by the company.

(d) The Company Law Board causes the notice of change to be served on the Registrar of Companies to enable him to offer his suggestions/objections.

(e) Copies of the order of the Company Law Board confirming the change have to be filed with the Registrars of both the States within a period of 3 months from the date of change.

(f) Certificates of transfer from both the Registrars have to be obtained by the company.

(g) The registered office of the company may then be shifted and a notice of the new address is to be given to the concerned Registrar within 30 days from the date of the change.

(h) Necessary alterations have to be made in the Memorandum and Articles of Association of the Company and copies thereof duly altered shall be filed with the Registrar of Companies.

(i) An advertisement in a local newspaper of appropriate circulation is to be published by the company advising the change.

Q. 12. What steps should be taken by the Company to change its 'Objects Clause'?

Ans. : Section 17(1) provides the circumstances under which the 'Objects Clause' of a company may be changed. The steps to be taken for the pupose are

(a) An Extraordinary General Meeting has to be convened and proper notice thereof together with the Explanatory Statement is to be forwarded to the members.

(b) A special resolution is required to be passed at the said meeting.

(c) A copy of the special resolution is to be filed with the Registrar of Companies within 30 days from the date of the meeting.

(d) A petition is to be made to the Company Law Board for its confirmation order. Reference is also to be made to the Company Law Bench Rules.

(e) A copy each of the altered Memorandum and the confirmatory order of the Company Law Board has to be filed with the Registrar within 3 months from the date of confirmation order.

(f) The Registrar will make the necessary changes in his register and arrange to issue a fresh certificate.

Q. 13. How are the Directors of a public limited company appointed? In case of resignation tendered by a Director elucidate (a) the date on which the resignation takes effect, and (b) whether the resignation relieves the director from liabilities and obligations already incurred (ICSI)?

Ans. : Refer to Sections 254, 256, 260, 262, 285, 313 and 408 of the Companies Act, 1956.

As there is no provision in the Companies Act as to acceptance of resignation tendered by the Directors, it will be decided by the provisions of the Articles of Association of the company. Conventionally, the resignation is effective from the date of the letter or from the date it is received by the company. However, in terms of the provisions of the Indian Contract Act, the resignation will not relieve the Director from the liabilities and obligations already incurred.

Q. 14. Define' Company Secretary' according to the Companies (Amendment) Act of 1988. How is a Company Secretary appointed? What are his principal functions or duties?
(C. U. 1967; B. U. 1967, ICSI)

Or, Who is a qualified Company Secretary? How is he appointed? What are his major functions? (C. U. 1999, 1998, 1994, 1991, 1982, 1980)

Or, Discuss the different capacities in which the Secretary of a company functions. Should every company have a Secretary? (V. U. 1987; C. U. 1981)

Or, 'A Company Secretary is not only a servant of the Company but also a servant of law.' Examine the Statement. (C. U. 1991)

Ans.: According to the provision of Section 2(45) of the Companies (Amendment) Act, 1988, "Secretary" means a Company Secretary within the meaning of clause (c) of sub-section (1) of Section 2 of the Company Secretaries Act, 1980, and includes any other individual possessing the prescribed qualifications and appointed to perform the duties which may be performed by a Secretary under this Act and any other ministerial or administrative duties. Thus, the recognition so far given to the members of the Institute in the rules is enshrined in the statute as in the case of the other two sister professions viz., Chartered Accountancy and Cost Accountancy. The definition has been so amended to bring the existing definition of Secretary in Section 2(45) in line with the definition of Company Secretary as contained in the Company Secretaries Act, 1980. According to Section 2(1)(c) of the Company Secretaries Act, 1980, "Company Secretary" means a person who is a member of the Institute of Company Secretaries of India. 'The present definition is an inclusive one and includes any other individuals possessing the qualifications as prescribed under the Companies (Secretary's Qualifications) Rules, 1975, and appointed to perform the duties which may be performed by a Secretary under this Act and any other ministerial of administrative duties'. The Companies (Secretary's Qualifications) Rules, 1975, have since been replaced by the Companies (Appointment & Qualifications of Secretary) Rules, 1988. In terms of the provision of Section 383 A(1), as amended by the Amendment Act of 1988, every company having such paid-up share capital as may be prescribed shall have a whole-time Secretary, and where the Board of Directors of any such company comprises only two Directors, neither of them shall be the Secretary of the company. However, according to Rule 2(1) of the Companies (Appointment & Qualifications of Secretary) Rules, 1988, as amended in 1993, vide GSR No. 372 (E) dated 13.4.1993 : "Every Company having a paid-up share capital of not less than Rs. 50 lakhs shall have a whole-time secretary."

Prescribed Qualifications

Qualifications for appointment as Secretary—The qualifications which a person shall possess in order to be eligible for appointment as a secretary shall be :

(a) in the case of a company having a paid-up share capital of rupees fifty lakhs or more [according to Section 383A of the Amendment Act , the amount shall be prescribed by the Central Government], the membership of the Institute of Company Secretaries of India, incorporated under the Companies Act, 1956 (1 of 1956) and licensed under Section 25 of that Act:

Provided that for a period of five years from the commencement of the Companies (Amendment) Act, 1974 (41 of 1974), a person who is a member of the Institute of Chartered Secretaries and Administrators, London, shall also be eligible for appointment as secretary of such company;

(b) in the case of any other company, one or more of the following qualifications, namely

(i) the qualifications specified in clause (a);

(ii) Pass in the Intermediate Examination of the Institute of Company Secretaries of India.

(iii) degree in law granted by any university;

(iv) membership of the Institute of Chartered Accountants of India constituted under the Chartered Accountants Act, 1949 (38 of 1949);

(v) membership of the Institute of Cost and Works Accountants of India constituted under the Cost and Works Accountants Act, 1959 (23 of 1959);

(vi) post-graduate degree or diploma in management sciences granted by any university or the Institute of Management.

(vii) post-graduate degree in Commerce granted by any university;

(viii) diploma in Company Law granted by the Indian Law Institute, New Delhi.

(ix) membership of the Association of Secretaries and Managers.

(x) Post Diploma in Company Secretaryship granted by the Institute of Commercial Practice, Delhi.

(xi) Diploma in Company Law and Secretarial Practice granted by the University of Udaipur.

EXPLANATION—In this rule, "University" has the meaning assigned to it in the University Grants Commission Act, 1956 (3 of 1956), and includes any university outside India which is recognised by the Union Public Service Commission for the purpose of recruitment to public services and posts in connection with the affairs of the Union or of any State.

Provision in relation to existing Secretaries

The qualification possessed by a person holding office as the Secretary of a company immediately before 30th October 1980 shall be deemed, for the purposes of these rules, to be the qualifications which he shall be required to possess in order to be eligible to continue in that office in that company. It has been further provided that where the paid-up share capital of such company is raised to rupees fifty lakhs or more, the company shall, within one year from the date of such increase, appoint a whole-time Secretary having membership of the Institute of Company Secretaries of India.

Appointment of a Company Secretary : A Company Secretary may be appointed in the following ways:

1. Ordinarily, the name of the first Secretary is mentioned in the Articles of Association of the company. In case, however, he is not employed by the company, he does not have any cause of action against the said company. (*Krishna Rao vs Anjaneyulu*).

2. One of the promoters with requisite qualifications may carry on the duties of Secretary before the incorporation of the company. He may subsequently be appointed by the promoters as the Secretary after the company is incorporated.

3. Subsequent appointment of Secretary may be made by the Board of Directors at its meeting. The resolution adopted by the Board contains detailed terms and conditions of appointment of the Secretary. As a matter of practice, a written agreement embodying the terms of appointment is entered into between the company and the Secretary.

Functions

The Company Secretary has to carry out all the duties that are assigned to him by the Board of Directors. He is to perform those duties which have been specified by the Companies Act. Besides, he is to perform some other duties which, of course, vary with the size and the organisational structure of the company. His duties may be discussed under the following heads :

(i) Statutory duties.

(ii) Duties to management.

(iii) Duties to shareholders.

(iv) Duties to the public.

(v) Duties in relation to the organisation of office.

(vi) Miscellaneous duties.

1. **Statutory duties** : The Secretary is to comply with the various legal requirements imposed on a company. Under the Companies Act, a company is to prepare and file documents, notice of the meetings, statements, returns like Memorandum and Articles of Association, Prospectus or Statement in lieu of Prospectus, annual list of members, etc., with the concerned Registrar of Companies. A company is required to maintain proper books of account and various registers such as the Register of Members, Register of Mortgages and Charges, Register of Debentureholders, Register of Directors, etc. The Secretary, being the Principal Officer of the company, is to ensure that all the statements, documents and returns are duly filed and the books and registers are maintained. He is required to maintain the Minutes Book at the registered office of the company.

The Indian Stamp Act imposes on the company a number of obligations. The Secretary is to ensure that the letters of allotment, share certificates, share warrants, debentures, etc. issued from his office are properly stamped in terms of the provisions of the Act.

According to the provisions of the Indian Income-tax Act, the Secretary is required to deduct income-tax at source from the salaries paid by the company to its employees and to submit the returns to the appropriate authority. He is also to submit a return to the income-tax authorities showing therein the income of the company. Besides, he used to issue income-tax deduction certificates to the shareholders in respect of the dividends paid by the company till the financial year 1996-97. No tax is deducted by the company on dividend paid to the shareholders following amendment of the Income-tax Act, 1961, from the financial year 1997-98.

Under the Capital Issues (Control) Act, 1947, the Secretary is required to make the estimation of the total cost of the project while the company makes an application to the Securities Exchange Board of India for their consent to the issue of capital.

Under the Industries (Development and Regulation) Act, 1951, the Secretary is required to familiarise himself with the estimation of annual production, requirements of raw materials—both in quantity and the value—when the company makes an application to the Central Government for the purpose of establishing a new industrial undertaking.

Under the Monopolies and Restrictive Trade Practices Act, 1969, the Secretary has to play a very important role, e.g.,

(i) While submitting a notice to the Central Government of the intention of expansion of the company, the Secretary is concerned with the description of goods manufactured, supplied, distributed or services rendered including the value, cost, price, quantity of capacity of each of the goods or services, etc.

(ii) In submitting an application for establishment of a new undertaking, the Secretary is concerned with the proposed installed capacity and estimated annual production, turnover in quantity and in value together with the basis of estimation.

(iii) While the company appoints dealers, the Secretary is required to make some cost analysis.

Moreover, the Secretary is required to comply with the provisions of the Sales Tax Act, Factories Act, Payment of Wages Act, Shops and Establishments Act, Estate Duty Act, Foreign Exchange Regulation Act, Stamp Act, etc., if and when applicable to his company.

2. **Duties to Management** : The Secretary acts under the direct control and guidance of the Board of Directors. In the eyes of law, he is a servant of the directors. If the directors are called the brains of the company, the Secretary may be said to be its ears and hand. He serves as the connecting link between the directors and the shareholders. He cannot act without the authority from the directors. The directors cannot act without a meeting and it is the Secretary who arranges for such meetings. He is to fix date, place and time, to prepare agenda and to issue proper notice of the meeting. He is required to advise the directors and other officers on problems relating to law, accounts, income-tax, etc.

3. **Duties to shareholders** : The shareholders are the real owners of the company and the Secretary should show them proper courtesy and give their problems careful consideration. The Secretary may be said to be a medium of communication between the directors (the brains of the company) and the shareholders (the owners of the company). He is responsible for scrutiny of share applications, placing them before the Board, issuing allotment letters, call notices, share certificates, share warrants, dividend warrants, etc. He is also to notify the shareholders regarding payment of dividends and closure of transfer registers of the company.

4. **Duties to the public** : A Company Secretary is the medium of communication between the directors of the company and the third parties including the creditors and debenture-holders of the company. In the matter of public interest, he must not discriminate while disclosing any confidential information.

5. **Duties in relation to organisation of the office :** As the principal officer of the company, the Secretary has a number of departments under him. The office can be said to be his domain. Besides secretarial department, shares department, filing, records and correspondence departments, accounts department, etc. remain under his control. He is responsible for close co-operation and co-ordination between various departments. He should see that each of the departments is well-equipped and properly manned and the staff are contented. In a nutshell, he is responsible for the efficient organisation of the office.

6. **Miscellaneous duties :** The Secretary is also required to perform several routine duties. These include attending to legal, social, and economic matters pertaining to the company. He has to arrange for meetings of various types. His duties in this regard are in three stages, viz., before the meeting, at the meeting and after the meeting.

Q. 15. (a) Describe the provisions of the Companies Act, 1956, regarding compulsory appointment of a secretary. (b) Explain the role of a company secretary in the functioning of a company. [ICSI]

Ans. : (a) Section 383-A of the Companies Act, 1956, read with Rule 2(1) of the Companies (Appointment and Qualifications of Secretary) Rules, 1988, as amended in 1993, vide GSR No. 372E dated 13.4.1993, provides that every company having a paid-up capital of not less than Rs. 50 lakhs shall have a whole-time secretary and where the Board of Directors of any such company comprises only two directors, neither of them shall be the secretary of the company. Rule 2(2) provides that only a member of the Institute of Company Secretaries of India constituted under the Company Secretaries Act, 1980, can be appointed as a whole-time secretary.

(b) During the last three decades the role of a company secretary has undergone a tremendous change. From the status of a mere clerk, the secretary has risen to the level of an officer in the company and he is seen to travel in the society of the chairman, managing director, directors and other senior officers of the company. He is sometimes regarded as the 'kingpin' of the company's administrative hierarchy. The role of a company secretary is four-fold, viz. (i) as a statutory officer; (ii) as a co-ordinator; (iii) as an administrative officer and (iv) as a liaison officer.

(i) As a Statutory Officer—*Refer to page 25.*

(ii) As a Co-ordinator—As a co-ordinator, the Company Secretary has a very important role to play in the organisation. He is a link between the top and other levels of management and co-ordinates the actions of other executives vis-a-vis the Board of Directors of the company. He has to convey the policy decisions of the Board to the concerned functional executives for proper implementation. As the 'watch-dog', he is responsible for reporting on the proper implementation or otherwise of the tasks assigned to the functional managers to the top management. Apart from internal co-ordination, he has to co-ordinate with the shareholders, depositors, Government and the society.

(iii) As an Administrative Officer—In this capacity, the secretary has to ensure that the activities of the company are in conformity with its laid-down policies. He will see to it that the properties of the company are adequately insured against loss, theft, fire etc. *(Now add (5) from page 27).*

(iv) As a Liaison Officer —The Company Secretary has to maintain close liaison with the trade unions, auditors, shareholders, depositors, Government and the society. He should be careful with the officials of the trade union during the course of discussions or negotiations. Apart from the statutory audit, an auditor's certificate is required under various statutes. The Secretary has, therefore, to maintain close liaison with the company's auditor. He has to maintain relationship with the shareholders and depositors of the company. He has to ensure timely inspection of books and registers by the shareholders as per the provisions of the Companies Act. Letters received from them should be promptly replied by him bearing in mind the statutory provisions. With adoption of ideal of a welfare state, the government regulations and control over the corporate sector have increased manifold. The Company Secretary has to ensure that the company is implementing the Government policies in their true spirit and there is no contravention of the provisions of the various legislations. He is also expected to ensure that the company meets responsibilities of the society to the maximum extent possible.

Q. 16. What is the difference between an 'Occupation' and a 'Profession'? Is Company Secretaryship a 'Profession'? Who can be a member of the Institute of Company Secretaries of India? (C. U. 1995, 1988, 1987)

Ans. : According to the Webster's Dictionary, the term 'occupation' means "the principal business of one's life" or "an activity in which one engages" himself to earn his livelihood. A 'profession', on the other hand, according to the same dictionary, is "a calling requiring specialised knowledge and long and intensive academic preparation". Though both the terms are loosely used, there is, indeed, a difference between them. Since company secretaryship satisfies all the characteristics which are required of a profession, it is indeed a profession. It may be added here that this profession has also won the legal and public recognitions as a 'profession'.

The Institute of Company Secretaries of India (ICSI) was registered in 1968 in terms of the provision of Section 25 of the Companies Act, 1956. Subsequently, following passing of the Company Secretaries Act in 1980, the Institute is a statutory body. It arranges oral/postal coaching for the registered students, holds examinations twice a year, arranges practical training for those who pass the final examination of the Institute with the approved companies. It also arranges conferences/seminars in collaboration with the Institute of Chartered Accountants of India and/or Institute of Cost & Works Accountants of India on such subjects which benefit the students, members of the Institutes and executives of various companies.

On completion of the Final Examination of the Institute, a candidate is eligible for practical training in any of the companies recognised by the Institute and in the office of the Registrar of Companies for a total period not exceeding four months. The candidate remains attached to the Company Secretary and is imparted on-the-job training in various departments with special emphasis on the work of the Secretarial Department. In the office of the Registrar of Companies, the candidate remains attached to the Registrar and learns some of the important work being handled by that office. Reports on the performance of the candidate are sent by the Company and the Registrar of Companies where he was trained to the Institute. If the reports received by the Institute on the candidate are good and the candidate applies for membership, the Council may enrol him as a member. Membership of the Institute is of two types — Associateship and Fellowship. The Associate Members and Fellow Members may write after their names the letters A.C.S. and F.C.S., respectively, until and unless their memberships are cancelled by the Institute.

Q. 17. Discuss the provisions of the Companies Act governing the appointment of the secretary of a company having a paid-up capital of Rs. 60 lakhs. What is the procedure for appointing an associate of the erstwhile managing agents of the company as a Secre-

tary? Draft the resolution for the appointment of a secretary who is not associate of the erstwhile managing agents of the company. (ICSI, June 1971)

Ans. : *Refer to pages 23-25.* In this connection, if the associate of the erstwhile Managing Agents is an individual possessing the prescribed qualifications, he can be appointed as the Company Secretary with the prior approval of the general meeting as well as the Central Government.

Q. 18. What are the duties and functions of a Company Secretary (i) before the meeting, (ii) at the meeting and (iii) after the meeting? (V. U. 1988; C. U. 1999)

Ans. : A Company Secretary has to deal with all kinds of meetings, viz., Shareholders' meetings, Board meetings and special meetings. It is quite obvious that his duties and functions will differ for different types of meeting. Broadly speaking, his duties and functions in regard to any meeting may be summarised as under :

Before the Meeting

1. On receipt of instruction from the Board of Directors, he is to arrange for accommodation of the meeting.

2. He is to prepare the agenda for the meeting and draft the Chairman's speech, in case the Chairman is to deliver a speech.

3. He is to issue proper notice convening the meeting.

4. He is to gather all the relevant papers which may be required at the meeting, i.e., documents, letters, transfer deeds, new certificates, company's seal, etc.

5. In case of general meetings, he is required to give details of proxies along with the notice. He is also required to state the particulars with regard to ordinary or special resolution.

6. In case of an annual general meeting, he is to issue notice to the members and auditors of the company. He is also to see that copies of the annual accounts reach the hands of the shareholders well in time.

At the meeting

1. He is to see well in time that the accommodation is adequate and all the items of stationery which may be required at the meeting are ready.

2. He is to keep ready at hand all the documents, reports, copies of Memorandum and Articles of Association, copies of audited balance sheets, details of proxies lodged, Minutes Book, Register of Members, etc.

3. He is to take attendance of the members and/or directors.

4. He is to keep ready the Registers of Directors and shareholders.

5. He has to take note of the proceedings of the meeting.

6. He is to draft the resolutions to be moved at the meeting.

7. He reads the notice of the meeting. If necessary, he has to read the Minutes of the last meeting.

8. He is to assist the Chairman for smooth conduct of the meeting.

After the Meeting

1. He has to write the Minutes of the meeting.

2. He has to carry out the instructions of the meeting.

3. He has to convene next meeting or meetings as and when required.

4. He has to file the returns with the Registrar of Companies within the stipulated time. In case of the statutory meeting, the Secretary is to file the statutory report. In case of an Annual General Meeting, he is required to file within 30 days from the date of the meeting three copies of balance sheet and profit and loss account of the company. He must file with the Registrar of Companies the annual return within 60 days from the date of the meeting.

Q. 19. What are the qualities a Secretary must possess to perform his functions efficiently? (C. U. 1998)

Ans. : In order to perform his duties efficiently, a Secretary must have a good education, knowledge and training. He must have a thorough knowledge about the provisions of the Companies Act, Monopolies and Restrictive Trade Practices Act, Income-tax Act, Factories Act, Trade Union Act, Shops and Establishments Act, Estate Duty Act, etc. The qualifications and training essential for a successful Company Secretary are detailed below :

1. **Academic Attainment :** The Company Secretary should have a sound general education. He must be a member of the Institute of Company Secretaries of India if he is appointed as Secretary of a company whose paid-up share capital is Rs. 50 lakh or more.

2. **Office Organisation and Methods** : He should know the best systems of filing and indexing for useful application to his office. He should also be aware of the labour-saving devices for adoption in the office.

3. **Staff Matters :** He must know the methods of selection and control of the staff. He should be able to post the right man for the right job. This will help efficient and smooth running of the office.

4. **Knowledge of Mercantile Law :** For the day-to-day working, he must be well-versed with the provisions of various Acts, such as Contract Act, Insurance Act, Banking Regulation Act, Sale of Goods Act, etc.

5. **Knowledge of Accountancy :** Though he is not expected to be a professionally qualified accountant yet he should know the basic principles of accountancy and laws relating to income-tax.

6. **Meeting :** He should be thorough in the laws and procedures of various types of meetings.

7. **Knowledge of the Business :** He should be quite familiar with the line of business pursued by the company.

8. **Personality :** He should be a man of personality and should have initiative, drive, tact, intelligence, sincerity, responsibility and self-confidence.

9. **Wide Reading :** He is often asked to give his advice on various matters and, to do proper justice to his job, he should be a man of wide reading.

Q. 20. "The position of the Secretary in the administrative set up of a company is quite high, coming closely next to the Managing Director or the General Manager."—Examine the statement and determine the legal position of the Secretary.

(C. U. 1982; ICSI Final Exam.—Adapted)

Or, Discuss the legal and actual position of a Company Secretary.

(C. U. 1999, 1997, 1995, 1989)

Or, "A Company Secretary has no power of his own, yet he enjoys enough of it."—Discuss. **(C. U. 1996, 1987)**

Ans. : According to the provision of Section 2(45) of the Companies Act, 1956, as amended by the Amendment Act of 1988, a Secretary is appointed to perform the duties which may be performed by a Secretary under this Act and any other duties of ministerial or administrative nature. To determine the actual position of the Secretary in the administrative set-up of a company, one must know the work performed by him (Secretary).

In terms of Section 2(45), the Secretary is a mere employee of the company. But in actual practice, he commands considerable influence with the Board of Directors and plays a very vital role. From this point of view, he enjoys a very unique position in the company's management. He remains in close touch with the Directors and thus gains a very intimate knowledge of the internal and confidential affairs of the company. He is frequently consulted by the Chairman in regard to the policy and administration of the company. In all these cases, he is very often given executive powers of management. He is thus a guiding spirit of the Board of Directors of the company and not a mere puppet in the hands of the top management. In respect of routine work of his department, he has functional responsibility to the Managing Director of the company. "The Company Secretary is a mere servant with no rights and responsibilities"—as conceived by Lord Escher, —cannot be said to be true in the present-day management.

The Secretary is seen to travel in the society of the Chairman, Managing Director and other directors of the company. In formulating the objectives and policies of the company, the Board of Directors has to perform a variety of tasks. They have to determine the general policies to be followed, provide for legal responsibilities towards the community and search for avenues for survival and growth of the company. The Secretary, besides the functions relating to his own department, has to help the directors in performing their above functions in an efficient manner. From this perspective, he seems to be a member of the top executives and thus justifies his designation of the principal officer of the company. He is required to advise the Board in such a way as to enable it to manage the affairs of the company in compliance with the provisions of laws as well as various rules and regulations. The directors may delegate some of their functions to the Secretary. Once he wins the confidence of the directors, the Board will delegate to him more and more executive powers of management. He may, therefore, be said to be the guiding force of the Board of Directors.

On a careful consideration of the status, rights and duties of the Secretary under the law and in the organisation structure of the company, it is quite apt to remark that he quite fits into the role of the functional executive. By virtue of this, he is responsible only to the Board of Directors of the company. The various policies laid down by the Board of Directors at its meetings need to be interpreted by the managing or executive director to the line executives for implementation. In actual practice, however, the Secretary communicates the policies of the Board to the executives. He is the official spokesman of the directors for publication and announcement of all corporate decisions.

To determine his position in the administrative set-up of the company, one should analyse the type of work performed by a Secretary. If he performs the routine work and acts as the agent of the Board and does "as he is told to do", he is nothing but a ministerial or administrative employee of the company. On the other hand, besides the routine functions, he may become an executive, create his own openings for advancement and render valuable advices to the Board. In this case, he is termed a dynamic Secretary and is vested with the powers "as delegated to him" by the Board of Directors of the company.

Q. 21. "A Secretary is a mere servant : his position is that he is to do what he is told, and no person can assume that he has any authority to represent anything at all."

"He is no longer a mere clerk. He regularly makes representations on behalf of the company and enters into contracts on its behalf which come within the day-to-day running of the company's business..... All such matters now come within the ostensible authority of a company secretary."

Discuss these statements with reference to the company secretary's actual powers, rights, duties and responsibilities. (ICSI)

Or, "While the Directors are the brains of the Company, the Secretaries are the ears, eyes and hands." Elucidate the Statement with reference to the functions of the Company Secretary. (V. U. 1987)

Ans. : *Pages 26-28 & 31-32.*

Q. 22. What are the rights and powers of a Company Secretary? What are his liabilities? How can a Company Secretary be dismissed? (C. U. 1990; ICSI)

Ans. : The Companies Act does not confer any special powers on the Company Secretary. The Board of Directors delegates some of its executive functions to the Secretary and, in doing so, very much counts on the capabilities of the Secretary. The Secretary cannot do anything without obtaining the express or implied authority from the Board of Directors. He can neither be called a trustee nor an agent of the company. He is merely a salaried official having no original or inherent powers. The rights and powers of a Secretary may be summarised as follows :

1. He has the right to superintend, direct and control his own department.

2. In the event of winding-up of the company, he can claim his salary for 4 months or Rs. 20,000/-, whichever is less, inasmuch as he is an employee of the company. [Section 530]

3. Unless authorised by the directors or unless the Articles of Association empower the directors to delegate powers, the Secretary cannot allot shares to the applicants.

4. Unless authorised by the Board, the Secretary cannot register transfer of shares.

5. As one of the principal executive officers of the company, he has the right to sign the documents of the company.

6. The Company Secretary, unless so authorised by the Board, cannot bind the company by his acts.

7. He can serve notices under Sec. 53 of the Companies Act.

Liabilities : If the Secretary fails to perform his duties entrusted to him by the various Acts (e.g., Companies Act, Income-tax Act, Stamp Act, Monopolies and Restrictive Trade Practices Act, Sales Tax Act, Shops and Establishments Act, Factories Act, etc.), he will be held statutorily liable to the company. On the other hand, if he fails to discharge his duties as per the Service Agreement, he will be deemed to be contractually liable to the company. Hence, his liabilities may be either statutory or contractual, or both. These liabilities may, again, be both civil and criminal and normally arise from acts of omission or commission or from actual cases of default or negligence.

Statutory liabilities : Under the provisions of the Companies Act, 1956, as amended uptodate, the Secretary may be held liable for—

(i) *default in making ready the share certificates and debentures within three months after allotment and two months after application of transfer;* [Section 113]

(ii) *failure to record entries in the Register of Members on the issue of share warrant*; [Section 115]

(iii) *default in filing the particulars of charges with the Registrar of Companies*; [Section 142]

(iv) *failure to get the name and address of the registered office or place in which its business is carried on*; [Section 147]

(v) *failure to maintain register and index of members and debentureholders*; [Sections 150-152]

(vi) *default in holding the statutory meeting and filing statutory report with the Registrar and circulating it to the members entitled to attend and vote at the meeting*; [Section 165]

(vii) *default in holding the annual general meeting in terms of Section* 166; [Section 168]

(viii) *default in circulating members' resolution of which due notice has been given by them to the company*; [Section 188]

(ix) *failure to record the minutes of the meetings*; [Section 193]

(x) *failure to give notice of Board Meeting to the directors*; [Section 286]

(xi) *failure to maintain register of directors, manager and secretary*; [Section 303]

(xii) *failure to maintain register of directors' shareholdings, etc. and make it available at and during the continuance of the meeting*; [Section 307]

(xiii) *failure to file with the Registrar three copies of balance sheet and profit & loss account together with other documents*; [Section 220]

(xiv) *failure to maintain register of directors, etc.*; [Section 303(1)]

(xv) *failure to file with the Registrar a return containing the particulars specified in the registers of directors, etc., and changes therein, if any*; [Section 303(2)]

(xvi) *failure to disclose his other offices, if any, for maintaining the register of directors, etc., uptodate*; [Section 305(1)]

(xvii) *failure to make, submit and verify the statement as to the affairs of the company to the Official Liquidator.* [Section 454]

Statutory Liabilities under other Acts

(i) In terms of the provisions of the Income-tax Act, 1961 (as amended uptodate), the Company Secretary is responsible for payment of corporation tax. He is also responsible for deduction of income-tax from the salaries of the staff and payment to the Income-tax department. He was responsible for deduction of income-tax from dividends paid to the shareholders, interest paid to debenture-holders and payment thereof to the Income-tax Authorities till the financial year 1996-97. Since then, tax on dividend is paid by the company.

(ii) According to Section 2 of the Monopolies and Restrictive Trade Practices Act, the Secretary is a principal officer of the company and in that capacity he is responsible for giving notice and verifying various statements required in connection with establishment of a new undertaking, expansion, acquisition and merger/amalgamation.

(iii) In terms of the provisions of the Indian Stamp Act, it is the responsibility of the Secretary to verify as to whether the documents bear the requisite stamps.

(iv) Under the Shops and Establishments Act, Sales Tax Act and Factories Act, the Company Secretary is recognised as the principal authority as to administrative requirements of these statutes.

Contractual Liabilities : Apart from the statutory liabilities, the Company Secretary may be held liable for some other liabilities which may arise out of his service agreement with the company. These are known as contractual liabilities and may be enumerated below :

(i) He is responsible to the Board of Directors for proper discharge of his duties. He must carry out the orders of the directors and fulfil the obligations which emerge from his service agreement.

(ii) He must not divulge any confidential information to the detriment of the interests of the company or members thereof.

(iii) He is liable for negligence and wilful misconduct. But if he discharges his duties with sufficient care and skill, he will not be held liable.

(iv) He will be held liable if he acts in contravention of the rules and regulations of the company or if he acts beyond his authority. [Re : *The Panorama Development (Guildford) Ltd. vs. Fidelis Furnishing Fabrics Ltd.*]

(v) He may be held liable if, in the course of his employment, he violates the company's rules, makes any breach of trust or commits any fraud.

Removal : The Articles of Association may empower the directors to remove the Secretary. Since he is an employee of the company, his suspension or dismissal is determined by the terms of appointment offered by the company and accepted by him. He may, however, be dismissed without any notice from the company if he makes secret profits. He may also be dismissed for his permanent disability, wilful misconduct, disobedience, incompetence, etc.

Q. 23. "A Secretary is a mere servant of the Company". "A Secretary is an officer of the Company with extensive duties and responsibilities"—Which of these two statements is correct and why? (C. U. 1981)

Ans. : If and when the Secretary performs only the routine work and does "as he is told to do" by the Board of Directors, he is nothing but a ministerial or administrative employee of the Company, as defined in Section 2(45) of the Companies Act. Here "A Secretary is a mere servant of the Company." On the other hand, besides performing the routine functions, he may create his own openings for advancement, render valuable advices to the Board and thus become an executive in the truest sense of the term. Here "A Secretary is an officer of the Company with extensive duties and responsibilities."

Q. 24. What are the duties of a Company Secretary (a) before the incorporation of the company (b) after the incorporation of the company?

Ans. : The duties of a Company Secretary prior to incorporation of the company may be summed up as under :

1. He is a competent person to help the promoters in finalising their new venture. The prospects and weaknesses of their venture are spotlighted by the Secretary and, thus, he comes into prominence.

2. When the promoters finally decide to start the business, it is the Secretary who helps them in finalising the financial plan of the company.

3. He ascertains from the office of the Registrar of Companies whether the name proposed by the promoters is available for registration.

4. He decides the situation of the registered office of the company.

5. He drafts the Memorandum and Articles of the company.

Duties after incorporation

After the company is incorporated, the decisions in regard to various matters will be taken by the Board of Directors at its meetings. The Secretary has, therefore, to arrange for calling Board meetings in order to settle the following issues :

1.(i) to elect a chairman of the meetings;

(ii) to receive the report from the Solicitors;

(iii) to appoints the company's bankers, brokers, managing director, etc.;

(iv) to approve a common seal;

(v) to get his appointment as the Secretary of the company confirmed and get his appointment letter;

(vi) to fix up the time and date of the next meeting of the Board of Directors;

(vii) to sign prospectus or statement in lieu of prospectus;

(viii) to make share allotment;

(ix) to apply to the Registrar of Companies for the commencement of business in case it is a public limited company.

2. He is to carry on the day-to-day activities of the company.

3. He is to comply with the provisions of the Companies Act and other enactments.

4. He is to look after the work of his own department.

Q. 25. What are the duties and functions of a Company Secretary in connection with formation of a company?

Ans. : The persons who conceive the idea of forming a company and explore all the possibilities by way of taking active part in its formation are called the promoters. The Company Secretary renders valuable service to the promoters from the time when they conceive the idea of forming a company. His functions are enumerated below :

1. He helps the promoters in preparing the Memorandum and Articles of Association of the company.

2. He helps the promoters in finalising underwriting arrangements and preliminary contracts.

3. He keeps the minutes of the meetings of the promoters.

4. He has to ascertain from the Registrar of Companies whether the name chosen by the promoters has the approval of the Registrar.

5. He has to obtain the sanction of the Central Government/Securities Exchange Board of India if the company is to have a paid-up capital of more than Rs. 1 crore.

6. He is to arrange for obtaining a licence under the Industries (Development and Regulation) Act, 1951, if the company desires to take part in an industry which comes under the purview of the Act.

7. He is to arrange for submission of the application form for registration, duly signed by the promoters of the company. The application form should be properly stamped and it

should accompany necessary registration and filing fees. Besides, the following documents should be attached to the application form :

(a) Memorandum of Association.

(b) Articles of Association (Unless Table 'A' of the Companies Act is complied with).

(c) A duly signed list of persons who have consented to act as Directors with their addresses, occupations and other particulars.

(d) A declaration by any one of the following persons to the effect that all the requirements of the Act have been complied with, viz., an Advocate, a Pleader, a Chartered Accountant, or a person named in the Articles as Directors, Manager or a Secretary of the company. After the above requirements are complied with, the Secretary is to obtain the Certificate of Incorporation. A private limited company can commence its business just on receipt of the certificate but a public limited company has to comply with certain other requirements before commencing its business. The following steps should be taken by the Secretary at this stage :

  (i) He should arrange for issuing prospectus or statement in lieu of prospectus and getting the same registered with the Registrar of Companies.

  (ii) He should submit the company's application for listing of the shares to the Stock Exchange.

  (iii) He should see that allotment of shares is made only after the raising of the minimum subscription.

  (iv) He should arrange for election of the Chairman and appointment of the Managing Director, Auditors, etc.

  (v) He is to arrange for opening company's account with the bank. After the above requirements are met and if the Registrar of Companies is satisfied, he will issue the Certificate for Commencement of Business. It is the duty of the Secretary to procure the certificate before the company commences its business. It may be mentioned that private limited companies do not require this certificate.

Q. 26. Discuss the procedure for securing Stock Exchange Enlistment.

And. : A Stock Exchange refers to an organised market which maintains list(s) of shares and/or debentures of the companies for purchase and sale. Listing of shares/debentures means entry of these securities in the official list of the Stock Exchange(s). Section 73 of the Companies Act, 1956, provides for the listing arrangement. The following steps are required to be taken for securing stock exchange quotation :

(a) An application in the prescribed form of the Stock Exchange has to be made by the company. If the company desires its securities to be listed in more than one Stock Exchange, separate applications have to be submitted.

(b) Copies of agreements entered into between the company and its sharebrokers/bankers have to be forwarded along with the application.

(c) The company has to file along with the application copies of share application, letter of allotment, etc. duly approved by the SEBI with the concerned Stock Exchange.

Q. 27. Enumerate the steps to be taken by the company which wishes to issue shares to the public.

Ans. : The decision regarding the issue of shares at par or premium must be in terms of the SEBI guidelines. The steps involved are enumerated below :

(a) Compliance with SEBI guidelines.

(b) A general meeting of the shareholders has to be convened for obtaining their consent to the proposed issue in case the Articles so provide (applicable to an existing company which proposes to issue additional shares).

(c) Intimation to Stock Exchange.

(d) Appointment of managers to the issue.

(e) Appointment of various agencies like Registrars to the issue, collecting bankers to the issue, advisors to the issue, brokers to the issue etc.

(f) Drafting of prospectus.

(g) Approval of the prospectus by legal advisors/solicitors/stock exchange etc.

(h) Vetting of prospectus by SEBI and filing of draft prospectus with the Stock Exchange(s).

(i) Approval of Board of Directors to prospectus and other documents.

(j) Registration of prospectus with the Registrar of Companies.

(k) Application to Stock Exchange(s) for the permission of enlisting shares.

(l) Printing and distribution of prospectus and application forms.

(m) A certificate from a Chartered Accountant/Company Secretary— in practice to the effect that the promoters' contribution in its entirety has been brought in advance before the public issue opens—should be forwarded to SEBI.

(n) Announcement regarding the proposed issue should be made at least ten days before the subscription list opens should be made. Advertisement has to be made bearing in mind the SEBI guidelines.

(o) Subscription list for public issue is to be kept open as required by the SEBI.

(p) Dates of opening and closing of the subscription list should be intimated to all the collecting branches of the bank.

(q) SEBI requirement regarding minimum subscription has to be complied with.

(r) Basis of allotment has to be decided in consultation with the concerned stock exchange(s).

(s) Filing of necessary Forms with the Registrar of Companies.

(t) As per SEBI guidelines, over-subscription should not be retained by the company.

(u) Refund of over-subscription amount.

(v) Lead managers have to forward a report within 45 days from the date of closure of the issue along with a compliance certificate from statutory auditors/practising Chartered Accountant/practising Company Secretary to the SEBI.

(w) Share Certificates must be issued by the company within three months after allotment of the shares.

Q. 28. What do you mean by bonus shares? What are the current guidelines in respect of issue of bonus shares?

Ans. : When a company is prosperous and accumulates a large surplus, it converts this surplus into capital and divides the capital among the members pro rata. This is done by issuing fully paid-up shares representing the increased capital. These shares which are issued to the existing members of the company free of cost are known as bonus shares. Bonus shares go by the modern name of 'capitalisation of shares'. If the Articles of Association of the company so provide, the company can capitalise profits and/or reserves and issue fully-paid shares to its existing members. A resolution for capitalising the profits has to be passed by the Board and this has to be approved by the members in a general meeting. Permission of the SEBI has to be obtained before issuing the bonus shares.

The SEBI guidelines on issue of bonus shares are enumerated below :

(i) No bonus shares shall dilute the other issues of the company.

(ii) Bonus shares can be issued only out of free reserves built out of genuine revenue profits or share premium collected in cash.

(iii) Revaluation reserve cannot be capitalised for issue of bonus shares.

(iv) Bonus issue shall not be made in lieu of dividend.

(v) Partly paid shares are not eligible for bonus shares. Such shares, if any, should be made fully paid-up before bonus issue is contemplated.

(vi) The company shall not have defaulted in the payment of interest or principal in respect of public deposits and interest payment of debentures or repayment of principal on redemption of debentures. The company shall not have defaulted in respect of any statutory payments.

(vii) A company which announces bonus issue after the Board approval must implement the proposal within six months.

(viii) A bonus proposal cannot be withdrawn by the company.

(ix) The Articles of Association of the company should have a provision for capitalisation of reserves; otherwise, the Articles need to be amended.

(x) If and when necessary, before action on bonus issue is taken, the company shall increase its authorised capital to permit the proposed bonus issue.

(xi) The above SEBI guidelines apply to all listed companies.

(xii) A compliance certificate stating that the terms and conditions of bonus shares have been observed has to be signed by the company and countersigned by its statutory auditors or a practising company secretary and forwarded to SEBI.

Q. 29. Enumerate the steps to be taken by the company for reduction of its share capital. Draft a resolution to be passed in this regard.

Ans. : Sections 100 and 103 of the Companies Act deal with the provisions for reduction of share capital. The following steps are required to be taken for reduction of share capital :

(a) The Memorandum and Articles of Association shall empower the company to reduce its share capital.

(b) A meeting of the Board of Directors has to be convened to discuss the plan in question.

(c) An Extraordinary General Meeting has to be convened and a special resolution passed to this effect.

(d) A copy of the special resolution has to be filed with the Registrar of Companies within 30 days from the date of the meeting/resolution.

(e) A petition is to be filed by the company with the Government for its order of confirmation.

(f) A certified copy of the Government order confirming the reduction of share capital together with the statement/minutes detailing all the particulars of reduction shall be filed with the Registrar within 3 months from the date of the Government order.

(g) Copies of Memorandum and Articles duly altered have to be filed with the Registrar.

(h) The Certificate of Registration will be issued by the Registrar within 30 days from the date the company files a certified copy of the Government order.

Special Resolution to be passed :

'Resolved that the capital of the company be and is hereby reduced from Rs. 10 lakhs divided into 1,00,000 equity shares of Rs. 10/- to Rs. 5 lakhs divided into 1,00,000 shares of Rs. 5/- each and the amount so obtained be utilised to write-off the debit balance of profit and loss account (Rs. 4 lakh) and discount on issue of shares (Rs. 1 lakh)."

Q. 30. Explain the principles laid down in the following cases with facts of the cases :

(i) Barnett Hoares & Co. vs The South London Tramways Co.

(ii) Panorama Development Ltd. vs Fidelis Furnishing Fabrics Ltd.

(iii) Turner Morrison & Co. Ltd. vs Hungerford Investment Trust Ltd. **(ICSI)**

(i) *Barnett Hoares & Co. (BHC) vs South London Tramways Co. (SLTC)*

The South London Tramways Co. engaged contractors to construct certain tramline.

The terms of the contract, *inter alia,* provided keeping of retention money by the Tramways Co. until completion of the maintenance period. The contractors sought to borrow money from BHC and offered as security for the advance the retention money lying with the Tramways Co. BHC happened to enquire of the Secretary of the SLTC about the retention money. On the basis of the Secretary's certificate, BHC sued the SLTC for the retention money.

It was held in 1887 that "A Secretary is a mere servant, his position is to do what he is told and no person can assume that he has any authority to represent anything at all." The Secretary of the SLTC had no authority to certify on behalf of the company and the company was not liable for the action of its Secretary.

(ii) *Panorama Development (Guildford) Ltd. vs Fidelis Furnishing Fabrics Ltd. (1971).*

In the olden days, the Company Secretary was considered as a mere servant having no authority to make any representation on behalf on the company. This stand was current in the 19th century (1887). However, in the Court of Appeal, England, Lord Denning overruled the legal decision of 1887 and pronounced that "A company secretary is a much more important person now-a-days than he was in 1887." He is an officer of the company with extensive duties and responsibilities. This is amply clear as per the Companies Act as amended up-to-date and further corroborated by the role he assumes in the day-to-day administration of the company's affairs. He makes representations on behalf of the company and enters into contracts on its behalf. He may be regarded to have authority to do such acts on behalf of the company as and when authorised by the Board. He has the ostensible authority to sign contracts which relate to the administrative side of the company.

(iii) *Turner Morrison & Co. Ltd. (TMCL) vs. Hungerford Investment Trust Ltd. (HITL)*

In this case, Turner Morrison appealed to the Supreme Court that the amount of income-tax and super tax paid by it as an agent or on behalf of HITL be reimbursed to it.

Despite the fact that a number of resolutions were passed by the company at the meetings of Board of Directors and shareholders, the Secretary of TMCL filed a suit without the prior consent of the Board. The defendants objected as to maintainability of the suit on the ground that the directors of the applicant company were not aware of the case and prior sanction of the Board for filing the suit was not obtained.

However, the Board of Directors subsequently ratified the action of the Secretary. The Articles of the TMCL provided, *inter alia*, that the Secretary could file a suit with prior permission of the Board. In view of the above, the Court held that there could be a valid objection as to maintainability of the suit.

While dismissing the main suit, the Court held the Secretary liable to pay the costs of both the parties in this Court. It was further stated that the suit was engineered by Mr. Mundhra so as to enable him to serve his own purposes and, practically speaking, there was no justification of bringing the suit. "We think it proper to direct Hormasji (Secretary) to bear the costs of both the parties in this Court."

Q. 31. Define the terms : (a) Share (b) Stock (c) Share Scrip (d) Share Warrant (e) Share Certificate (f) Debenture (g) Common Seal (h) Sweat Equity Shares (i) Dividend Warrant.

Ans. : (a) According to Section 2(46) of the Companies Act, 1956, "Share" means share in the share capital of a company and includes stock except where a distinction between stock and shares is expressed or implied." A share reflects the contribution of a shareholder towards the share capital of the company. In other words, it is a unit of account for measuring a member's interest in the company. Share capital of a company may be of two types — preference share capital and equity share capital. Preference shares enjoy preferential right both in respect of payment of dividend and return of capital in the event of winding-up of the company. Preference shares may be of the following types :

(i) Cumulative preference shares;

(ii) Non-cumulative preference shares;

(iii) Redeemable preference shares;

(iv) Irredeemable preference shares; and

(v) Participating preference shares.

Equity shares—which are usually known as the risk capital—confer on their holders the residue of rights of the company. These shares ordinarily carry the main financial risk if the company is unsuccessful, but they carry the greatest prospects of financial reward if the company succeeds in its venture.

(b) Stock can be defined as the aggregate of the fully paid-up shares legally consolidated, portions of which aggregate may be transferred or split up into fractions of any amount without regard to the original nominal amount of the shares. If so authorised by its Articles, a company limited by shares or limited by guarantee with a share capital can convert the whole or part of its paid-up shares into stock, and vice versa. Shares can be converted into stock only after they are paid in full.

(c) A share scrip is a provisional share certificate in lieu of the share certificate. After receipt of the information from the company that the share certificates are ready, the holders of the scrips may surrender the scrips for obtaining the share certificates.

(d) A share warrant is a document issued by a company under its common seal stating that the bearer thereof is entitled to the shares mentioned therein. The company issuing such warrants may arrange for coupons or otherwise for payment of dividends to the holders of such warrants. Section 144 requires that the following conditions should be fulfilled by the companies before issuing share warrants :

(i) The Articles of Association of the company must authorise it.

(ii) Prior approval of the Central Government/SEBI is necessary.

(iii) Shares must be fully paid-up.

(e) A share certificate, as the name suggests, is a document issued under the common seal of the company specifying the number of shares held by the person mentioned therein. It is a documentary evidence to the effect that the person mentioned in the certificate is the holder of the shares as specified therein. A company is now required not only to keep the share certificates ready for delivery, but also to deliver the same to the allottees within three months from the date of allotment and to the transferee within two months from the date of application for registration of transfer of shares, debentures or debenture stock.

(f) Section 2(12) of the Companies Act, 1956, defines the term debenture as 'debenture' includes debenture stock, bonds and any other securities of a company, whether constituting a charge on the assets of the company or not. In the ordinary business sense, a debenture generally means a document—but not necessarily under the common seal of the company—acknowledging a debt and securing repayment thereof by mortgage or charge on the company's property and undertaking. The document also provides that, until repayment, interest will be paid thereon at a fixed rate, payable either half-yearly or yearly on fixed dates, Debenture interest is normally payable whether or not the company earns profits. Debentures may usually be of the following types :

(i) Bearer Debentures;

(ii) Registered Debentures;

(iii) Secured Debentures;

(iv) Unsecured or Naked Debentures;

(v) Redeemable Debentures;

(vi) Convertible Debentures;

(vii) Collateral Debentures;

(viii) Perpetual Debentures;

(ix) Debentures with *pari passu* charge.

(g) The seal is a relic of the past when medieval barons—who were illitereate—used their rings to make a characteristic impress. While, with the growth of literacy, seal has given place to the signature by hand, it continues to serve as the physical impression made upon written documents executed by the corporate bodies. The purpose of affixing the seal is to supplement the signature of the corporate officers and, thereby, authenticate the documents. The Articles of Association of the company provide that the seal shall not be affixed to any instrument except by the authority of the Board of Directors or a Committee of the Board and in the presence of one Director and Company Secretary. The said two officers of the Company shall sign every instrument to which the common seal is affixed. Section 48 of the Companies Act, 1956, states the provisions for affixing the common seal of the company.

(h) According to the Companies (Amendment) Ordinance, 1998, Section 79A which deals with issue of sweat equity shares has been incorporated in the Companies Act, 1956. Notwithstanding anything contained in Section 79, a company may issue sweat equity shares of a class of shares already issued if the following conditions are fulfilled, namely

(i) the issue of sweat equity shares is authorised by a resolution passed by the company in the general meeting;

(ii) the resolution specifies the number of shares, their value and the class or classes of directors or employees to whom such equity shares are to be issued;

(iii) not less than one year has, at the date of the issue, elapsed since the date on which the company was entitled to commence business;

(iv) the sweat equity shares are issued in accordance with the regulations made by the Securities Exchange Board of India in this behalf.

The expression 'Sweat Equity Shares' means equity shares issued at a discount or for consideration other than cash for providing know-how or making available rights in the nature of intellectual property rights or value additions, by whatever name called.

(i) Section 206 of the Companies Act, 1956, provides that no dividend shall be paid by a company in respect of any share therein except to the registered holder of such share or to his order or to his bankers. The instrument (which looks like a cheque) by which dividend is paid by a company to its shareholders is known as dividend warrant. Like cheques, the dividend warrants remain valid for 6 months unless the issuing companies reduce the period. However, the holders of the warrants can request the issuing companies for revalidating the warrants for a further period.

Q. 32. Who is a member of a company? How can a membership be acquired and when does it cease?

Ans. : Section 41 of the Companies Act, 1956, defines the term member. The subscribers of the Memorandum of Association of the company, every other person who agrees in writing to become a member of a company and whose name is entered in its register of members, shall be a member of the company. Moreover, every person holding equity share capital of a company and whose name is entered as beneficial owner in the records of the depository shall be deemed to be a member of the concerned company. A person can be a member of a company in any one of the following ways:

(a) By subscribing to the Memorandum of Association of the company.

(b) When the directors agree to purchase qualification shares and forward the undertaking to the Registrar of Companies.

(c) By agreeing in writing to become a member of a company and after his name is entered in the register of members. His name will be so entered when he has paid all the moneys due on application/allotment/calls.

(d) By transfer of share by the seller to the buyer.

(e) By transmission of shares in favour of the heirs from the deceased shareholder.

Section 41 of the Companies, Act, 1956, states the circumstances under which a person may cease to be a member of a company :

(a) by a valid surrender;

(b) by the trustee in bankruptcy of an insolvent member disclaiming his shares;

(c) by transferring his shares to another person;

(d) by rescission of the contract of membership on the ground of misrepresentation or mistake;

(e) by his shares being sold by the company under some provision in its Articles and the purchaser being registered as holder in his place;

(f) by his shares being forfeited;

(g) by death of the shareholder, when by transmission his legal representative becomes the owners of the shares.

Q. 33. Explain the following terms and discuss the functions or duties of the Company Secretary in connection with :

(a) Allotment of shares, (b) Share certificate, (c) Calls, (d) Forfeiture of shares, (e) Re-issue of forfeited shares, (f) Transfer and transmission of shares, (g) Bonus shares, (h) Rights issue or Rights share (i) Dividend.

Ans. (a) Allotment of shares

(i) The Secretary has to make arrangement with the bankers to receive application forms and application moneys. All moneys received by the bank on account of application and allotment are credited to the company's "Application and Allotment Accounts."

(ii) When the last date of subscription is over, the Secretary has to arrange for sorting the applications alphabetically and entering them in the Application and Allotment sheets. The total of the "Cash received column" should tally with the balance at the bank.

(iii) He has to arrange a meeting of the directors for making allotments.

(iv) If the allotment is made, a Letter of Allotment must be forwarded to each of the allottees. A "Letter of Regret" should be sent to those whom allotment could not be made.

(v) In terms of Section 75(1), return of allotment should be filed by the Secretary with the Registrar within thirty days of allotment.

(vi) Ordinarily, an allottee has the right to renounce his title to shares in favour of another person. Along with the Letter of Allotment, a Letter of Renunciation is also sent to the allottees. Those who desire to renounce their titles in favour of the nominees have to fill in the Letter of Renunciation. The nominees will have to write to the company a Letter of Request together with the Letter of Renunciation to enroll them on the Register of Members. After allotment of shares is over, the share registers are prepared and the share certificates are made ready. The company will have to arrange for despatching the shares to the allottees.

(b) Share Certificate

The functions of the Company Secretary in connection with issue of share certificates are :

(i) The share certificates are written-up from the particulars entered in the Register of Members. Before issuing the certificates, these are carefully checked.

(ii) The Company's Seal is affixed on all the certificates and the share certificates are signed according to the provisions of the Act and the Articles of Association.

(iii) A Circular Letter is issued to all the allottees advising them that the share certificates are ready. The share certificates are to be despatched to the allottees by the company.

(iv) The certificates are delivered to the allottees, or their authorised persons, on production of the necessary documents and giving a receipt to the company.

Duplicate Share Certificate

If the original certificate is lost, the company may issue a duplicate certificate after compliance with the following procedure :

(i) The shareholder will have to request the company for issuing a duplicate share certificate to him. His letter should clearly state that the certificate has been lost.

(ii) A stamped letter of indemnity duly signed by the shareholder and two sureties is to be forwarded to the company. In case the company has to face any loss in future for issuing the duplicate certificate, the letter of indemnity will enable the company to claim indemnification from the shareholder.

(iii) The shareholder will have to undertake to bear all costs or expenses that are incurred by the company in connection with the issue of duplicate certificate.

(c) Calls

A call is a demand by the company on its shareholders to pay the whole or part of the balance remaining unpaid on each share. After the shares are allotted, the Board of Directors may decide to make calls. The Secretary's duty is to issue letters of call to the shareholders. On receipt of the call moneys, proper postings are made in the Share Register. The Secretary is to send suitable reminders to the defaulting shareholders. The last reminder should clearly state that if the call money is not received by the company within a certain specified date, the shares will be forfeited. In the event of non-payment of call money(s) by the allottees, the company reserves the right to forfeit those shares. The forfeited shares can be re-issued by the company to other persons.

(d) Forfeiture of shares

The Secretary places the names of the shareholders who have defaulted in paying call money(s). Ordinarily, the Board of Directors decides to forfeit the shares if the Articles so provide. The Secretary has to arrange for necessary entries in the books of account and the Share Register of the company.

(e) Re-issue of forfeited shares

If the Articles so provide, the Secretary may arrange to re-issue the forfeited shares. A resolution duly passed by the Board of Directors in connection with re-issue of forfeited shares is required to be obtained. He is to see that the amount at which the forfeited shares are re-issued must not be less than what is due on the shares.

(f) Transfer and Transmission of shares

The shares are movable property and, as such, these are transferable. The Companies Act empowers the shareholders to transfer shares, subject to the provisions of the Articles.

The Secretary's duty is to see that the following procedure is adopted :

(i) A proper instrument of transfer duly stamped and executed by both the transferor and the transferee is to be delivered to the company together with the scrips.

(ii) The instrument of transfer must be in the prescribed form and must be presented to the prescribed authority duly filled in and stamped.

(iii) An application of transfer may be made either by the transferor or by the transferee. When the transferor submits the application and the shares to be transferred are partly paid-up, notice to that effect is to be given by the company to the transferee.

(iv) All transfers must have the approval of the Board of Directors. After the approval is obtained, endorsement on the back of the share certificate is made or a new certificate is issued. The Secretary should see that entries for transfer are made in the Share Register.

Transmission of shares : Where the right to deal with shares is acquired by operation of law, it is called transmission of shares. The secretary's duties in this connection are

(i) To examine the legal status of the representative before he is allowed to deal with the interest of the deceased shareholder.

(ii) In case the shareholder dies leaving a valid will, the executors will be required to produce before the company the probate of the will. In case, however, he dies intestate—without leaving a will, his legal representative will be required to produce the Letter of Administration issued by the Court.

(iii) Details of probate, etc. and transmission are to be entered in the Register of Members.

(g) Bonus Share

The Companies Act does not define bonus shares. However, a bonus share can be defined as a further issue of capital by the company as fully-paid shares or treating the partly paid-up shares as fully paid-up shares, to its existing shareholders without taking any payments from them. In other words, a company issues the share certificates to its shareholders in lieu of payment of bonus in cash. The duties of the Secretary in connection with issue of bonus shares are enumerated below :

(i) Consideration and decision of the Board of Directors to issue such shares.

(ii) The matter is placed in the form of a special resolution before a meeting of the shareholders for their approval.

(iii) The transfer books of the company are closed in order to ascertain the members entitled to bonus shares.

(iv) The list of members, detailing their names, addresses, holdings and the number of bonus shares they are entitled to receive, etc., is placed before the Board meeting. The bonus shares are then allotted.

(v) Letter of allotment for bonus shares together with a circular explaining how the allotment has been made and a transfer form is sent.

(vi) The allottee may, subject to the approval of the Board, transfer the shares in favour of other person.

(vii) Notice is sent to all the shareholders asking them to collect the share certificates from the company on surrender of the allotment letters.

(viii) Within 30 days from the date of allotment of bonus shares, a return detailing the particulars of allotment, allottees and a copy of the resolution authorising the issue of bonus shares are filed with the Registrar of Companies.

(h) Rights Issue or Rights Shares

In terms of Section 81 of the Companies Act, when a company decides to issue further share capital, the new offer has to be first made to the existing shareholders in proportion to their shareholdings. These newly offered shares are known as rights shares or rights issue. In other words, the existing shareholders get this offer as a matter of their rights.

(i) Dividend

The term 'dividend' is derived from a Latin word *dividendum* which means "that which is to be divided or shared". In relation to companies, it is that portion of the profit which is to be distributed amongst the members of the company in proportion to their shareholdings. At the end of the financial year, the final accounts of the company are prepared and are duly audited by the company's auditors. A provisional statement as to disposal of profits is prepared and placed before the Board. The Board finalises the rate of dividend and approves of the dividend notice and warrant and recommends payment of dividend to the general members for their approval. Dividend is finally declared at the annual general meeting. The Board also determines the period for which the Register of Transfers is to be kept closed. The Secretary's duties in this context are :

(i) To send to all the members of the company and also to get published in the newspapers a notice as to the date of the annual general meeting, the period for which the Register of Transfers is to remain closed and the date on/after which dividend warrants will be issued to the shareholders if the dividend, as recommended by the directors, is declared at the annual general meeting.

(ii) A list of members showing the names, addresses, holdings, gross dividend due, income tax to be deducted (abolished after the financial year 1997-98) and the net amount due to each is prepared.

(iii) On completion of the dividend list, work relating to dividend warrants is taken up.

(iv) Arrangements are finalised with the company's bankers to accept the signature of the Secretary or other officer for purpose of honouring the dividend warrants.

(v) Dividend warrants are posted to the members within forty-two days from the date of the annual general meeting.

[*For further discussion on 'Dividend', refer to* **Chapter 11 — Miscellaneous**]

3

OFFICE ORGANISATION

[**Contents** : Office—its Role & Functions—Office Organisation—Importance—Location of an ideal Office—Office Layout—Good working conditions—Office Manual—Large Open Office vs a series of Small Offices—Centralization & Decentralization of Office Services—Centralised Correspondence vs. Decentralised Correspondence—Flow of Work—O & M Department—Office System & Procedure—Organisation Chart—Secretary's Duties as regards Office—Telex, Teleprinter—RSVP—Television—M O—TMO—Postal Order—Postal Parcel—Registration—Insurance—VPP—Book Post—Certificate of Posting—Late Posting—Express Delivery—Post Restante—Business Reply Cards & Envelopes—Identification Cards—Postal Guide—Post Box—Post Bag—Registered Telegraphic Address—Employment Exchange—MT—TT—Courier, Speed Post, Metro Mail Service—Functioning of the Secretarial Department.]

Q. 1. Evaluate the role of an office in a large commercial enterprise. (C. U. 1998; ICSI)

Or, Elucidate the statement of Prof. Dicksee that "The office is to a business what the mainspring is to a watch."

Or, "The office has an important role to play in the management of business enterprises."—Could you justify the statement?

Or, What is an office? Enumerate the important functions of an office. What is its importance to a business enterprise? (C. U. 1988, 1981, 1980)

Or, (a) Discuss the functions of office. (b) Elucidate the importance of an office. (C. U. 1984)

Ans. : Though actual production takes place on the shop floor yet it is the joint result of thought and endeavours of the management and the employees working in the office as well as on the shop floor. Without an efficient office, it is a futile effort to expect worthwhile production. The activities of a business enterprise are multifarious. The work of co-ordinating these activities, rendering assistance in the preparation of various schemes and policies of the management and in taking final decisions and actions on various matters is the functions of an efficient office. The role of an office in this sphere is similar to a playback singer of the cinema or theater. In other words, an office helps the manufacturing divisions indirectly. The principal role played by an office is to supply the correct information to the right person at the appropriate time. The functional managers (for example, Sales Manager, Purchase Manager, etc.) need information on purchase, sales, production, personnel, machines, costs, prices etc. and the chief executive may ask for a synopsis of the various data as he does not have much time to go through the detailed particulars.

These particulars are collected by an office and produced before the managers in such a form as to help them take various decisions. For this purpose, data are processed, recorded and communicated to those persons who need them. When data are complete, accurate and timely, the decisions taken at the appropriate time may prove useful. On the other hand, incomplete, inaccurate and back-dated data may lead the management to take wrong decisions—the results of which may be disastrous. The needs for data and information process are more complex.

The purpose of the office is to provide for the services of records and communication. The office may, therefore, be regarded as an aid to management.

Another purpose of the office is to co-ordinate the departmental activities in such a way as to maximise the efficiency of the enterprise. The office may be called the nerve centre of the business unit. Its function in this respect may be compared to that of the mainspring of a watch. If the mainspring of a watch goes wrong, the watch cannot perform its function. Similarly, if the office does not work well, the business enterprise cannot expect a good production at proper or reasonable cost.

The functions of an office may be summarised as follows :

(a) Collection of data from various sources and preservation of records of all kinds.

(b) Processing of data and posting of entries.

(c) Communication through letters, circulars, notices, etc.

(d) Reporting matters to the proper levels of management to foster the growth of business.

Q. 2. (a) What do you mean by office organisation? (b) What is its importance? (c) Describe the organisation of a modern office. (C. U. 1998, 1991)

Ans. : (a) Henri Fayol, in his book : "General and Industrial Management", has defined the term 'organisation' as follows : "To organise a business is to provide you with everything useful to its functioning : raw materials, tools, capital, personnel." According to G. E. Milward in his book "Large Scale Organisation" : "Organisation is a process of dividing work into convenient tasks or duties, of grouping such duties in the form of posts, of delegating authority to each post, and of appointing qualified staff to be responsible that the work is carried out as planned."

The management experts opine that because of great variety of organisations in existence, it is not desirable to standardise the principles of office organisation. They have, nevertheless, designed certain principles which can be used as guidelines depending on the circumstances obtaining in the organisation. The principles can be enumerated as follows :

(i) The objective of the organisation must be clear and means of achieving it must be indicated in sufficient detail.

(ii) The organisation structure must be flexible to take care of the changing circumstances.

(iii) Every employee should be responsible to only one supervisor.

(iv) Authority to be granted to the employees must be commensurate with responsibility.

(v) Every effort should be made for an even distribution of work amongst the employees and maximum utilisation of their abilities.

(vi) There must be effective co-ordination between various units/divisions/sections of the organisation.

(b) and (c) : *pages 50 and 62-64.*

Q. 3. Discuss some of the important factors which need careful consideration in selecting the location of an ideal office. (C. U. 1998, 1996)

Or, What are the factors that are usually taken into consideration while selecting the site for the Head Office of a large manufacturing concern? (C. U. 1978)

Or, Discuss the factors that are generally kept in view in selecting the site for head office of a company. (C. U. 1984)

Ans. : The various operations of any undertaking—whether manufacturing or trading—are controlled by its office. The work of co-ordinating these operations or activities, rendering assistance in the preparation of various schemes and policies of the management and taking final decisions and actions on various matters, are some of the important functions of an office. In this perspective, the importance of an office cannot but be emphasised. In order to derive the maximum benefit from an office, its location should be ideal. But it is really very difficult to lay down any hard and fast rules for an ideal location of the office as because the circumstances obtaining in any business are peculiar to its own. The circumstances determine the need and the need, in its turn, determines the conditions of location. Broadly speaking, the following factors shall be given careful consideration while selecting the location of an office :

(a) **Accessibility to customers :** New offices are established in that area where the offices of any particular industry are already in existence. This localisation helps the customers in that they are in a position to contact a number of suppliers/traders/producers/service-providers before purchasing a particular product.

(b) **Accessibility to Bank, Post Office, etc. :** Every office, whether big or small, is required to contact the Bank, Post Office, Railway Station, Government Departments for various purposes. The office staff are required to visit these places off and on. The nearness of office to these places will enable quick communication and this, in turn, will save a lot of time and money.

(c) **Proximity to other departments of the concern :** Proximity of the office to its factory, warehouse, sales office, etc., enables it to have quick communication. This, in turn, helps the organisation as a whole to save time and money.

(d) **Availability of personnel :** Different categories of staff are required to man the office and run it smoothly. Therefore, it should be borne in mind that the lower level staff, i.e., Clerks, Technical Assistants, etc., are available locally as far as possible.

(e) **Availability of adequate communication :** Facilities of transport communications should be adequate as these will help the employees as well as the customers.

(f) **Climatic conditions :** Climatic conditions have a direct impact on the health and mind of the human beings. Moderate (i.e., temperate) climate is congenial to the office staff for rendering the maximum service.

(g) **Complementary and Competing Industries :** The area where there are both complementary and competing industries is most helpful for establishment and expansion of office.

Q. 4. What is meant by office layout? Indicate the principles that should guide its planning. (ICSI; C. U. 1999, 1997, 1995 1988, 1971)

Or, What principles would you take into consideration in planning the layout of the new office premises in which your company proposes to move? (ICSI, 1967—Adapted)

Or, What are the factors that should be taken into consideration while selecting the location of an office of a big mercantile firm? (C. U. 1981)

Or, What do you mean by layout of an office? Discuss the factors which should be taken into consideration while planning the layout of an office. (V. U. 1987; C. U. 1982)

Ans. : Layout of an office implies the arrangement and location of all its departments and placement of personnel and equipment with a view to deriving the maximum all-round efficiency with the minimum loss of time and manpower. The following factors deserve careful consideration while planning the layout of an office :

(i) Size and shape of the building and the available space.

(ii) The number of departments into which the office is to be divided, nature of functions of each of the departments, departmental heads and the various categories of staff.

(iii) The total number of employees and the nature of their responsibilities.

(iv) The type of office equipment and appliances to be provided.

(v) Provision for future expansion.

There are a number of principles which provide specific guidance to the manager planning the layout. Some of the guiding principles are enumerated below :

(a) Work is to continuously flow forward as far as practicable in a straight line.

(b) Departments having more or less similar functions should be placed close to one another.

(c) Private offices or chambers should be provided to the top executives.

(d) Stenographers'/Typists' pool, filing room, etc., should be placed centrally.

(e) Adequate space allowances are to be provided for smooth handling of the work and comfort of the employees.

(f) Equipment and furniture should, as far as practicable, be of uniform size and make.

(g) Easy and clear access to 'Exits' should be provided for the sake of safety of the personnel.

(h) Employees should face in the same direction as far as practicable.

(i) Noisy equipment need be placed in an enclosed room.

(j) Sufficient scope for privacy should be provided for those who need it. In this connection, necessary private offices are to be located where interference is the least.

(k) Suitable lighting and air-conditioning arrangements should be made and it should be ensured that healthy working conditions are created.

(l) Scope of future expansion and, consequently, need for more men and equipment, should not be lost sight of.

Q. 5. "Working conditions obtaining in an office have a direct bearing on the efficiency of its employees." Discuss the statement with special reference to the proper working conditions required for the office staff.

And. : Work performed by office employees involves more of mental exercise than physical. Most of the office work is of routine or repetitive nature. Adverse conditions affect the mental and physical health of the employees whose work is mostly monotonous. This, in turn, adversely affects the output and, hence, profitability of the organisation. The impelling need for providing congenial working conditions cannot, therefore, but be emphasised. The management of every progressive organisation fully appreciates this need and tries its level best to create such an atmosphere which would help its employees to render the best possible services.

The following are some of the considerations which enable the employees to render their best services :

(a) **Layout :** Office layout implies the arrangement and location of all its departments and placement of personnel and equipment with a view to deriving the maximum all-round efficiency with the minimum loss of time and manpower.

(b) **Accommodation :** Each employee must get adequate space to work without any hindrance or interruption.

(c) **Lighting :** Good work cannot be expected without good lighting. The cost incurred to provide good lighting may be quite considerable but the benefits derived are sure to more than offset the former. That is why the modern organisations very much care for providing proper and adequate lighting arrangements.

(d) **Ventilation and Heat :** Proper health of the employees can be maintained only when proper ventilation system is provided. In this context, in extreme climatic conditions, air-conditioning machines may be installed to provide healthy working conditions.

(e) **Freedom from Noise and Dust :** Noise and dust are two deterring factors in the smooth working of the employees. Every endeavour should, therefore, be made to create an atmosphere which is free from noise and dust as far as possible.

(f) **Furniture, Fittings and Stationery :** Good furniture, fittings and stationery—if and when provided to the employees—help them work better.

(g) **Miscellaneous :** This includes facilities for cheap canteen, toilets, medical arrangements, etc. Provision for these facilities is sure to raise the morale of the employees and this, in turn, increases productivity and profit.

Q. 6. Write a short note on 'Colour Conditioning'. (C.U. 1988, 1981)

Ans. : The term 'Colour conditioning' may be defined as use of colours most effectively and efficiently so that the employees working in an organisation are in a position to render their best services. This, in turn, increases productivity and profitability of the business enterprise.

Q. 7. What do you mean by an office manual or organisation manual? What are its principal contents? Why is it so important for any expanding organisation?

Ans. : Office Manual : It is a document which sets out the duties and responsibilities of the employees, the rules and regulations under which they have to work and the principles and objectives of the business enterprise in general. The manual is a record of information and instructions to the employees to work in such a manner as to enable the organisation to reach the desired goal. In fact, it is a guide book.

The principal contents of an office manual are enumerated below :

(a) A brief history of the organisation.

(b) An organisation structure showing the authority and responsibility of different categories of staff.

(c) Policies, practices and objectives of the organisation.

(d) Instructions for doing standard as well as non-standard work.

(e) Various forms to be used by the employees together with the instructions for use of the forms.

(f) Facilities available to the various categories of staff.

(g) The date of publication of the manual, name and designation of the person who authorised its publication, etc.

(h) Instructions as to how to use the manual.

The impelling need for office manual in any modern business organisation cannot but be emphasised. The need is much more for the organisations which are growing. The reasons for this are as follows :

(a) Reference to the manual may help the employees to solve most of the problems arising out of routine matters.

(b) This helps the employees to gain confidence and makes them prepared to shoulder responsibility.

(c) Executives are not required to advise the junior employees for the routine work and the time thus saved may be utilised for important and complicated policy matters.

(d) Flow of work remains smooth and uninterrupted.

(e) In the growing organisations, recruitment, promotion and transfer take place frequently. Presence of office manual and its proper use will help the employees to perform the routine work smoothly.

(f) Senior employees handling important matters may leave the organisation or retire. In such circumstances, the office manual comes to the rescue of those who fill in these positions.

Q. 8. Discuss, in brief, the comparative advantages and disadvantages of a large open office and a series of small separate offices. Which one would you recommend for a modern expanding organisation and why? (C. U. 1991)

Ans. : In recent years, there has been a growing tendency for large open office in preference to a series of small separate offices.

Some of the advantages which are derived from the adoption of open office are

(a) Better supervision of the staff is possible.

(b) Better and easier communication is facilitated.

(c) Better utilisation of space which leads to cost reduction.

(d) The speed and efficiency of the employees may increase due to the fact that each employee's work can be observed by his colleagues.

(e) Uniformity may be maintained in regard to provision of office furniture, lighting and ventilation. This leads to economy in cost.

(f) Employees feel contented as there is no discrimination in regard to provision of desks, shelves, filing cabinets, etc.

Adoption of open office is attendant with a number of disadvantages some of which are mentioned below :

(i) Identity of the various departments/sections is lost. The departments/sections handling private and confidential matters are at a very helpless, undesirable and precarious position.

(ii) Uniform lighting and ventilation may not suit all the employees.

(iii) This may lead to noise and disturbance which deter the smooth functioning of the office.

(iv) The office becomes overcrowded sometimes and this results in dislocation of work.

(v) Opening and closing of doors and windows pose a problem and may result in friction between the employees.

Q. 9. Discuss the comparative merits and demerits of centralisation and decentralisation of office services. Which one do you recommend for a growing concern?

(C. U. 1998, 1994, 1990)

Ans. : The term centralisation in relation to an office connotes the following two possibilities :

1. When all the employees of an office are placed at a particular place and the work is carried according to the instructions of a particular executive, it is known as central control with central location.

2. When the employees of an office are placed in its different departments and they are controlled by a central executive, it is known as central control with physical dispersal.

Advantages of Centralisation (or, Disadvantages of Decentralisation)

(a) **Increased efficiency :** Employees hardly get any time to spare as leisure. Continuous work increases efficiency of the employees.

(b) **Cost reduction :** Better utilisation of men, machines and other facilities leads to reduction in cost.

(c) **Specialisation :** Centralisation of office work enables the employees to be specialised in their respective fields.

(d) **Standardisation of payment :** Methods of payment to centrally placed employees may be standardised. This ensures equitable distribution of payment amongst the employees.

(e) **Standardisation of methods :** Office procedures and forms may be standardised and uniform methods may be adopted for the office as a whole.

(f) **Creation of healthy atmosphere :** A healthy atmosphere for working is created and the relations amongst the staff are improved.

Disadvantages of Centralisation (or, Advantages of Decentralisation)

The possible disadvantages of centralisation of office work are summed up as under :

(a) Centralisation of the activities involves more time of the executive for the purpose of control. This wastage of time is wastage of money.

(b) The executive cannot give proper attention to the work of all the individual employees.

(c) It is very difficult to maintain privacy even though the work is of a confidential nature.

(d) Centralisation produces a number of specialists but very few generalists.

Centralisation or decentralisation in its entirety is neither feasible nor desirable. In a growing concern, according to the exigencies of the situation, decentralisation of office services may be permitted because this leads to better progress and higher productivity. On the other hand, some specialised services like accounting, personnel, etc. are better performed if these are centralised. This also leads to cost reduction for the organisation as a whole.

Q. 10. In a big office, the centralised correspondence is more useful than the decentralised one. Discuss the statement. **(C. U. 1987)**

Ans. : The choice between centralisation and decentralisation of correspondence depends mainly on the size and nature of a business organisation. Centralisation demands specialisation which proves profitable only when the volume of work is high to employ specialist staff. It is, therefore, not worthwhile for small and even medium size organisations to go in for centralisation of correspondence. The main advantages of centralisation of correspondence may be enumerated as under :

(i) More even distribution of work which results in improvement in quality and savings.

(ii) Concentration of a number of small sections to a department resulting in saving in accommodation and better supervision.

(iii) Most end-products of the department, i.e., letters written by the specialists, reach a high literary standard.

(iv) Interruption to work on account of noise pollution is minimised as the typists, and stenographers are usually accommodated in a corner of the office.

The disadvantages of the system may be summed up as under :

(i) Departments lose close touch with their correspondents/customers since the correspondence staff write the letters on the basis of information/particulars obtained by them from the respective departments.

(ii) Stenographers/typists are not likely to remain attached to one officer only as a result of which they lack the advantage of becoming familiar with one voice/hand-writing. *Now refer to pages 56-57.*

Q. 11. What is meant by 'Flow of Work'? Discuss some of the common difficulties which stand in the way of getting an ideal flow of work in the office. (C. U. 1991)

Ans. : Flow of work refers to the rate at which the work moves in any way or direction from one operation to another or one desk to another. It is a function of the top management and very often it poses a serious problem to them. Despite the best endeavours, the management cannot exercise absolute control over the flow of work. If the flow of work remains continuous and uninterrupted, the employees, the customers, the suppliers and the visitors are satisfied. This, in turn, creates a good image of the organisation. A direct benefit derived from the ideal flow of work is reduction in cost and, consequently, increased profitability.

Some of the difficulties which are experienced by the management in getting the ideal flow of work are discussed below :

(a) **Unequal volume of work :** There are daily and seasonal fluctuations in the workload. For example, work received in the first mail is mostly heavy compared to that received subsequently. This problem cannot be fully solved despite planning.

(b) **Lack of standards :** Actual performance of the employees can be judged properly against the fixed standards. Non-fixation of standards very often results in unequal distribution of work amongst the employees. This not only deters the smooth work-flow but also creates dissatisfaction amongst the employees. It may be pointed out that it is not always possible—and desirable too—to fix up standards for each job, process or operation.

(c) **Interruption of work :** Non-availability of materials, skilled labour, power and direction results in interruptions of work. It may be mentioned that some of these factors may be controlled by proper planning.

(d) **Lack of planning and scheduling :** Lack of planning or defective planning is dangerous for any venture and it is quite obvious that without good planning no scientific scheduling is possible. It is, therefore, apparent that without good planning and scientific scheduling work-flow is sure to face obstruction.

Q. 12. (a) Explain the term departmentation and its need. (b) What are the principal factors for departmentation? (c) What are the bases on which departmentation is effected? (C. U. 1995)

Ans. : (a) Departmentation can be defined to be a process of grouping common or similar activities into various departments according to the need of the organisation. The need for departmentation in any organisation can be summarised as follows :

(i) This helps an organisation to grow smoothly.

(ii) This ensures proper utilisation of the available facilities to the best advantage of the organisation.

(iii) This enables the organisation to build up a number of specialists in all the departments.

(iv) This enables the employees to work more efficiently and effectively which, in turn, helps the organisation to increase its output and profit.

According to the conditions obtaining in the organisation and bearing in mind its peculiar needs, departmentation is usually effected. It may be effected on the following basis :

(i) **Function-wise :** There are various functions in an organisation viz., purchase, personnel, finance, liaison, research and development etc. Here departmentation is effected on the basis of function. Each of the departments is headed by a qualified and experienced person who is usually a specialist in the line.

(ii) **Product-wise :** A multi-product company usually adopts departmentation on the basis of products being handled by the organisation. Each of the departments is headed by a professionally qualified and experienced person.

(iii) **Territory-wise :** In a large organisation handling a number of products and having all-India market, departmentation is effected on the basis of territory or geographical regions. These territories or regions are headed by Territory/Regional/ Zonal Managers. Such a division helps the Regional Managers to adapt themselves to the peculiar needs and problems of the regions. This leads to better customer satisfaction which, in its turn, helps the organisation to grow further.

(iv) **Customer-wise :** When departmentation is effected on the basis of customers of varied interests, it is known as customer-wise departmentation. Though this is customer-friendly, it poses problems in co-ordinating the activities of various departments.

(v) **Process-wise :** When departmentation is effected on the basis of different processes, it is known as process-wise departmentation. This is suitable for large manufacturing concerns whose final products turn out after a few distinct processes. Each of the process departments is under the control of a technically qualified and experienced person. There should be close co-ordination between the various process departments so as to enable the organisation to perform efficiently.

Q. 13. What do you mean by 'O & M' department in a big organisation? What are its main functions? What are its advantages and disadvantages? Could you justify formation of 'O & M' department in the growing concerns?

Ans. : "O & M" is the abbreviation of Organisation and Methods. Organisation ("O") mainly consists of arrangement of work, division of activities, allocation of duties, authorities and responsibilities, etc., within the concern. Methods ("M"), broadly speaking, refer to work procedure or office systems. With the growth of organisation, workload increases manifold and operational techniques change considerably. Work operations require continuous as well as systematic review with a view to finding better and easier ways of performing the **work**, minimising waste and maximising efficiency. The job can be well-accomplished by the "O & M" department.

Functions

(a) Improvement of the organisation structure.

(b) Ensuring proper delegation of authority amongst the various officials of the business enterprise and extent of decentralisation warranted.

(c) Finding out easier and better ways of doing work.

(d) Improvement of recruitment and promotion policies and training system.

(e) Introduction of the techniques of job evaluation and examination of pay structure and fringe benefits for different categories of staff.

(f) Examination of the existing furniture, fixtures, fittings, equipment, machines, etc. and improvement of these according to the needs of the organisation.

(g) Examination and improvement of the system of forms management.

(h) Examination of and improvement in the methods of filing and indexing.

(i) Fixation of standards of work—both as regards quantity and quality.

(j) Examination of the system of work flow and suggesting improvement.

Advantages

(a) Elimination of waste in every direction which, in turn, increases the profitability of the organisation.

(b) Codification of work procedures.

(c) Improvement in the work-flow and minimisation of the chances of interruption.

(d) Fixation of work standard helps to improve the output of the employees—both qualitatively and quantitatively.

(e) Evaluation of the systems and procedures of work.

(f) Improvement of the overall efficiency of the organisation.

Disadvantages

(a) Application of 'O & M' techniques involves considerable time and entails a lot of expenditure.

(b) A feeling of insecurity arises amongst the office staff and that is why they cannot but oppose it.

(c) The cost incurred in introducing the 'O & M' techniques does not match the benefits derived in the initial stages.

Formation of 'O & M' department in a growing concern is all the more important. In a growing concern, workload increases manifold and operational techniques change quite considerably. It is also not unlikely that in such a situation objectives of the business enterprise will change. Work operations necessitate continuous as well as systematic review with a view to finding better and easier means of accomplishing the work, minimising waste, maximising efficiency and increasing the overall profitability of the organisation.

Q. 14. (a) What do you mean by Office System and Office Procedure? (b) What are the purposes of such systems and procedures in office work? (C. U. 1990)

Ans. : (a) Every office has its own 'systems' and these are usually known as 'office procedures'. The office systems vary with the type as well as size of business, knowledge and wishes of the office managers. According to N. C. Deyner, in his book 'Office Management', "the term 'Office Procedures' is used to describe office systems, and such 'procedures' are said to be made up of 'operations', an operation being the smallest step in a procedure, although the amount of work involved in an operation will depend on the circumstances." Neuschel, in his book "Streamlining Business Procedures", has defined the terms 'System' and 'Procedure' as : 'System' is a network of related procedures developed according to an integrated scheme performing a major activity of the 'business.' 'Procedure' is a sequence of operations usually involving several people in one or more departments established to ensure uniform handling of a recurring transaction of a 'business.' "An office system is the standard sequence of operation in a particular business activity and is concerned with how these operations are performed as well as with where and when they are performed."

(b) **Importance of office systems** : The importance of office systems has been acknowledged throughout the world. The reasons for which so much importance has been attached to office systems are enumerated below :

(i) Good systems which are conducive to smooth working of the office help to reduce bottlenecks in work-flow.

(ii) Systems are based on the methods employed and, as such, they help in speedy disposal of work.

(iii) Systems which include internal checking help to minimise frauds and maximise control over work.

(iv) Good systems result in reduction in direct and indirect expenses.

(v) Good systems improve the overall co-ordination between various departments of the organisation.

(vi) Good systems help the office staff to work almost error-free which, in its turn, improves the overall efficiency of the organisation.

Principles or characteristics of office systems : The general principles or characteristic features of office systems are laid down as follows :

(i) to seek simplicity for complicated systems to make them understandable to general office staff;

(ii) to make the system effective for the purpose for which it has been designed;

(iii) to achieve a good work-flow with no or minimum bottlenecks;

(iv) to minimise errors and maximise speed and accuracy;

(v) to avoid unnecessary checking and writing to keep the paper work to the barest minimum;

(vi) to make the best use of specialisation;

(vii) to make the best use of machines;

(viii) to seek reduction in expenditure;

(ix) to provide for dynamism and adaptability to suit the changing future needs of the organisation;

(x) to use, as far as practicable, the principle of 'management by exception'; and

(xi) to make as few exceptions to the rule as possible.

Q. 15. Describe the main departments of a modern business illustrating your answer with a simple organisation chart. (V. U. 1987 & C. U. 1966)

Or, What do you mean by an organisation chart? Give a specimen organisation chart showing therein the position of the Company Secretary.

Or, Mention the principal departments to be found in a modern business office and briefly describe the functions of any department. (ICSI April, 1970)

Ans. : Just like a tree, any organisation must have its base, body, branches and an apex. The organisation structure of any business is its foundation. The Chairman or President of the Company is at the apex and all actions lie with him or the Board of Directors. The policies of the company are formulated by this top level executive. He is assisted by deputies who are in charge of controlling the major functions. These deputies, in turn, are assisted by the functional managers. An organisation chart, (*refer to page 63*) as the name suggests, is a chart detailing the structure of the concern and the inter-relationships of the various departments.

An organisation chart of a public limited company is given below :

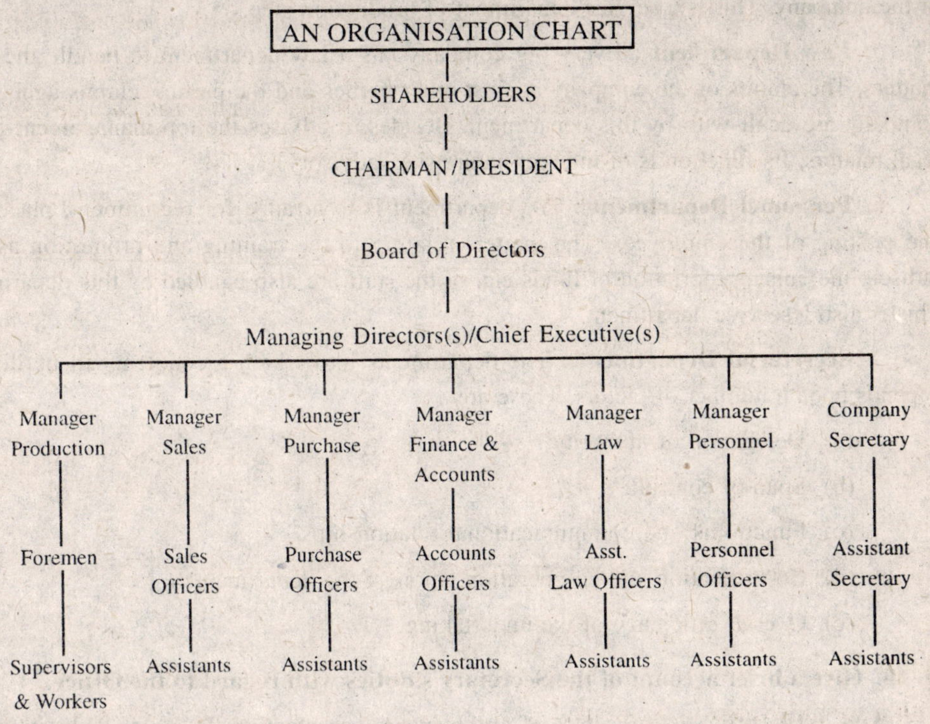

From the chart, it is evident that a company should normally have the following departments :

1. **Production Department :** The main function of this department is to carry on production according to the production schedule. Every effort is made to attain the targeted level of production fixed in the production budget.

To simplify production and economise the operations, it is considered necessary to design the product correctly before production is taken up. So the need for a planning and design section cannot but be emphasised.

2. **Sales Department :** The role of the sales department is a very important one because the overall budget of the company is largely influenced by it. Success of an undertaking is to a great extent dependent on the efficiency of this department. Better profits can easily be earned by effecting higher sales at the existing or higher prices.

3. **Purchase Department :** The function of this department is to arrange for economic purchase of raw materials and spare parts of the appropriate quality/specifications and at the appropriate time so that the production department does not experience any difficulty or bottleneck. The overall profit earned by a company is directly and largely influenced by the success or failure of this department.

4. **Finance and Accounts Department :** This department keeps the proper books of

account so that the position of a business enterprise is ascertained at periodical intervals. It also advises the top management as to profitable and economic use of finance at the disposal of the company. This is a service department of production side.

5. **Law Department :** Every big company has a law department to handle the legal matters. The claims of the company against other parties and the parties' claims against the company are dealt with by this department. Besides, it advises the top management on all legal matters. Its function is of indirect nature (i.e., advisory).

6. **Personnel Department :** The department is to arrange for recruitment, placement and posting of the employees. The matters relating to the training and promotion as also indiscipline, misappropriation of funds etc. of the staff are also handled by this department. This is also a service department.

7. **Secretarial Department :** The departments into which a concern will be divided depends upon a number of factors. These are

(a) Delegation of authority.

(b) Span of control.

(c) Functional and communicational relationships..

(d) Co-ordination and co-operation amongst the departments.

(e) Overall efficiency of the undertaking.

Q. 16. Give a brief account of the Secretary's duties with regard to the Office.

Ans. : The office is the centre of any business organisation. It is a co-ordinating link between production and distribution. It controls and directs the activities of the functional managers. The principal function of the Secretary is to supervise the office work in general. The duties are numerous and these include both routine and non-routine, important and unimportant work. His duties largely vary with the size of the organisation and type of business handled by it. Broadly speaking, the duties performed by a Secretary comprise the following :

(a) Receiving the incoming mail and sorting and distribution thereof.

(b) Drafting of letters, circulars, notices, etc.

(c) Placing the important and complicated letters which involve policy matters before the concerned executives.

(d) He is to look after the work of the Despatch Section.

(e) He is to see that incoming letters and copies of replies to them are filed properly.

(f) He is to arrange for indexing of office files and records.

(g) He helps his boss in fixing up the appointments. He also reminds his boss so as to enable him to keep his appointments.

(h) The persons seeking interviews with his principal are interviewed by him at first (as a private secretary).

(i) Ordinarily, he is authorised to purchase office stationery, forms and equipment.

(j) He has to record the proceedings of various meetings.

(k) Staff matters—selection and posting, etc.—are sometimes handled by him in small organisations.

Besides, a Company Secretary has to organise various meetings and to comply with the provisions of the Companies Act, Monopolies and Restrictive Trade Practices Act, Foreign Exchange Regulation Act, Income-tax Act and various other legislations.

Q. 17. Write short notes on

1. Office Manual, 2. Telex, 3. Teleprinter, 4. R. S. V. P., 5. Television, 6. Money Order, 7. Telegraphic Money Order, 8. Postal Order, 9. Postal Parcels, 10. Registration, 11. Insurance, 12. VPP, 13. Book Post, 14. Certificate of Posting, 15. Late Posting, 16. Express Delivery, 17. Post Restante, 18. Business Reply Cards and Envelopes, 19. Identification Cards, 20. Postal Guide, 21. Post Box, 22. Post Bag, 23. Registered Telegraphic Address, 24. Employment Exchange, 25. M. T., 26. T. T. 27. Courier, 28. Speed Post, 29. Metro Mail Service.

Ans. : 1. **Office Manual :** It is a document which sets out the duties and responsibilities of the employees, the rules and regulations under which they have to work and the principles and objectives of the business enterprise in general. The Manual is a record of information and instructions to the employees to work in such a manner as to enable the organisation to reach the desired goal. In fact, it is a guide book.

2. **Telex :** The teleprinter service maintained by the Department of Telecommunications is known as Telex. The teleprinters are supplied by the Department on rental basis. According to the arrangement, messages can be transmitted round the clock from one subscriber to another. The machine is connected by a Post Office line to the nearest exchange. The subscribers are allotted individual numbers and the transmission of messages between the subscribers is routed through the central teleprinter exchange. The telex operator has to dial the particular number and, after he gets it, he starts typing the message to be transmitted. If there is an operator at the other end, he will receive the message on the machine; otherwise, the machine itself will record the message. The telex machine partly looks like a typewriter and it works like a typewriter. As soon as typing of the message is complete, transmission thereof is also complete and the message gets recorded at the other end almost instantaneously. The operator receiving the message sends a copy thereof to the particular person.

3. **Teleprinter :** This is an electro-mechanical device which is designed to transmit messages instantaneously. It facilitates communication between Head Office and its branch offices or between branch offices located at different parts of the country. The combined advantages of a written letter and a telephone can be derived from the use of a teleprinter. The message to be conveyed is typed in capital letters on a machine which is just like a typewriter. This is simultaneously reproduced over telegraph wires at the other centre or centres having receiving machines. Very large organisations which have to frequently send and receive important messages may install teleprinter exchange with advantage. Teleprinter may be purchased straightaway or it may be taken on rent from the Department of Telecommuniucations.

Teleprinter is essential for the large business houses, newspaper offices, news agencies, etc.

4. **R. S. V. P. :** This is the abbreviation of the French words r'espondez s'il vous plait. The meaning of the terms is respond or reply if you please. In case of some invitation letters, the invitees are requested to reply as to whether they would attend the invitation.

5. **Television :** This is a device by which data recorded in bound books, documents kept in central files, reports, etc., can be transmitted by the sender and viewed on the screen at the receiving end. It has got three parts, viz., camera, master-viewer and power unit. According to the requirements of the organisation, extension viewers may be attached to the master-viewer. In accordance with the instructions given to the filing assistant, the files, documents, papers, records, etc. are placed before the camera which project a clear picture at the receiving end. Installation of television entails huge capital expenditure and this can only be afforded by large organisations. This is an ideal audio-visual aid. The TV system may be usefully employed in traffic monitoring.

6. **Money Order :** Remittance of money between two persons residing in different places may be easily made by way of Money Order. Money Order may be inland or foreign. According to the procedure of the Postal Department, the sender of money is to fill in a standard form which can be had at any Post Office on payment. The form is so designed as to contain the particulars of names and addresses of the sender as well as the payee, the amount to be remitted, date and place of remittance. Besides, the remitter may write a short letter to the payee in the space provided in the form. The Post Office agrees to remit the amount to the addressee on receipt of the amount to be remitted and the requisite fees at the prevalent rate. On receipt of the money, the payee signs an acknowledgement which is sent back to the sender in due course.

7. **Telegraphic Money Order (T. M. O.) :** For quick remittance, the sender has to fill in the standard Money Order Form in the usual manner with the special instruction "By Telegraph". Besides the prescribed fees, the sender has to pay the charges for telegram. The Post Office receiving the money for remittance advises the paying Post Office by way of a telegram to pay the money to the addressee (i.e., payee). 'TMO' is the abbreviation of the term "Telegraphic Money Order."

8. **Postal Order :** A Postal Order—as the name suggests—is an order by a Post Office from which it is purchased to another Post Office where it is presented by the payee or holder for payment of the money mentioned therein. In India, Postal Orders are available in multiples of Re. 1 but up to a maximum limit of Rs. 100. For broken amount of less than Re. 1, postage stamps not exceeding three in number may be affixed on the Postal Order. It is a convenient means of remittance of small amount. The purchasers are required to pay a commission to the Post Office at the prescribed rate in addition to the face value of the Postal Order. The remitters often cross the Postal Orders to ensure that the amount is received by the person for whom it is meant. A crossed Postal Order can be encashed only when it is presented through a bank or a Post Office.

The validity period of a Postal Order is six months calculated from the last date of the month of issue. After this period, a Postal Order becomes stale. A stale Postal Order may be revalidated for another period of six months on payment of a commission at the original rate. On expiry of this period, a Postal Order becomes invalid once for all.

9. **Postal Parcel :** It is a means by which articles of small size and maximum weight of 5 kgs can be sent by an individual or firm to another individual or firm on payment of the postal charges to the Post Office. Parcels weighing more than 5 kgs but up to 20 kgs are required to be registered when these are known to be Registered Postal Parcels.

10. **Registration :** The Postal mail may be sent by registered post to ensure due transmission. In addition to the usual postal charge, the sender is to pay the registration fee. If he desires to have an acknowledgement from the addressee, he has to fill in an Acknowledgement Form supplied by the Post Office, pay an additional charge and mark the cover with the words 'Registered with Acknowledgement Due'. On receipt of the article by the addressee, the acknowledgement form is signed by him in token of his acceptance and the same comes back to the sender in due course through Post Office.

11. **Insurance :** The Post Office does not accept any liability for loss or damage of the articles and parcels sent by registered post. Registered articles, viz., letters, parcels and VPP (Value Payable Post), may be insured to cover all risks of loss or damage during the period of transmission. The articles to be insured must be marked "Insured for Rs. ..." and contain the names and addresses of both the sender and the addressee. The Post Office issues a receipt to the sender in token of accepting the article. In addition to usual postage and registration fees, insurance fees at the prescribed rate (which depend on the values for which the articles/parcels are insured) are to be paid. The Post Office acts as an insurer. On receipt of the articles, the addressee signs the Acknowledgement Due (A. D.) Form which is delivered to the sender in due course.

12. **VPP :** This is the abbreviation of the term Value Payable Post. It is an arrangement between the sender of articles and the Post Office according to which the latter recovers the value of the posted articles from the addressee and hands over the specified amount to the sender. This helps the businessmen and traders in sending articles to their various customers and realising the value through the Post Office. The sender is to fill in a prescribed application form supplied by the Post Office. The particulars to be incorporated in the form are the names and addresses of both the sender and the receiver, the amount to be remitted to him (i.e., sender), etc. He has to declare that the VPP article is being sent by him in execution of a proper order. Only the registered articles can be sent by VPP cover. It recovers from the addressee the amount indicated by the sender plus the prescribed fees of its own and remits the sender his amount by Money Order.

13. **Book Post :** Books, Newspapers, Periodicals, etc. may be sent by Book Post but no personal letters are allowed by the Postal Department in these packets. To facilitate checking of the contents by the postal people, the packets are posted in unsealed envelopes or in covers open at both ends. The covers should be clearly marked with the words 'Book Post'. Transmission of books, printed papers, etc. by way of 'Book Post' is cheaper than that of registered post and ordinary post.

14. **Certificate of Posting (C. U. 1990) :** The Post Offices do not issue any receipt to the sender of ordinary postal articles. As such, there remains no documentary evidence with the sender as to whether postal article has been sent. When the sender is in need of producing or retaining the evidence, he has to fill in the "Certificate of Posting" form which is supplied free by the Post Office. A postage stamp for Rs. 2 is to be affixed on the form and the Post Office date-stamps it which provides space for entering particulars of three articles. The Certificate of Posting certifies that the articles mentioned therein have been posted but the Post Office is not liable to the sender or the addressee in any way for the damage or loss of the articles.

15. **Late Posting :** When the Scheduled time for last clearance from the letter box is over, the sender may arrange for posting a letter by paying late fee by way of additional postage. This facilitates immediate arrangement for despatch of urgent letters. The facility or late posting is available at any Post Office, RMS (Railway Mail Service) Office or in the RMS Van of a train. This has since been discontinued by the Department of Posts.

16. **Express Delivery :** On payment of additional postage, the sender of letters, post-cards, book-posts, etc., may mark these as 'Express Delivery'. These are treated as ordinary articles and sent by ordinary mail. As soon as the articles reach the Post Office of the addressee, the letters, etc. are delivered like telegrams. This is not in vogue at present.

17. **Post Restante :** This is a French expression which means care of Post-Master or to remain in the Post Office until called for. When postal articles are mailed to a person having no exact address (e.g., salesman, medical representative, etc.), these are marked 'Post Restante'. In such an eventuality, the articles are handed over to the addressee when he calls at the Post Office within a reasonable time and discloses his identity. Otherwise, the articles are returned to the sender.

18. **Business Reply Cards and Envelopes : (C. U. 1990)** For the purpose of promoting sales, the traders and businessmen usually send business reply cards/envelopes along with the literatures, brochures, etc. to their prospective customers. The addressees desirous of placing orders have to fill in the order forms and mail them without affixing any postage stamps. The senders of business reply cards have to apply, together with requisite fees, for permission of the postal authorities before issuing the cards. Permission is accorded to the applicants to issue the cards or envelopes as per the prescribed design and size by way of allotting Permit Numbers which are to be inserted in the cards. According to the arrangement with the Postal Department, the postage is collected from the sender of business reply cards/envelopes (i.e., businessmen/traders) on delivery. This induces the addressees to place orders immediately which would not have been placed at all or placed at a later date.

19. **Identification Cards :** The Post Offices issue these cards to those persons who desire to establish their identity for the purpose of receiving postal articles. The cards contain particulars like names, addresses, descriptions, etc. together with their passport-size photographs affixed thereon. After making discreet enquiries to the satisfaction of the Post Offices, they issue these cards. To obtain such cards, the persons have to submit applications to the Post Office together with the requisite fees. The cards may be renewed on payment of the requisite fees.

20. **Postal Guide** : The book which is published by the Postal authorities contains detailed rules and regulations of the postal department. The names of all the Post Offices together with their respective Pin Code Numbers are also available in this guide.

21. **Post Box : (C. U. 1991, 1984, 1982, 1980).** Big Post Offices maintain a number of numbered post boxes which are allotted to any individual, firm or a body corporate on rental basis. Those who desire to have post box facilities have to apply in the prescribed form. Besides rent, prescribed amount of deposit is also to be lodged with the Post Office. When a box is allotted to any one, the relative key and the delivery ticket are also handed over. The duplicate key is retained by the Post Office. The advantages derived from the maintenance of a post box may be summarised below :

(a) The identity of the renter is concealed.

(b) Postal address is shortened.

(c) Mail may be collected by the hirer or renter according to his convenience but during the working hours of the Post Office.

(d) Sorting of mail by the postal people is quickened and facilitated.

22. **Post Bag : (C. U. 1982, 1980)**. To ensure safe delivery and secrecy of postal articles, both from and to the Post Office, business houses may hire post bags on payment of the prescribed fees. A post bag may be hired in addition to a post box. The hirer or renter hands over a lock with duplicate key to the Post Office and the latter issues a delivery ticket which is meant for the messenger of the renter. The Post Office arranges to put all the incoming mail in the bag and the locked bag is handed over to the representative of the renter during the specified hours on production of the delivery ticket. The post bag may be used for outgoing mail also.

23. **Registered Telegraphic Address : (C. U. 1990)**. Telegram charge depends on the number of words used by the sender. It is hardly possible to shorten the name and address of the addressee of the telegram. Large business houses, therefore, arrange with the postal authorities according to which they are allowed to use abbreviated name and address or a code on payment of the prescribed fee to the postal department. For example, THISTLE, Calcutta is the registered telegraphic address of State Bank of India, 1 Strand Road, Calcutta 700 001.

24. **Employment Exchange :** Labour Departments of each of the State Governments maintain a registered Employment Exchange and a number of Sub-Regional Employment Exchanges. Unemployed persons of different categories register their names with any of the offices of the Employment Exchange showing documentary evidences of their age, qualifications, experience, etc. Even employed persons are allowed to register their names for better jobs. The employers— especially in the public sector—are required to notify the Employment Exchange as and when vacancies arise in their offices. On receipt of requisitions from the prospective employers, this office informs the suitable candidates with the instructions to contact the company/firm to get the proper men without incurring a lot of expenditure by way of advertisement in the dailies.

25. **Mail Transfer (M. T.) :** Any individual, firm or a company, irrespective of the fact that he/it maintains an account with the bank, may request the banker to transfer any sum of money for credit to the account of any person or firm being maintained in any of the branches of that bank anywhere in India. What he/it has to do is to deposit the money to be remitted unless he/it maintains an account with the branch of that bank and it does not have sufficient balance. This mode of remittance—which is usually extended by the banks free-of-charge—is known as Mail Transfer (M. T.).

26. **Telegraphic Transfer (T. T.) :** The individuals or firms who desire to remit funds from their accounts to the accounts of others being maintained in any of the branches of that bank in India may request their banks for the facility of remittance by telegraphic transfer. The persons or corporates who do not even maintain any accounts with a bank can also avail of this facility. In addition to the usual charges for remittance, the banks recover telegram charges also. As the message of remittance of fund is sent by telegram, this mode of transfer of money is very quick.

27. **Courier :** The dictionary meaning of the term is messenger. A courier is usually a person or firm that arranges to deliver the letters, parcels, documents etc. collected or received by it to the addressees—usually within 24 hours if the addressees are located in India, or 72 hours if they are located abroad. A courier collects from the individuals and offices of various organisations the mail for delivery to the addressees who may be located it any important centre in India or abroad. The charge for any item to be couriered depends on its weight and distance of the place where it has to be delivered. With the complexities of the modern-day-business and opening-up of the Indian economy, the importance of fast and safe communication has increased manifold. As a result, during the last two decades, a large number of firms have ventured into this flourishing business.

28. **Speed Post :** This is a special quick delivery service introduced by the Department of Posts a few years ago. This facility is available in big Post Offices and the letters, envelopes, parcels etc. received by the Post Offices are usually delivered to the addressees within 24 hours to 48 hours from the time of receipt. The charge for sending any item by speed post is more than registered post charge. The speed post charge depends on the weight of the cover and distance. However, the minimum charge for first 200 gmsintra-city speed post is Rs. 15/- and for inter-city delivery the amount is Rs. 45/-.

29. **Metro Mail Service :** It is a special postal service introduced by the Department of Posts a few years ago for quick delivery of the ordinary mail only at five metro cities of India viz. Delhi, Mumbai, Calcutta, Chennai and Bangalore. The special post boxes painted in blue colour for easy identification are provided at big post offices and important centres and these can be used by the public at large who would like to avail the metro mail service for delivery of their letters. The postal charge for this service is the same as one charged for ordinary post.

Q. 18. Describe the procedure and functioning of the Secretarial Department and use of labour-saving devices by it. (ICSI, October 1975)

Ans. : The executive function of the company is handled by the Managing Director,

Executive Director or General Manager while the administrative function is performed by the Company Secretary. Depending on the size of the organisation and the type as well as volume of business handled by it, the duties and functions of the Secretary vary largely. Though he heads the Secretarial Department, he may have to supervise the works of Accounts Section, Cash Section, Mailing Section, Personnel and Administrative Section, Statistical Section, etc. The procedure and functions of Secretarial Department may be summarised as follows:

(a) **Meetings** : The department helps the chairman to fix up the dates of various meetings of the company. It also performs the various duties before, at, and after the meetings.

(b) **Maintenance of Statutory Books** : The various books required under the Companies Act are maintained by the department.

(c) **Issue of Shares and Debentures** : The work relating to issue of shares and debentures is performed by it and various books/registers required therefor are maintained by it.

(d) **Common Seal** : The common seal remains under the custody of this department (usually with the Secretary) and affixing of the seal on various documents/papers is the responsibility of the Secretary.

(e) **Transfer and Transmission of Shares** : The work relating to transfer and transmission of shares is handled by it.

(f) **Resolutions** : Drafting of resolutions to be passed at the meetings is undertaken by the department.

(g) **Filing of Returns, etc.** : Copies of various returns and special resolutions as required by the Companies Act are filed by the department with the Registrar of Companies.

(h) **Minute Book** : Maintenance of Minute Book for various meetings and making the Minute Book in respect of general meetings available for public inspection is its responsibility.

(i) **Registration and Satisfaction of Charge** : When the company borrows moneys from banks and/or term lending institutions against the securities of industrial assets of the company, the charge has to be created and registered with the Registrar of Companies and on liquidation of the loan(s), the charge is to be satisfied. This is the duty and responsibility of the department.

(j) **Personnel, Administration and Taxation** : The work relating to personnel, administration and taxation is more often than not handled by this department.

The labour-saving devices used by the Secretarial Department largely vary depending on the size of the company and the volume of work handled by it. However, depending on the actual requirements of the individual companies, all or some of the following devices may be used :

(a) Typewriter.

(b) Duplicator.

(c) Addressograph (Bradma).

(d) Signing machines (for facsimile signatures).

(e) Tod Cheque Signer.

(f) Loose leaf Minutes Book.

(g) Punching Machine.

(h) Sorting Machine.

(i) Tabulating Machine.

Q. 19. Discuss the various service facilities available to an office from the Department of Posts.

Or, Discuss the various service facilities provided by the Department of Posts to the business community.

Ans. : All the countries of the world have Departments of Posts which render very essential services to all sections of the people. In India, this department is run under the direct control of the Central Government. The services provided by the department are available to all individuals, firms or bodies corporate. The services available to the business community at large are enumerated below :

(a) Post Box and Post Bag.

(b) Post Office Savings Bank facilities inclusive of National Savings Certificates, National Savings Scheme, Indira Vikas Patra etc.

(c) Telegram.

(d) Post Restante.

(e) Money Order and Telegraphic Money Order.

(f) Registered Parcel.

(g) Registered letters.

(h) Insured Parcel.

(i) Value Payable Post (VPP).

(j) Business Reply Card/Envelope.

(k) Book Post.

(l) Certificate of Posting.

(m) Abbreviated Telegraphic Address.

(n) Prepaid Postage.

(o) Speed Post.

4

CORRESPONDENCE, OFFICE FORMS & OFFICE COMMUNICATION SYSTEM

[**Contents** : Incoming & Outgoing Mail—Purposes & Functions of Office Forms—Forms Control—Central Pool System of Stenographers & Typists vs Personal Staff—Internal Communication System of an Office.]

Q. 1. Suggest a suitable procedure for handling incoming and outgoing mails in a big office and mention at least two important records to be maintained as well as two mechanical devices to be used in this connection.

(C. U. 1994, 1969, 1964; B. U. 1966: ICSI April 1970—Adapted)

Or, Discuss sequentially the procedure of handling 'Inward Mail' of a company which has a number of departments. (C. U. 1990, 1987, 1981 & V. U. 1987)

Ans. : Office is said to be the nerve centre in any concern receiving and despatching communications. Correspondence implies communication by letter, circular, notice or memorandum. Communication by way of correspondence is preferred to other media because it enables the sender to convey the message properly. Besides, as this is a documentary evidence, the possibility of any dispute in future can be ruled out. The mail in an office can broadly be divided into two categories :

1. Inward or incoming mail and
2. Outward or outgoing mail.

Handling Inward Mail

The practice of handling mail differs from concern to concern. Ordinarily, big offices usually have central receiving departments for handling the incoming mail. The following procedure may be adopted for handling the inward mail :

1. **Receiving the incoming mail :** This is, practically speaking, the starting point of work of the correspondence department. Most of the large organisations have a post box or post bag at the post office wherefrom letters, etc. are collected by a person once or twice a day. Besides, some letters are delivered by the postman which do not bear the number of post box/bag. Moreover, quite a number of letters is received at the counter through the "Peon Book" of the sender. It is to be ensured that the incoming mail is placed in the custody of a responsible officer and nobody gets any chance to pilfer away or tamper with any of the letters and their enclosures.

2. **Opening the mail :** The next stage starts at opening the mail. The mail is normally opened by the principal executive or the proprietor himself in small offices. However, in large organisations, there is a central receiving department. The clerical staff of this department open the mail in the presence of a responsible officer. The officer goes through the letters and checks up whether the enclosures as stated in the letters are actually enclosed. The letters addressed by names (or marhed 'PERSONAL' should not be opened and these should be forwarded to the concerned persons for their direct disposal. Large organisations handling voluminous mail may profitably use the electric letter opener. The empty covers may either be attached to the respective letters or retained for a few days to check up the address or date of stamp of Post Office.

3. **Scrutiny and Sorting** : The contents of all the covers should be carefully checked up. The letters enclosing cheques, postal orders, bank's pay-orders, etc. need careful attention. Any discrepancy should be immediately noted on the forwarding letter.

4. **Date-stamping the mail :** Prevalent practice of most of the organisations is to put a stamp on all incoming mail. The stamp is so designed as to include the particulars like date and time of receipt, serial number, signature of the receiving clerk, etc. Large organisations may gainfully use 'Dating', 'Numbering' and 'Time Recording' machines to get this work done.

5. **Recording the receipt of mail :** The details of the incoming mail are entered in the 'Letters Received Register'. The purpose of this Register is to check how the letters are disposed of as well as to keep track of the letters. This system does not find favour with modern large organisations. They maintain central receiving section which prepares a list, in duplicate, of the incoming mail, department-wise. The duplicate copies of the lists having the initials/signatures of the officers of the receiving departments are filed in the Central Receiving Section. This system is proved to be more economic and effective too.

6. **Distribution of mail :** After proper sorting, letters are distributed to the concerned departments.

7. **Routing :** Occasion arises when a letter needs the attention of a number of persons in different departments. In such a case, a routing slip containing the names of persons to whom the letter is referred is attached and the letter is forwarded for necessary action to each of them. Alternatively, photocopies may be sent to the concerned persons.

8. **Follow-up :** The world at large judges a business enterprise on its efficiency in correspondence. Business correspondence can be said to be the substitute for a dialogue. To create a good image of the organisation in the eyes of the people, all letters must be replied to with promptitude and copies of replies retained for future reference. The departmental managers should ensure that prompt and suitable replies are sent to all the letters. This is known as 'follow-up' of the inward mail or keeping track of the mail.

Handling Outward Mail

The procedure for handling outward mail can be discussed under the following heads :

1. **Drafting letters :** Letters may be of two types, viz., (a) important letters and (b) routine letters or form letters. The important letters are ordinarily replied by the senior and responsible officers. Before drafting the reply, the relative file and the relevant papers have to be made ready. The senior executives do not have much time for drafting the letters. They normally utilise the services of stenographers for this purpose. The replies to various letters are dictated by the executive to his stenographer. The dictation taken by the stenographer is thereafter transcribed by him on a typewriter. The executive may also ask the stenographer to type out drafts of the dictated letters. While going through the drafts, he makes the necessary corrections. These drafts are then returned to the stenographer or the typist for final typing on the letterheads of the undertaking with the number of copies as desired.

Use of dictaphone is becoming very popular. The busy executive can dictate the replies to various letters at his spare time when the services of stenographer may not be available. The stenographer or the typist can type out the dictated matter when the disc containing the dictation is played back on the transcribing machine at such a speed at which he/she can type. The machine is both labour saving and time saving.

In replying to routine letters, what is required is to fill in the appropriate standard printed forms. These 'Form' letters are mostly signed by the junior officers or the senior assistants of the concern.

2. **Signature and Seal :** After the letters are typed by the stenographers or the typists, these are placed before those persons who have the powers to sign. The unimportant routine letters are, however, signed by the junior officers or the senior clerks. The original letters, together with the endorsement, if any, are signed in full and the copies are initialled by the person concerned.

3. **Referencing :** All the outgoing letters are marked with some symbol or marking which facilitates easy identification and placement of the letters in the appropriate files. This is the process of referencing. The addressees are requested to give the reference numbers of the letters while replying. The symbol consists of words, abbreviations and numbers and it is designed in such a way as to indicate the department wherefrom the letter originated and the concerned file.

4. **Despatch :** After the letters are signed, these are sent to despatch section for despatch to the addressees. Large offices generally have a central despatch section which handles the correspondence received from all the departments for final despatch. The process of despatch involves the following stages :

(a) Checking up of the addresses on the envelopes and the letters.

(b) Checking up the number of enclosures said to have been forwarded with the letter.

(c) Folding the letters and inserting the enclosures to the letters in the envelopes. Where the volume of work warrants, use of folding and inserting machines may be used with advantage.

(d) **Sealing the envelopes, flaps or covers as the case may be :** Large offices handling voluminous correspondence may profitably use the sealing machine.

(e) **Stamping or franking the outgoing mail :** Small offices affix the postage stamps on the letters by hand but large offices perform this work mechanically by way of a franking machine.

(f) **Recording :** Most of the offices maintain an outward mail register showing the details of the letters sent under the columns suitably designed. Normally the columns are for date, serial number, reference number, names and addresses of the addressees, subject, enclosure(s), sender, postage, remarks (if any), etc.

(g) **Delivery :** Ordinarily, letters addressed to the local parties as well as the urgent letters are sent through messengers after entering the details of the letters in Peon Book. Telegrams, registered letters and letters sent by speed post may be entered in different registers for convenience.

Q. 2. (a) Discuss sequentially the different steps involved in handling 'Incoming' mail of a fairly large business undertaking.

(b) Give the proforma ruling to two books of record which are usually maintained by the correspondence department of a business concern. (C. U. 1990, 1986, 1983)

Ans. : *(a) Write 'Handling Inward Mail' portion from the previous answer.*

(b) Two commonly used books of records in the correspondence department are Letters Received Book and Letters Despatch Register (or Outward Mail Register). As the names suggest, the Letters Received Book records the details of the incoming letters and Letters Despatch Register records detailed particulars of the outgoing mail. A proforma of each of the said registers is given below :

Letters Received Book

Date of Receipt	Reference number	Name & Address of sender	Short Subject	Enclosure(s), if any	Referred to	Disposal	
						Date of Reply	Signature

Letters Despatch Register

Serial Number	Date	Name & Address of the Addressee	Short Subject	Enclosure(s), if any	Postage Stamp	Remarks

Q. 3. Describe the purposes and functions of office forms. Why is it important to consider the designing and physical appearance of an office form?

Or, What are the important considerations which should govern proper form design? (ICSI)

Ans. : A form is a printed or cyclostyled piece of paper or card which contains a number of columns asking for various information or instructions and providing space to incorporate the information/instruction. The purposes of the forms may be enumerated as under :

(a) Presentation of information in such a systematic manner as to make it easily understandable.

(b) To ensure efficient office-work.

(c) To save valuable time.

Functions

(a) Essential tools for clerical and routine work.

(b) Form helps to record transactions, convey information and expedite filing.

(c) It ensures uniformity in operation and the copying work is minimised.

(d) Helps both who designs the forms and who fills in the same.

(e) Standardisation of forms entails cost reduction.

(f) Information on various heads may be obtained through a well-designed form.

(g) Office methods and procedures are simplified and uniformity can be maintained.

(h) Serves as work guide.

Though the designing of forms is the function of a specialist, the office manager should be in touch with the designer and offer his suggestions so as to make the forms helpful and useful to the office. The design of a form has a direct bearing on the efficiency or otherwise of an office. The importance of an office form stems from the following facts :

1. Purpose of its use is the most important consideration.

2. The amount of information that a form requires determines the size of the form.

3. The quality/type of paper to be used for the form depends on its use, frequency of handling and period of storage, etc.

4. The main function of the form is to simplify and systematise the routine works. In planning the layout of a form this point should not be lost sight of. A good form should normally contain three parts, viz., heading or caption, body and footing.

5. A well-designed form should lend itself to easy typewriting, punching, etc.

Appearance of form : Where a form is meant for use by the outsiders, its physical appearance deserves special consideration. Every effort should be made by the office sending the forms to the outside parties to make these attractive. Quality paper and colour can be used even though the cost may be somewhat high. A good form creates a good impression and image of the firm.

Q. 4. Discuss the steps necessary for operating an effective forms control system in an office. (ICSI October 1976)

Or, Write Short Notes on Forms Control. (C. U. 1981)

Ans. : Forms control may be said to be a method of exercising control by the management over the day-to-day affairs of any enterprise. The main function of forms control is to evaluate the design and ensure that the forms in use meet the requirements of the office and contribute to the efficiency and productivity of the organisation. The following steps may generally be taken to achieve an effective forms control system :

(a) **Office systems :** The first step is to ascertain the systems, routines and procedures followed by the office. This job should preferably be entrusted to an officer. A close study of the office procedures and systems will help him properly integrate the forms.

(b) **Improvement :** Expansion of the organisations leads to diverse needs. Obviously, the forms already in use may need addition, alteration or deletion of certain particulars/ information. The office systems and procedures may require some changes. Taking these factors into consideration, a critical review of the existing forms should be made by the forms supervisor. He should accept the suggestions from those who use the forms. A register may be maintained by the Forms Control Section wherein changes suggested by the various departments/sections and employees may be entered for subsequent consideration.

(c) **Recommendation :** The forms supervisor should carefully examine the individual suggestions and thereafter offer his recommendations to the higher level of management.

(d) **Purchase and Procurement :** On receipt of approval of all the departments/sections, the Forms Control Section arranges for placing the order through the purchase department. The stores department receives the forms for subsequent supplies to the various departments according to their needs.

(e) **Standardisation :** Standardisation of office forms helps the work-flow to be smooth inasmuch as both the employees and the constituents of the organisation are equally benefited. This results in cost reduction and increased profitability.

Q. 5. Discuss the merits and demerits of a central pool system for stenographers and typists as compared to personal staff for the same.

Ans. : According to the central pool system, the services of the stenographers and the typists are placed in common pool which works according to the instructions of a specialised supervisor. Most of the large and modern offices are switching over to this system for its inherent advantages.

Merits

The merits of the pool system can be enumerated as under :

1. Work received from various departments is allotted to the stenographers and typists in such a manner that none of them is over-worked or remains idle. This is based on the principle of equity.

2. The idle time is minimised which saves avoidable costs. For example, a department which has ten officers will require ten stenographers for each of the officers. Under a pool arrangement, the services of six or seven stenographers will be sufficient to cope with the same work load. It is, however, true that a few executives may like the services of one or two of the stenographers of the pool. In such an eventuality, the executives will be given priority for their preference.

3. Senior executives who have to handle confidential and important matters would require their concerned stenographers for the purpose.

Advantages or Merits of personal staff or departmental arrangement :

1. The stenographer or the typist who is attached to a particular executive becomes

familiar with the peculiarities of his boss. Clear understanding between the executive and his staff helps to produce better work.

2. The stenographer/typist becomes habituated with the peculiarities and the technicalities of his departmental work. This increases his efficiency and improves his quality of work further.

3. The executive can get the services of his stenographer/typist according to his sweet will.

4. A sense of loyalty grows in the minds of the personal staff and they render their best services for the sake of their respective officers as well as for the department as a whole.

Demerits/Disadvantages

1. Due to uneven and unfair distribution of work amongst the staff, someone may be overworked and someone may sit idle for hours. It is a source of displeasure and discontentment amongst the staff.

2. This system entails employment of more stenographers and typists than are actually required. Therefore, this arrangement proves more costly.

3. According to departmental arrangement, placement of stenographers/typists within each of the departments is sure to disturb the other staff.

Q. 6. "Communication is the principal function of any office"—Elucidate and explain categories of internal communication system. (ICSI)

Or, What do you mean by internal communication? What are the methods usually adopted for internal communication? (ICSI)

Ans. : Communication is the process of conveying message or thought. The office acts somewhat like a clearing house. It receives information from outside and transmits the required information to the proper person or the department. When an office communicates with outside parties, this is known as external communication. When the communication is restricted to two persons or departments of the same organisation, it is known as internal communication. Communication may be made verbally or in writing. An office—especially large—is required to provide facilities for communication amongst the employees and the departments of any organisation. The efficiency of a large and modern office largely depends upon the provision of inter-communication facilities.

The methods of internal communication usually adopted by large offices can be discussed under the following two heads :

1. **Oral or verbal :** This can again be subdivided into (a) transmission in person and (b) transmission through mechanical and electrical devices. Face-to-face conversation is an example of transmission in person. Transmission of message by way of speaking tubes, dictating machines, signals, telephones, etc. are examples of communication through mechanical and electrical devices.

2. **Communication in writing :** Internal communication may be made in writing or by way of mechanical devices.

Messages in writing can be conveyed by one person or department to another person or department through the messenger as and when necessary. In some offices, the internal mail service is still in vogue. According to this arrangement, the messengers are to collect messages according to a time-table from the departments/employees for onward transmission to those for whom these are meant.

Another mode of transmitting written messages is by way of mechanical devices. Transmission by mechânical devices proves economic and more effective when the office is to handle voluminous communications and that too very frequently. Messages may be conveyed by mechanical carriers or by transmitters. Examples of mechanical carriers are wire carriers, pneumatic tubes, etc. Television, telefax, telex, computers are some of the examples of transmitters.

Q. 7. Write short notes on (1) Telewriter, (2) Mechanical conveyor, (3) Pneumatic Tube, (4) RABMN, (5) SWIFT.

Ans. : 1. **Telewriter :** It is a mechanical device of transmitting handwritten message. The message to be transmitted is written with a metal stylus on a metal platen after switching on the machine. As soon as the message is written at one end, it is almost instantaneously reproduced at the other end, i.e., the receiving point. The limitation of this machine is that transmission is possible within a very limited distance. Telewriter is also known as telautograph.

2. **Mechanical Conveyor :** This is a communicative device which is suitable only when volume of work is always large. The conveyor may be of different types and the particular type which will be suitable for a particular business house depends on distance, weight, etc. of what is to be conveyed.

3. **Pneumatic Tube :** It is a mechanical device of conveying messages, papers, documents, blue-prints, etc. from one point to another by means of a cylindrical pipe. The papers etc. are carried by pneumatic (i.e., air) pressure through the tube for ultimate delivery to the persons/departments/offices concerned. The initial cost of introducing this device is much on the high side but it proves quite economical provided the volume of work is large and continuous.

4. **RABMN :** The Department of Telecommunications has recently set up the Remote Area Business Message Network (RABMN) which is a satellite-based network capable of linking far-flung areas of the country. Output of a computer in the form of simple text/file is beamed on to the satellite revolving at an altitude of 33,000 kms from the earth. The information which is reflected by the satellite is picked up by the main earth station where it gets routed via the satellite to its ultimate destination. The speed of transmission is about 15 words per second. The network is not affected by natural calamities like rains, floods, cyclones, earthquakes etc. and, as such, is ideally suitable for establishing communication links with remote areas which are vulnerable to natural calamities.

5. **SWIFT :** It is the abbreviation of Society for Worldwide Inter-bank Financial Telecommunications. Security, standardisation and efficiency are the hallmark of SWIFT which transmits 15,00,000 messages per day. It works through standardised message tapes developed by the Society. The members of the Society—which are generally financial institutions, commercial banks, brokers, exchanges, trust companies and nominee services—can use this facility for the exchange of essential information relating to a broad range of transactions.

5

FILING AND INDEXING (MAINTENANCE OF RECORDS)

[**Contents** : Filing and its Importance—Filing System, Requirements, Centralised vs Decentralised Filing System—Procedure of Filing—Selection of Filing Equipment—Classification of Files—Filing Systems (Old vs New)—Indexing—Types & Purposes—Disposal of Old Files—Card Index & its Uses]

Q. 1. Define Filing and explain its importance. **(ICSI)**

Or, What is filing and what are its objects and importance?
(C. U. 1996, 1986, and often subsequently)

Ans. : Filing has been defined as "the process of so arranging and storing original records and copies of them that they can be readily located when required." In other words, it refers to the preservation of business records (e.g., incoming letters, replies to them, documents, etc.) in a systematic way.

Objects and Importance

The principal object of filing lies in preserving the records of a business house in such a manner as to facilitate easy referencing. In conducting the day-to-day affairs of any office, very often it becomes necessary to refer to past records. If the records are systematically filed, it will be very easy to trace out the particular record which is required by a particular employee. Records are, so to say, the evidence of the transactions effected by any business enterprise. In this context, it may be mentioned that the principal role of an office in a business enterprise is to supply the correct information to the right person at the appropriate time. For this purpose, reference to various records needs to be made. This is very much facilitated if and when a proper and systematic filing system is in vogue.

The importance of filing in a modern business house cannot but be over-emphasised. With the growing complexity of the business—both in size and magnitude—the volume of correspondence and other documents is increasing. As a sequel to this, it has been imperative on the part of any office to maintain a systematic filing system. The main functions of a filing system or the advantages derived from the filing system may be summed up as under :

1. All incoming letters can be attended to without any delay. Prompt replies to the outsiders create a good image of the business house in their minds.

2. Future plan of action and policy decisions may be easily and effectively taken by reference to past records.

3. Records are the documentary evidence of various facts and figures and these can be used as legal proof in the settlement of disputes.

4. Referencing is facilitated. The customers feel disturbed if and when they are asked to supply copies of previous communications.

5. The files enable one to know the life history of the business house.

Q. 2. State in general terms the fundamental requirements which should be fulfilled by a good filing system for office correspondence and records.

Or, What factors would you take into account when designing a filing system? (ICSI)

Or, What are the essentials of a good filing system? (ICSI—Adapted; C. U. 1976, 1970)

Or, What is meant by filing? What are the requisites of a good filing system? Why filing is important in office? (C. U. 1998, 1989, 1982; V.U. 1988)

Ans. : Any organised activity is preceded by a system and this is true for all office activities. A good filing system ensures efficient working of the filing department in particular and the organisation as a whole in general. There is no ideal system of filing which can be safely recommended to suit all the circumstances. Every system is attendant with its peculiar merits and demerits. The system to be adopted will largely depend upon the needs of the organisation and the circumstances obtaining. It should, however, be ensured that the following essential characteristics are present in the system to be installed :

(a) **Simplicity :** It should be simple so that even an employee of average intelligence can master the system.

(b) **Suitability :** It must suit the peculiar needs of the organisation. A system suitable to a particular type of organisation may not suit others.

(c) **Serviceability :** The system should be such as would ensure the work of speedy and accurate tracing, easy handling and quick referencing. In other words, the system should guarantee that adoption of routine steps will entail minimum loss of time.

(d) **Consistency :** The method once adopted should, as far as practicable, be followed consistently because frequent deviations lead to great confusion.

(e) **Elasticity :** The system should be so elastic that it can be easily expanded or contracted with the changing needs of the business house.

(f) **Safety** : Use of proper type of filing equipment ensures safety of the papers and records against loss by fire, insects or theft.

(g) **Economy :** The system should pass the test of cost-benefit analysis. In other words, the cost to be incurred for the introduction of the system must match the benefits to be derived therefrom. Economic use of space is very important—

especially in big cities—where rent is abnormally high. The difficulty can be partly overcome by using special equipment which takes comparatively less space and, in turn, attracts less rent.

(h) **Cross-reference** : The system to be designed should provide for the facility of cross-reference so that a particular document may be traced out under different headings.

Q. 3. What are the comparative advantages and disadvantages of centralised and decentralised filing? (ICSI—Adapted; C. U. 1997, 1986, 1973)

Or, What do you know about the organisation of the filing department?

Ans. : The problem of deciding as to whether filing work should be centralised or decentralised is said to be the organisation of the filing department. Centralisation in this connection refers to the placement of filing equipment and staff centrally in such a way as to benefit the working of all the departments of the organisation. On the other hand, when filing work is done and run by the department, it is known as departmental or decentralised filing. Here, the location of the filing equipment and staff is arranged within the department.

Decentralised filing : The advantages and disadvantages of this arrangement are outlined below :

Advantages

1. It ensures better control over filing staff and arrangement.

2. It facilitates quick disposal of matters.

3. Secrecy of the department can be maintained inasmuch as the papers and documents of confidential nature are kept within the department.

4. The papers and documents which are the concern of only one department can be maintained departmentally to make these easily accessible to the employees of that department.

Disadvantages

1. It is more expensive since much space is wasted and considerable amount of money is blocked in purchasing quite a number of filing equipment.

2. Standardisation of filing work will hardly be possible inasmuch as every individual department will follow its own system.

3. As the filing clerks will not have sufficient work for the whole day, they will normally be called upon to do other jobs. Consequently, they will not be able to acquire specialisation.

4. Filing of those papers and documents which will be required by a number of departments poses a special problem.

Centralised filing : The advantages and disadvantages of this arrangement may be summed up as follows :

Advantages

1. Economic use of space and filing equipment entails savings in cost.

2. Standardisation of filing work is possible.

3. The filing staff acquire specialisation and render efficient service to the organisation.

4. Installation of modern filing equipment is facilitated by this arrangement.

Disadvantages

1. Secrecy of the individual departments cannot be maintained as the papers and documents of confidential nature pass through a number of persons.

2. Delay in obtaining the files from the central filing department may interrupt the departmental work.

Q. 4. What is the procedure of filing? What factors need consideration in the selection of filing equipment?

Ans. : After the finalisation of the filing system, a carefully planned filing procedure is to be devised and this should be followed by the filing staff. With a view to making the procedure successful, the following steps may be taken :

1. **Checking the papers, etc. :** The papers earmarked for filing should be filed. The filing clerks should ensure that the papers relating to pending matters are not filed.

2. **Classification and sorting :** The filing clerks should read the papers for the purpose of their proper classification and subsequent sorting.

3. **Order of filing :** The papers passed on for filing should be arranged date-wise in such a way that the most current letter remains at the top.

4. **Removal of paper :** Whenever any paper is removed from any file, indication by way of placing a substitution card or out-guide should be given.

5. **Diarising :** Matters requiring follow-up action should be properly marked by way of tags.

Equipment : The prerequisites for an efficient filing work are proper selection of the equipment and employment of trained men. The following points should be carefully considered in selecting the filing equipment :

1. The shape and size of the equipment will have to be decided on the basis of the space available for use.

2. The services to be rendered by the equipment and the ease with which the same can be handled.

3. The cost incurred should match the benefits to be derived therefrom.

Q. 5. What is meant by classification of files? What are the various methods of classification of files? (C. U. 1991, ICSI)

Ans. : The term 'classification of files' implies assigning individual items to a particular group or category on the basis of some common characteristics. Proper classification ensures efficiency of the filing system and the papers or documents required may be traced out by any employee very easily. Big business houses often have several types of files and each type, in turn, contains a large number of folders.

To ensure easy accessibility to files, these should be given proper titles. Classification and grouping of files should be based on some fixed or pre-determined principle. Several methods of classification of files are in vogue and the particular method to be introduced in an office depends on its suitability for the purpose. Some of the methods are discussed below :

(a) **Alphabetical classification :** This refers to classification of folders according to the first alphabet of the correspondent. This method is recommended when the names of the correspondents are important. The working of this method is similar to the working of a dictionary or a telephone directory. The advantages of this system are

(i) This is very simple.

(ii) The working under this system is so elastic that any change may be incorporated subsequently.

(iii) No indexing is required in this system.

(b) **Numerical classification :** This implies allotment of numbers to each folder or record and then placing the files in the strict numerical order. The best advantage of this system is that it is elastic since new files can be easily accommodated. For tracing out a paper or making a reference under the system, the index is to be referred. So indexing is a 'must' under the system.

(c) **Alpha-Numerical classification :** According to this system, filing is firstly alphabetical and subsequently there are a number of folders under each letter or alphabet. This combines the elements of alphabetical and numerical classification and, as such, it is also known to be the combination system.

(d) **Subject classification :** According to this system, all the papers/documents pertaining to a particular subject are collected for filing in a particular file, e.g., Purchase, Sales, Agencies, etc. The titles of the files have to be very clear, unambiguous and short. It is, therefore, considered unwise to leave this job in the hands of junior clerks.

(e) **Geographical classification :** Under this system, files are arranged according to the location or address of the individuals/firms. This system requires indexing.

(f) **Chronological classification :** Under this system, papers are placed strictly datewise.

Q. 6. What are the filing systems (both old and new) of an office? Examine the relative advantages of each of the system. (C. U. 1991; ICSI)

Ans. : The systems of filing may be discussed under the following two heads :

1. Old methods.

2. Modern methods.

The old methods of filing are still very useful to those business houses whose volume of work is small. In other words, offices handling a small number of documents, papers, etc. may continue to use the old methods. The filing equipment to be used may be any one of the following :

(a) **Lever arch files :** These files consist of heavy cardboard covers wherein the papers/documents are retained by means of stout arch-shaped wire loops.

(b) **Guard Books :** These are bound books in which papers are pasted in strict chronological order.

(c) **Metal holders :** The papers which are required for small duration may be filed in the metal holders. This is a very back-dated method and used by a few small offices.

(d) **Spike files :** All the papers meant for filing are just put through a spike fixed to small metal or wooden base. This method suits small one-man businesses.

(e) **Pigeon-hole :** The papers, documents, etc. meant for filing are placed into a wooden box having a number of squared holes. Usually the box contains twenty-six holes in alphabetical order.

(f) **Box files :** These are provided with spring clips and alphabetically arranged manila sheets which facilitate quick filing.

(g) **Loose-leaf binders** : The papers and documents meant for filing are loosely kept together. These look like bound books.

(h) **Expanding alphabetical cases :** These are made of cardboard and these contain a number of pockets where papers can be placed alphabetically.

(i) **Press Copy Book :** All outgoing letters are copied in this book. This involves incurring of avoidable cost and suits only small concerns whose volume of business is small.

Modern methods : The old methods of filing discussed above have made way to the new methods which can broadly be divided into the following three categories :

1. Flat or Horizontal system.

2. Vertical system.

3. Lateral system.

1. **Flat or Horizontal system :** This refers to the system under which papers and documents inserted in the files or folders are kept in cabinets or drawers in horizontal position. The great advantage of this system is the arrangement and placement of papers in chronologi-

cal order. The main disadvantage, on the other hand, is that since the drawers can accommodate lesser number of files, the space available is not economically and effectively utilised. Consequent upon expansion of business, volume of papers and documents also increases and this necessitates reorganisation of the drawers. Some of the important types of horizontal filing are described below :

(i) **Flat Files :** According to this system, the covers are made of cardboard or thick paper and these are arranged in the flat form one upon the other, subject-wise or customer-wise. This is an improvement on the pigeon-hole system. The papers etc. lie flat in each drawer fixed with a pilot. Papers relating to more than one file should be copied so that each of the files gets a copy thereof. The files are placed horizontally. The system necessitates proper numbering of files and indexing. Movement of files from one employee to another should be properly recorded.

(ii) **Lever Files :** These too are made of cardboard wherein metal arches are fixed. These files are operated by lever. For the purpose of inserting any paper, the lever is moved upward which opens the metal arches and the lever is pressed down after the insertion of the paper. The most important advantage of the system is to place any paper at the desired place and take out any paper from the file without disturbing the order of other papers and documents. Another advantage is that the papers etc. are protected from loss or misplacement. The system makes economic use of the available space.

(iii) **Desk Filing :** The executives may like to have all the relevant papers in regard to any matter near at hand. To cater to the needs of these executives, their desks are provided with deep drawers. The papers may be fastened or clipped or may be kept loose. On completion of the specific job, the relative papers are removed from the deep drawers for the purpose of permanent filing.

(iv) **Open Shelf Filing :** Under this system, for the purpose of placing the papers and/or files, steel racks or open shelves are used. The demerit of the system is that papers remain uncovered here.

2. **Vertical System :** As the name suggests, this refers to the system by which the files or folders are placed vertically in the drawers of the filing cabinet. This system requires steel or wooden cabinets in which equipment for hanging folders is fixed. The files are kept in the folders. Each of the folders has a jutting-out portion which indicates the number or subject-matter of the file. This helps quick location of the required file.

The vertical filing system is superior to horizontal system, and that is why the former has been widely accepted by modern and large business houses. The merits of this system are outlined below :

(a) **Economy :** Economic use of space ensures saving in avoidable cost.

(b) **Ready Reference :** The papers are easily accessible and withdrawal or placement of papers does not pose any problem.

(c) **Flexibility :** Increase in volume of correspondence can be met by increasing the number of folders. The vertical system lends itself to provision for future expansion.

(d) **Adaptability :** The system can be adapted to any type of classification, e.g., subject-wise, correspondence-wise, geographical.

(e) **Safety :** The papers and documents are placed in the folders and thus kept free from dust and worms.

(f) **Applicability :** Variety of records, viz., letters, orders, invoices, estimates, tenders, quotations, etc. can be preserved.

3. **Lateral system :** A variant of the vertical filing system is known as lateral system. As the name suggests, the folders are suspended by hooks and stored laterally. This system ensures economic use of space and thus saves avoidable cost.

Q. 7. What is indexing? Mention the principal types of index and the purposes for which they may be used. (ICSI; C. U. 1997, 1977)

Or, Write short notes on indexing. (C. U. 1991, 1986, 1981)

Ans. : Index means pointer, guide or indicator and, as such, indexing may be said to be a system which readily indicates the whereabouts of the files or the folders. In other words, indexing is the key to filing. If the files are arranged alphabetically or geographically in alphabetical order, index is not necessary. In other cases, an index is required to be maintained with a view to keeping a condensed record of customers and the correspondents. To make it more useful, the particulars of the correspondents and customers—such as their addresses, telephone numbers, credit reports, etc.—may also be recorded. Indexes are also used with ledgers and other registers.

Types of indexes : Indexes used by the business houses are of several types. Some of these are crude and rigid and, therefore, involve less cost, whereas some are highly sophisticated and modernised and, therefore, costly. The choice of a particular type of system depends largely on the need of the business. Indexes of files which are commonly used by business houses are enumerated below :

1. **Book Index :** As the term suggests, it is in the form of a bound book or register wherein names of persons, documents or other information are arranged in alphabetical order. The merit of this index is that it is not costly and is not likely to be misplaced. The disadvantage is that this is not flexible and, as such, too many additions or alterations cannot be incorporated. Another disadvantage is that, excepting the reference to location of an account/paper, no other information can be recorded herein. This is useful to small concerns.

2. **Vowel Index :** This is the improved form of Book Index. Here, the pages of the index book reserved for each alphabet are divided into six sub-sections A, E, I, O, U and Y. The names of the correspondents are recorded on the page reserved for its initial letters and next by the first vowel following the initial letter. This type of index is generally used with loose-leaf or bound ledgers. Since it lends itself to limited expansion, its use is restricted to medium-size organisations.

3. **Loose-leaf Book Index :** This is a variant of the Book Index. This book comprises single removable sheets fitted into metal hinges or screws. Index is prepared on these sheets.

In case a new leaf is to be inserted, the book may be unscrewed to insert the sheet in the proper place. The loose-leaf books are commonly used for maintaining the Customers' Ledgers, Registers of Members, etc.

4. **Fixed Index :** Instead of a separate index for ledger and other books maintained by a business house, an index is bound or fixed with the book concerned. This type of index is found in all books. Fixed index may appear in either of the following two forms :

(a) Self Index.

(b) Extended Index.

5. **Card Index :** This is prepared by allotting a separate card to each piece of information, e.g., a customer, a document, etc. The cards should be of uniform size and arranged in alphabetical, numerical or geographical order. Sometimes two cards are prepared from the same information but the cards are arranged in two different ways. This facilitates quick location of the cards. In libraries, cards may firstly be arranged title-wise (of the books) and then name-wise (of the authors). The cards are put in steel drawers and a rod is put through them to hold them in proper places. The purpose of this is to avoid the risk of misplacement. The cards are of immense help to the libraries, banks and other business houses.

6. **Visible Index :** Under this system, the cards are held flat in transparent covers in a shallow metal tray. These cards are placed in such a way that a part of the lower portion of the cards is visible all the time. Each tray contains as many as fifty cards. The trays may be fitted horizontally into cabinets or vertically to metal stands. The cards may be arranged alphabetically, numerically or in some mixed orders. The entries may be made in the cards without removing them from the trays.

Purposes of Index

1. The main purpose is to facilitate location of the required file.
2. To make an orderly list of correspondents readily available.

Q. 8. "Filing and Indexing are the two very important aspects of record keeping,"— How can you justify the statement?

Ans. : *Write 'Objects and Importance' from Answer to Question Number 1 and the first paragraph of Ans. No. 7, pages 81-82 and 88-89.*

Q. 9. (i) What are the reasons for keeping old office records? (ii) What are the various considerations involved in the disposal of old files and records? (C. U. 1972)

Ans. : (i) Maintenance of records is an important part of office management. Management has to take important decisions and the prerequisite for decision-making is information. The required information may be available if proper records are maintained in a methodical manner. Some of the objectives for maintenance of office records are enumerated below :

(a) Records are required for future reference.

(b) In case of disputes, records may be required to be produced before the Court.

(c) Records help the management to take vital decisions properly.

(d) Records help the organisation to measure its progress. Comparison of its performance with other concerns in the same line of business is also possible.

(e) Remedial measures for cost reduction and increased profitability may be adopted if proper records are available.

(f) Chances of errors are minimised and prevention and detection of frauds is facilitated if proper records are maintained.

(g) Records are required to be maintained for compliance with legal requirements.

(ii) Old and inactive files which are hardly required by the business house are generally destroyed. Every concern develops its own retention schedule based on certain factors or considerations. Some of them are enumerated below :

1. Legal requirements.
2. Governmental requirements.
3. Operational requirements.
4. Historical requirements (i.e., value).
5. Requirement of future reference.

The retention period may vary from three years to ten years. The old and inactive files —until destroyed—are normally kept in a separate room. The files which should be destroyed are normally kept in a separate room. The files should be destroyed in the presence of a responsible officer of the firm/company bearing in mind the legal provisions for retention period of different types of documents.

Q. 10. What do you mean by 'Card Index' and what are its advantages? Discuss the various uses of 'Card Index'.

Ans. : *Write the paragraph on Card Index from pgs. 88-89. Ans. to Q. No. 7.*

Advantages

(a) According to the expansion or contraction in the volume of business, the number of drawers/trays can be increased or decreased. In other words, this system of indexing offers the maximum flexibility.

(b) The order in which the cards are arranged and/or the order in which the drawers/trays are arranged can be changed without any difficulty.

(c) The cards for dead files can be withdrawn and the cards for new files can be inserted without any difficulty.

(d) The system offers the advantage of using the cards by a number of employees at the same time.

(e) The cards can be taken out from the drawers for incorporating some more data and then inserted in their proper places. This does not pose any problem to the users.

(f) Apart from the purpose of indexing, the cards are also, so to say, the store-house of vital information.

(g) Compared to other forms of indexing, the system offers economy.

(h) The facility of cross-referencing is available to this system.

(i) Unlike Book Index, blank cards need not be inserted.

(j) It takes very little time to trace out a particular card as the cards are easily visible.

Uses

(a) **Office :** The Personnel or Staff Department of any office is required to maintain particulars of the various categories of staff on its roll.

(b) **Bank :** The banks are to record the specimen signatures of their customers.

(c) **Life Insurance Corporation/General Insurance Cos. :** Life Insurance Corporation and General Insurance Companies record the names, addresses, etc. of the lives assured/items insured for sending premium notices.

(d) **Banks/Lending Institutions :** They are required to record the details of the borrowers for frequent reference.

(e) **Public Limited Companies :** The public limited companies having a large number of shareholders are to record the details of the names, addresses, etc. of the shareholders for sending notices/letters/dividend warrants, etc.

(f) **Manufacturing Organisations :** Large manufacturing concerns have to carry hundreds of items in their stores. The details of these items may be recorded on the cards to facilitate inventory control.

(g) **Trading Concerns :** The firms/companies who sell by instalments are required to record the details of the transactions as well as the customers. These organisations can well use the card index.

(h) **Libraries :** Libraries are required to maintain a large number of catalogues for the books. The card index system serves their purpose very well.

6

OFFICE EQUIPMENT & LABOUR-SAVING DEVICES

[**Contents** : Labour-saving devices—advantages and disadvantages; Consideration for selection of machines; Bound and loose-leaf registers; Microfilm; Duplicating machines; Accounting machines—advantages; Addressing Machine, Letter Opening Machine, Envelope Sealing Machine, Folding Machine, Inserting Machine, Stamping and Franking Machine, Electronic Calculator, Punch Card Machines, E.D.P. Machines, Cheque writing machine, Dating and numbering machines, Tod-Cheque signer, Comptometer, Cash Register, Billing machines, Time recording machine, Log Book, Internal Check, Continuous Stationery, Loose-leaf registers, Office furniture, Telephone Exchange, PMBX, PABX, Intercom, Extensions, Phonogram, Local Calls, Toll Calls, Trunk Calls, Demand Trunk Call, STD, ISD, Internet Ready Reckoner, Slide Rules, Automatic Typewriter, Electric Typewriter, Adding Machines, Calculating Machines, Automatic Calculator, Facsimile Telegraphy, Microfilming]

Q. 1. What do you understand by 'Labour-Saving devices'? What are their advantages and disadvantages? Name a few such devices which are commonly used in modern offices. (ICSI)

Ans. : Modern era is the age of machines. The machines cannot work on their own. Human brain directs the machines to get the things done according to the requirement. From this perspective, man plays as the thinker and machines act as the workers. The machines which save or reduce human labour are known as labour-saving devices. The office machines are ordinarily known to be the labour-saving devices.

Advantages

The advantages derived from the use of labour-saving devices may be outlined below :

1. The machines save labour time and, thus, labour cost also. Time so saved may be utilised for higher production at comparatively low cost.

2. Greater efficiency and better production improve productivity and reduce cost of production.

3. Cost reduction results in increased profits the share of which is enjoyed by the shareholders/partners/proprietor/employees.

4. Accurate and uptodate records are very useful to the various levels of management.

5. The drudgery of monotonous work performed by the employees is eliminated.

6. Better communication between the company and its staff on the one hand and between the company and its shareholders as well as the customers on the other is possible.

7. Better service to the public creates a good image of the organisation.

8. Uniformity of work performed by machines helps an organisation to standardise its work.

9. Cost of maintenance of a machine is ultimately cheaper than the cost of maintaining a man on the pay roll.

Disadvantages

The disadvantages or demerits which are attendant with the introduction of these machines are enumerated below :

1. The expenditure incurred is often quite considerable and this strains the liquid position of the firm installing the machines.

2. Breakdown of machines often creates bottleneck in work.

3. Trained operators may not be available within the organisation and the firm may have to recruit men from outside to run the machines.

4. Sometimes volume of work is not adequate to keep the machines fully engaged.

5. Some of the machines occupy much space.

6. Depreciation is high and operational cost is often higher than estimate.

7. Replacement of machines which involves sizable investment poses a serious problem to the management.

Types of machines : The machines available may be classified under the following categories :

1. Typewriters including electronic typewriters.

2. Duplicating machines, e.g., Hectograph, Mimeograph, Multigraph, etc.

3. Accounting and Tabulating Machines such as Adding Machines, Calculating Machines, Cash Register Machines, Billing Machines, Punch Card Machines, etc.

4. Copying Machines, viz., Photostat, Diazo, Microfilming, etc.

5. Electronic Data Processing (EDP) Machines.

6. Desk-top Computers/Personal Computers are used by the employees of many organisations for accessing the database captured/collected by the EDP Department.

Q. 2. When will you favour the use of machines and equipment?

Or, What consideration should weigh with the management in selecting machines for a large office?

Or, What principles should be taken into consideration before purchasing any new office machines and equipment? (ICSI)

Ans. : The impelling need for suitable mechanical devices in a modern office cannot but be emphasised. The main purpose of installing the machines is speedy but accurate work at comparatively low cost. The workers feel contented when they are provided with modern tools to work with. But great care and caution should be taken before deciding on the issue of installation. The following considerations should weigh with the management :

1. **Cost-Benefit Approach :** The cost to be incurred in connection with purchase and installation of the machine must match the benefit to be derived therefrom during the period of its life.

2. **Volume of Work :** Volume of work must be sufficient to constantly feed the machines, otherwise installation proves uneconomical.

3. **Availability of machines and spare parts :** It should be ensured that machines as well as their spare parts are easily available.

4. **Availability of trained personnel :** The machines cannot work on their own. They need to be operated by trained men. It should, therefore, be ensured that there is no dearth of trained operators.

5. **Repair and Maintenance :** It should be ensured that facilities of repair and maintenance are available from the suppliers of machines as and when occasion arises.

6. **Opposition from the Employees/Union :** Installation of machines is often opposed by the trade unions inasmuch as the services of quite a number of employees become redundant. In case of retrenchment, payment of compensation to the workers poses a problem.

7. **Organisational difficulties :** Due to change in the existing set-up and the system of work, the concern may have to experience a number of difficulties. Besides, the employees are, in general, allergic or averse to mechanisation.

8. **Accommodation :** It should be ensured that the machines to be installed can be accommodated in the space available.

Q. 3. Discuss the methods of copying without repeating the original process of preparing office correspondence and documents. (C. U. 1977, 1976, 1965)

Or, Describe the methods of making copies (not carbon copies) of letters or documents. State briefly the advantages and disadvantages of the method you choose for an office where thousands of circulars are sent every day.

Or, Name three machines for copying letters without repeating the original process of preparing the letters. (C. U. 1986, 1982)

Ans. : Copying refers to production of a few copies either by hand or on a typewriter/computer. When the number of copies required are more than the capacity of typewriters but not so much as to justify printing, the use of duplicating machines is recommended. However, personal computer can generate as many copies as required.

Irrespective of the size of office and volume of work handled by it, use of typewriter cannot but be emphasized. Operation of a typewriter is very simple and it can produce six copies on ordinary paper and ten copies on manifold paper. However, modern offices are switching over to personal computer/lap-top computer in preference to typewriter. Typewriters may be of different sizes and types—the most common being standard typewriter of standard size. Besides, there are Portable Typewriter, Electric Typewriter, Automatic Typewriter and Electronic Typewriter.

Duplicating Machines : Some of the important processes and machines for duplication are described below :

1. **Hectograph :** The master copy is hand-written or typewritten on a paper with special ink or carbon. It is then placed on the gelatine surface and the duplicating papers pressed on the gelatine bed take the impression. Gelatine duplicators which use the hectographic process may be of three types, viz., (a) Flat-bed, (b) Rotary and (c) Liquid Spirit. Approximately 200 copies may be obtained from one impression.

2. **Mimeograph :** It is the name of the machine which is commonly used for obtaining copies under the stencil process. A stencil is a special type of coated tissue paper. The matter which needs to be copied is type-written, hand-written/drawn by stylus. The stencil is then fastened to the cylinder over the ink pad. While the cylinder revolves, the stencil comes in contact with the duplicating papers fed to the machine. This is also known as stencil duplicator. The principal types of this machine are Roneo and Gestetner. By this process, 1,000 to 5,000 copies may be obtained and the stencil may be retained for future use. This machine is used by most of the business houses.

3. **Offset duplicator :** Master copy of metal paper plate is prepared on the typewriter or by hand/photographic methods. The master copy is so fixed with the cylinder that it gives a negative impression on another cylinder. It is then possible to get positive impressions from the negative. This machine is recommended to those who require thousands of copies as well as need retention of the master copy.

4. **Multigraph :** Multigraph machine can be said to be a small printing press in an office. As purchase and installation entail huge cost, installation of this machine is beneficial where the volume of work warrants it. A multigraph machine, which is driven by a motor and automatically fed with blank sheets, can make out approximately 3,000 copies per hour. Here the type is hand-set and printing through a ribbon and inking the type make out copies like printed ones.

5. **Photostat Machine : (C. U. 1986) :** This machine can reproduce the exact copy of any writing, printing or drawing by way of taking a direct photograph on the photographic paper. This machine does not require any film or plate to produce the photo. According to the requirement, the photograph to be taken may be made smaller or larger than the original, Besides, use of filter in the machine enables it to produce coloured copies of the photographs.

6. **Blue printing :** This method of copying is of limited use. It is a semi-photographic process according to which the matter to be copied is written or drawn on a special semi-transparent paper. Afterwards, it is set in a printing frame and it comes in contact with the specially coated paper and is exposed to sunlight/artificial light. The positive copy thus obtained is developed and washed like a photograph.

7. **Micro-filming :** A complete micro-filming unit comprises (a) micro-film, (b) pro-

jector, (c) developing machine and (d) printing machine. The matter to be copied is photographed on a thin film in miniature. The film may be retained for future use. Papers fed into a chute are automatically photographed on a single roll of film. The machine operates at such a high speed that as many as 6,000 photographs may be taken in an hour. The advantages of microfilming are enumerated below :

(i) Safe preservation of records is possible.

(ii) Photographs may be obtained speedily and accurately.

8. **Personal Computer (C. U. 1997) :** A Personal Computer (PC) is basically a small, relatively cheap, general purpose, single user microcomputer based on microprocessor chip technology with all functional elements found in larger systems. It usually consists of a keyboard, a Central Processing Unit (**CPU**) and a monitor.

Q. 4. What do you mean by Accounting Machines? What are the principal advantages of mechanised accounting?

Ans. : Where the volume of accounting and book-keeping work is so much that it is not possible to handle the work manually with efficiency and speed, use of accounting machines becomes essential. Accounting machines may be broadly divided into two categories, viz., (a) Typewriter-cum-calculator which can type both in words and in figures. (b) Typewriter which prints figures only indicating the nature of the entry, i.e., Debit (Dr.) or Credit (Cr.). Some of the important and commonly used machines are as follows :

1. Adding/Listing machines manufactured by the Remington Rand of India Ltd.
2. Calculating machines for additions, subtractions, multiplications, divisions, etc.
3. Cash register and Coin handling machines.
4. Billing and book-keeping machines.

The advantages derived from machine accounting may be summed up as under :

(i) Machines work much more quickly than men.

(ii) Accuracy is ensured and the customers are satisfied as to the correctness of the calculations.

(iii) Accounts can be maintained neatly.

(iv) Handling voluminous data is a drudgery and the machines come to the rescue of the clerical staff.

(v) Preparation of final accounts is facilitated as the books are posted uptodate.

(vi) Clerical expenditure is reduced.

(vii) Most of the machines can be used for more than one purpose.

(viii) The data available from the machines can be profitably used by management for better control.

However, the organisations which have partly or fully computerised their operations can use appropriate softwares with advantage in preference to the old accounting machines.

Q. 5. Make a comparative study of the advantages and limitations of bound and loose-leaf registers. (C. U. 1978)

Ans. : Modern business houses have to maintain a number of registers either of necessity or for compliance with the statutory requirements. These registers may be maintained either in the form of bound books or in loose-leaf form.

Loose-leaf book is a variant of the book index. This book comprises single removable sheets fitted into metal hinges or screws. Index is prepared on these sheets. In case a new leaf is required to be inserted, the book may be unscrewed to incorporate the sheet in the proper place.

The advantages which accrue by loose-leaf registers may be summarised as under :

1. Location of any name or subject is facilitated.

2. This system lends itself to flexibility inasmuch as the number of leaves may be withdrawn or increased as and when required.

3. As the system is more or less self-indexing, no separate index needs to be maintained.

4. The registers can be easily handled.

5. Error in posting or transferring data/information from one sheet to another is minimised.

6. The system saves much labour inasmuch as a completely new register need not be written when the same is filled-up.

7. The leaves can accommodate more data/information than the cards.

8. The system lends itself to adaptability since the order/arrangement of the leaves can be changed easily.

The loose-leaf registers are attendant with a number of defects and limitations. These may be summed up as under :

1. Compared to bound books, the initial cost is much on the high side.

2. The possibility of misplacement or accidental loss of the leaves cannot be ruled out.

3. It facilitates fraud inasmuch as the unscrupulous employees get an opportunity of replacing or destroying some of the leaves.

4. A Court of Law does not accept the loose-leaf records as documentary evidence.

The advantages of bound books are discussed hereunder :

1. Compared to the loose-leaf registers, cost of the bound books is on the low side.

2. As the sheets or leaves are bound, there is hardly any possibility of loss or misplacement of the pages.

3. Possibility of fraud by the employees is undoubtedly minimised.

4. Unlike loose-leaf registers, bound books are accepted as documentary evidence in a Court of Law.

The defects and limitations of bound registers are outlined below :

1. The system is neither flexible nor adaptable.

2. Separate index is required to be maintained.

3. Bound books/registers cannot be easily handled.

4. Insertion of new pages and withdrawal of old pages according to requirement pose a problem.

5. Bound books are not suitable for the modern growing organisations handling voluminous transactions.

In the light of the above, it may be concluded that modern big business houses should go in for loose-leaf registers/books which, in fact, they actually do.

Q. 6. What do you mean by microfilming and what are its main uses in an office? (C. U. 1988)

Ans. : Microfilming is a means of recording and retaining information by photography of 16 mm or 35 mm cinematograph film. The matters/documents/records so microfilmed may be seen by projection on to a screen. The machine which is used for the purpose is known as 'Viewer'.

The use of microfilming has already been very popular with big business houses with modern outlook. The uses to which microfilming may be put to are :

(a) Saving of office space, especially in these days of exorbitantly high rent, is possible by replacing the files/records, etc., by spools of film.

(b) Safety of the original documents is ensured inasmuch as microfilm may be referred to for general use of the staff.

(c) Compared to security and durability of the paper records, microfilming is undoubtedly better and longer lasting.

(d) Compared to other methods of copying, microfilming is better because it takes the minimum time in copying.

(e) Cost of freight may be reduced to a great extent if, instead of sending bulky files, spools of film are sent.

(f) Microfilm may be a part of the office system.

(g) Cost of filing equipment and floor space also is considerably saved.

(h) Microfilm is, so to say, a permanent record.

Q. 7. Name the principal office machines used in the following departments and describe their functions :

(a) Mailing department.

(b) Cash department.

(c) Accounting and billing department.

(d) Share and secretarial department. (ICSI)

Ans. : (a) (i) Inserting Machine, (ii) Envelope Sealing Machine, (iii) Folding Machine, (iv) Addressing Machine, (v) Stamping and Franking Machine.

(b) (i) Cash Register, (ii) Billing Machines.

(c) (i) Electronic Calculator, (ii) Comptometer, (iii) Cash Register, (iv) Cheque-Writing Machine, (v) Billing Machine.

(d) (i) Adding Machine, (ii) Comptometer or Facit, (iii) Electric Typewriters, (iv) Bradma Addressing Machine.

For functions of the machines, refer to Ans. to next Question.

Q. 8. Write short Notes on : (1) Addressing Machine, (2) Letter Opening Machine, (3) Envelope Sealing Machine, (4) Folding Machine, (5) Inserting Machine, (6) Stamping and Franking Machine, (7) Electronic Calculator, (8) Punched Card Machines, (9) EDP Machines, (10) Cheque Writing Machine, (11) Dating and Numbering Machines, (12) Tod Cheque-Signer, (13) Comptometer, (14) Cash Register, (15) Billing Machines, (16) Time Recording Machine, (17) Log Book, (18) Internal Check, (19) Continuous Stationery, (20) Loose-Leaf Registers, (21) Office Furniture, (22) Telephone Exchange, (23) PMBX, (24) PABX, (25) Intercom, (26) Extensions, (27) Phonogram, (28) Local Calls, (29) Toll Calls and Trunk Calls, (30) Demand Trunk Call, (31) Ready Reckoner, (32) Slide Rules, (33) Automatic Typewriter, (34) Electric Typewriters, (35) Adding Machines, (36) Calculating Machines, (37) Automatic Calculator, (38) Facsimile Telegraphy, (39) S. T. D., (40) I. S. D., (41) Internet, (42) E-mail, (43) E-commerce, (44) V-SAT, (45) Computer, (46) Personal Computer, (47) Laptop, (48) Pager, (49) Mobile Phone.

Ans. : 1. **Addressing Machine :** The addressing machine makes a great contribution to the smooth and efficient running of business by providing the means of imprinting repetitive information quickly, accurately, neatly and at low cost. Where letters, circulars, advertising literatures are sent frequently to the same persons, an addressing machine serves the purpose very well. The machine is commonly used by the companies for issuing shares, dividend warrants, balance sheets, etc. to their shareholders, by the insurance companies for sending policies, premium notices, by big organisations for preparation of pay-roll, etc.

The machine may be of the following three types :

(i) uses stencils;

(ii) uses embossed zinc plates;

(iii) uses hectographic carbons as the printing medium.

The operation of the machine is very simple. Names and addresses are placed on 'masters' and the latter are made to pass through a machine which imprints the information at the desired place.

2. **Letter Opening Machine** can open envelopes very quickly and this is adjustable to any size of envelope. Where volume of incoming mail is quite considerable, this machine may be used with advantage. This may be operated by electricity or hand. An electrically operated machine can open up to 500 envelopes of different sizes in a minute.

3. **Envelope Sealer** moistens and presses the flaps of envelopes for pasting. This machine may be hand-operated or electrically operated. An electrically operated machine can seal approximately 300 envelopes of different shapes and sizes per minute.

4. **Folding Machine** folds letters in the manner desired and at a very high speed. Where the volume of work is large, this machine may be used with advantage.

5. **Inserting Machine** inserts or places the enclosures in the envelopes and thus saves much time of the clerical staff.

6. **Stamping Machines** are used by small offices for affixing postage stamps. Stamps of various denominations are supplied by Post Office in rolls and these are kept locked in the machines. The machines are so designed as to moisten and affix the stamps. The total amounts of stamps used is recorded on an automatic counter. The machines may be hand-operated or electrically-operated.

Offices handling voluminous outgoing mail prefer **franking machines** to stamping machines mainly because of the speed at which they work. These machines enable printed impressions of stamps to be made on all types of outgoing mail such as envelopes, postcards, parcels, etc. The name or an advertisement of the user may be incorporated along with the stamps. The machines may be purchased or taken on rental basis from the supplying companies licensed by the postal authorities. The users of franking machines are required to comply with the following conditions :

(a) Holding a Post Office licence.

(b) Depending on the amount prepaid to the Post Office, the machine is set and locked. The machine ceases to work as soon as the amount prepaid is exhausted and it starts functioning when reset by the Post Office after advance payment by the user.

(c) A statement showing the daily readings of the meter should be forwarded to the postal authorities at the end of the week.

7. **Electronic Calculator** works like a mathematical wizard and with lightning speed. Additions, subtractions, multiplications and divisions as also squaring, square-rooting etc. of any simple or complex figures can be done instantly.

8. **Punched Card Machines** consist of three main processes, viz., (a) Card Punching, (b) Sorting, (c) Tabulating. The advantages of punched card accounting system are outlined below :

(i) It eliminates the work relating to posting of data in journals and ledgers.

(ii) The cards which are permanent records may be used anytime.

(iii) It ensures quick and accurate preparation of various statements.

9. **EDP** is the abbreviation of the term Electronic Data Processing. It refers to the processing of data through electronic computers. These computers are nothing but electronic devices and they comprise electro-mechanical equipment. These are capable of handling

various types of complicated work in the quickest possible time. Smooth work flow is ensured and this, in turn, improves the overall efficiency of the organisation.

10. **Cheque Writing Machine** is also known as the cheque protector. The main purpose of the machine is prevention of fraudulent alteration of amounts in figures as well as in words. Some machines perforate the cheques with pin-print type in such way as to make any alterations practically impossible.

11. **Dating and Numbering Machines :** Irrespective of the size of the organisation, these machines are used for stamping date, time and number on letters. The machines are not at all expensive but they render very useful service to the organisation.

12. **Tod Cheque Signer** is a machine which is used when a large number of cheques are required to be signed simultaneously. The function of this device is very simple. The specimen signature is reproduced on the cheques and this hardly gives any scope for forging. This machine is electrically operated and kept locked in a cabinet so that it cannot be used by undesirable persons.

13. **Comptometer** is designed to perform a great variety of calculations. Additions, subtractions, multiplications and divisions in whole numbers, decimals or fractions, etc. can be done with ease, speed and accuracy.

14. **Cash Register :** This machine is largely used by the big offices on their sales counters, particularly where cash transactions are voluminous. This machine serves two main purposes :

(i) As and when customers pay against a cash memo, receipts are issued by the machine to the customers.

(ii) The daily cash sales are totalled and verification of actual cash in hand of the cashier with the amount recorded in the machine is facilitated. NCR (National Cash Register) is the most commonly used machine.

15. **Billing Machines :** Big offices handling large number of bills, invoices, etc. may use the billing machine with advantage. The modern machine is, practically speaking, a combination of typewriter and calculator. The machine is so devised that in the event of a wrong posting the automatic devices lock the machine. Various types of billing machines are available.

16. **Time-recording Machines :** There are several methods by which time of arrival and departure of workers and other employees can be recorded. Some of the methods are outlined below :

(i) **Time Clock Method :** The details can be recorded on a card by means of clock recorder. The advantages of this method are that it is economical and chances of fraudulent entries are minimised.

(ii) **Dial Recorder :** This recorder is so designed that there are a number of holes around the dial. Each of the holes represents a number which has already been allotted to individual workers. The working of the recorder is very simple. The workers are to press the dial arm into a hole to record the time.

(iii) **Key Recorders :** Each key recorder consists of a number of keys and the keys bear the corresponding ticket numbers of the workers. To record the time and the card number, the individual workers are to put their keys at the appropriate holes and give a turn.

17. **Log Book** is maintained separately for individual vehicles to record details of trips made by each of the vehicles throughout the day. The book contains a large number of information such as Vehicle Number, Make and Specification, Date of Purchases, Name of Driver, Name (or Number) of Route, Time of Starting, Time of Return, Distance Covered, Weight Carried, Details of Delays, Supplies of Petrol or Diesel, Lubricating Oil, grease, etc. Maintenance of log books enables the management to keep a track of the fleet of vehicles and wastage of running capacity is minimised.

18. **Internal Check :** This has been defined by the Institute of Chartered Accountants in England and Wales as the checks on the day-to-day transactions which operate continuous as part of the routine system, whereby the work of one person is provided independently or is complementary to the work of another, the object being the prevention or early detection of errors and frauds.

19. **Continuous Stationery :** It is a device by which rolls of office forms together with the means of copying are continuously fed into the machine. There are some special devices attached to the machine by which as soon as a set is typed, it is automatically separated and makes way to the next set. It saves time and enables the user to get a larger number of copies according to the requirement.

20. **Loose-Leaf Registers :** These comprise single removable sheets which by means of a suitable device are fixed in a binder. These are used with advantage by companies for the purpose of maintaining the Register of Members, Minutes Book, Wages Book (Payroll), etc. The advantages of Loose-Leaf Registers may be summed up as under :

(i) Names can be quickly located.

(ii) It does not require separate indexing.

(iii) Handling is easy inasmuch as insertion of new leaves and extraction of old leaves do not pose any problem.

(iv) Both sides of the leaves can be used without any difficulty.

(v) It saves much labour as new books need not be written at any time.

(vi) This lends itself to flexibility.

(vii) The chances of error in posting are minimised.

The defects of the system are :

(a) It facilitates fraud.

(b) Initial cost is higher than that of Card Index System.

(c) A Court of law may not accept the loose leaves as evidence.

21. **Office Furniture :** Office furniture comprise chairs, tables, cabinets, cupboards, lockers, etc. As office work is mainly paper work by different categories of employees, suitable furniture should be provided to them according to their individual requirements and positions. Broadly speaking, an office requires the following three types of furniture :

(i) For the executives;

(ii) For special purposes;

(iii) For the clerks and other assistants.

Selection of office furniture needs careful consideration of the management for the following reasons :

(i) A close relation between furnishing the office and the welfare of staff exists.

(ii) Cost of furniture is quite significant.

(iii) Appearance of the office largely depends on the type of furniture used.

The following points may be noted in connection with selection of furniture :

(i) Economic use of space.

(ii) Use of standard furniture should be made as far as practicable.

(iii) Cost involved.

22. **Telephone Exchange :** The telephone system of any country is normally under the direct control of the Department of Telecommunications of the Government. In this connection, in India, Mumbai and New Delhi are the only two cities which are served by Mahanagar Telephone Nigam Ltd. Excepting these two cities, the rest of India is served (from 1st October 2000) by Bharat Sanchar Nigam Ltd. (B.S.N.L.).

The local areas which are served by the telephone system have an 'exchange' for each. Big cities and towns normally have more than one exchange. A telephone exchange may be run manually or automatically. In a manual exchange, the caller has to quote the required number to the operator and the latter connects the caller. In an automatic exchange, the required connection can be obtained simply by dialling the particular number.

23. **PMBX :** Private Branch Exchange (PBX) may be of two types, viz., manually operated type which is known as Private Manual Branch Exchange (PMBX) and Private Automatic Branch Exchange (PABX). In (PMBX), the board is operated by a number of operators and the number of operators depends on the number of telephone lines as well as extensions. Since the board is operated manually, the system is known as Private Manual Branch Exchange (PMBX). Both incoming and outgoing calls are controlled by the operators and, as such, service to the extensions tends to be slow. The system has the following advantages :

(a) Callers requiring particular numbers need not dial themselves and waste their valuable time. What they are supposed to do is to lift the receivers and quote the required numbers when the operator responds. The operator dials the particular number, gets it and connects the line to that extension wherefrom the request for the number emanated.

(b) As desired by the busy executive, the operator at first gets the particular person on the line (trunk or local) and then connects the line to the particular extension.

(c) Transfer and call back facilities are available.

(d) Connection between any two extensions is very easy.

The disadvantages are that service is slow compared to what is available in PABX system and employment of operators involves considerable amount of overhead expenses.

24. **PABX :** This is the abbreviation of Private Automatic Branch Exchange. This is the unique combination of Private Manual Branch Exchange (PMBX) and automatic dialling system. It is manual in the sense that all incoming calls are at first received by the operator before passing them to appropriate extensions. These extensions are fitted with dial instruments and have distinctive numbers. The callers from the extensions may contact the operator by dialling '9' for the purpose of getting an external number. However, the system is automatic in the sense that the caller from any extension can get another extension simply by dialling the particular number. These extension numbers normally consist of three/four digits. To get an external line without the intervention of the operator, the caller has to dial '0' first to be connected to the exchange and then he/she has to dial the desired number. The system proves to be of much advantage where the number of external (outgoing) calls far outweigh the number of incoming calls as because the number of operators to be employed depends on the volume of incoming calls.

25. **Intercom (C. U. 1991) :** In large organisations where the volume of internal calls between various departments or sections of the same department is quite large and cannot be conveniently handled by the PMBX operators, installation of PBX (Intercom) system proves to be of much advantage. This is a private automatic exchange and is popularly known as Intercom. Each telephone has its distinctive number consisting of two or three digits. Any person desirous of contacting another person has simply to dial the particular number. The installation of this telephone systems involves huge capital expenditure and can be borne only by the large business houses.

26. **Extensions :** Large offices having a number of departments and staff cannot instal individual outside telephones (direct lines) for each of the departments and the senior staff. With a view to avoiding this difficulty and deriving certain benefits, most of the modern large and medium-size offices have their own Private Branch Exchange run by one or more than one operator. A number of lines which are drawn from the PBX board and connected to the departments and the chambers of the executives are known as extensions. All the incoming calls are received by the operator at first and then passed on to the appropriate extensions. The persons desirous of getting outside numbers are to lift the receivers and quote the numbers to the operator. The operator notes down the numbers and connects the outside line to the extension wherefrom that number was quoted.

27. **Phonogram :** With a view to sending a telegraphic message, the telegram form is to

be filled in by the sender and it is to be forwarded to the Post/Telegraph Office. This process involves much time and effort. In order to avoid this difficulty, there is special telephone service available at Central Telegraph Offices located in State capitals/important places. The message to be cabled may be conveyed by the sender to the nearest telegraph office over the telephone and this special service is known as 'Phonogram'. The charge for making a phonogram—which is the same as telegram charge—is included in the telephone bill.

28. **Local Calls :** Telephone calls within the areas served by the local telephone exchanges are known as local calls.

29. **Toll Calls and Trunk Calls :** The telephone calls which are outside the limits served by the local exchanges may be either toll calls or trunk calls. When a call falls outside the area of operation of the local telephone exchanges but is within a certain radius of the city or the town, it is known as toll call. If, on the other hand, the distance between the two places is much, the call is known as a trunk call. Toll calls have, however, since been discontinued.

30. **Demand Trunk Call :** In recent time, arrangements have been made by the Department of Telecommunications and Mahanagar Telephone Nigam Ltd. by which trunk lines in between a number of cities may be obtained by the subscribers on demand. This is also known as lightning call through the Central Telephone Exchange. Compared to the charges of ordinary trunk calls, charges for demand trunk calls are much on the high side.

31. **Ready Reckoner (C. U. 1991, 1976) :** As the name suggests, it reckons or calculates readily. It is a device by which the results of complicated calculations may be obtained by a single reference. Use of ready reckoner is not only popular but also a 'must' for banks, insurance companies and big organisations. Where purchase of calculating machines or computer is not warranted because of insufficient work or cost involved, ready reckoner may be used with advantage. Sometimes, ready reckoner proves to be even faster than the machines.

32. **Slide Rules :** These are devices for rapid and accurate calculation. Use of Slide Rules is very popular with engineering concerns. Compared to the calculating machines, these are cheap and sometimes faster than the machines in the hands of efficient user.

33. **Automatic Typewriter :** This is controlled by perforated paper tape prepared by a typist. Details of letter are coded by means of punched holes and these, in turn, control the operation of the typewriter. In recent years, magnetic tape is largely being used in place of punched paper tape. This machine may be advantageously used to reproduce identical copies of letters at a very high speed. This is equally helpful for sending letters to shareholders, inviting tenders, sending greetings, etc. The output of an automatic typewriter is roughly four times of an ordinary typewriter. However, because of many advantages, computers have almost replaced the automatic typewriters.

34. **Electric Typewriter :** This may be either fully or partly electrically driven. An electric motor is fitted with a standard typewriter which saves a lot of human energy and fatigue. In a fully electrically operated machine, all the operations such as depressing the keys, throwing of carriage, use of shift keys, space bars, back-space, etc. are performed electrically. Compared to the standard typewriters, this is expensive but the output is better, both

qualitatively and quantitatively. However, computers have almost replaced the electric typewriters.

35. **Adding Machines :** These machines, which are either manually or electrically operated, are used for addition—the most common computing operation. Based on these machines, accounting and posting machines, calculators, etc. have been introduced. Most of the adding machines have a roll of paper which is known as 'tally roll'. Figures are typed on this roll. Such a machine is known as listing machine because in addition to addition, figures are listed simultaneously.

36. **Calculating Machines (C. U. 1991) :** Calculating machines can perform additions, subtractions, multiplications and divisions of a set of simple or complex figures very quickly. These have largely eliminated the routine calculations and thus contributed to efficiency of the business enterprise. These machines are available in different forms to suit the needs of individual businesses.

37. **Automatic Calculator :** This machine is of recent origin and operated by electricity. A mere pressing of the button sets the machine in motion and the data can be stored in the machine according to the requirement. Various types of computations can be performed on this machine automatically and at a very high speed.

38. **Facsimile Telegraphy :** It is a device by which written messages, formulae, drawings, etc. can be quickly transmitted between two points (machines) connected by a telegraph line. This machine has three control points, viz., 'Send', 'Receive' and 'Stop'. The matter to be transmitted is reproduced on electro-sensitive paper. The paper is wrapped round the cylinder and then it is inserted in the machine. Now as soon as the 'Send' and 'Receive' buttons are switched on, the transmission commences almost immediately.

39. **STD :** STD stands for Subscriber Trunk Dialling. Any subscriber may dial directly any other distant subscriber in the specified cities and important towns in India—without the help of any operator of the Telephone Exchange—within a few seconds. He is not required to wait indefinitely for the call to mature. The charge for such a call depends on the distance between the two places, the time taken for conversation and the time when the call was made.

40. **ISD :** ISD stands for International Subscriber Trunk Dialling. The facility is available between Indian cities and foreign countries. At the written request of the subscribers to the concerned Telephone Exchange, the telephone authorities extend ISD facility. Any subscriber having ISD facility on his telephone can get any telephone number in, say, London, New York etc., after dialing the ISD code, country code and then the local subscriber's telephone number. ISD works like STD with the only exception that it is operated through Intercontinental automatic system. This enables fast communication but the service is very expensive. ISD call charges depend on distance between the two places, duration of conversation and the time of making the calls.

41. **Internet :** Internet is the inter-connection between several computers of different types belonging to various networks all over the globe. It is a network of networks. To send data within a matter of seconds to someone or to receive the same from someone almost

instantaneously was unthinkable before the advent of the Internet. The Internet has more than a million computers connected to it, from which arises the need for proper addressing system for communicating through the Internet.

The Internet application that is drawing the most attention is the *World Wide Web* (WWW). WWW is a series of servers that are interconnected through hypertext. Hypertext is a method of presenting information in which certain text is highlighted that, when selected, displays more information on the particular topic. These highlighted items are called hyperlinks and allow the users to navigate from one document to another that may be located on different servers. The user can use the browsing software such as Internet Explorer, Mosaic or Netscape Navigator to navigate the web. A *browser* is a software that helps the users to navigate the WWW.

42. **E-mail :** E-mail is the most used feature of Internet. It is the sending of messages through the internet as a mail on a definite address. Many sites on the Internet provide free E-mail facility. Data files can be attached to mail as attachment. It is the most convenient mode of transferring messages across the countries using the Internet.

43. **E-commerce :** E-commerce means Electronics Commerce, i.e., buying and selling on the Web. It is a way of enabling business over the Net. Products and services can be offered through sites on the Internet. Banks and other financial institutions are working on various methods, protocols and standards to enable such transactions over the Web. The transactions are mostly done through credit cards and, therefore, security as well as secrecy is very important for a trustworthy electronic commerce solution over the Web.

E-commerce also refers to automation of all the business processes that are associated with trade and commerce. E-commerce demands investments in computers including hardwares and softwares, trained personnel and telecom infrastructure.

44. **VSAT :** VSAT (Very Small Aperture Terminal) is a satellite-based Network technology and has several advantages over traditional networking methods. VSATs provide an enabling technology in rapidly building a reliable communication backbone. Besides providing communication channels of high quality and availability, VSATs can be installed and operated in widely dispersed locations irrespective of the distance and terrain. There are three points of operation—Satellite, Hub and VSATs. Distance insensitivity-cost of a link in a VSAT based Network is not sensitive to distance. The Network is entirely under the control of owner organisation and is independent of intermediary agencies (e.g., DoT) once the necessary approvals and satellite resources are obtained. Broadcast transmission capacity of satellites enables signals to be sent to a wide geographic area. In countries with hostile terrain and little existing infrastructure, satellites are an attractive idea.

45. **Computer :** Computer is defined as an electronic information processing device capable of receiving inputs (i.e., raw information), storing sets of instructions for solving problems (i.e., set of software called programs) and generating outputs (i.e., results) with high speed and accuracy. The term computer is often meant to include various components like printer, video monitor, keyboard, disk drive etc. which are technically called computer peripherals. A computer system is run on the basis of a set of instructions called the software

program developed by a person who is a computer software professional and he is called the programmer. The instructions of the programmer are in a computer language in the form of computer program(s) and are called computer software. It can perform a vast variety of mathematical calculations ranging from simply adding and subtracting to solving complicated mathematical equations that involve thousands of steps and can repeat a complicated calculation trillions of times without error.

46. **Personal Computer :** With the development of technology, the size of the computer—which in earlier days could run into large rooms—began to reduce gradually and standardised into a Personal Computer or desktop computer, i.e., the modern day PC. A personal computer can be fitted on a standard office table and can be operated by a single individual. A personal computer has now become a everyday tool.

47. **Laptop :** A laptop is the improvised version of the personal computer. It refers to very small personal computer which can fit on a person's lap, operates on battery, weighs a few kilos and can be easily carried in a car, train or plane and provides the comfort of working on a computer while on jouney. It incorporates all the features of a PC, e.g., it can be connected to printer, modem, internet, LAN (Local Area Network) etc.

48. **Pager :** A pager is a portable wireless receiver which receives messages from various callers into audio-visual form. A user of pager can receive the messages even when he is mobile. On receipt of the message, he can initiate necessary action. Even if the user of the pager does not carry it with him, he can see the messages when he returns home or to his work place. Pager service is reliable as it is not dependent on the conventional telephone lines which are under the control of the Department of Telecommunications.

49. **Mobile Telephone :** A mobile telephone or cellular phone enjoys the combined facilities which are available to a pager and standard telephone service provided by the Department of Telecommunications. A cellular phone is a trans-receiver which can receive messages like pagers and can transmit messages which is done by the telephone service run by the Government. This phone has all the features of a pager as well as of a telephone instrument together with an antenna for wireless communication. The macro-cellular technology proves coverage of wide area and the facility to make calls by the user while he is in a flying aircraft or a running car/train. This is very popular nowadays with busy people of the society whether they are working in offices or self-employed persons. Compared to the call charges of pager and Department of Telecommunications' telephones, the call charges of mobile telephones are on the high side.

Q. 9. Briefly describe the functions and working of three labour-saving devices commonly used in modern offices.

Ans. : *Write about any three machines from the Answer to Question No. 1 of this chapter, pages 92-93.*

7

MEETINGS OF CO-OPERATIVE SOCIETIES, CLUBS AND STUNDENTS' UNIONS

[**Contents** : Rules governing meetings of Co-operative Societies, Clubs, Students' Unions—Notice—Agenda—Minutes]

Q. 1. What are the rules which govern the meetings of (a) Co-operative Societies and (b) Clubs and Students' Unions?

Ans. : The meetings of the Co-operative Societies are governed by the Co-operative Societies Act, Co-operative Societies Rules and bye-laws annexed to the Act.

The Clubs and Students' Unions are registered under the Societies Registration Act, 1940. Within the framework of the Act, they can frame their own rules for conducting various types of meetings. However, when the organisation does not frame its rules and there is no legal provision for conducting the meetings, it should follow the custom. In the event of non-availability of rules for conducting the meetings, the meeting itself or the Chairman of the meeting himself can frame the rules.

Q. 2. Draft a notice of the Annual General Meeting of a Co-operative Credit Society together with agenda.

Ans. :

Sahapur Co-operative Credit Society Ltd.

Registered Office
75/57 S. N. Roy Road
Calcutta 700038
Dated the 20th May 2000

NOTICE

Notice is hereby given that the Third Annual General Meeting of the members of the Society will be held at its Registered Office on Friday, the 12th June 2000, at 10 A. M. to transact the following business :

1. To confirm the minutes of the last meeting.
2. To consider and approve the reports of the Directors and Auditors of the Society.

3. To consider and approve the audited accounts for the year ended 31st March 2000 and balance sheet as at that date.
4. To appropriate the profit and declare dividend.
5. To elect Directors and other office-bearers as per Rules of the Society.
6. To consider ways and means of increasing the share capital of the Society.
7. To consider raising the amount of loan from Rs. 15,000/- to Rs. 20,000/- per member.
8. To consider any other business with the permission of the Chair.

By Order of the Board,
M. V. Prabhu
Secretary

Q. 3. Draft a Notice of the First meeting of the Directors of a Co-operative Credit Society.

Ans. :

Sahapur Co-operative Credit Society Ltd.

Registered Office :
75/57 S. N. Roy Road
Calcutta 700038
Date : 20th May 2000

Shri T. S. Narayanaswarmy, Director,
Sahapur Co-operative Credit Society Ltd.
P-674, 'O' Block
New Alipore
Calcutta 700053

Dear Sir,

Re : First Board Meeting

I have been directed by the Board to inform you that the first meeting of the Board of Directors of the Society will be held at its Registered Office on Friday, the 12th June 2000, at 11 A. M. to transact the following business :

Agenda :

1. To approve the Bye-laws of the Society.
2. To approve and adopt the Common Seal of the Society.
3. To decide on opening operation of the Bank Account.
4. To consider the applications for loans received from the members.
5. To consider any other business with the permission of the Chariman.

You are requested to make it convenient to attend the meeting.

Yours faithfully,
P. S. Iyenger
Secretary

Encl : Agenda Papers

Q. 4. Draft a Notice convening the meeting of the Directors of a Co-operative Credit Society (not being the first meeting).

Ans. :

Sahapur Co-operative Credit Society Ltd.

Registered Office :
75/57 S. N. Roy Road
Calcutta 700038
Dated 12th June 2000

NOTICE

Notice is hereby given that the Third Meeting of the Board of Directors of the Society will be held at its Registered Office on Wednesday, the 24th July 2000, at 11 A. M. to transact the following business :

Agenda :

1. To confirm the minutes of the last Board Meeting held on 31st March 2000.
2. To ascertain the progress made by the Society on the basis of the instructions of the last meeting.
3. To consider and, if thought fit, approve the appointment of a full-time Accountant.
4. To consider sanction of loan applications received from the members.
5. To consider any other business with the permission of the Chairman.

By Order of the Board,
P. Awasthi
Secretary

Q. 5. Draft a suitable notice convening an Annual General Meeting of a Club.

Ans. :

East Bengal Athletic Club

Registered Office :
Eden Gardens
Calcutta 70000
Date : 20th May 2000

NOTICE is hereby given that the twenty-first Annual General Meeting of the Club will be held at the University Institute Hall, College Square, Calcutta 700009, on Monday the 12th June 2000 at 3 P. M. to transact the following business :

1. To consider and approve the Secretary's Report.
2. To consider and approve the annual audited accounts of the Club for the year ended the 31st March 2000.
3. To elect office-bearers.
4. To appoint auditors of the Club for the year 2000-2001.
5. To consider and if thought fit to approve the appointment of Shri Subrata Bhattacharya (Arjun Award Winner) as Football Coach of the Club.

6. Any other business with the permission of the Chairman.

By Order of the Board,
S. C. Basu
Secretary

Q. 6. Draft a suitable notice convening a meeting of the Executive Committee of a College Students' Union.

Ans. :

Sydenham College of Commerce Students' Union.

'B' Road
Churchgate
Mumbai 400020
Date : 31st January 2000

NOTICE

It has been decided to hold a meeting of the Executive Committee of the Union on Saturday, the 28th February 2000, at 2-30 P. M. to transact the following business :

All the members of the Executive Committee are hereby requested to make it convenient to attend the meeting.

Agenda :

1. To confirm the minutes of the last meeting.
2. To consider matters, if any, arising out of the minutes.
3. To consider arrangement for the annual social function of the College sometime by the end of the next month.
4. To finalise the subject matter and date of debate.
5. To consider awarding of prizes to the students who stood first in the last annual examination (both Pass and Honours Courses).
6. Miscellaneous.

Trisul Halder,
General Secretary

Q. 7. Draft the Minutes of a meeting of the Directors of a Co-operative Credit Society.

Ans. :

Evershinenagar Co-operative Society Ltd.

Registered Office :
Evershinenagar
Malad (West)
Mumbai

Minutes of the meeting of the Directors of the Society held at its registered office on Friday, the 1st January 2000, at P. M.

Present :

1. Shri M. N. Dandekar, Chairman

2. Shri S. M. Gavaskar, Director
3. Shri D. Vengsarkar, Director
4. Shri L. Lonekar, Director
5. Shri S. Sivalkar, Director
6. Shri H. N. Mangeskar, Director.

In Attendance :

1. Shri W. Walingkar, Secretary
2. Shri P. Pednekar, Auditor.

Shri M. N. Dandekar, Chairman, presided over the meeting.

Confirmation of the Minutes of the last Meeting : The minutes of the last meeting of the Society held on Wednesday, the 30th November 1999 were read, approved and confirmed.

Increasing loan amount from Rs. 15,000/- to Rs. 20,000/- : The issue was discussed in detail. In view of the inflationary conditions obtaining in the country, it was " Resolved that the existing borrowing limits of the members be and are hereby increased from Rs. 15,000/- to Rs. 20,000/-".

Sanction of Loan : There was only one application for a long term loan of Rs. 20,000/- from Shri M. Moolgaonkar for the purpose of alteration/renovation of his residential flat. The issue was discussed and it was "Resolved that a long-term loan of Rs. 20,000/- (Rupees twenty thousand only) be and is hereby sanctioned to Shri M. Moolgaonkar payable in sixty equal monthly instalments".

Appointment of Accountant : With sizable increase in volume of work of the Society following admission of 200 new members during the last few months, it was considered essential to appoint a full-time Accountant. It was, thereafter, "Resolved that the Secretary of the Society be and is hereby authorised to make necessary arrangements for insertion of an advertisement in the Times of India (English) and Lokasatta (Marathi) and finalise appointment of an Accountant for the Society".

Next Meeting : It was decided that the next Board Meeting will be held at the Registered Office of the Society on Wednesday, the 16th March 2000, at 4 P.M.

Vote of Thanks : Shri S. M. Gavaskar proposed and Shri D. Vengsarkar seconded a hearty vote of thanks to the Chairman for presiding at the meeting. The Chairman replied suitably and terminated the meeting.

Dated Bombay, M. N. Dandekar
the 15th January 2000 Chairman

Q. 8. Draft the proceedings of a meeting of an Annual General Meeting of a Club.

Ans. : Minutes of the Thirty-eighth Annual General Meeting of the Mohun Bagan Athletic Club, Eden Gardens, Calcutta 700001 held at Mahajati Sadan, Chittaranjan Avenue, Calcutta on Monday, the 2nd January 2000 at 4 P. M.

Present :

1. Shri Sailen Manna, President
2. Shri Chuni Goswamy, General Secretary and 368 members whose names appear in the attendance sheet.

Shri Sailen Manna presided over the meeting.

Secretary's Report : The Secretary read the Annual Report of the Club. A number of questions on the Report were raised by a few members which were replied to by the Secretary. Thereafter, the Report was approved.

President's Speech : The President delivered a short but heartening speech to the members on the excellent performances of the Club in different sports and games. He also dwelt upon the future plans and programmes of the Club.

Annual Accounts : The annual accounts for the year ended the 31st October 1999 together with the Auditor's Report were placed before the members. After detailed discussions, the accounts were approved unanimously.

Election of the Executive Committee Members : Shri Putan Ghosh proposed the names of Sarvashri Umapati Kumar, Sunil Guha, Subhasish Guha Thakurata, Pranab Ganguly and Kesto Pal for election to the Executive Committee and Shri Dilip Chatterjee seconded. The proposal was unanimously approved.

Election of President : Shri Satyajit Chatterjee proposed that Shri Sailen Manna should continue for another year as the President of the Club and the proposal was approved unanimously.

Election of Secretary : Shri Shibaji Banerjee proposed the name of Shri Subrata Bhattacharya for election to the post of General Secretary and this was seconded by Shri Rabi Das. The proposal was carried unanimously.

Appointment of Auditors : Shri Sanat Seth proposed that Messrs. Chakraborty & Nath, Chartered Accountants, who are the present auditors of the Club, may be allowed to continue for another year with an honorarium of Rs. 10,000/- and this was seconded by Shri Fancy Banerjee. The proposal was carried unanimously.

As there was no other business to be transacted, the meeting terminated with a vote of thanks to the Chair.

Dated Calcutta — Sailen Manna,
the 22nd January 2000 — Chairman

Q. 9. Draft the proceedings of the meeting of the Executive Committee of a College Students' Union.

Ans. : Minutes of the meeting of the Executive Committee of the Sydenham College of Commerce, 'B' Road, Churchgate, Mumbai 400020, held on Wednesday, the 16th March 2000 at the Union Office at 5 P. M.

Members Present :

1. Shri P. Awasthi, President

2. Shri N. M. Damle, Vice-President
3. Shri Murli Raghavan, General Secretary
4. Shri M. V. Prabhu, Cultural Secretary
5. Shri S. Panigrahi, Sports Secretary
6. Shri K. Ketkar, Member
7. Shri M. G. Ranade, Member
8. Shri M. M. Sharma, Member
9. Shri M. W. Shivalkar, Member

Shri P. Awasthi presided over the meeting.

The minutes of the last meeting were read, discussed and approved.

It was decided to hold the Annual Social of the College Union on the 1st May 2000 and Shri M. V. Prabhu and Shri M. M. Sharma were requested to make necessary arrangements therefor within the budgeted expenditure of Rs. 10,000/-

The Committee finalised the subject-matter of the debate to be held on the Foundation Day of the College. It was thereafter "Resolved that the subject-matter of the debate for the current year would be 'Students and Politics' and the Principal, Vice-Principal and the Head of the Department of Political Science of the College be and are hereby requested to be the judges for the Competition".

It was "Further Resolved that the candidates getting the first five places in order of performance be awarded suitable prizes at a total cost not exceeding Rs. 3,000/-".

There being no other business, the meeting terminated with a vote of thanks to the Chair.

Dated Mumbai,
the 31st March 2000

P. Awasthi,
President

Q. 10. Prepare the draft minutes of proceedings of the Annual General Meeting of a Co-operative Society. **(C. U. 1967 and 1962)**

Ans. : Royd Multipurpose Co-operative Society Ltd.

Minutes of the 3rd Annual General Meeting of the Society held at the Registered Office of the Society, Parry Park, Calcutta 700034, on Friday, the 29th July 2000 at 2-30 P. M.

Shri H. Sinha Roy, Chairman of the Managing Committee of the Society, took the Chair.

1. **Quorum :** The Chairman declared that the quorum was present and started the meeting.

2. **Confirmation of the Minutes :** The minutes of the last Annual General Meeting held on 23rd July 1999 were read, approved and signed by the Chairman of the meeting.

3. **Secretary's Report :** The Secretary placed his report before the meeting detailing the activities of the Society for the year ended 31-3-2000. The report was unanimously accepted by the meeting.

4. **Adoption of Accounts and Auditor's Report :** The Secretary read the Auditor's Report for the year ended 31-3-2000. The Chairman stated that as the accounts were in the hands of the members for quite sometime, they might be taken as read. The queries of the members were satisfactorily replied to by the Secretary and finally the accounts were unanimously adopted.

5. **Payment of Dividend :** It was resolved "That a dividend of 6% on the paid-up value of shares be declared and arrangement for payment of dividend be made by the Secretary to those members whose names appeared on the Register of Members as on the 23rd April 2000".

6. **Annual Budget** : The budget estimate for the year ending the 31st March 2001was placed before the meeting. A number of questions were raised by the members and these were replied to by the Chairman. The budget was thereafter adopted by the meeting unanimously.

7. **Election of Members** : According to the Bye-laws of the Society, Sarbasri S. Soni and G. Grover retired from the Managing Committee. It was resolved "That the vacancies in the Managing Committee be filled in by Sarvasri M. Modak and P. Pathak".

8. **Vote of Thanks** : The meeting terminated with a vote of thanks to the Chair.

Dated the 25th August 2000

H. Sinha Roy,
Chairman

8

LOCAL BODIES, PANCHAYATS AND THEIR MEETINGS

[**Contents** : Municipal Secretary—Qualifications, Powers, Duties & Functions—Secretary of a Zilla Parishad—Power, Duties, Functions—Removal—Panchayat Samiti—Its Secretary, Qualifications, Powers, Duties & Functions—Organisational structure of a local Self-government—Municipal Service—Commission—Mayor—Municipal Commissioner—Zilla Parishad—Sabhadhipati—Sahakari Sabhadhipati—Executive Officer of Zilla Parishad—Sabhapati and Sahakari Sabhapati—Executive Officer of Panchayat Samiti—Pradhan & Upa-Pradhan—Gram—Meetings of Zilla Parishad, Panchayat Samiti & Gram Panchayat—Notices, Agenda & Minutes.]

Q. 1. Define the term 'Municipal Secretary'. How is he appointed and what are his qualifications? What are his powers and functions? Discuss in brief the duties to be performed by the Municipal Secretary. (C. U. 1999)

Ans. : According to Section 14(j) of the Calcutta Municipal Corporation Act, 1988, the Municipal Secretary is an officer of the Corporation. In terms of Section 39(1) of the Act, the Municipal Commissioner is the principal executive officer of the Corporation who appoints the Secretary under the rules and regulations of the Corporation. All the officers of the Corporation including the Municipal Secretary are subordinate to him.

Appointment of the Municipal Secretary is statutory. He may be appointed by the Managing/Executive Committee of the Municipal Corporation or by the concerned State Government. He may be elected on honorary basis or appointed as a salaried employee of the Corporation.

If the appointment of the Secretary is honorary, he is entitled to conveyance allowance and other allowances as may be decided by the Corporation. In case he is a salaried employee, he is entitled to monthly salary and allowances as provided in the Act or as decided by the appointing authority.

No statutory qualifications have been prescribed for appointment of the Municipal Secretary. However, he should preferably have the following qualifications :

(i) He should have a sound general education.

(ii) He should be thorough in secretarial function.

(iii) He should have thorough knowledge of the Municipal Corporation Act especially and other relevant enactments in general.

(iv) He should be thorough about the rules and procedures of the Corporation meetings.

Section 42 of the Act states the powers and functions of the Municipal Secretary which are as follows :

1. The Municipal Secretary shall be the Secretary to the Corporation and the Municipal Accounts Committee, and shall exercise such powers and discharge such functions as are conferred on him by the Municipal Commissioner.

2. The Municipal Secretary shall be responsible for the custody of all papers and documents connected with the proceedings of the Corporation, and the Municipal Accounts Committee, and shall preserve the same in such manner and for such period as may be determined by regulations.

The duties of the Municipal Secretary may be enumerated as under :

(i) He has to supervise and control the officers and staff of his own Department.

(ii) He has to prepare the notice and agenda papers of the meetings of the Corporation and its committees in consultation with the Municipal Commissioner.

(iii) He has to send the notice of the meeting to all the eligible members well in advance.

(iv) He has to help the Chairman for smooth conduct of the meeting.

(v) He has to place the notice before the Chairman which he receives from any Councillor or Alderman under Section 186 of the Act. He will have to circulate the notice among the members as per the rules of the Corporation.

(vi) He has to initiate action for supply of the statement to the Councillor or Alderman from whom he received a notice asking for a statement on an urgent matter relating to the administration of the Corporation.

(vii) He is responsible for recording the proceedings of the meetings (i.e., Minutes) in the Minutes Book kept for the purpose.

(viii) He has to place the Minutes before the presiding officer (i.e., Chairman) of the meeting for his signature at the next meeting.

(ix) Section 110 of the Act requires the Secretary to forward to the State Government a copy of the Minutes of the proceedings of each meeting of the Corporation or Committee thereof within a period of ten days from the date of the meeting.

(x) He has to liaise between various Departments of the Corporation for better coordination.

Q. 2. Define the term 'Secretary of a Zilla Parishad'. How is he appointed and what are his qualifications? Can he be transferred or removed? Enumerate the powers, duties and functions of the Secretary of a Zilla Parishad. (C. U. 1998, 1996)

Ans. : According to Section 166(2) of the West Bengal Panchayat Act, 1973 : "The State

Government may appoint a Secretary for a Zilla Parishad on such terms and conditions as may be prescribed." The first Secretary of the Zilla Parishad following its constitution is appointed by the Government for a period of four years from amongst the senior W. B. C. S. (West Bengal Civil Service) officers. He is a gazetted officer and exercises the powers and performs the duties as delegated to him by the Executive Officer, i.e., the District Magistrate. The subsequent appointments are made by the Zilla Parishad for periods of five years.

A Zilla Parishad Secretary is required to have the following qualifications :

(i) He has to be a W. B. C. S. officer with a fair level of seniority.

(ii) He should have good knowledge of modern office organisation, its functioning, various office equipment and labour-saving devices inclusive of computers etc.

(iii) He should be thorough about the rules and procedures of Zilla Parishad meetings.

The Secretary of the Zilla Parishad may be transferred by the Directorate of Panchayat on the recommendation of the Executive Officer and there is no provision in the Act for his removal.

In terms of the provision of Rule 4 of the West Bengal Panchayat Rules, 1978 : "Notwithstanding anything contained in Rule 3, the Executive Officer may, by order in writing, delegate all or any of his powers and functions under sub-rules (1) and (3), clauses (a), (b) and (c) and sub-clauses (i) and (v) of clause (d), of sub-rule Parishad." The Secretary shall exercise such of the powers, perform such of the functions and discharge such of the duties of the Executive Officer as may be delegated to him by the Executive Officer. He shall render all assistance to the Executive Officer in the discharge of his responsibilities. The principal duties and functions of the Secretary may be summed up as under :

(i) Supervision and control of the office of the Zilla Parishad.

(ii) Custody of office records and conduct of official correspondence.

(iii) Preparation of notice inclusive of agenda together with relative notes for the meeting of the Zilla Parishad.

(iv) Attending the meetings of the Zilla Parishad on behalf of the Executive Officer.

(v) Co-operation with the Sabhadhipati and Sahakari Sabhadhipati in the conduct of the meetings.

(vi) Execution of the decisions of the meetings.

(vii) Signing of the Cash Book daily and examining the Zilla Parishad Pass Book issued by the Treasury/Bank from time to time.

(viii) Proper maintenance of accounts of the Zilla Parishad.

(ix) Preparation of quarterly reports of expenditure of the Zilla Parishad and submitting the same to Artha-O-Sansthan Sthayaee Samiti.

(x) Preparation of the draft budget estimates.

(xi) Preparation of the schemes of planning and development.

(xii) Supervision of the audit of the books of account of the Zilla Parishad.

Q. 3. What do you mean by a Panchayat Samiti? Who can be the Secretary of a Panchayat Samiti and how is he appointed? Can he be transferred or removed? What are the powers, functions and duties of the Secretary of the Panchyat Samiti? (C. U. 1994)

Ans. : According to Section 94 of the West Bengal Panchayat Act, 1973 : "For every Block, the State Government shall constitute a Panchayat Samiti bearing the name of the Block". Every Panchayat Samiti will be a body corporate having perpetual succession and a common seal and shall by its corporate name sue and be sued.

In terms of Section 119(1A) of the said Act : "There shall be a Secretary for every Panchayat Samiti and the Executive Officer, Panchayat, shall be the ex-officio Secretary." The Secretary is appointed either directly through the W. B. C. S. Examination conducted by the West Bengal Public Service Commission or by departmental promotion. He may be transferred by the Directorate of Panchayat but cannot be removed from his service.

The Executive Officer of the Panchayat Samiti (Block Development Officer of the concerned Block becomes the ex-officio Executive Officer) delegates his powers to the Secretary. The powers, duties and functions of the Secretary are enumerated below :

(i) The Secretary of the Panchayat Samiti shall work under the overall control of the Executive Officer and shall be responsible to the Samiti for his work.

(ii) The Secretary shall carry on routine correspondence of the Panchayat Samiti. He shall, however, keep the Executive Officer informed of the correspondence made by him.

(iii) He shall call the meetings of the Panchayat Samiti. The list of businesses to be transacted at every meeting shall be prepared by him under the guidance of the Executive Officer and the Sabhapati or the Sahakari Sabhapati of the Panchayat Samiti. He shall also attend the meetings of the Samiti.

(iv) He shall exercise such of the powers, perform such of the functions and discharge such of the duties of the Executive Officer as may be delegated to him by the Executive Officer.

(v) He shall render all such assistance as may be required by the Executive Officer in the discharge of his responsibilities.

Q. 4. Define the terms 'Gram' and 'Gram Panchayat'. What is the term of office of Panchayat and what are the sources of its revenue?

Ans. : Section 3 of the West Bengal Panchayat Act, 1973, states that "The State Government may, by notification, declare for the purposes of this Act any 'mouja' or a part of a 'mouja' or parts thereof to be a 'Gram'." The notification shall specify the name of the 'Gram' by which it shall be known and shall specify the local limits of such a 'Gram'. From time immemorial, gram panchayat or village panchayat has been playing a very important role in the social and economic life of India. The word 'Panchayat' means a team or council of five elderly and respectable persons of a village. The villagers have high regards for the Panchayat and they abide by or obey the decisions of the Panchayat. Rural self-government in India is based on a three-tier system which is :

(i) Village/Gram Panchayats (base level)

(ii) Panchayat Samiti (intermediate level)

(iii) Zilla Parishad (top level).

The term of office of a Panchayat is usually three years through the process of elections. However, the period can range from three to five years. If the Panchayat cannot perform its duties as required, it can be dissolved by the Government before expiry of its term. A Sarpanch who is the head of a village or Gram Panchayat can be removed from his office if two-thirds of the members (Panchas) vote against him. However, removal of a Sarpanch needs prior approval of the concerned district authorities.

Panchayat takes part in various developmental activities of the village and this necessitates availability of sufficient funds at its disposal. The main sources of income of a Panchayat are enumerated below :

(i) Income from local duties, cesses, fees, etc.

(ii) Income from village lands.

(iii) Grants from the State Government and local authorities.

(iv) Income from levy of tax on houses.

(v) Voluntary donations.

(vi) Income from fisheries and sale of refuse as well as cow-dung.

(vii) Income from levy of tax on fairs and festivals held in the village.

Q. 5. Define the term 'Secretary' of a Gram Panchayat. Who can be appointed a Secretary and how is he appointed? Can he be transferred or removed from his office? What are his duties? (C. U. 1997, 1995)

Ans. : According to Section 4 of the West Bengal Panchayat Act, 1973 : "For every Gram the State Government shall constitute a Gram Panchayat bearing the name of the Gram." Section 35(1) of the Act states that "There shall be a Secretary for every Gram Panchayat appointed by the State Government or any authority empowered by the State Government in this behalf." The appointing authority is the Director of Panchayat on behalf of the State Government.

Section 31 of the Act dwells upon the qualifications, age and period of probation etc. of the Secretary. No person shall be appointed a Secretary unless he has passed the Madhyamik or School Final Examination of the West Bengal Board of Secondary Education or equivalent examination. He shall be between 18 and 35 years of age.

The Secretary may be transferred by the Directorate of Panchayat on the recommendation of the District Panchayat Officer within the district. He may be removed from his office as and when the allegations brought against him by the Pradhan/Upa-Pradhan/villagers are proved on the basis of an enquiry. The enquiry is made by the Block Development Officer or the District Panchayat Officer on the basis of the order issued by the concerned District Magistrate.

Rule 35 of the West Bengal (Gram Panchayat Administration) Rules, 1981, states the duties to be performed by the Secretary of a Gram Panchayat which are :

1. The Secretary of a Gram Panchayat shall be in charge of the office of the Gram Panchayat. He shall act under the direct supervision of the Pradhan or the Upa-Pradhan and shall be responsible to the Gram Panchayat through the Pradhan or the Upa-Pradhan, as the case may be.

2. Notwithstanding anything contained in any other rules, the Secretary shall

(a) prepare the assessment list in due time;

(b) prepare the budget in due time;

(c) be responsible for maintaining the Cash Book and other books of account. He shall also be responsible for preparing the monthly and quarterly statements of account and placing the same before the Gram Panchayat;

(d) be responsible for keeping all records of the Gram Panchayat in safe custody;

(e) be responsible for producing all records before the auditors or inspecting officers as and when directed by the Pradhan;

(f) be responsible for maintaining all registers relating to Dafadars and Chowkidars;

(g) be responsible for preparing and sending to the appropriate Authority necessary reports and returns relating to Dafadars and Chowkidars;

(h) be responsible for bringing to the notice of the Pradhan all important information furnished by Dafadars and Chowkidars;

(i) be responsible for submission to the appropriate Authority in due time all grant-in-aid bills;

(j) be responsible for allotting duties to Dafadars and Chowkidars when they report to the Gram Panchayat office for duty;

(k) perform such other duties in respect of the work of the Gram Panchayat and of the State Government as the Pradhan, the Upa-Pradhan or the State Government may direct.

Q. 6. Show the organisational structure of the local self-government which is also known as 'Panchayati Raj'.

Ans. : The organisation of local self-government—which is also known as Panchayati Raj—is shown in the next page.

Local Self-Government

	Gram or Village Panchayat	Panchayat Samiti	Zilla Parishad
1. **Level**	Village	Block or Circle	District
2. **Composition**	Minimum 10 and maximum 30 members directly elected	Sarpanches of all village panchayats, MPs, MLAs and concerned BDO.	Dy. Commissioner, Chairman of Panchayat Samitis, MPs, and MLAs of the districts.
3. **Presiding Officer**	Sarpanch	Chairman	Chairman
4. **Functions**	Provision of civic amenities, primary education and health, looking after sanitation and management of common property.	Coordination of the working of Panchayats, provision of secondary and college education, hospital and health services and developments of agriculture.	Coordination of the working of Panchyat Samitis, recommendations for grants-in-aid, implementation of various plans and liaison with the State Government.
5. **Sources of Income**	Tax on lands and houses, fair tax, grants-in-aid etc.	Government grants, levy on Panchayats etc.	Government grants, tax collected from fairs, etc.

Q. 7. Write short Notes on : (a) Municipal Service Commission, (b) Powers of Mayor, (c) Powers of Municipal Commissioner, (d) Zilla Parishad, (e) Sabhadhipati and Sahakari Sabhadhipati, (f) Executive Officer of Zilla Parishad, (g) Sabhapati and Sahakari Sabhapati, (h) Executive Officer of Panchayat Samiti, (i) Pradhan and Upa-Pradhan, and (j) Gram.

Ans. :(a) **Municipal Service Commission :** According to Section 26 of the Calcutta Municipal Corporation Act, 1980, the Corporation shall, as soon as may be, after the commencement of the Act, constitute a Municipal Service Commission consisting of—(i) a Chairman, and (ii) two other members.

(b) **Powers of Mayor :** The Mayor shall exercise such powers and discharge such functions as are conferred on him by or under the Act.

(c) **Powers and functions of the Municipal Commissioner :** According to Section 39 of the Act "The Municipal Commissioner shall be the principal Executive Officer of the Corporation and shall, subject to the supervision and control of the Mayor

(i) exercise the powers and perform the functions specifically conferred or imposed upon him by or under this Act or by any other law in force for the time being ;

(ii) assign the duties, and supervise and control the acts and proceedings, of all officers and employees of the Corporation. According to Section 39(2) of the Act : "All officers and employees of the Corporation shall be subordinate to the Municipal Commissioner."

(d) **Zilla Parishad :** In terms of the provisions of Section 140(1) of the West Bengal Panchayat Act, 1973, "for every district (except the district of Darjeeling) the State Government shall constitute a Zilla Parishad bearing the name of the district." Every Zilla Parishad shall be a body corporate having perpetual succession and a common seal and shall by its corporate name sue and be sued.

(e) **Sabhadhipati and Sahakari Sabhadhipati :** According to Section 143(1) of the West Bengal Panchayat Act, 1973, "Every Zilla Parishad shall, at its first meeting at which a quorum is present, elect, in the prescribed manner, one of its members to be the Sabhadhipati and another member to be the Sahakari Sabhdhipati of the Zilla Parishad." Both the Sabhadhipati and Sahakari Sabhadhipati shall, subject to the provisions of Section 146 and to their continuing as members, hold office for a period of five years. They shall be paid out of Zilla Parishad Fund such honoraria and allowances and shall be entitled to leave of absence for such period or periods and on such terms and conditions, as may be prescribed.

(f) **Executive Officer of the Zilla Parishad :** The executive officer is the chief officer or executive head of the office. The District Magistrate is ex-officio Executive Officer of the District.

(g) **Sabhapati and Sahakari Sabhapati :** Section 98(1) of the West Bengal Panchayat Act, 1973, states that "Every Panchayat Samiti shall, at its first meeting at which a quorum is present, elect in the prescribed manner, one of its members to be the Sabhapati and another member to be the Sahakari Sabhapati of the Samiti." The Sabhapati and Sahakari Sabhapati shall, subject to provisions of Section 101 of the Act and to their continuing as members, hold office for a period of five years. They shall be paid out of the Panchayat Samiti Fund such honoraria and allowances as are admissible under the Act.

(h) **Executive Officer of Panchayat Samiti :** The Executive Officer is the chief officer or executive head of the office. The Block Development Officer (B. D. O.) is the Executive Officer of a Panchayat Samiti.

(i) **Pradhan & Upa-Pradhan** : "Pradhan" and "Upa-Pradhan" mean a Pradhan and Upa-Pradhan of a Gram Panchayat elected under Section 9 of the West Bengal Panchayat Act, 1973. The Section states that "Every Gram Panchayat shall, at its first meeting at which a quorum is present, elect in the prescribed manner, one of its members to be the Pradhan and another member to be the Upa-Pradhan of the Gram Panchayat". The Pradhan and Upa-Pradhan shall, subject to the provisions of Section 12 and to their continuing as members, hold office for a period of five years.

(j) **Gram :** Section 3 of the West Bengal Panchayat Act, 1973 states that, "The State Government may, by notification, declare for the purposes of this Act any mouja or a part of a mouja or group of contiguous moujas or parts thereof to be a Gram." The notification shall specify the name of the Gram by which it shall be known and shall specify the local limits of such of Gram.

Q. 8. Describe the important rules for conducting the meetings of Zilla Parishad.

Ans. : The rules which govern the meetings of the Zilla Parishad are enumerated below :

(a) **Period :** A Zilla Parishad is required to hold at least one meeting in every three months.

(b) **Time and Place :** The time and place of the meeting of Zilla Parishad shall be decided by its previous meeting. In other words, the current meeting fixes the time, date and place of the next meeting.

(c) **Convenor :** While the first meeting of the newly-constituted Parishad shall be convened by the concerned District Magistrate, the subsequent meetings are convened by its Secretary in consultation with the Sabhadhipati.

(d) **Chairman :** It is the Sabhadhipati or, in his absence, the Sahakari Sabhadhipati who presides over the meetings of a Zilla Parishad. However, in case both of them are absent, the members present at the meeting will elect one of themselves to preside at the meeting.

(e) **Quorum :** The quorum for a meeting of a Zilla Parishad shall be one-fourth of its total number of members. However, if the meeting is adjourned for any reason, no quorum is necessary for such a meeting.

(f) **Decision :** All the items of the agenda will be decided by a majority of votes.

(g) **Casting Vote :** The Chairman of the meeting is empowered to use his casting vote (in addition to his vote as a member of the Parishad) in case there is a tie on any issue.

(h) **Executive Officer** : The District Magistrate, who is the Executive Officer of a Zilla Parishad, shall attend and participate in the meetings.

(i) **Requisition Meeting :** When one-fifth of the total number of members of a Zilla Parishad requisition in writing for holding of a meeting, the Sabhadhipati shall have to convene the requisition meeting within ten days. In the event of his failure to do so, the requisitionists themselves can convene the meeting after giving seven days' notice in writing.

Q. 9. Draft a Notice of the first meeting of a Zilla Parishad.

Ans. :

Burdwan Zilla Parishad
P. O. & Dist. Burdwan
Pin : 713101

Dated the 10th January 2000

Notice is hereby given that the first meeting of the recently-constituted Parishad will be held in the Office of the Zilla Parishad on Friday, the 24th February 2000 at 3 P. M. to transact the following business :

Agenda :

1. Election of the Sabhadhipati and Sahakari Sabhadhipati of the Parishad.
2. Formation of the Sthayee Samities.
3. Any other business with the permission of the chair.

Prabir Mukherjee
District Magistrate
Burdwan District

Q. 10. Draft a Notice of the meeting of a Zilla Parishad (other than the first meeting).

Ans. :

Burdwan Zilla Parishad
P. O. & Dist. Burdwan
Pin. 713101

Dated the 1st January 2000

Notice is hereby given that an ordinary meeting of the members of the Parishad will be held at the office of the Zilla Parishad on Friday, the 24th January 2000 at 2-30 P. M. to transact the following business :

Agenda :

1. To confirm the Minutes of the last meeting held on 2nd December 1999.
2. To consider implementation of the various development schemes in the District.
3. To consider allocation of moneys received from the Government of West Bengal to Panchayat Samitis and Gram Panchayats for construction of roads, sinking tube-wells, construction of new school buildings, etc.
4. To consider and approve the budget estimates of the Panchayat Samitis.
5. Miscellaneous.

S. C. Basu
Secretary

Q. 11. Draft the Minutes of the first meeting of a Zilla Parishad.

Ans. : Minutes of the first meeting of the Burdwan Zilla Parishad, P. O. & Dist. Burdwan, held on Wednesday, the 12th January 2000 at 2-30 P. M. at the office of the Parishad :

Members Present : 101 members were present at the meeting whose names and signatures appear in the Attendance Register.

In Attendance : Shri Rameshwar Ghosh, Secretary.

Chairman : Shri Prabir Mukherjee, District Magistrate, presided over the meeting.

Election of Sabhadhipati and Sahakari Sabhadhipati : Shri Rai Chand Baral proposed the names of Sarbashri Hemanta Mukerjee and Shyamal Mitra as Sabhadhipati and Sahakari Sabhadhipati and the proposal was seconded by Shri Manna Dey. It was, thereafter, unanimously "RESOLVED that Sarbashri Hemanta Mukherjee and Shyamal Mitra be and are hereby elected Sabhadhipati and Sahakari Sabhadhipati of the Burdwan Zilla Parishad."

Formation of Sthayee Samitis : Sk. Abdul Quadir proposed the names for Nine Sthayee Samitis which Sk. Sajjad Ali seconded. It was thereafter "Resolved that nine Sthayee Samitis be and are hereby formed with the following members :

1. **Artho O Sanstha** :

(a) Shri Hemanta Mukherjee, Sabhadhipati, ex-officio

(b) Shri Dwijen Mukherjee

(c) Shri Tarun Banerjee

(d) Shri Satinath Mukherjee

(e) Shri Jatileswar Mukherjee

(f) Shri Asit Chatterjee

and three more members to be nominated by the Government.

2. **Janaswastha** :

(a) Shri Hemanta Mukherjee, Sabhadhipati, ex-officio

(b) Shri Pijush Pramanik

(c) Shri Ratan Roy

(d) Shri Himadri Bhattacharya

and three more members to be nominated by the Government of West Bengal.

3. **Purta Karya** :

(a) Shri Hemanta Mukherjee, Sabhadhipati, ex-officio

(b) Shri B. S. Sadasiv

(c) Shri Prabhat Roychowdhury

and three more members to be nominated by the State Government.

4. **Krishi, Sech O Samabaya** :

(a) Shri Hemanta Mukherjee, Sabhadhipati, ex-officio

(b) Shri Bhabananda Maji

(c) Shri Debendra Debnath

(d) Shri Bipin Mandal

and three more members to be nominated by the Government.

5. **Siksha** :

(a) Shri Hemanta Mukherjee, Sabhadhipati, ex-officio

(b) Shri Nil Ratan Das

(c) Shri Ajit Chowdhury

(d) Shri Dipen Bhattacharya

and three other members to be nominated by the Government.

6. **Khudra Shilpa, Tran O Janakalyan** :

(a) Shri Hemanta Mukherjee, Sabhadhipati, ex-officio member

(b) Shri Shyamal Mitra

(c) Shri Milan Ghosh

(d) Shri Nihar Bhattacharya

and three other members to be nominated by the Government.

7. **Unnayan Parikalpana O Bhumi Sanskar** :

(a) Shri Hemanta Mukherjec, Sabhadhipati, ex-officio member

(b) Shri Akhil Bandhu Ghosh

(c) Shri Dipak Moitra

(d) Shri Priyanko Moitra

and three other members to be nominated by the Government.

8. **Matsa O Pashupalan** :

(a) Shri Hemanta Mukherjee, Sabhadhipati, ex-officio member

(b) Shri Shyamal Mitra, Sahakari Sabhadhipati

(c) Shri Shyamsundar Debnath

(d) Shri Radheshyam Debnath

and three other members to be nominated by the Government.

9. **Khadya O Sarbaraha** :

(a) Shri Hemanta Mukherjee, Sabhadhipati, ex-officio member

(b) Shri Natabar Maharana

(c) Shri Giridhari Nayak

(d) Shri Omprakash Maharaj

and three other members to be nominated by the Government."

As there was no other business, the meeting terminated with a vote of thanks to the Chairman.

Confirmed.

R. Ghosh — Prabir Mukherjee
Secretary — Chairman
Date : 20.02.2000 — Date : 21.02.2000

Q. 12. Draft the Minutes of a Meeting of a Zilla Parishad (other than the first meeting). (C. U. 1995)

Ans. : Minutes of the meeting of the Burdwan Zilla Parishad, P. O. & Dist. Burdwan, Pin : 713101, held in the Parishad Office on Friday, the 24th January 2000 at 2-30 P. M.

Present :

1. Shri Hemanta Mukherjee, Sabhadhipati
2. Shri Shyamal Mitra, Sahakari Sabhadhipati

and 101 members whose names and signatures appear in the Attendance Register.

In Attendance :

1. Shri Prabir Mukherjee, Executive Officer
2. Shri Rameshwar Ghosh, Secretary.

Shri Hemanta Mukherjee, Sabhadhipati took the Chair. He ascertained the quorum and called the meeting to order.

Confirmation of the Minutes of the last meeting : The Minutes of the last meeting held on 2nd December 1999, were read by the Secretary and confirmed by the meeting. It was, thereafter, "Resolved that the Minutes of the last meeting be and are hereby confirmed."

Implementation of Development Schemes : The various development schemes which were placed before the meeting were discussed in detail. It was then "Resolved that the scheme for eradication of illiteracy be and is hereby approved for its immediate implementation."

Allocation of Government Grant : The matter was discussed in detail. It was then "Resolved that a sum of Rs. 5 lakhs each be and is hereby allocated to Parulia, Sijna, Dainhat and Kaigram villages for development and construction of roads and arrangements be made immediately for disbursement of 50% of the allocated amounts to the said villages."

Budget Estimates of Panchayat Samitis : The budget estimates of Palla Road and Nabagram Panchayat Samitis as placed before the meeting were discussed and approved. "Resolved that the budget estimates of Palla Road and Nabagram Panchayat Samitis be and are hereby approved."

Vote of Thanks : As there was no other business, the meeting terminated with a vote of thanks to the Chair.

Confirmed.

Rameshwar Ghosh	Hemanta Mukherjee
Secretary	Sabhadhipati
Date : 31.1.2000	Date : 31.1.2000

Q. 13. Enumerate the important rules which govern the meetings of a Panchayat Samiti.

Ans. : The rules which govern the meetings of a Panchayat Samiti can be summed up as under :

(a) **Period :** A Panchayat Samiti is required to hold at least one meeting in every three months.

(b) **Time & Place :** The time and place of the meeting shall be decided at the previous meeting. In this connection, the place of the meeting may be anywhere within the local limits of the concerned Block.

(c) **Convenor :** While the first meeting of the newly-constituted Samiti shall be convened by the Sub-Divisional Officer (SDO), the subsequent ones shall be convened by the Secretary in consultation with the Sabhapati.

(d) **Chairman :** It is the Sabhapati or Sahakari Sabhapati in absence of the former who presides over the meetings of a Samiti. If, however, both of them are absent, the members present will elect one from amongst themselves to preside at the meeting.

(e) **Quorum :** The quorum for a meeting of a Samiti shall be one-fourth of its total number of members. However, an adjourned meeting requires no quorum.

(f) **Decision :** All the items of the agenda will be decided by a majority of votes.

(g) **Casting Vote :** In addition to his usual vote as a member, the Chairman can use his casting vote (additional vote) in case of a tie.

(h) **Executive Officer :** The Block Development Officer (BDO) is the ex-officio Executive Officer of the Panchayat Samiti. He shall attend the meetings of the Samiti and participate therein.

(i) **Requisition Meeting :** If and when one-fifth of the total number of members of a Panchayat Samiti requisition in writing for holding of a meeting, the Sabhapati shall convene the meeting within seven days. In the event of his failure to do so, the requisitionists themselves can convene the meeting after giving seven days' notice in writing.

Q. 14. Draft the Notice of the first meeting of a Panchayat Samiti.

Ans. :

Nabagram Gram Panchayat Samiti
Vill. & P. O. Nabagram
Dist. Burdwan

Dated the 1st January 2000

Notice is hereby given that the first meeting of the newly-constituted Samiti will be held in the Samiti Office on Friday, the 24th January 2000 at 3 P. M. to transact the following business :

Agenda :

1. Election of Sabhapati and Sahakari Sabhapati
2. Formation of nine Sthayee Samities.

Bidyut Barman
Sub-Divisional Officer
Nabagram Sub-Division

Q. 15. Draft the notice of a meeting (other than the first meeting) of a Panchayat Samiti. (C. U. 1994)

Ans. :

Parulia Panchayat Samiti
Vill. & P. O. Parulia
Dist. Burdwan

Dated the 19th January 2000

Notice is hereby given that an ordinary meeting of the members of the Samiti will be held at its office on Friday, the 12th February 2000, at 3 P. M. to transact the following business :

Agenda :

1. To confirm the Minutes of the last meeting held on 13th January 2000.
2. To consider the proposal for construction of school buildings and renovation/ extension of existing ones.
3. To consider approval of Budget Estimates of Gram Panchayats.
4. Miscellaneous.

Ilyas Ali Mollah
Secretary
Parulia Panchayat Samiti

Q. 16. Draft the proceedings of the first meeting of a Panchayat Samiti.

Ans. : Minutes of the first meeting of Parulia Panchayat Samiti, P. O. & Vill. Parulia, Dist. Burdwan, held on Wednesday, the 12th January 2000, at 2 P. M. at Panchayat Office.

Members Present : Thirty members were present at the meeting and their names and signatures appear in the Attendance Register.

In Attendance :

1. Shri Sriniwas Sarma, B. D. O.
2. Shri M. M. Modak, Secretary.

Chairman : Shri Bidyut Barman, S. D. O. presided over the meeting.

Election of Sabhapati and Sahakari Sabhapati : Shri K. K. Kar proposed the names of Sarbashri S. Sawant and M. G. Ranade as Sabhapati and Sahakari Sabhapati and the proposal was seconded by Shri S. Sabde. It was thereafter "Resolved that Sarbashri S. Sawant and M. G. Ranade be and are hereby elected Sabhapati and Sahakari Sabhapati, respectively, of the Samiti."

Formation of Sthayee Samitis : Shri A. Aslam proposed the names of the members of nine Sthayee Samitis, which Md. Nurul Islam seconded. It was then "Resolved that nine Sthayee Samitis be and are hereby formed as per the list of members submitted before the meeting."

As there was no other business, the meeting terminated with a vote of thanks to the Chair.

Confirmed.

M. M. Modak	Bidyut Barman
Secretary	Chairman
Date : 23.1.2000	Date : 24.1.2000

Q. 17. Draft the Minutes of a meeting (other than the first meeting) of a Panchayat Samiti.

Ans. : Minutes of the ordinary meeting of Parulia Panchayat Samiti, Vill. & P. O. Parulia, Dist. Burdwan (Parulia Sub-Division) held in Samiti Office on Friday, the 16th March 2000 at 3 P. M.

Present :

1. Shri S. Sawant, Sabhapati
2. Shri M. G. Ranade, Sahakari Sabhapati

and thirty members whose names and signatures appear in the Attendance Register.

In Attendance :

1. Shri Bidyut Barman, S. D. O.
2. Md. Ilyas Ali Mollah, Secretary

Shri S. Sawant, Sabhapati, took the Chair.

Confirmation of Minutes : The Minutes of the last meeting held on 31st December 1999 which were circulated amongst the members were considered as read, approved and confirmed. "Resolved that the Minutes of the last meeting held on 31st December 1999 be and are hereby confirmed."

Construction/Renovation/Extension of School Buildings

There was a threadbare discussion on the proposal for construction/renovation/extension of the school buildings situated within the precincts of the Samiti. It was thereafter "Resolved that Vidyasagar School, Dr. S. N. Mukherjee Vidyalaya and Sarkar Vidyapith be and are hereby granted sums of Rs. 10 lakhs, Rs. 5 lakhs and Rs. 2 lakhs, respectively, for construction, renovation and extension of the proposed existing school buildings."

Approval of Budget Estimates of Gram Panchayats

The Budget Estimates of Teghara and Mandira Gram Panchayats placed before the meeting were discussed in detail. It was then "Resolved that the Budget Estimates of Teghara and Mandira Gram Panchayats as placed before the meeting be and are hereby approved."

Vote of Thanks : As there was no other business for discussion, the meeting terminated with a vote of thanks to the Chairman.

Confirmed.

Ilyas Ali Mollah — S. Sawant

Secretary — Chairman

Date : 24.3.2000 — Date : 24.3.2000

Q. 18. Describe the rules which govern meetings of Gram Panchayat.

Ans. : The rules which govern the meetings of Gram Panchayat are summed up as under :

(a) **Period :** A Gram Panchayat is required to hold at least one meeting in each month.

(b) **Time & Place :** The time and place of the meeting shall be decided in the preceding meeting. The place of the meeting shall be within the local limits of the concerned Gram.

(c) **Convenor :** While the first meeting shall be convened by the Block Development Officer (BDO), the subsequent one shall be convened by the Secretary in consultation with the Pradhan.

(d) **Chairman :** It is the Pradhan or, in his absence, the Upa-Pradhan who presides at the meetings. If, however, both of them are absent, the members present shall elect one of them to preside at the meeting.

(e) **Quorum :** One-fourth of the total number of members of the Gram Panchayat, subject to a minimum of four members, shall be the quorum. However, an adjourned meeting does not require any quorum.

(f) **Decision :** All the decisions to be taken at the meeting shall be by a majority of votes.

(g) **Casting Vote :** In addition to his ordinary vote as a member, the Chairman can exercise his casting (additional) vote in case there is a tie.

(h) **Executive Officer :** The Block Development Officer (B. D. O.) is the ex-officio Executive Officer of the Gram Panchayat. He shall attend the meetings of the Gram Panchayat and participate in the discussions.

(i) **Requisition Meeting :** If and when one-fifth of the members of the Gram Panchayat, subject to a minimum of four, requisition in writing for holding a meeting, the Pradhan shall convene the meeting within seven days. If the Pradhan fails to do so, the requisitionists themselves can convene the meeting after giving seven clear days' notice in writing.

Q. 19. Draft the notice of the first meeting of a Gram Panchayat. (C. U. 1999, 1996)

Ans. :

Chowhati Gram Panchayat

Vill. & P. O. Chowhati

Dist. 24 Parganas (South)

Date : 1st April 2000

Notice is hereby given that the First Meeting of the newly-constituted Gram Panchayat will be held in the Panchayat office on Tuesday, the 23rd April 2000 at 2 P. M.

All the members are requested to make it convenient to attend the meeting.

Agenda :

1. To elect the Pradhan and Upa-Pradhan.
2. To form a Committee for eradication of illiteracy in the Gram.
3. Miscellaneous.

Amalendu Sinha
Block Development Officer
Sonarpur Block

Q. 20. Draft the notice of an ordinary meeting (other than the first meeting) of a Gram panchayat.

Ans. :

Chowhati Gram Panchayat
Vill. & P. O. Chowhati
Dist. 24 Parganas (South)

Date : 15th April 2000

Notice is hereby given that an ordinary meeting of the members of the Gram Panchayat will be held at the Panchayat office on Wednesday, the 10th May 2000 at 3 P. M. to transact the following business.

All the members are requested to attend the meeting.

Agenda :

1. To confirm the Minutes of the last meeting held on 23rd March 2000.
2. To consider establishment of a Girls' School.
3. To consider possible solutions to unemployment problem of the Gram.
4. To consider grant of relief to the affected villagers.
5. Miscellaneous.

Purna Chandra Gorai
Secretary

Q. 21. Draft the Minutes of the first meeting a Gram Panchayat.

Ans. : Minutes of the First Meeting of Chowhati Gram Panchayat, Vill. & P. O. Chowhati, held on Tuesday, the 23rd April 2000 at 2 P. M. at the Gram Panchayat office.

Members Present : Twenty-one members were present at the meeting whose names and signatures appear in the Attendance Register.

In Attendance : Md. Abbas Ali Baig, Secretary.

Chairman : Shri Amalendu Sinha, B. D. O., took the Chair.

Election of Pradhan and Upa-Pradhan : Shri Jagannath Mukherjee proposed the names of Sarbashri Srikanta Sar and Balaram Bal as Pradhan and Upa-Pradhan, respectively. Shri Samar Nath seconded the motion. It was then unanimously "Resolved that Sarbashri Srikanta Sar and Balaram Bal be and are hereby elected as Pradhan and Upa-Pradhan, respectively, of the Chowhati Gram Panchayat".

Development of Education : There was a threadbare discussion as to how basic education can be reached to almost all the villagers. Shri Akhil Ansari proposed the names of Sarbashri Amarendra Adak, Head-Master, Chowhati School, Khagen Khasnabis and Susanta Sanyal as the Chairman and members of the Education Development Committee. It was then "Resolved that Sarbashri Amarendra Adak, Head-Master, Chowhati School, Khagen Khasnabis and Susanta Sanyal be and are hereby elected as the Chairman and members of the Education Development Committee."

Vote of Thanks : As there was no other business, the meeting terminated with a vote of thanks to the Chair.

Amalendu Sinha
Chairman

Q. 22. Draft the proceedings of an ordinary meeting of a Gram Panchayat.

Ans. : Minutes of the Ordinary Meeting of Chowhati Gram Panchayat, Vill. & P. O. Chowhati, held on Wednesday, the 10th February 2000 at 3 P. M. at the office of the Gram Panchayat.

Present :

Shri Srikanta Sar, Pradhan, and eleven members whose names and signatures appear in the Attendance Register.

In Attendance :

Shri Purna Chandra Gorai, Secretary.

Chairman : Shri Srikanta Sar, Pradhan, took the Chair.

Confirmation of Minutes : Minutes of the last meeting which were circulated amongst the members were taken as read and approved. It was then "Resolved that the Minutes of the last meeting held on Wednesday, the 23rd January 2000 be and are hereby confirmed."

Establishment of a Girls' School : There was a detailed discussion as to how a Junior Girls' School can be started in the Gram. All the members present agreed to donate and collect donations from villagers as well as outsiders so that at least 25% of the cost of the project can be contributed by the village itself. For the balance amount, the Pradhan agreed to take up the matter with appropriate authorities. It was thereafter "Resolved that all the necessary arrangements for establishment of a Junior Girls' School be and are hereby made as early as possible."

Development of Gram : Discussion on the ways and means of developing the Gram was made. It was then "Resolved that the programmes for plantation of plants/saplings and construction of roads be and are taken up in the first week of the next month."

Vote of Thanks : As there was no other business for transaction, the meeting terminated with a vote of thanks to the Chair.

Confirmed.

Purna Chandra Gorai	Srikanta Sar
Secretary	Pradhan
Date : 20.2.2000	Date : 20.02.2000

Q. 23. Draft a notice convening an ordinary meeting of the Commissioners of the Rajpur Municipality.

Ans. : Notice is hereby given that an ordinary meeting of the Commissioners of the

Rajpur Municipality will be held on Monday, March 16, 2000 at 3.00 P. M. at its main office building to transact the following business. Please make it convenient to attend the meeting.

Kausik Debnath
Chairman

Agenda :

1. To grant leave of absence, if any.
2. To confirm the minutes of the last meeting held on February 1, 2000.
3. To consider the monthly departmental reports.
4. To consider and approve the recommendations of the Standing Committee.
5. To consider and approve the Adult Education Scheme for implementation in phases.

Q. 24. Draft the minutes of an ordinary meeting convened by a Municipality.

Ans. : Minutes of the meeting of the Commissioners of the Rajpur Municipality held on Monday, March 16, 2000 at 3.00 P. M. at its main office building.

Present :

1. Shri Kaushik Debnath, Chairman
2. Shri Tushar Mukerjee, Commissioner
3. Shri Dhiren Basu, Commissioner
4. Shri Madan Paul, Commissioner.

In attendance :

Shri Buddhadev Nath, Secretary.

Sr. No.	Subject	Details
1.	Leave of Absence	Leave of absence was granted to Shir Samar Nath, Commissioner, who had earlier communicated his inability to attend the meeting.
2.	Confirmation of Minutes	Minutes of the last meeting held on February 1, 2000, were confirmed.
3.	Monthly departmental reports	The members present took note of the contents of the departmental reports placed before the meeting.
4.	Recommendations of the Standing Finance Committee	Recommendations of the Standing Finance Committee were discussed and the members present approved the recommendations unanimously.
5.	Adult Education Scheme	It was decided by the members present to implement in phases the Adult Education Scheme recently approved by the Government of West Bengal.
6.	Vote of Thanks	The meeting terminated with a vote of thanks to the Chair.

Dated Rajpur
March 23, 2000

Kausik Debnath
Chairman

Q. 25. Draft a notice of the meeting of the Councillors of the Calcutta Municipal Corporation.

Ans. :

Calcutta Municipal Corporation
Surendra Nath Banerjee Road
Calcutta 700 013

Notice is hereby given that an Ordinary Meeting of the Councillors of the Corporation will be held on Monday, March 31, 2000 at 3.00 P. M. at the Conference Room of the Central Office of the Corporation, Calcutta, to transact the following business. Please make it convenient to attend the meeting.

Agenda :

1. To grant leave of absence, if any.
2. To confirm the Minutes of the last meeting held on February 28, 2000.
3. To take note of the contents of the monthly reports of the departments.
4. To take note of the complaints received on unauthorised encroachment of footpaths by the hawkers in Gariahat and Shyambazar areas and consider remedial measures.
5. To consider any other business with the permission of the Chair.

Babul Bose
Chairman

Q. 26. Draft the minutes of a meeting of the Councillors of the Calcutta Municipal Corporation.

Ans. : Minutes of meeting of the Councillors of the Calcutta Municipal Corporation held on Monday, March 31, 2000 at 3.00 P. M. at the Conference Room of the Central Office of the Corporation, Calcutta.

Present :

Shri Babul Bose, Chairman

Shri Chanchal Chatterjee, Councillor

Shri Debasish Debnath, Councillor

Shri Even Eaphen, Councillor

Shri Falguni Fernandes, Councillor.

In attendance : Shri M Pohnerkar, Secretary.

Sr. No.	Subject	Details
1.	Chairman of the Meeting	Shri Babul Bose took the Chair, ascertained the quorum and declared the meeting to be in order.
2.	Leave of Absence	Leave of absence was granted to Shri Gajendra Ghosh who had earlier informed about his preoccupation.
3.	Confirmation of the Minutes	Minutes of the last meeting held on February 28, 2000 were confirmed.
4.	Complaints on encroachment of footpaths	All the letters of complaints received were discussed and necessary remedial actions were suggested by the members. It was also decided that Shri Chanchal Chatterjee would be in charge of the Action Committee.
5.	Any other business/Vote of Thanks	As there was no other business to be transacted, the meeting terminated with a vote of thanks to the Chair.

Dated Calcutta
the 3rd April, 2000

Babul Bose
Chairman

9

COMPANY MEETINGS (A)
GENERAL

[**Contents** : Meeting—Types, Requisites, Lawful & Unlawful, Private & Public—Notice—Agenda—Chairman, Appointment, Qualifications, Duties, Powers, Responsibilities—Slander & Libel—Motion & Resolution —Types of Resolutions—Amendment—Ordinary & Special Business—Resolutions & Agreements to be filed with the Registrar of Companies—Sense of a Meeting—Poll—Proxy—Requisites, Interruptions to Debate—Privileges in Speeches—Absolute & Qualified Privilege, Admission of Press to Company Meetings, Minutes—Points to be noted—Legal Requirements for maintenance of Minutes—Minutes & Reports—Confirmation of Minutes—Minutes of Narration & Decision—Alteration of Minutes.]

Q. 1. What do you mean by a meeting? What are the different kinds of meetings held by companies? Give short description of each.

(C.U. 1998, 1996, 1969, 1967, 1962; ICSI—Many times)

Or, Define a meeting. Distinguish between private meeting and public meeting. Enumerate the different types of company meetings. (C.U. 1982)

Or, Describe briefly the following classes of meetings of a public co. (a) Meeting of Board of Directors other than the first meeting of the Board, (b) Annual General Meeting, (c) Extra-ordinary General Meeting, (d) Creditors' Meeting.
Mention the nature of business conducted at each one of them. (C.U. 1999)

Ans. : A meeting is an assembly of two or more persons to transact any lawful business. According to the Shorter Oxford Dictionary, a meeting is "an assembly of a number of people for entertainment or the like." According to the Webster's Dictionary, a meeting is "an act or process of coming together." A meeting, therefore, is a gathering of two or more persons with an object in view or for certain specific purposes. However, when all the shares of a particular class in a company are held by one person that person will constitute the quorum and a valid meeting too of the shareholders of that class. A committee meeting also may be validly held with one member. But it must be made clear here that every gathering or an assembly will not be considered as a meeting. A number of conditions have to be complied with before a meeting can be said to be validly convened and properly conducted. Meetings of various types of organisations are governed by the various statutes governing such organisations. There may be some meetings which are not controlled by any statutes but by some customs and conventions. In this connection, a meeting may be of two kinds, viz. public meeting and private meeting.

The meetings held by companies may be classified under the following categories :

1. Meeting of shareholders which may be subdivided into :

   (i) Statutory Meeting.

   (ii) Annual General Meeting.

   (iii) Extra-ordinary General Meeting.

   (iv) Class Meeting.

2. Meetings of debentureholders.

3. Meetings of creditors—these may be subdivided into two types :

   (i) When the company is wound-up.

   (ii) When the company is not wound-up.

4. Meetings of Directors.

1. (i) **Statutory Meeting :** Section 165 of the Companies Act, 1956, states the provisions regarding statutory meeting and statutory report. Every public limited company must hold a general meeting of the members within a period of not less than one month and not more than six months from the date of commencement of business. This meeting which is held only once during the lifetime of a company is known as the statutory meeting. The members discuss at this meeting the report (Statutory Report) drafted/presented by the directors of the company. Any matter relating to formation of the company can be discussed at this meeting even though no previous notice therefor has been given.

(ii) **Annual General Meeting :** Section 166 of the Companies Act, 1956, states the provisions for this meeting. According to this Section, every company must hold its first annual general meeting within eighteen months of its incorporation. If such a meeting is held within the period of eighteen months as above, no such meeting is required to be held in the year of incorporation of the company or the following year. The interval between two annual general meetings must not exceed fifteen months. The Registrar of Companies may, in some special cases, extend this time by a period not exceeding three months.

Every annual general meeting shall be called during the business hours on a working day at the registered office of the company or at some other place within the town/village where the registered office is situated.

The notice must specify that it is a notice for annual general meeting. According to Section 171, a general meeting requires a clear 21 days' notice in writing. A meeting with a shorter notice may be allowed to be held if it is agreed to by all the members entitled to vote thereat.

If the company defaults in holding an annual general meeting in terms of the provisions of Section 166, the Company Law Board may call or direct the calling of a general meeting on the application of any member of the company (Section 167).

Non-compliance with the provisions of Sections 166 and 167 makes the company and its officers liable to a fine of Rs. 5,000 (maximum) and for continuing default a further sum of Rs. 250/- per day (Section 168).

Ordinary business, viz., approval of annual accounts, declaration of dividend, appointment of directors and appointment of auditors and other business (i.e., special business) can be transacted at this meeting.

(iii) **Extra-ordinary General Meeting :** The purpose of calling this meeting is to deal with an extraordinary matter which falls outside the scope of annual general meeting. Besides this, such a meeting is also held to transact such urgent business as cannot be deferred till the next annual general meeting.

According to the provisions of Section 168, the Board of Directors of a company can be compelled to hold such a meeting on request or requisition made for it. The requisition must be signed by members holding at least 1/10th of the paid-up share capital of the company (having a share capital) or 1/10th of the total voting power (in case of other companies). The requisition must clearly state the matters to be discussed at the meeting as it must be deposited at the registered office of the company. If the Board of Directors does not hold the meeting within 45 days from the receipt of requisition, the requisitionists themselves can arrange for calling the meeting. Under Section 186, the Company Law Board may call such a meeting. Resolutions properly passed at this meeting are binding on the company. No ordinary business can be transacted at such a meeting.

(iv) **Class Meeting :** The meeting of a particular class of members/shareholders is known as class meeting. The Articles of Association may contain rules regarding holding of this meeting. Ordinarily, to make the consent binding, a majority of three-fourths of the shareholders'/members' votes in favour of the proposed change are required. The circumstances under which a class meeting may be called are enumerated below :

(a) When a company issues different types of shares and confers different rights.

(b) When the Court deems it fit that a compromise or an arrangement between the company and its members should be made.

2. **Meetings of Debentureholders :** A company may issue debentures to raise loans and, as such, debentureholders are a class of creditors. The rules and regulations in connection with meeting of debentureholders are incorporated in the Trust Deed or Debenture Bond. These rules are, therefore, binding upon both the company and its debentureholders.

Modification of the terms of their rights comprises

(a) variation in the rate of interest on debentures;

(b) enabling the company to raise further loans by way of issuing fresh debentures;

(c) relaxation of some of the stringent provisions contained in the Deed.

3. (i) & (ii) **Meetings of Creditors** may be of two types. A company may hold such a meeting either in the event of its winding-up or as a running concern. Sections 391-393 of the Companies Act provide the details in this regard. The Act authorises a company to make

compromise with its creditors and lays down the procedure to be adopted. These meetings are, strictly speaking, not the meetings of a company.

4. **Meeting of Directors :** Meetings of the directors of a company are called Board meetings. The Board is the executive authority and manages the affairs of the company. The following are some of the business which are usually transacted at a Board meeting :

(a) Management of affairs of the company.

(b) Allotment of shares.

(c) Making calls.

(d) Passing of transfers.

(e) Forfeiture of shares.

(f) Re-issue of forfeited shares.

(g) Finalisation of accounts for onward transmission to the auditors for certification.

(h) Appropriation of profit and recommendation for dividend.

(i) Appointment of officers.

The Companies Act provides for the following rules in regard to meetings of the Board of Directors of a company :

(i) Section 285 provides that such meeting should be held at least once in every three months and four times in a year. The Central Government may, by notification in the official Gazette, exempt any class of companies—partly or fully—from compliance with this rule.

(ii) Section 286 provides for giving notice in writing to all the directors for the time being in India and for others at their usual residential address in India.

(iii) Section 289 provides for the rules of circulating the resolution to the directors and its approval by the Board.

Q. 2. (a) Define a meeting. (b) What are the features of a meeting? (c) What is the importance of a meeting?

Ans. : (a) *Please refer to first paragraph of Answer to the previous question.*

(b) The important features of a meeting can be summed up as under :

(i) It is an assembly of two or more persons.

(ii) The object of the meeting must be lawful.

(iii) It must be held at a lawful place.

(iv) The persons or members who attend the meeting must have interest in the subject matter of the meeting.

(c) In a democratic managerial set-up, meetings have a unique place which provide the best means of communication. The members present get an opportunity to discuss face-to-face, exchange ideas and views as well as arrive at collective decisions. Such decisions are sound and matured. Therefore, these can be enforced for the best interest of the organisation.

The problems of the institution/organisation can also be chalked out in a meaningful way in the meeting.

Q. 3. What are the requisites of a Valid Meeting? **(N.B.U. 1977; ICSI)**

Or, "A company meeting must be duly convened and properly constituted."—Discuss. **(C.U. 1974; ICSI)**

Or, State the requisites of a valid meeting. **(C.U. 1983, 1980)**

Or, (a) Explain the requisites of a valid meeting. (b) How will you distinguish between a lawful meeting from an unlawful meeting? **(C.U. 1984)**

Ans. : Unless the business of a meeting is validly transacted, the resolutions adopted or decisions taken will not be binding on the organisation. The requisites or requirements of a valid meeting may be enumerated as under :

1. Proper convention (i.e., calling) of the meeting. This means that :
   (a) It must be convened by an authorised person.
   (b) Proper notice of the meeting must be given to the members and other persons/ parties who are entitled to attend it.
   (c) Communication of notice of the meeting by appropriate means.
2. Proper constitution of the meeting. This signifies the following :
   (a) Minimum number of members (i.e., quorum) must be present during the currency of the meeting.
   (b) The meeting must have, and it must be conducted, by a duly elected Chairman.
   (c) The proceedings of the meeting must be conducted according to the rules governing the meeting.

For the statutory bodies, prescribed rules for conducting their meetings are available but, in case of non-statutory bodies, these have got to be framed. In case of companies, the Articles of Association provide the rules for the conduct of the meetings.

Some organisations which do not have their written rules may adopt the following principles for conducting their meetings :

(a) Rules established by custom should be followed.

(b) In case there is no such custom, each meeting or the Chairman of the meeting must decide the rules.

Q. 4. What is meant by lawful and unlawful meeting? What are the provisions of the Indian Penal Code relating to unlawful assembly? **(C.U. 1980)**

Or, Distinguish between lawful meeting and unlawful meeting. **(C.U. 1995, 1982)**

Ans. : A meeting to be valid must be properly convened (i.e., called) and conducted according to the law/rules governing the meeting. The law of meetings under various statutes/

Acts enumerates a number of conditions which should be complied with to make the meeting valid. Non-compliance with one or more than one of the statutory requirements will make the meeting invalid. An invalid meeting may be lawful or unlawful. A meeting will be termed lawful if it is held in a proper place for a lawful purpose and is not aimed at endangering the peace and tranquility of the locality. A meeting, even though lawfully held, may become invalid because of some technical reasons. If the above requirements are complied with, the meetings of different companies, societies, clubs, political parties, schools, colleges, etc. will be considered as lawful ones. A meeting which has not been properly called or convened will be called an invalid meeting. An invalid meeting, therefore, is not an unlawful meeting. A meeting is unlawful if and when it is held in contravention of the provisions of the concerned Act and is against the public policy/interest. A meeting called for an unlawful purpose or called at a place where holding of meeting is specially prohibited because of certain reasons will be termed as unlawful meeting. A meeting which disturbs the peace of the people of the locality or terrorise them will be considered as an unlawful meeting.

Section 141 of the Indian Penal Code dwells on unlawful assembly and reads : "An assembly of five or more than five persons having for common object, one or other of the five objectives specified below, will constitute an unlawful assembly :

(i) to overcome by criminal force, the government or any public servant in lawful discharge of its/his duty;

(ii) to resist the execution of any law or of any legal process;

(iii) to commit any offence, mischief or criminal tresspass;

(iv) to obtain forcible possession of any movable or immovable property by means of criminal force, dispossess any person of such property or to enforce any right or supposed right;

(v) to compel any person by force to do a wrong which he is not legally entitled to do or to omit to do what he is bound to do".

Q. 5. 'A meeting becomes unlawful if it is held for an unlawful purpose.' Under what other circumstances can a meeting become unlawful?

Ans. : If the purpose of the meeting is unlawful, the meeting too becomes unlawful. Some of the instances, where a meeting becomes unlawful, are :

(a) Meeting at any public place without the permission of the appropriate authority.

(b) Meeting at a place specifically prohibited for law and order situation of the area. (e.g. where Criminal Procedure Code 144 is in force).

(c) Any meeting which will make the local people panicky for nothing and destroy their peace.

Q. 6. A private meeting is going to be held in a public park. Will it be a lawful meeting? (C.U. 1988)

Ans. : A private meeting may be held in the office premises of that organisation or in a rented hall. A private meeting which is going to be held in a public park will, therefore, be treated as an invalid or unlawful meeting.

Q. 7. Distinguish between a public meeting and a private meeting.

Ans. : A public meeting, as the name suggests, is meant for the general public and, as such, anybody can attend such a meeting. A private meeting, on the other hand, is meant for members of that organisation only which may be a company, firm, association or club. A public meeting deals with the public interest and is held in an open place, park or inside a building. A private meeting deals with such matters in which the members only are interested and is held inside the office building of that organisation or any other building/hall. While no formal notice and quorum are necessary for a public meeting, these are essential for a private meeting.

Q. 8. What is a Notice? What are its requisites? (B.U. 1962)

Or, What are the essential requisites of a valid notice for a General Meeting of a Company in regard to length of time, contents and manner of service? (V.U. 1988; C.U. 1985)

Or, What is a notice of a meeting? Outline the rules governing the issue of notice for a company's general meeting. Under what circumstances can the length of notice of a general meeting be reduced? (ICSI; C.U. 1999, 1997)

Or, Discuss the requisites of a valid notice for a General Meeting of a company. (C.U. 1998, 1995, 1969, 1967)

Or, What are the essentials of a valid notice? (C.U. 1981)

Ans. : Notice implies a proper and adequate intimation to those members who have the right to attend the meeting and vote thereat.

A meeting to be valid must be properly constituted and conducted. Proper constitution of the meeting refers to due intimation to those persons about the time, place and date of the meeting who are entitled to attend it. The convenor of a meeting must be an authorised person and the means of communication of the intimation may be verbal or written. Ordinarily, the Company Secretary is authorised by the Chairman or the Board of Directors to issue notice.

Essential requisites of a valid notice :

1. It must clearly specify the date, time and place of the meeting with a view to ensuring convenience to the majority of the participants. In case of meetings of the Board of Directors and its committees, the current meetings fix up the date and time of the next meetings (Section 172).

2. The business to be transacted at the meeting must be clearly specified in the notice. That is why the agenda form a part of the notice. In some cases, copies of resolutions, reports, etc. are forwarded along with the notice.

3. According to the provisions of Section 172(2), notice of every meeting shall be given to every member who is entitled to attend it.

4. Section 171 of the Companies Act states the rules regarding length of notice. A general meeting may be called by giving not less than 21 clear days' notice. In case of annual general meeting, if all the members entitled to note agree to a shorter notice, the meeting may be validly held. In case of other meetings, meeting with a shorter notice may be held if it is agreed to by :

(a) members holding not less than 95% of the paid-up share capital of the company and entitled to vote at the meeting; or

(b) members holding not less than 95% of the total voting power at the meeting.

5. Notice must be issued by proper authority.

6. It must be written in clear and unambiguous terms; it must be explicit and unqualified (i.e., unconditional).

7. It must be served in the manner provided in the rules of the organisation. It is desirable to send a notice in writing. A verbal notice followed by written confirmation may also serve the purpose equally well.

8. Issuance of notice may be dispensed with in those cases where meetings are fixed to be held on a specified day of the week or the month.

Q. 9. What will be the consequences of a general meeting of a public limited company :

(a) where the notice was despatched to a wrong address?

(b) where the notice was despatched within the scheduled date, but due to postal delay which was known to the company, the notice failed to reach within due time?

(c) where the legal successor of one of the shareholders lives in a remote village in the Himalayas and the notice failed to reach him?

(d) where one shareholder lived in Japan and the notice reached him after the meeting was over? (ICSI)

Ans. : (a) Despatch of notice to a wrong address will not invalidate the proceedings at the meeting. However, the member who has not received notice—due to despatch thereof to a wrong address—may take action against the company for oppression on the minority if he holds more than 10% of the paid-up capital.

(b) In terms of Section 53(2) (b) of the Companies Act, 1956, the company is not liable. But since, in the instant case, the postal delay was known to the company, it should have taken proper precaution so that the notice would reach the member in due time. Obviously, it is a wilful default on the part of the company. The aggrieved member may take action against the company but he cannot invalidate the proceedings of the meeting.

(c) As per the provisions of Section 172, read with Section 53 the Companies Act, 1956, the company is not liable in the instant case. The legal successor can neither take any action against the company nor can he invalidate the proceedings of the meeting.

(d) In terms of the provision of Section 53(3), advertisement of the notice in the neighbourhood of the registered office of the company shall be deemed to be duly served on every member of the company who has no registered address in India and has not supplied to the company an address within India for sending notices to him. Therefore, the shareholder can neither make the company liable nor can he invalidate the proceedings of the meeting.

Q. 10. Can a Company Meeting be held on any day, at any place and at any time? (C.U. 1981)

Ans. : Section 166 of the Companies Act provides that an Annual General Meeting should be held on a working day and during the normal business hours of the company. According to the clarification of the Department of Company Affairs, if the adjourned annual general meeting comes to be accidentally held on a public holiday, there is no violation of Section 166(2). So a general meeting other than the annual general meeting may be held beyond the business hours of the company. Annual general meeting may be held at the registered office of the company or at some other place within the town/village where the registered office of the company is situated. A statutory meeting may be held on any day including a public holiday and at a place other than the registered office of the company. A Board Meeting may be held on any day including a holiday and anywhere in the country. The rules regarding date, time and place of holding an extra-ordinary general meeting are the same as those applicable to the Statutory and Board Meetings.

Q. 11. (a) What is a notice? (b) On whom is the notice of a meeting required to be served? (c) In this connection, explain the term 'Clear Days'. (d) Under what circumstances service of notice is not necessary?

Ans. : (a) *Refer to pages 145-46.*

(b) Section 172(2) specifies the persons to whom notice of every meeting shall be given. In terms of this Section, notice shall be given to the following persons/parties :

(i) Every member of the company;

(ii) Every person on whom the shares of the deceased (by means of transmission) or insolvent have devolved.

(iii) The auditor or auditors for the time being of the company.

Section 172(3) provides that the accidental omission to give notice to, or non-receipt of notice by, any member or other person to whom it should be given shall not invalidate the proceedings at the meeting.

(c) **'Clear Days' :** The term 'clear days' implies the number of days between the date of serving notice to the members and the scheduled date of meeting (exclusive of both these days). The members entitled to attend the meeting must get proper and adequate number of 'clear days' notice in terms of the provisions of the Companies Act.

(d) Service of notice is not obligatory, i.e., service of notice can be waived under the following circumstances :

(i) When the members present at a meeting decide when they will meet next.

(ii) When the Board or committee members decide that they will meet on a particular date of a month or at particular intervals of time.

(iii) When a meeting is adjourned, no notice of adjourned meeting needs to be served and the meeting will be held in the next week on the same day, at the same day, time and place.

Q. 12. What is meant by 'Agenda'? Why is it necessary? Will you put the routine items of agenda first in order? Why? Draft a specimen agenda for an Annual General Meeting of a Public Limited Company. (C.U. 1997, 1995; ICSI)

Or, Draft a notice for the general meeting of a limited company setting out in serial order the ordinary business to be transacted at the meeting. (ICSI)

Ans. : The term 'Agenda' implies 'things to be done' or 'business to be transacted' at a meeting. Agenda comprises a list of things and a summary of points to be considered at a meeting.

Every meeting—whether of the shareholders or of the directors—must have an agenda with a view to ensuring that all the items to be transacted are discussed at the meeting. It also helps the members to think on the matters in the agenda and form their opinion thereon prior to the meeting. The agenda should be so prepared as to help quick disposal of the business to be transacted. It is usually the duty of the Secretary to prepare the agenda in consultation with the Chairman of the meeting.

It is conventional—and desirable too—to put the routine items of agenda first in order. The reason for this is to dispose of the routine matters first inasmuch as they take comparatively less time than the contentious or controversial matters. Due to insufficient time or non-availability of the quorum at any stage of the meeting, the unfinished business can be taken up for discussion later. Since the controversial or contentious matters take more time for discussion, these are put in the agenda later.

Specimen of Notice and Agenda

The A.B.C. Co. Ltd.

Notice to Members

The Third Annual General Meeting of the Members of the A.B.C. Co. Ltd. will be held at the Registered Office of the Company, 6 Clive Row, Calcutta 700001, on Monday the 31st January 2000 at 4 p.m.

Agenda :

1. The Secretary to read the Notice convening the meeting.
2. Minutes of the last meeting.
3. Directors' Report.
4. Declaration of Dividends.
5. Election of Directors.
6. Appointment of Auditors.
7. Vote of thanks.

The Register of Members and the Transfer Registers of the company will remain closed from the 26th to 31st January 2000, both days inclusive.

Note : A member entitled to attend and vote at the above meeting may appoint one or more proxies to attend the meeting and vote instead of him and the proxy or proxies so appointed need not be members of the Company.

By Order of the Board
The A.B.C. Co. Limited
A. Ghosh
Secretary

Registered Office :
6 Clive Row
Calcutta 700001
5th January 2000

Q. 13. Explain what do you mean by the term 'Agenda Book'.

Ans. : The paper containing the list of things to be done or business to be transacted at the meeting is called the Agenda paper. It is prepared by the Company Secretary in consultation with the Chairman or the Managing Director of the Company. The agenda papers meant for the Chairman and the Secretary are prepared in large sheets of paper having sufficient space for making necessary notes thereon by them. Some companies make use of an Agenda Book for this purpose. The Secretary takes note of the discussions of the meeting in this book. The notings made at the meeting help him to write the minutes of the meeting with ease and authenticity.

Q. 14. Define a Chairman. What are the qualifications of a successful Chairman? What are the circumstances under which the Chairman can eject or expel a member from the meeting?

Or, Who is a Chairman? How is he appointed? What qualifications should a successful Chairman possess? (C.U. 1997; N.B.U. 1976)

Or, "A Chairman is born, not made"—Elucidate. (V.U. 1987)

Ans. : A Chairman is the person who presides over and conducts the proceedings of a meeting. Before a meeting can start its business, it must have a Chairman. The Articles of Association of the company may provide for the appointment of a Chairman. The first Chairman of the company is generally named in the Articles. If the Articles do not so provide, the Chairman may be chosen or elected from amongst the members present. A Chairman is mostly a member of the body over which he is to preside.

The Companies Act does not prescribe any qualifications which a Chairman must possess. It is, however, a fact that success of any meeting largely depends on the capabilities of the Chairman. The qualifications which a Chairman should have may be enumerated below :

1. .He should be conversant with the law and procedure of conducting a meeting.

2. He should have a standard general education and he should be able to address the meeting in the same language in which proceedings thereof are conducted.

3. He should be aware of his powers and duties.

4. He must be a man of personality and resourcefulness.

5. He should be cool and patient.

6. He should have a judicial mind and be able to command the respect of the meeting.

7. He must be absolutely impartial in his rulings.

8. He should be firm in his decisions but must not be an autocrat.

One of the most important duties of the Chairman is to maintain order and decorum at the meeting. In case there is no proper order in the meeting, no business can be smoothly conducted and the very purpose of the meeting is frustrated. In the event of a few members behaving in a disorderly manner, the Chairman, at the first instance, advises them to behave properly. This is as good as warning to these members. Despite this, if these members continue to disturb the meeting and disobey the Chairman, he may expel or eject the members from the meeting. If these members do not leave the meeting on their own, the Chairman can take steps to have them evicted by force. In the course of eviction, no greater force should be used than is actually necessary. Otherwise, the Chairman may be held liable and the ejected members may take action against him for damage on account of assault. In extreme cases, the Chairman is constrained to adjourn the meeting.

Q. 15. Describe the powers, responsibilities and duties of the Chairman of an Annual General Meeting of a Company. (ICSI Adapted; C.U. 1976)

Or, Discuss the rights and duties of the Chairman of a Meeting.
(C.U., 1987, 1983, 1973, 1971, 1968, 1966)

Or, "The success or failure of a meeting depends on its Chairman"—elucidate.
(ICSI; N.B.U. 1977)

Or, Enumerate the rights and duties of the Chairman of a meeting. (C.U. 1994, 1981)

Ans. : A company delegates the authority to the Chairman either by the Articles of Association or by the meeting which appoints him as such. It has aptly been said by C. J. Jervis in the case of Taylor vs. Nesfield that "The Chairman collects, as it were, his authority from the meeting." The powers and duties of a Chairman are summed up hereunder :

Powers

1. **To maintain order and decorum at the meeting :** If the meeting gets disorderly, the Chairman can suspend or adjourn it. He has the power to maintain order and decorum at the meeting.

2. **To decide points of order :** When a member is speaking on a certain motion, another member may get up and enquire as to whether the statement of the speaker is in order. This is what is known as raising a point of order. The Chairman has the power to give his ruling on that point. His ruling, whether right or wrong, is final and binding on all members.

3. **To decide priority of speakers :** Frequently a number of persons get up and wish to

speak on the motion. In the circumstances, the Chairman decides the order in which the members will speak. His ruling in the matter is final.

4. **To maintain relevance and order :** He has the power to stop any irrelevant discussions or restrain use of unparliamentary language.

5. **To stop discussion on a matter :** When a motion is under discussion for a considerable period of time, he can stop the discussion and put the motion to vote.

6. **To eject disorderly persons :** When any member has been warned by the Chairman for his disorderly behaviour and he continues to disobey him, the Chairman can eject the member.

7. **To adjourn a meeting :** The Chairman is empowered to adjourn a meeting when :

(a) the number of members present falls below the quorum;

(b) the meeting demands it;

(c) the meeting becomes disorderly; and

(d) the business is complete before time.

8. **To exercise the casting vote :** Unless the Articles otherwise provide, the Chairman does not have the casting vote. In case he is entitled to a casting vote, he can exercise it when there is a tie. This vote is in addition to his ordinary vote (or deliberative vote) as a member of the company.

Duties

1. The chairman should see that the meeting is duly convened and properly constituted.

2. He is to ensure that the proceedings are conducted strictly according to rules.

3. He should see that the business of the meeting is taken up for consideration in the same order in which it appears in the agenda. He, however, can alter the order with the consent of the meeting.

4. He is to see that the motions and amendments are in order and within the scope of the meeting.

5. He must not allow any discussion unless there is a specific motion in this regard before the meeting.

6. He has to ensure that proper order in the meeting is maintained.

7. He should see that the minority is properly heard at the meeting.

8. He has to sign the Minutes of the last Board meeting.

9. He has to ascertain the sense of the meeting and to put all motions and amendments to vote.

Q. 16. "The Chairman is the umpire of debate." How far does it apply to the Chairman of a meeting? (C.U. 1987)

Ans. : An umpire is the controller, judge and supreme authority in a cricket match whose decision is final and binding on the contesting teams. Similarly, a chairman is the supreme authority in a meeting whose decision is final and binding on all the members attending the meeting. So the comparison of the Chairman in a meeting with the umpire in a cricket match has been aptly made.

Q. 17. Distinguish between "slander" and "libel".

Ans. : A slander refers to a false and defamatory statement—whether verbal or oral—in transitory form which intends to injure the reputation of another without any lawful justification or excuse.

A "libel", on the other hand, may be said to be a publication of a false and defamatory statement in some permanent form which tends to injure the reputation of another person without any lawful justification or excuse.

Points of distinction :

1. While a slander is spoken defamation, a libel is a written one.

2. While slander is a criminal wrong, libel is both a civil and a criminal offence.

3. Slander is, save in some special cases, actionable only of proof or special damage; whereas libel is actionable *per se*.

Q. 18. Distinguish between a 'Motion' and a 'Resolution'. What are the requisites of a Motion? Explain how a 'Motion' is moved. (ISCI; N.B.U. 1975)

Or, Point out the rules regarding Motion. (ICSI)

Or, Define a Motion and describe the rules as to its form, presentation and disposal. (V.U. 1987; B.U. 1963)

Or, What is a Motion? When does it become a Resolution? (C.U. 1999, 1998, 1996, 1990, 1982)

Ans. : Though the terms 'Motion' and 'Resolution' are indiscriminately used, there is a lot of difference between the two. Motion refers to a proposition placed before the meeting for discussion and final decision. It is also known as observation. A Motion is subject to alteration or amendment before it is adopted by the meeting. A Resolution is such a Motion which has already been voted upon and passed by the meeting with or without any amendments. A Resolution ultimately finds place in the Minutes of the meeting.

Before a Motion is brought before the meeting, it is the practice to give a notice therefor. A Motion is in writing and signed by the mover. A Motion needs to be seconded though it is not a 'must'. A Motion must be within the scope and power of the meeting. It should be worded in clear and unambiguous terms. As a matter of convention, a Motion is in the affirmative and starts with the word 'That'.

Requisites for a valid Motion :

1. A Motion should be in writing and signed by the mover, i.e., the proposer.

2. Only one Motion is permitted at a time for discussion.

3. A Motion is worded in the affirmative and it starts with the word 'That' so that with a slight alteration (or no alteration) it is turned into a resolution.

4. It must be within the powers of the meeting and scope of the notice.

5. It should be worded in clear, definite and unambiguous terms.

6. A Motion, before being brought before the meeting, ordinarily requires previous notice. However, motions for the purposes of appointment of Chairman, dissolution of the meeting, etc. do not require previous notice.

7. Unless the rules specifically provide for seconding of a Motion, it need not be seconded.

Moving a Motion : Subject to the rules of the organisation, a Motion is generally handed over to the Secretary before the meeting or the Chairman at the meeting. As a matter of procedure, the proposer rises, 'secures the floor' and addresses the Chairman of the meeting. He thus presents the Motion. If his Motion is not seconded, the Chairman rejects it outright and the Motion is then said 'to fall to the ground'. If, on the other hand, it is seconded, the Motion is said to be 'before the meeting'. The proposer is then given an opportunity to fully express his views. With the permission of the Chair, any member can speak on the Motion. No member is allowed to speak on the Motion more than once. However, the mover of the Motion may be allowed to speak twice, of course, before it is put to vote. When sufficient discussion has been made on a Motion, it may be put to vote by the Chairman. The Motion may be adopted by the meeting unanimously by the majority votes. If the majority of the members vote in favour of the Motion, it is said to be 'carried'. If, on the other hand, majority of the members vote against the Motion, it is said to be 'lost'. It is the Chairman who announces the results. The Motion, when adopted by the meeting, is known to be a Resolution.

Q. 19. What is an amendment and how can it be moved? What is the procedure adopted for moving an amendment? How does a Chairman deal with several amendments to the main motion and an amendment to an amendment? (ICSI)

Or, An amendment to a motion cannot be to negate the original motion. Discuss. (C.U. 1981)

Or, Write explanatory notes on 'Amendment'. (C.U. 1996, 1994, 1980)

Ans. : Amendment refers to any alteration of the original Motion which is under discussion and yet to be voted upon. The alteration may be in the term or wording of the Motion. Amendment is generally seconded by another member, but seconding is not compulsory. An amendment should normally be in writing and the terms thereof should be clear, unambiguous and in the affirmative. It should be relevant to the original Motion and must be within the scope and notice of the meeting. The Chairman is empowered to accept or reject an amendment on any reasonable ground.

Moving an amendment : An amendment is usually moved in one of the following ways :

(a) by way of omitting a few words or phrases from the original motion;

(b) by adding or inserting a few words or phrases;

(c) by deleting a few words or phrases of the original motion and substituting new ones;

(d) by altering position of the words or phrases.

When an amendment is proposed and duly seconded, the discussion on the main motion ceases. If the amendment is lost, discussion on the main motion is resumed. If, on the other hand, it is carried (i.e., accepted), the amendment is incorporated in the main motion and the amended motion is known as substantive motion. It may so happen that a number of amendments to the main motion or an amendment to an amendment is proposed. The Chairman insists on submission of amendments in writing. This helps him to consider the original motion. The Chairman is empowered to exercise his sole discretion to decide the order of the amendments. Usually, he does not accept more than one amendment to any amendment. It may sometimes happen that the number of amendments are considerable and complicated. In the circumstances, as a matter of practice, the original motion is withdrawn with the consent of the meeting and a new motion is placed instead.

Q. 20. Distinguish between a "motion" and an "amendment". Can a Chairman reject an amendment? If so, what are the grounds on which an amendment may be rejected?

Ans. : An amendment to a motion may be rejected by the Chairman of the meeting on the following grounds :

(a) If the amendment negatives the original motion;

(b) If the amendment introduced is purely a new one or contrary to the original motion;

(c) If it is not relevant to the original motion;

(d) If the amendment is not definitely clear and in the affirmative;

(e) If it is an amendment to an amendment;

(f) If it is proposed by a member who has already spoken on the original motion or moved an amendment to the main motion;

(g) If it is proposed as formal or dilatory motion.

Q. 21. Explain the meaning of ordinary and special resolutions. Mention the circumstances under which each is required to be passed by the company. (ICSI; B.U. 1962)

Or, When does a Motion become a Resolution? How does an ordinary resolution differ from a special resolution? (C.U. 1980)

Or, Explain the two types of resolutions which may be passed in a General Meeting of a Company. Name an ordinary business which should be passed by a special resolution. (C.U. 1998, 1982)

Ans. : When a motion is put to vote by the Chairman and found to have the requisite majority, it is said to be a resolution. In other words, resolution refers to the decision of the members present at a properly constituted meeting. According to the Companies Act, 1956, resolution may be of two types, viz., ordinary and special. Section 189(1) defines an ordinary resolution. An ordinary resolution is one which is passed by a simple majority of members entitled to vote, including the casting vote of the Chairman, if any. The votes cast in favour of the proposal by the members entitled to vote, either in person or by proxy, must exceed the votes cast against the resolution. The majority referred to above means majority of those members entitled to vote and not the majority of those who are attending the meeting. Ordinary resolution needs no notification in the agenda. The following are some of the business which a company can transact by way of passing an ordinary resolution :

1. Adoption of annual accounts of the company.

2. Appointment of directors.

3. Removal of director(s).

4. Appointment of auditor at the annual general meeting.

5. Declaration of dividends.

6. Issue of shares at a discount.

7. Alteration of share capital.

8. Voluntary winding-up of the company when the period fixed for its duration has expired.

A special resolution is one which is necessary for discussion of important matters and passed by a majority of three-fourths of the members voting. The voting in this regard may be by show of hands or on a poll and either in person or by proxy. The notice calling the general meeting must specify that a special resolution will be moved. Section 189(2) states the rules regarding special resolution. The following are some of the cases where a special resolution is required :

1. Change of the name of the company.

2. Transfer of its registered office from one State to another or alteration of its objects (Section 146).

3. Alteration of its Articles of Association (Section 31).

4. Reduction of share capital, subject to confirmation of court (Section 100).

5. Payment of interest out of capital (Section 208).

6. Allowing a director to hold an office of profit under the company (Section 314).

7. Getting the affairs of the company investigated by inspectors appointed by the Central Government (Section 237).

8. Determining that any portion of share capital shall not be called up except in the event of winding-up of the company (Reserve Share Capital—Section 99).

9. Voluntary winding-up of the company (Section 484).

10. Disposal of books and papers after the completion of voluntary winding-up of a company (Section 550).

Q. 22. The number of directors of a company is to be increased from 9 to 14. Give necessary resolution with requisite procedure for the same. (ICSI)

Ans. : The necessary resolution to be passed at the meeting as a special resolution is as follows :

"Resolved that subject to the approval of the Central Government, the number of existing directors, i.e. 9, be and is increased to 14 and Sarbashri Udayan Chakraborty, Jayanta Ghosh, Samar Sen, D. K. Deb and Biswanath Banerjee be and are hereby appointed as additional directors of the company."

"Further resolved that Shri T. K. Ganguly, a Director of the company, be and is hereby authorised to take necessary steps for obtaining permission of the Central Government in this behalf."

Procedure :

(i) The Articles of Association must have provision for the proposed increase.

(ii) Consent of the Company in general meeting is required (Sec. 258).

(iii) An ordinary resolution needs to be passed (Sec. 258).

(iv) Approval of the Central Government is necessary (Sec. 259).

Q. 23. Explain special business and the manner of its transaction by one example for each of the types of resolution required. Draft a resolution for appointment of another auditor in place of the retiring auditors as per notice given by one of the members. (ICSI)

Ans. : *For the first part, write paragraph 1 of Ans. to Q. No. 21, page 154.*

Special business may also be transacted at the annual general meeting with proper notice therefor. Ordinary business is transacted with ordinary resolution while special business may be transacted by ordinary or special resolution. Appointment of auditors is an item of ordinary business and, as such, requires an ordinary resolution. But the appointment or re-appointment of auditors requires a special resolution if not less than 25% of the subscribed share capital of the company is held, whether singly or in any combination, by a public financial institution/Government Company/Central Government/State Government/ nationalised bank/insurance company, etc. (Sec. 224A).

In terms of the provisions of Section 225, a special notice of not less than 14 days has to be given to move a resolution for appointment of another auditor in place of the retiring auditors. The following resolution is required to be passed by the general meeting :

"Resolved that Messrs. Ganguly, Gupta and Das Gupta, Chartered Accountants, regarding whose removal special notice has been received under Section 225 of the Companies Act,

1956, shall not be and are not re-appointed and Messrs. M. Dhar & Co., Chartered Accountants, 1 Hare Street, Calcutta 700001, be and are hereby appointed auditors of the company for the ensuing year and until the conclusion of the next annual general meeting at a fee of Rs. 15,000/- (Rupees Fifteen Thousand only) per annum plus out-of-pocket expenses".

Q. 24. (a) What type of resolution is required to transact the following business :

1. Consolidation of shares;

2. Appointment of retiring auditors of a public company in which 30% of the subscribed capital of the company is held by public financial institution;

3. Adoption of Statutory Report;

4. Appointment of the additional director as regular director;

5. Changing registered office of the company from one state to another?

(b) Draft suitable resolutions in respect of the above matters.

Ans. Hints : (a) 1. Ordinary Resolution (Section 94);

2. Special resolution (Section 224A);

3. Ordinary resolution (Section 165);

4. Ordinary resolution Ssection 189 (1)];

5. Special resolution (Section 17).

(b) Refer to ICSI Questions-Answers pages, 400-405.

Q. 25. Distinguish between a special resolution and a resolution requiring special notice. Quote a few instances of each. **(C.U. 1991; ICSI)**

Ans. : *For special resolution and instances thereof, write paragraph 2 of Q/Ans. 21, pages 155-56.*

Resolution requiring special notice : Sub-sections (1) and (2) of Section 190 state the provisions of special notice. Resolution requiring special notice may be an ordinary or a special resolution. The usual rules of passing the resolutions (i.e., simple majority for ordinary and three-fourths majority for special) are also applicable here. The notice of the intention to move such a resolution should be given to the company at least 14 days before the date of the meeting at which the resolution is to be moved. In calculating the days, the date of serving the notice and date on which the meeting is scheduled to be held are not taken into account. The company, on receipt of such a notice, shall give notice of the resolution to its members as per rules of notice. In case it is not practicable, the company must give at least 7 clear days' notice by advertisement in a newspaper having an appropriate circulation or in any other mode allowed by the Articles. The following matters require a special notice :

(a) At an annual general meeting to appoint a person as auditor in place of the retiring auditor (Section 225).

(b) A special resolution, at an annual general meeting, stating that the retiring auditor shall not be re-appointed (Section 225).

(c) a special resolution to appoint certain persons as directors of the company.

(d) a resolution to remove a director or appoint a director in place of the director removed/to be removed (Section 284).

Q. 26. What are the points one should remember while drafting resolutions?

Ans. : Resolutions are the decisions arrived at the meeting. These should, therefore, be drafted in clear, lucid and unambiguous terms to facilitate quick understanding. Ordinarily, a resolution consists of two parts, viz. preamble part and operative part. The first part explains the reasons for adopting the resolution and begins with "Whereas" and the second part spells out the decision and begins with "Resolved that". Some of the more important points which should be borne in mind in drafting the resolutions are enumerated below :

(a) All the important particulars/information must be included in the resolution.

(b) Superfluous and meaningless words and phrases must be excluded from the resolution.

(c) Resolutions, when adopted in pursuance of provisions of any Act, the relevant Section must be mentioned.

(d) Resolution should confine itself to one subject-matter only.

(e) Resolution requiring approval of the Central Government/Company Law Board must contain the information in it.

(f) Lengthy resolutions should be avoided as far as practicable. These should be divided in paragraphs according to the sequence of the subject-matter.

(g) Resolution may be made effective immediately or from a specified date and this should be mentioned in the resolution itself.

(h) The various documents approved at the meeting should be initiated by the Chairman and this fact should be noted in the resolution.

Q. 27. Distinguish between "Ordinary Business" and "Special Business" in a general meeting. What business can be conducted in an extra-ordinary general meeting? Can special business be conducted at an annual general meeting? Elaborate your answer.

Ans. : Any business transacted at the extra-ordinary general meeting will be deemed as special. Special business can be transacted at an annual general meeting. *Write Ans. to Q. No. 21.*

Q. 28. (a) State the resolutions and agreements which are required to be filed by a company with the Registrar of Companies. (b) What are the details which have to be included in the register of directors' shareholdings? Who can inspect the register and require a copy thereof and when? (ICSI)

Ans. : (a) Refer to Sections 192, 293(1) (a) (d) (c), 294 and 484 (1) of the Companies Act, 1956.

(b) In terms of Section 307 of the Companies Act, 1956, every company has to keep a register showing the number, description and amount of shares in or debentures of the company held by the directors. The register can be inspected by the members, debentureholders, officers/employees of the Central Government and the Registrar of Companies. It shall be open to inspection at the registered office of the company for not less than two hours daily on all working days. The Central Government or the Registrar of Companies may ask for a copy of this register or any part thereof at any time.

Q. 29. How is the sense of a company meeting ascertained?

(C.U. 1996; N.B.U. 1975; ICSI)

Or, What are the different methods of voting in the company meeting? (C.U. 1976)

Or, How does the Chairman ascertain the sense of the house of meeting?

(V.U. 1987; C.U. 1971)

Or, Explain the different methods of ascertaining the sense of a meeting.

(C.U. 1990, 1988, 1980; V.U.1987)

Ans. : The sense of the meeting refers to the view or attitude of the members as to a question before the meeting. It is ascertained in such a way as to clearly show the numerical strength of the supporters of and the opposers to a motion or an amendment to a motion or an amendment to an amendment. The view of the majority is considered to be the sense of the meeting. One of the important duties of the Chairman is to ascertain the sense of the meeting to the satisfaction of the members attending it. For this purpose, he has to put the question to vote. The methods usually adopted to ascertain the sense of the meeting are discussed below :

1. **By Acclamation :** Formal motions (viz., giving thanks to the Chairman, etc.) are usually adopted unanimously or nearly so by applause or cheering. The Chairman, in such a case, feels the sense of the meeting by the applause. The method is very simple but not suitable where a controversial issue is to be decided upon.

2. **By Voice Vote :** This method is more or less similar to No. (1). Here the Chairman reads out the motion and asks the members to indicate their approval (by 'yes') and disapproval (by 'no'). If the volume of voices is largely in favour of the proposition, he declares the result by saying that " 'The 'Ayes' have it' ". In the other extreme, when the volume of voices is heavily against the proposition, he declares that "The 'Nays' or 'Noes' have it".

3. **By Show of Hands :** Section 177 states that "At any general meeting, a resolution put to the vote of the meeting shall, unless a poll is demanded under Section 179, be decided on a show of hands". Here the Chairman asks the members to raise their hands who are in favour of the motion. He may personally count the number or ask the Secretary to do it. He then proceeds to count the number of members who are against the motion. Then he declares the result. The difficulties of this method of voting are :

(a) Proxies are not allowed to vote.

(b) Irrespective of number of shareholding, each member is entitled to one vote only.

4. **By Division :** Here the room for the meeting is divided into two parts marked 'Ayes' and 'Nays' or 'Noes'. The Chairman asks the members to go to 'Ayes' side if they are in favour of the proposition and to 'Nays' side if they are against it. The sense of the meeting is ascertained when counting is over by tellers.

5. **By Ballot :** Voting by ballot ensures secrecy. Every member records his vote on the ballot paper and puts it into the ballot box. This method is largely used in political elections. Section 283A empowers the Articles of those companies which do not distribute dividend or work for profit to elect directors by this method.

6. **By Poll :** Voting by poll is the most suitable method for company meetings with large attendance. The voting rights of the members are in proportion to their respective holdings. Section 179 provides that poll may be taken only when the Chairman or a number of members are not satisfied with the result of voting by show of hands or when a certain number of members demand a poll. The poll may be demanded by :

(a) the Chairman of the meeting of his own motion;

(b) five persons having voting rights and present in person or by proxy, if not more than 7 members are personally present and by 2 such members if more than 7 members are personally present (in the case of public company);

(c) one member having the right to vote and present in person or by proxy, if more than 7 members are personally present and by 2 such members if more than 7 members are personally present (applicable to private companies);

(d) any member or members present in person or by proxy and having not less than 1/10th of the paid-up capital, through shares having voting rights.

(e) any number of members present in person or by proxy and holding shares on which an aggregate sum has been paid-up, which is not less than 1/10th of the paid-up capital, through shares having voting rights.

A poll which is demanded on the question of an adjournment or on the question of election of the Chairman must be taken forthwith. In other cases, it must be taken within 48 hours.

The demand for poll may be withdrawn at any time. A proxy has equal right of a member to demand a poll.

The Chairman appoints two scrutineers to scrutinise and count the votes and to report to him. One of these two persons must be a member (but not an officer or employee) of the company. The votes cast are recorded by the scrutineers on a form prepared by the Secretary. The form contains the list of shareholders entitled to vote, number of shares held by each of them, number of votes to which they are entitled, etc. The scrutineers distribute the voting papers. The members or their proxies fill in and sign the voting papers. These are then collected by the scrutineers. After counting of the votes for and against the motion is over, they report the numbers to the Chairman. The results of the poll are then declared by the Chairman.

Q. 30. (a) What is a poll? (b) When and how can a voting by 'poll' be demanded? Explain the proper procedure for taking a poll. Who can participate in a voting by poll?
(B.U. 1966; ICSI)

Or, Write notes on Poll. (C.U. 1995, 1981)

Ans. : *For answer to (a) and (b) write paragraph (6) of Q/Ans. No. 29, page 160.*

Procedure for taking a poll : It is one of the duties of the Secretary to prepare a statement detailing the names of the shareholders entitled to vote, number of shares held by each of them and number of votes to which they are entitled. The two scrutineers appointed by the Chairman hand over these forms to those members who are entitled to vote either in person or by proxy. After the forms are filled in and signed by the members, these are collected by the scrutineers. After due scrutiny and counting, they intimate the numbers to the Chairman. The results of the poll are finally declared by the Chairman.

All the members present at the meeting, either in person or by proxy, are entitled to vote by poll.

Q. 31. Discuss and explain the difference between special notice, special business and special resolution. (ICSI)

Or, What is special business? State the statutory requirements as regards the notice of a meeting at which a Special Business is proposed to be transacted. (C.U. 1982)

Ans. : Special Notice : Where, by any provision contained in this Act or in the Articles, special notice is required of any resolution, notice of the intention to move the resolution shall be given to the company not less than fourteen days before the meeting at which it is to be moved, exclusive of the day on which the notice is served or deemed to be served and the day of the meeting. [Section 190(1).]

The company shall, immediately after the notice of the intention to move any such resolution has been received by it, give its members notice of the resolution in the same manner as it gives notice of the meeting, or if that is not practicable, shall give them notice thereof, either by advertisement in a newspaper having an appropriate circulation or in any other mode allowed by the articles, not less than seven days before the meeting. [Section 190(2)]

Special Business : According to the provision of Section 173(1) (a), in the case of an annual general meeting, all business to be transacted at the meeting shall be deemed special, with the exception of business relating to :

(i) the consideration of the accounts, balance sheet and the reports of the Board of Directors and Auditors;

(ii) the declaration of a dividend;

(iii) the appointment of directors in the place of those retiring and

(iv) the appointment of, and the fixing of the remuneration of, the auditors; and

In the case of any other meeting, all the business shall be deemed special. [Section 173(1)(b)]

According to Section 173(2), where any item of business to be transacted at the meeting is deemed to be special as aforesaid, there shall be annexed to the notice of the meeting a statement setting out all material facts concerning each such item of business, including, in particular, the nature of the concern or interest, if any, therein of every director and the manager, if any.

Special Resolution : *Write paragraph 2 of Q/Ans. 21, page 155.*

Q. 32. (a) What do you understand by the term "quorum"? (C.U. 1999, 1997, 1994, 1983)

(b) What is the quorum required for :

(i) a public company meeting;

(ii) a private company meeting;

(iii) a Board meeting?

(c) What should the Chairman of a meeting do if the quorum is not present? (d) Is quorum necessary at an adjourned meeting? (e) What is the need for making provision for quorum in Company Law? (ICSI)

Or, What should you do as the Chairman of a General Meeting of a public limited company if you find that there is no quorum at the appointed time for commencement of meeting? (V.U. 1988; C.U. 1982)

Or, Write explanatory notes on quorum. (C.U. 1982)

Ans. : (a) The term "quorum" means the minimum number of members required for proper constitution of the meeting. Section 174 of the Act states the provisions for quorum. According to the regulation 49 of Table A, the quorum need not be present throughout the currency of the meeting. A similar ruling was given in Re Hartley Baird Ltd. case. But the quorum must be present throughout during the currency of the Board Meeting (Re : Henderson vs Louttit).

(b) In terms of Section 174(1), unless the Articles of the Company provide for a larger number, five members personally present in the case of public company (other than a public company which has become such by virtue of Section 43A) and two members personally present in the case of any other company shall be the quorum for a meeting of the company. In the case of a Board Meeting, Section 287(2) provides that at least two non-interested directors or one-third of the total strength of the Board (any fraction rounded-off as one), whichever is higher, shall be the quorum.

(c) As per Section 174(3), if within half an hour from the time appointed for holding a meeting of the company, a quorum is not present, the meeting, if called upon the requisition of members, shall stand dissolved. Section 174(4) provides that in any other case, the meeting shall stand adjourned to the same day in the next week, at the same time and place, or to such other day and at such other time and place as the Board may determine.

(d) Section 174(5) states that if at the adjourned meeting also a quorum is not present within half an hour from the time appointed for holding the meeting, the members present shall be the quorum.

(e) The need for making provision for quorum is to enable the members present to act in association and exercise their powers for the interest of the majority. Where there is no provision for quorum in the Companies Act, any smaller number could have been fixed to form a quorum and decisions taken would have hampered the interests of the owners of the company, i.e., the shareholders.

Q. 33. What is meant by quorum? State the statutory provisions relating to 'Quorum' for different kinds of company meetings. (ICSI)

Ans. : *For the definition of quorum, write paragraph (a) of Q/Ans. No. 32, page 162.* Unless the Articles of Association provide otherwise, if the quorum is not present within half an hour of the appointed time of the meeting, it shall stand dissolved (in case of requisitioned meeting). But in case of other meetings, these shall be adjourned to the same time and place in the next week. In case there is no quorum in the adjourned meeting, the member(s) present shall form the quorum. In case of Board Meetings of the public limited companies (but not so under Section 43A), five members personally present shall form the quorum. In case of private companies, two members personally present shall form the quorum for the Board Meetings. The Articles may, however, prescribe a larger number. Section 287 of the Companies Act, 1956, provides that the quorum for a Board Meeting must comprise two non-interested dirçctors or one-third of the total strength of the Board, whichever is higher (any fraction should be rounded-off as one). The term disinterested quorum means that the persons forming the quorum must not be interested in the business to be discussed at the meeting. In case there is no quorum in a Board meeting within half an hour of the appointed time, it shall be adjourned to the same time and place in the next week unless the Articles do not specifically provide otherwise.

Q. 34. When can a Company Meeting be held with a one-member quorum? (C.U. 1991, 1989, 1981)

Ans. : (a) When a company has shares of several classes and all the shares of a particular class are held by a single member. (b) Under Sec. 156, if default is made in holding the annual general meeting, the Central Government may call/direct to call such a meeting. In such a meeting, one member in person or proxy will constitute a valid meeting, (c) In a bankruptcy proceeding, if only one creditor has proved a liability or debt, that person alone will form the quorum/valid meeting. (d) A committee meeting may be validly held with one member.

Q. 35. How will the following persons be counted for the purpose of quorum : (a) Chairman, (b) proxy-holder, (c) Preference shareholder, (d) joint shareholder, (e) public trustee, (f) legal representative, (g) authorised representatives of a body corporate, (h) an employee/officer of the company holding 10% of the total equity capital, (i) lady member, (j) a member of the company who is also representing a company?

Ans. : (a) Chairman—If the chairman of the meeting is also a member of the company, he will be counted as one member. (b) Proxy-holder is not counted, (c) Any one or both of them will be counted as one member. (d) A preference shareholder can attend the meeting if it affects his interest and if he attends the meeting, he will be counted as one member. (e) A public trustee is counted as one member. (f) If the name of legal representative has been entered in the Lists of Members, he will be counted as one member. (h) The employee/officer will be counted as one member irrespective of his shareholding. (i) For the purpose of the quorum, there is no difference between a lady and a gentleman. The lady will be counted as one member. (j) The member will be counted as two persons for the purposes of quorum since he is attending the meeting in two different capacities. A leading case on the subject is M'Leod and Sons Ltd. (1976) Scott Case. 16.

Q. 36. The following persons attend the annual general meeting of a public company :

(i) A member holding 1/10th of paid-up equity capital of the company;

(ii) A preference share-holder;

(iii) A proxy-holder;

(iv) The public trustee;

(v) Joint shareholders;

(vi) Representative of company-member.

How are they counted for purposes of quorum and what are their voting rights?

Ans. : (i) The member holding 1/10th of paid-up equity capital shall be counted as one member only for quorum. On voting by show of hands, he will have one vote and, on poll being taken, his voting right will be proportionate with his holding of shares.

(ii) Refer to Section 87(2) (b) and 87 (2) (c) of the Companies Act, 1956.

(iii) A proxy is counted for the purposes of quorum.

(iv) For purposes of quorum, the public trustee is counted.

(v) For the purposes of quorum, the joint shareholders will be considered as one member only.

(vi) He will be considered as one member for the purposes of the quorum. Also refer to Section 187 of the Companies Act, 1956.

Q. 37. (a) Distinguish between voting "by show of hands" and "voting by poll". (b) Discuss the rights of the 'Proxy' in regard to voting by these two methods. (c) Does a proxy enjoy all the rights of the members by whom he is so appointed? (ICSI)

Ans. : (a) *Write paragraphs (3) and (6) of Q/Ans. 29, pages 159-60.*

(b) Unless the Articles of the company provide otherwise, a "proxy" does not enjoy any right to vote under the method of voting "by show of hands". Though the proxy has the rights to demand a poll, he is not entitled to speak at the meeting. Under "voting by poll", he has the right to vote.

(c) In terms of the provisions of Section 176 of the Companies Act, 1956, and unless the Articles of Association of the company provide otherwise, a proxy shall not be allowed to vote except on a poll. He does not enjoy the right to vote "by show of hands". Obviously, he does not enjoy all the rights of the members by whom he is appointed.

Q. 38. Explain the voting rights of a shareholder in person, by proxy and by an authorised representative on a voting by show of hands and on a poll at a general meeting. (ICSI)

Ans. : In terms of Section 87(1) of the Companies Act, 1956, an equity shareholder is entitled to vote on every resolution placed before the company. This right cannot, in any way, be curtailed by the Articles of Association of the company. According to the provisions of Section 87(2), a preference shareholder is entitled to vote on resolutions which directly affect his rights attached to his preference share and resolution for winding-up of the company.

In view of the above provisions, a shareholder is entitled to vote both by show of hands and by a poll.

A proxy is not entitled to vote except on a poll unless allowed by the Articles of Association of the company. He is not allowed to speak in the meeting. It is, therefore, quite obvious that a proxy can vote either by show of hands or by poll.

A body corporate (i.e., a company) which is a member of another company is entitled to appoint a proxy and that the proxy need not be a member of the company. According to Section 187A (1) of the Act, the President of India or the Governor of State, if he is a member of a company, may appoint such person as he thinks fit to act as his representative at any meeting of the company or at any meeting of any class of members of the company. According to Section 187 (A) (2), a person appointed to act as aforesaid shall for the purpose of this Act be deemed to be a member of such a company and shall be entitled to exercise the same right and powers (including the right to vote by proxy) as the President or, as the case may be, the Governor could exercise as a member of the company.

Q. 39. What is a proxy? What are the necessary conditions for a valid proxy? Can a proxy be revoked? Give a specimen proxy form.

(C.U. 1994)

Or, Draft a general proxy form of a limited company. (ICSI)

Ans. : A proxy may be defined to be a person who is authorised by another person to attend and act or vote at a company meeting. A proxy may also imply the document by which a person is so appointed (i.e., proxy). Common law does not recognise voting by proxy but in case of company meetings, this right is specifically given by law.

In view of the fact that proxies play an important role in regard to company meeting, certain important provisions have been made by Section 176 of the Companies Act. These are enumerated below :

1. Any member of a company who is entitled to attend and vote at a meeting of the company is entitled to appoint another person, whether a member of the company or not, as his proxy to attend and vote instead of himself. A proxy so appointed is not entitled to speak at the meeting.

2. Unless the articles otherwise provide :

(a) Rule (1) above is not applicable to a company not having a share capital;

(b) A member of a private company shall not be entitled to appoint more than one proxy to attend on the same occasion; and

(c) A proxy shall not be entitled to vote except on a poll.

3. The instrument which appoints a proxy must be in writing, signed by a member or his duly authorised attorney. If the appointer is a body corporate, the proxy form must bear the seal of the company as well as the signature of an authorised officer or duly authorised attorney.

4. Every notice of a general meeting which is issued to a member must clearly indicate that he is entitled to appoint a proxy to attend and vote at the meeting and that the proxy need not be a member.

5. A member is entitled to lodge the proxy form with the company not more than 48 hours before the meeting and any longer period fixed by the Articles is void (applicable to a public company or a private company which is a subsidiary of the public company).

6. Every member entitled to vote at a meeting of the company, or on any resolution to be moved thereat, is entitled during the period beginning 24 hours before the time fixed for the meeting and ending with the conclusion of the meeting, to inspect the proxies lodged, by giving not less than 3 days' notice in writing to the company intimating his intention therefor.

The relationship between the appointer of a proxy and the proxy is that of a principal and an agent. Their relation is, therefore, governed by the law of contract of agency and the proxy acts according to the instructions of his principal. When the appointer of the proxy personally attends the meeting, revocation of proxy takes place. A proxy is also revoked as soon as the company receives the notice of revocation following death, insanity etc. of the member who appointed the proxy.

ABC & Co. Ltd.

Regd. office : 6 Clive Row, Calcutta 700001

PROXY

I/We...

of...

being a Member/Members of the above-named company hereby appoint..............................or failing him...or.............................

of...or failing him

....of...

....as my/our proxy in my/our absence to attend and vote for me/us, and on my/our behalf at the annual general meeting of the company to be held on 27th March 2000 and at any adjournment thereof.

As WITNESS my/our hand(s) this..

day of..2000.

Signed by the said..(One Rupee Revenue Stamp)

Note : The proxy must be deposited at the Registered office of the Company, 6 Clive Row, Calcutta 700001, not less than 48 hours before the time of holding the Meeting.

Q. 40. (a) What are the requisites of a valid proxy?

(b) X, a shareholder of a public limited company, gives his proxy to Y in pursuance of which Y attends the meeting after satisfying all the requirements of law. X himself attended the meeting and voted on a particular resolution, but his vote was rejected. Advise X. (ICSI)

Ans. : (a) *Write paragraph 2 of Q/Ans. No. 39 pages 165-66.*

(b) Subject to the provisions in the Articles of Association of the company, a member can revoke his proxy, by giving an intimation to the company, before it is acted upon. Besides, a member can prevent the proxy to act by attending the meeting himself and voting thereat. Here, in the problem, since X attended the meeting personally despite his appointing Y as proxy, his vote cannot be rejected by the company. The company is liable to X for the wrong action taken by it.

Q. 41. Annual general meeting of a public company was scheduled to be held on 15.12.1989. Mr. X, a shareholder, issued two proxies in favour of Mr. A and Mr. B. The Proxy in favour of B was lodged on 12.12.1988 and the one in favour of Mr. A was lodged on 15.12.1989. The company rejected the proxy in favour of Mr. B as the proxy in favour of Mr. B was dated 12.12.1989 and that in favour of Mr. A was dated 13.12.1989. (ICSI)

Ans. : In terms of Section 178 of the Companies Act, 1956, since the proxy in favour of A has become invalid, the rejection of proxy in favour of B is not sustainable. In other words, the proxy in favour of B which was deposited with the company in time stands valid.

Q. 42. Discuss in brief the law relating to proxy. A proxy was appointed by a member on an instrument duly executed. Will the vote cast by the proxy be valid in the following cases, viz. (i) when the member himself attended and cast his vote at the meeting without revoking the authority of the proxy, and (ii) when the member died in the meantime?

Ans. : *Refer to pages 165-66.*

(i) the vote cast by the proxy will not be valid in the instant case.

(ii) the vote so cast by the proxy will be valid even though the member died in the meantime.

Q. 43. In how many ways can a Proxy be revoked? (C.U. 1981)

Ans. : A proxy may be revoked in any one of the following three ways : (a) when the member (appointer of the proxy) personally attends the meeting even after appointing the proxy, (b) When the company receives the written notice of revocation of proxy (for death, insanity, transfer of share of the member etc.) before commencement of the meeting and (c) when the appointer of the proxy appoints another proxy within the time limit prescribed by the Companies Act.

Q. 44. Discuss the different ways by which the main motion can be interrupted.

(C.U. 1998, 1977)

Ans. : While the discussion on the main motion is current, it may be interrupted due to any of the following :

1. **Point of order :** A point of order refers to the question in regard to procedure at a meeting. During the currency of the debate, a member may rise on a point of order when he observes any irregularity in the meeting. In such an eventuality, the Chairman is required to give his ruling as to whether the motion is in order or not.

2. **Amendment :** *Write paragraph 1 of Q/Ans. 19, page 153.*

3. **Previous question :** When a proposition is moved and seconded, some members other than the mover or seconder may consider it unwise or inconvenient to take the decision immediately. They may move "that question be not now put" and this motion is called the 'previous question'. This motion, if seconded, takes precedence over all other motions and it is put to the meeting immediately. No amendment to the previous question is allowed.

4. **Closure or Gag :** When discussion on a motion becomes too lengthy, any member can propose "that the question be now put to vote". This motion is termed as 'Closure' or 'Gag'. This is proposed with a view to transacting business expeditiously as well as saving time. If and when the closure motion is seconded, the Chairman puts the motion or amendment to vote immediately without any further discussion. There are two types of closure — Guillotine Closure and Kangaroo Closure which have been defined later in this chapter.

5. **Next Business :** When discussion on the original motion is current and it is intended to prevent a decision on the main question, such a move is taken. Any member may rise and propose "that the meeting proceeds to the next business". The object of this move is to drop the discussion of the motion which is before the meeting. It is put to vote after being duly moved and seconded.

6. **Adjournment :** It refers to the discontinuation of a meeting with a view to resuming it on a future date. Unless the rules expressly provide, a meeting duly convened and constituted cannot be postponed. There is, however, no such provision for adjournment. During the currency of the meeting, any member may propose "that the meeting be now adjourned" provided he considers that this motion is in the interest of the meeting. The motion is put to vote when it is duly seconded. The members may decide to adjourn the meeting at a later date or indefinitely. The meeting at which adjournment is decided fixes the date, time and place for the adjourned meeting. No notice for adjourned meeting needs to be served if it is held within 30 days from the date of adjournment.

If the rules so provide, the chairman can adjourn the meeting under the following circumstances :

(a) When the meeting is so disorderly that it is impossible to transact any business.

(b) When at any stage of the meeting the number of members falls below the quorum.

(c) When all the business cannot be transacted in that meeting.

7. **Postponement :** A properly convened meeting cannot be postponed unless the rules specifically provide for it. Even if it is considered necessary to postpone a meeting for a valid ground, the meeting cannot be cancelled but should be held as per notice and adjourned to a future date without transacting any business. In the event of adjournment, the rules regarding adjournment will apply.

In this context, it may be mentioned that discussion on a motion may be postponed under the following circumstances :

(a) When due to lack of sufficient information it is not possible or wise to carry on the debate.

(b) When there arises a difference of opinion on such a point which necessitates detailed clarification.

8. **Referring Back to Committee :** This type of formal motion is used when the motion proposed by a Committee is under discussion. The Committee may be asked to consider the developments that have taken place after submission of the report.

Q. 45. (a) What do you mean by "interruptions of debate"? (b) What is the difference between (i) "substantive motion" and "dilatory motion"; (ii) "closure motion" and "previous question motion"?

Ans. : (a) In a meeting, the proposer introduces a motion and the seconder seconds it or adds his observations thereon. Thereafter, the Chairman invites the members to debate on the motion. When the debate or discussion on the main motion is interrupted or diverted, it is known as "interruptions of debate". The devices by means of which a debate may be interrupted are as under :

(i) Amendments,

(ii) Formal or dilatory motions, and

(iii) Points of order.

(b) *Pages 177 and 178.*

Q. 46. (a) Distinguish between adjournment and postponement of a meeting.

(C.U. 1999)

(b) What are the different ways by which a meeting may be adjourned? (ICSI)

Or, When can the Chairman adjourn a meeting? (C.U. 1982)

Ans. : (a) *Write paragraphs (6) and (7) of rules regarding adjournment of meeting and the Chairman's power in that respect (Pages 168-69).*

The Chairman may adjourn the meeting in the following circumstances :

(i) If there is no quorum at any stage of the meeting, the Chairman can adjourn it.

(ii) If the meeting so directs or consents to adjournment, the Chairman can adjourn the meeting (Regulation 53 of Table 'A').

(iii) If the meeting is so disorderly that the business cannot be transacted, the Chairman, at his own discretion, can adjourn the meeting.

If, however, the Chairman attempts to adjourn a duly convened and properly constituted meeting improperly, the meeting may elect another person as Chairman to transact the business.

Q. 47. (a) Explain 'adjournment', 'postponement' and 'dissolution' in relation to a company meeting. (b) What is the effect of adjournment as regards notice, business and proxies? (ICSI)

Ans. : (a) *For 'adjournment' and 'postponement', write from pages 169-70.* Section 174 of the Companies Act, 1956, provides that if the quorum is not present within half an hour after the time appointed for holding a general meeting on requisition, the meeting stands dissolved. Here the term signifies a situation where the meeting no longer exists as such. *Write paragraph (6) of Q/Ans. No. 44, pages 168-69.*

Q. 48. What is meant by 'Privileges in speeches'? When can 'Absolute Privilege' and 'Qualified Privilege' be claimed?

Or, Privilege in speech is either absolute or qualified. Explain the two.

(V.U. 1987; C.U. 1997, 1994, 1982)

Ans. : In order to enable the speakers in a meeting to express their views in a free and fearless manner, the law allows certain defences to them. Statements made by the speakers—whether orally or in writing—are termed privileged—when the persons making the statements are not liable to any legal action. During the currency of the meeting, it may be necessary for any member of the meeting to make a comment in respect of another member. The comment so made may appear to be defamatory of the person to whom it was meant for. In normal circumstances, the member so defamed could have taken legal action against the speaker. But no action would lie against the speaker as the statement was made by him on a privileged occasion. With a view to getting the 'privileges in speech', it should be ensured that the statement was made in good faith, without malice and in the interest of all members.

The "privileges in speeches" so offered by law may be divided into two categories — "absolute privilege" and "qualified privilege". Absolute privilege refers to defamatory statement made by a speaker in the interest of the organisation or the public but without inviting any liability whatsoever. It is a right—and a moral duty too—of any individual to make a free and frank statement in respect of any member on matters of public interest. Even though the statement may subsequently appear to be false, the speaker will get the protection of law.

The circumstances in which an absolute privilege is allowed are enumerated below :

(a) Statements made by a judge, advocate, juryman, witness, or party in the course of and/or in connection with any judicial proceedings in a Court of law.

(b) Statements made by the Members of Parliament or Legislative Assemblies of the States within the Houses.

(c) Statements or reports published in the Parliamentary papers with the specific authority of either of the Houses.

(d) Statements of the officers of State in the course of their official duty.

(e) Published or broadcast report on Parliamentary or court proceedings during currency thereof made fairly and accurately.

Qualified privilege is allowed to any speaker only when the qualification or condition attached is complied with. Absence of malice (i.e., improper motive) is the qualification or condition which entitles a speaker to claim qualified privilege. Statements which are defamatory but not malicious enjoy such privilege and are not actionable in a Court of law. Whether an occasion enjoys such privilege depends on the facts of the case and any decision in this matter will be taken by the judge on the basis of the facts placed before him. Broadly speaking, such privilege can be claimed if :

(a) the defamatory statement is made by the speaker in response to his moral, legal or social duty with the condition that he has interest in making such a statement and the other members of the audience have the corresponding interest of hearing;

(b) the statement is made in order to protect some common interest of the parties between whom the statement passes;

(c) the statement is contained in a report of the Parliamentary/Court proceedings; and

(d) the statement is made in any meeting of public concern.

Q. 49. What are the circumstances in which the press can be admitted to a meeting? Is there any objection to their (i.e., press) admission to a meeting? Can the press claim privilege in reporting the proceedings of meetings? What is a press communique?

Ans. : There is no rule of law for the purpose of regulating admission of the press to meetings. Admission of the press to meetings of the Parliament, Legislative Assemblies of the States, Local Authorities, etc. is, however, regulated by existing law. The press is entitled to admission to any public meeting irrespective of the fact that its members are invited or not. On the other hand, a private meeting which transacts business of executive or administrative nature may invite the press to attend it and request them to publish the report after due payment. Unless invited, the press are not allowed any access to the private meetings. The press is also not inclined to attend these meetings as the subject matter of discussion in these meetings is of very little interest to the general public.

The press is usually not invited to private meetings because these meetings discuss business of controversial and confidential nature. Presence of the press and/or the outsiders may stand in the way of the members' free and frank discussion. Besides, publication of the proceedings of the meetings is hardly of any interest to the general public. On the other hand, such publication may hamper the reputation and interest of the concern. In case, however, the organisation feels that wide publicity of the proceedings of the meeting is essential, the meeting may invite the press for the purpose. An alternative to this is to issue a press communique i.e., summary of the proceedings of the meetings, for publication.

Press and Privilege : Reports of defamatory speeches published in the press are not privileged. The press is entitled to claim privilege if its members were present at the meeting in accordance with the custom or convention and they publish a fair and accurate report of the proceedings. The press cannot claim privilege when its members are expressly invited to be present at the meeting by the person making a defamatory statement. The press reports of private meetings are entitled to qualified privilege whereas press reports of Parliamentary meetings enjoy absolute privilege.

Press Communique : This refers to the summary of proceedings of a meeting which is handed over by the meeting to the press agent for publication in various newspapers. When the meeting considers that the presence of the press is undesirable and at the same time publication of the selected portions of the proceedings is essential for the benefit of the members in particular and the public in general, a press communique is usually issued.

Q. 50. (a) What are the 'Minutes'? (b) What points should be borne in mind by the Secretary while writing the Minutes? (ICSI; B.U. 1967, 1966)

Or, Discuss the principles which guide the secretary in drafting minutes of proceedings of a meeting. (C.U. 1999, 1998, 1996, 1995, 1991, 1983)

Ans. : (a) Minutes are the written records of the proceedings of the meetings of the shareholders or the directors of a company. In other words, the business transacted and the decisions arrived at by a meeting are recorded in the minutes. As soon as these are signed by the Chairman of the meeting, they become permanent official record. Great care and caution should, therefore, be taken to ensure that the minutes portray a true, fair and full picture of the proceedings.

(b) One of the important duties of the Secretary is to write-up the Minutes. He must make important notes during the currency of the meeting and should start writing-up the Minutes as soon as the meeting is over. While writing up the Minutes, the following points should, be borne in mind by the Secretary :

1. Minutes must have a heading to contain the particulars, viz., nature of the meeting, date, time and place where it was held.

2. The Minutes must contain the names of the Chairman, Secretary and other members (if and when practicable) who attended the meeting.

3. To ensure quick reference to any item in the Minutes, each item should have a heading or marginal note properly numbered.

4. Dates as well as figures should be incorporated in the Minutes.

5. The Minutes should be written up in accordance with the agenda of the meeting.

6. Details of the appointments made and expenditure authorised by the meeting are entered in the Minutes.

7. The Minutes contain names of the absentee directors who had applied for leave of absence.

8. The Minutes should contain the names of the mover and the seconder of a motion, manner of voting and results thereof.

9. The Minutes contain a statement that the minutes of the last meeting were read, confirmed and signed by the Chairman.

10. The Secretary should show the draft Minutes and obtain the approval of the Chairman of the meeting before he starts writing in the Minute Book.

Q. 51. Define "Minutes" and distinguish Minutes from a report of a meeting. What rules would you observe when framing Minutes? (C.U. 1991, 1977, 1970)

Ans. : *Write paragraph (a) of Q/Ans. 50, page 172 and add the following portion :*

Minutes and a report : A Report may be defined as the systematic presentation of information about some business activity. A report of a meeting is the statement of facts on the proceedings of a meeting and it is not a statement of information. The points of difference between the two may be summed up as follows :

1. The Minutes contain the names of mover and seconder of a motion and the resolutions/decisions adopted/taken at the meeting. A report, on the other hand, records the decision only unless, of course, it is a verbatim report.

2. The Minutes must record the exact resolutions adopted by the meeting but a report records the decisions only.

3. The Minutes are the documentary evidence and are acceptable as such in a Court but a report is not accepted by a Court of law.

4. The Minutes are prepared separately for each and every meeting whereas a report usually contains a summary of the discussions of a number of meetings.

Q. 52. (a) What are the requirements of the Companies Act, 1956, regarding the keeping of minutes? (b) What is the object of having minutes signed and who, for the purpose in view, may sign them? (c) What are rights of inspection given by the Act? (d) Can a company rely on a resolution of which no record has been made in the minutes?

(C.A. Final; C.U. 1999)

Or, Summarise the provisions of the Companies Act relating to minutes of the proceedings of general meetings of a company and the meetings of its Board of Directors.

(C.U. 1991; C.A. Final)

Or, What are the provisions of the Companies Act, 1956, with regard to the maintenance of the minutes of meetings?

Ans. : (a) Section 193 to 196 of the Companies Act, 1956, state the rules regarding minutes.

Rules regarding keeping of Minutes may be outlined as follows :

(i) Every company must keep the records of its meetings—whether shareholders' meeting or directors' meeting—in the books kept for this purpose the pages of which should be marked consecutively.

(ii) The Minutes must not be attached to any Minute Book. These must be entered in the book within a period of 30 days from the date of the meeting.

(iii) The Minutes of each meeting must contain a fair and correct summary of the proceedings inclusive of the appointments made at the meeting.

(iv) In case of meeting of the Board of Directors or a Committee thereof, the names of the directors present at the meeting and names of the directors who dissent from the resolutions passed at the meeting must be entered in the Minutes.

(v) The Chairman exercises an absolute discretion regarding inclusion or non-inclusion of any matter in the Minutes which he may consider to be defamatory of any person, irrelevant or immaterial to the proceedings or detrimental to the interest of the company.

(b) The signature of the Chairman in the Minutes is required to provide *prima facie* evidence of the proceedings of the meeting. Where the minutes are properly prepared and signed, until the contrary is proved, the meeting will be considered to have been duly called and held and proceedings properly conducted and all appointments of directors/liquidators properly made. The minutes of general meetings must be signed with date within 30 days of the meeting by the Chairman of the meeting. In case of meetings of the Board of Directors or Committees thereof, the minutes must be signed within 30 days either by the Chairman of that meeting or the successive meeting.

(c) The Minute Books containing proceedings of general meeting must be kept open for inspection of any member at the registered office of the company. Any member requiring a copy of the minutes is entitled to get it, on payment of the requisite fees, within 7 days of his request. The members of the company are, however, not allowed to inspect or get copies of the minutes of the meetings of Board of Directors or its Committees.

(d) The record of the proceedings of a meeting is the *prima facie* evidence only and it may, therefore, be refuted or repelled. If the minutes do not contain any mention of the resolution which has been passed at the meeting, the resolution will be deemed to be valid and operative only when it can be satisfactorily proved that the same was actually passed.

Q. 53. (a) What are the rules regarding signing of the minutes? (b) What is meant by "Confirmation of Minutes?" (C.U. 1990)

Ans. : (a) *Q/Ans. 52(b), page 173.*

(b) The signing of the minutes by the Chairman of the meeting is said to be "Confirmation of Minutes". Normally, the Chairman asks the Secretary to read the minutes of the last meeting. More often than not, the minutes are taken as read. Obviously this saves a lot of valuable time of the meeting. After these are read by the Secretary, the Chairman asks the members as to whether he may take the minutes to be a correct record of the proceedings. If no objection is raised, the Chairman writes the words "Read, Approved and Signed" and subscribes his signature and date thereunder. In case of any objection, the Chairman may make the necessary minor alterations only under his initials and then puts his signature towards confirmation of the minutes. After confirmation, these must not be altered on any account. Major or material alterations, if genuinely necessary, can be made by way of duly passed resolutions.

Q. 54. (a) Explain the terms "Minutes of Narration" and "Minutes of Decision/Resolution". (b) What are the provisions of the Companies Act as to inspection of Minute Books?

Ans. : (a) *Page 176.*

(b) Section 196 of the Companies Act deals with inspection of Minute Books of general meeting. The books containing the minutes of the general meetings must be kept at the registered office of the company and be open, during business hours, to the inspection of any member without any charge. Reasonable restrictions on inspection of Minute Books may be imposed by the Articles or the general meeting but these must remain open for inspection for not less than two hours daily on working days during the business hours.

The members have the right to ask for a copy of the minutes on payment of such sum as may be prescribed [Section 196(2)]. If inspection of minutes is refused or copy of the minutes is not furnished to any member, the Company as well as the defaulting officer(s) thereof shall be punishable with fine which may extend to Rs. 500/-.

In the case of any such refusal or default, the Company Law Board may, by order, compel an immediate inspection of the Minute Books or direct that the copy required shall forthwith be sent to the person requiring it [Section 196(4)].

Q. 55. As a Company Secretary, what points should be remembered in the preparation of minutes? Outline the general rules relating to :

(a) Inspection of Minute Books and

(b) Alteration of Minutes. (ICSI).

Ans. : *(a) Write Ans. to Q. No. 54 (b), as above.*

(b) In case of necessity, the minutes may be altered before they are signed by the Chairman even though they have already been written in the Minute Book. The alterations must be initialled by the chairman at the time of his signing the minutes. If, on the other hand, the minutes are signed, they should not be altered on any score. If, however, a resolution which has already been adopted requires variation, the variation must be carried out by way of a resolution passed at a subsequent meeting.

Q. 56. What are the provisions in the Companies Act, 1956, in relation to maintenance of minutes for both Board and General meetings? What is the legal provision relating to keeping of loose-leaf Minute books? (ICSI)

Ans. : *Pages 173-74.*

For the second part, some hints are given :

The minutes of the meeting—whether a General Meeting or a Board Meeting—must be recorded within 30 days from conclusion thereof in a bound book or in a loose-leaf book [Section 193(1) (2)]. The minutes must not be attached by way of pasting or otherwise [Section 193(1B)]. The only possible way, therefore, is to write the minutes by hand.

Q. 57. Write Short Notes on : (1) Dividend, (2) Interest, (3) Clear Days (B.U. 1963), (4) Minutes of Narration (ICSI), (5) Minutes of Decision (ICSI), (6) Meeting on Holidays (ICSI), (7) Substantive Motion, (8) Dilatory motion, (9) Standing Orders, (10) Carried Nemine Contradicente, (11) Reference back, (12) 'Two-way' Proxy Form, (13) Explanatory Statement, (14) Waiver of Notice, (15) Point of Order, (16) Chairman's Speech or Statement, (17) Guillotine Closure, and (18) Kangaroo Closure, (19) Resolution By Circulation.

Ans. : 1. The term **dividend** has its Latin origin (*dividendum*) meaning 'that which is to be divided or shared'. In relation to companies, the term implies that portion of the profit which is distributed amongst the members of the company in proportion to their shareholdings. Dividend can usually be paid only out of current or accumulated profits of the company. Payment of dividend is recommemded by the directors at the Board Meeting and declared by the shareholders at the annual general meeting.

2. **Interest** can be said to be the rent of capital. In other words, it is the amount paid by the borrower to the lender for the use of money. The consideration that the borrower gets is the use of money and that the lender gets is the amount of interest.

3. **Clear Days :** The term 'clear days' implies the number of days between the date of serving notice to the members and the scheduled date of meeting (**exclusive of both these days**). The members entitled to attend the meeting must get proper and adequate number of 'clear days' notice in terms of the provisions of the Companies Act.

4. **Minutes of Narration :** Minutes of a meeting may be recorded in two methods. According to one method, details of the discussions, voting, etc. on the resolution are recorded. This is known to be the 'Minutes of Narration'. In this method, details of the discussions on such matters on which no formal resolutions are passed are also recorded.

5. **Minutes of Decision :** Recording of minutes may be made under two methods. In one method, details of the discussions at the meeting are recorded and this is known as Minutes of Narration. In the other method, the resolutions which are finally passed by the meetings are recorded in the minutes. Minutes recorded in this method are known as 'Minutes of Resolution' or 'Minutes of Decision'.

6. **Meeting on Holidays :** An annual general meeting must not be held on a public holiday but this meeting, when adjourned to a public holiday, may be validly held. If a meeting is called on such a day which is subsequently declared as a public holiday, the meeting can be validly held.

An extraordinary general meeting may be held on a public holiday or adjourned to a public holiday.

A meeting of a Board of Directors of a company can be held on, or adjourned to, a public holiday and can be held at any time or place.

A statutory meeting may be held on, or adjourned to, a public holiday.

7. **Substantive Motion (C.U. 1991) :** When a motion is proposed and duly seconded, any one present in the meeting may move an amendment to the original motion. If the amendment is duly carried, the Chairman puts the amended motion to vote at the meeting. The amended motion is known as 'Substantive Motion'.

8. **Dilatory Motion (C.U. 1991) :** Such a motion, as the name suggests, delays the discussions in a meeting. The object of this motion is to adjourn or delay the debate. The mover of such a motion is allowed to speak on it. Examples of dilatory motion are previous question, adjournment, etc. The forms of such motion are 'that this meeting does proceed to the next business here', 'that the meeting be now adjourned', etc.

9. **Standing Orders :** To enable a meeting to be properly conducted, there must be a set of rules to govern it. Statutory bodies have their prescribed rules for conduct of the meetings. But the meetings of the non-statutory bodies are conducted by the rules framed by them or by custom or convention. Such rules governing the meetings of the Parliament are known to be Standing Orders.

10. **Carried Nemine Contradicente :** When a larger number of members present at the meeting vote in favour of the resolution and none votes there against, the resolution is said to be carried nemine contradicente or nem. con. (i.e., none contradicting).

11. **Reference back :** The reports are usually prepared by the Secretary and sometimes by other officers of the company. The reports are submitted at the meeting. If the meeting considers the report to be incomplete or not acceptable, it may refer back the report to a particular committee, sub-committee or an official of the company. On such an eventuality, the concerned authority reconsiders the report and revises it before the same is re-submitted at the subsequent meeting.

12. **Two-way Proxy Form :** A proxy may be defined to be a person authorised by another person (who is a member of the company) to attend and act or vote at a company meeting. A proxy, in common parlance, often refers to the document by which the person (i.e., proxy) is so appointed. Common law does not recognise voting by proxy but, in case of company meetings, this right is specifically given by law. A proxy may vote in a poll either in favour of or against the motion. When the proxy forms are so designed that the proxy-holders are in a position to vote either in favour of or against a motion, these forms are called two-way proxy forms.

13. **Explanatory Statement :** Section 173(2) of the Companies Act, 1956, provides that where an item of business to be transacted at the meeting is deemed special, there must be annexed to the notice of the meeting a statement mentioning all material facts concerning

the item of business, including, in particular, the nature of the concern or interest, if any, therein, of every director and the manager, if any. It has further been provided that if any item of business requires approval to a document by the members accordingly, the notice must specify the date, time and place where the document will be available for inspection.

14. **Waiver of Notice :** *Page 147-148*

15. **Point of order :** *Page 168.*

16. **Chairman's Speech or Statement :** The Chairman of an annual general meeting of a public limited company has to give a speech regarding the working and progress of the company during the year under review, its future developments and prospects in the light of the economic conditions obtaining in the country. In absence of the Chairman, a statement is submitted at the meeting which contains all the information. This is known as the Chairman's statement. Sometimes the Chairman makes a special statement on any aspect of the company's working. This, too, is known as the Chairman's statement. The Chairman's speech or statement is not obligatory (or mandatory) under law but this is a matter of custom or convention.

17. **Guillotine Closure :** When discussion on a motion is time-bound, i.e., to be completed within the fixed time, guillotine closure is applied. As soon as the stipulated time expires, the motion is put to vote.

18. **Kangaroo Closure :** When there are a number of amendments to the main motion, the Chairman of the meeting selects a few of the amendments and thereby jumps over a few other amendments. This system is known as 'Kangaroo Closure'. When one amendment covers a number of other amendments and where a large number of amendments are proposed, the application of 'Kangaroo Closure' is felt necessary.

19. **Resolution by Circulation :** Section 289 of the Companies Act, 1956, states the provisions regarding passing of resolution by the Board of Directors or a Committee thereof, by circulation. For passing such a resolution, it has to be circulated in draft together with necessary supporting papers to all the directors then in India and the same has to be approved by majority of the directors (the number should be not less than the quorum required for the Board or Committee Meeting, as the case may be). The resolution so passed has to be placed before the Board/Committee at its next meeting for confirmation. It may be mentioned here that this section enables a company to propose any resolution other than those which are required to be passed at the Board Meetings only and have it passed by circulation.

Q. 58. On what occasion and for what purpose the Chairman's Speech is delivered? Is it obligatory under law? Draft a brief speech of a Chairman with suitable headings for publication in newspapers.

Ans. : While welcoming the members at the annual general meeting, the Chairman of the meeting usually makes a speech or reads out a statement. This is known as the Chairman's speech. The main purpose of this speech is to inform the members of the company in particular and the public in general as to working of the company in the past year and its future plan. *Write on the lines of Q/Ans. No. 14, pages 242-43.*

9

COMPANY MEETINGS (B) BOARD MEETINGS

[**Contents** : Board Meeting & its Requisites—Secretary's Duties regarding Board Meetings—Director & Board of Directors—Rights, Duties & Powers of the Board—Appointment & Election of Chairman—Agenda—Minimum number of Board Meetings in a year—Resolutions by Circulation—Minutes of Board Meetings.]

Q. 1. (a) What is a Board Meeting? (b) Discuss, in brief, the requisites of a valid Board Meeting.

Ans. (a) *Refer to page 144.*

(b) The requisites of a valid Board Meeting are as follows :

(i) **Notice :** Section 286(1) provides that proper notice of Board Meeting must be given to all the directors who are present in India at their usual address.

(ii) **Agenda :** The Companies Act does not specifically provide as to whether the agenda should be sent along with the notice or incorporated in the notice itself. However, as a matter of convention, the agenda accompanies the notice to enable the directors to come prepared to the meeting.

(iii) **Quorum :** Under Section 287 of the Companies Act, if the Articles do not fix the quorum, at least two dis-interested directors or one-third of the total strength of the Board (any fraction rounded-off to one), whichever is higher, shall be the quorum.

(iv) **Chairman :** Regulation 76(1) of Table A provides that the Board may elect a Chairman of its meetings and determine the period for which he is to hold office. Regulation 76(2) provides that if no such Chairman is elected, or if at any meeting the Chairman is not present within five minutes after the time appointed for holding the meeting, the directors present may choose one of them to be the Chairman of the meeting.

(v) **Procedure at Meeting :** Before meeting is started, the Chairman is to ensure that the meeting is duly convened and properly constituted.

(vi) **Voting Right :** Each of the directors of the Board enjoys a vote. If the Articles so provide, the Chairman may have an additional vote which is termed casting vote.

(vii) **Powers and Duties :** Subject to the provision of the Companies Act, the Articles of the company mention the powers and duties of the Board of Directors.

(viii) **Resolution :** Any resolution passed by the directors is the decision of the Board. A Board Resolution is passed by simple majority.

Q. 2. Enumerate the duties of the Company Secretary in connection with the meeting of Board of Directors. (ICSI)

Ans. : The duties of the Secretary relating to the Board meetings may be discussed under three heads, viz., (a) before the meeting, (b) at the meeting and (c) after the meeting.

(a) Before the meeting

(i) The Secretary fixes up the date and time of the meeting on the requisition of any director and/or in consultation with the Chairman.

(ii) He prepares the notice and the agenda in consultation with the Chairman and issues the same to the directors in compliance with the provision of the Articles.

(iii) He is required to summon the Solicitors, Auditors and officials of the company to be present at the meeting only when their presence is necessary for any specific purpose.

(iv) He has to keep ready various documents, contracts, cases of pending transfers together with the relative share certificates for sealing and signing by the directors.

(v) He has to keep ready various statements detailing the financial position and trading results of the company.

(vi) He has to prepare the Attendance Book of the directors.

(vii) He has to keep ready copies of various Acts, Memoranda and Articles of Association, and annual accounts which may be required at the meeting.

(viii) He has to make necessary seating arrangements and provide stationery.

(b) At the Meeting

(i) He has to get the signatures of the directors as well as the persons in attendance in the Directors' Attendance Book.

(ii) He has to ascertain or help the Chairman to ascertain the presence of quorum.

(iii) He reads the notice convening the meeting if and when instructed by the Chairman.

(iv) He has to read the minutes of the last meeting if so directed by the Chairman. Thereafter, when the minutes are approved by the Board, he has to obtain the signature of the Chairman.

(v) He has to report to the meeting the request for leave of absence, if any.

(vi) He has to report to the Board the disclosure of concern or interest of the director(s) in relation to any contract or arrangement under discussion so that the interested directors do not vote or participate in the discussion.

(vii) He has to render able assistance to the Chairman, as and when required, for smooth conduct of the meeting.

(viii) He has to take note of the proceedings of the meeting.

(ix) He has to arrange for payment of sitting fees and travelling expenses to the directors.

(c) After the Meeting

(i) He has to carry out the instructions of the Board contained in the resolutions.

(ii) He has to write the draft Minutes of the last meeting and place the same before the Chairman.

(iii) He has to communicate the decisions of the meeting to the various functionaries.

(iv) He has to arrange for filing the resolutions with the Registrar as required under Sec. 192.

Q. 3. Define the terms 'Director' and 'Board of Directors'. What are the rights, duties and powers of the directors of a public limited company? Are there any restrictions on their powers?

Ans. : Section 2(13) of the Companies Act, 1956, defines a director to include any person occupying the position of director, by whatever name called. The directors are collectively called or known as the Board of Directors of the company. The Board is the executive authority of the company. The rights, duties and powers of the Board of Directors are as under :

Rights

(i) To attend the Board Meetings and participate in the direction of the company's affairs;

(ii) to receive the remuneration and fees;

(iii) to receive compensation from the company for premature termination.

Duties : The duties to be performed by the directors are embodied in the Articles of Association of the company which are prepared bearing in mind the provisions of the Companies Act. The duties so imposed on them must be performed with reasonable skill and diligence. The Managing Director or Executive Director is a whole-time employee of the company and, as such, he is required to give continuous attention to the affairs of the company. His duties can be outlined as under :

(i) to determine the objectives of the business of the company and frame policies for achievement of the objectives;

(ii) to finalise various actions to be taken for implementation of the policies and delegate powers;

(iii) to initiate actions for periodical reviews of the performance of the company;

(iv) to appoint employees of various cadres so that the day-to-day operations of the company are carried on undisturbed;

(v) to disclose the details of shareholdings and nature of interest in any contract or arrangement to be entered into by the company.

Powers of Directors : The directors derive their powers from the Articles of Association of the company as well as from the Companies Act. It has to be borne in mind that a director individually does not have any authority over the management and control of the company unless such powers are delegated to him by the Board of Directors of the company. Barring the delegated powers, all other powers of the directors are exercised by the Board collectively by means of resolutions. In terms of Section 292, the Board exercises the following powers by means of resolutions passed at meetings of the Board :

(i) to make calls on shareholders in respect of money unpaid on their shares;

(ii) to issue debentures;

(iii) to borrow moneys otherwise than on debentures;

(iv) to invest funds of the company; and

(v) to make loans.

Restrictions on the powers of the Board : Section 293 of the Companies Act imposes certain restrictions on the powers of the Board. The Board shall not, except with the consent of the company in general meeting :

(a) sell, lease or otherwise dispose of the whole, or substantially the whole of the undertaking of the company or any of its undertakings where it owns more than one such undertaking;

(b) remit or give time for the repayment of any debt due by a director (except renewal of advance made by a banking company);

(c) invest otherwise than in trust securities the sale proceeds of acquisition of any undertaking as mentioned in (a) above or properties used for any undertaking;

(d) borrow moneys where the moneys to be borrowed together with moneys already borrowed will exceed the aggregate of the paid-up capital and free reserves of the company;

(e) contribute to charitable funds or other funds not directly relating to the business of the company or welfare of its employees any amount the aggregate of which will, in any financial year, exceed Rs. 50,000 or 5% of its average net profits during the last three financial years, whichever is more.

Q. 4. (a) What is the maximum number of directors who can be appointed in a public company on non-rotational basis, i.e., not subject to retirement in an annual general meeting? How is the appointment of such directors regulated in a private company? (b) What are the restrictions on the powers of the Board of Directors of a company? Can members in general meeting change a decision taken by the Board? What powers can be exercised by the Board only at its meetings? (ICSI)

Ans. : (a) In terms of Section 255(1) of the Companies Act, unless the Articles of Association of the company provide otherwise, two-thirds of the total directors of a public limited company and a private company which is a subsidiary thereof shall retire by rotation. However, this rule is not applicable to a private company. The Articles of private company may provide for any mode of appointment of directors.

(b) Refer to Section 291(1) of the Companies Act (for restrictions on powers of Board of Directors). The members cannot change the Board's decision provided it is within the powers of the Board of Directors of the Company. Refer to Sections 292, 262, 297, 293A, 299, 308, 316, 386, 372 and 488(1) of the Companies Act (for powers to be exercised only at Board Meetings).

Q. 5. (a) Who can be the Chairman of a Board Meeting? (b) Does the Companies Act prescribe any specific qualifications for the Chairman? (c) Distinguish between appointment and election of Chairman.

Ans. : (a) Every meeting—whether general or Board—must be presided over by a Chairman. Regulations 76 and 78 of Table A provide for election of Chairman. The Chairman shall be a shareholder or a duly authorised representative of the shareholders of the company. Ordinarily, the seniormost director is elected as the Chairman and another director as Vice-Chairman of the Board Meetings. Usually, elections take place in the first Board Meeting.

(b) The Companies Act does not prescribe any academic qualifications for the Chairman. It is, however, expected that he is conversant with law and procedures of meeting, a man of high personality, cool and patient, absolutely impartial and of judicial mind.

(c) The Articles of Association of the company usually provide for the appointment of Chairman and the name of the first Chairman is contained in the Articles. The Chairman so appointed usually presides over both the Board Meetings and the general meetings. If the Articles do not specifically provide for appointment of Chairman in terms of Regulations 76 and 78, the Chairman may be elected from amongst the directors.

Q. 6. Draft a specimen Agenda for the First Board Meeting. (ICSI; C.U. 1967)

Or, Draft a notice of the First Board Meeting of a Public Company containing a complete agenda. (C.U. 1988, 1980, 1964)

Or, Draft the notice along with agenda of the first meeting of the Board of Directors of a public company. (C.U. 1998, 1991, 1984)

Ans. :

Kettlewell Bullen and Co. Ltd.
30 Chittaranjan Avenue
Calcutta 700013

Dated the 3rd July 2000

Notice

This is to inform you that the first meeting of the Board of Directors of the Company will be held at the Registered Office of the Company on Saturday the 25th July 2000 at 10 a.m. Your presence at the meeting is solicited.

R. Halder
Director

Agenda :

1. Election of the Chairman of the Meeting.
2. Production of Certificate of Incorporation and Certificate for Commencement of Business.
3. Appointment of the Managing Director(s).
4. Appointment of the Directors.
5. Appointment of the Secretary.
6. Election of the Chairman of the company.
7. Appointment of Auditors.
8. Appointment of bankers.
9. Adoption of the common seal of the company.
10. Appointment of underwriters and brokers to the issue of shares.
11. Any other business with the approval of the Chairman.
12. Fixation of the date of the next meeting.

Q. 7. Directors normally act through Board Meetings at which their decisions are recorded as Resolutions. Discuss the above statement pointing out exceptions, if any.

(ICSI)

Ans. : The Articles contain a list of powers which may be exercised by the directors of the company. It may be mentioned that a director does not have any authority over the affairs of the company except as regards matters which have been specifically delegated to him by the Board. Ordinarily, the authority and powers of the directors are collectively exercised by the Board by means of resolutions. It has, therefore, been aptly said that the "directors normally act through Board Meetings at which their decisions are recorded as resolutions."

The exceptions to the above rule refer to the restrictions on the powers of the Board of Directors. Section 293 of the Act imposes a number of restrictions which are summed up as under.

The Board of Directors of a public company or a private company which is subsidiary of a public company shall not, except with the consent of the company in general meeting :

(a) sell, lease or otherwise dispose of the whole or substantially the whole of the undertaking of the company or any of the undertakings owned by the company;

(b) remit or give time for the repayment of any debt due by a director;

(c) invest otherwise than in trust securities the sale proceeds of any acquisition of the company;

(d) borrow moneys, where the moneys to be borrowed together with the moneys already borrowed by the company (exclusive of any temporary loans obtained by it from its bankers in the ordinary course of business) will exceed the aggregate of the paid-up capital and free reserves; or

(e) contribute to charitable and other funds not directly relating to the business of the company of the welfare of its employees, any amount the aggregate of which will, in any financial year, exceed Rs. 25,000/- or 5% of its average net profits during the immediately three preceding financial years, whichever is greater.

According to Section 293A, the Board of Directors is not allowed to contribute to any political party or political purpose.

According to Section 293B of the Act, the Board may contribute to National Defence Fund or any other fund approved by the Government of India, for purpose of national defence and this should be disclosed in the profit and loss account of the company.

Q. 8. ABC Ltd. held five Board Meetings in 1986 on 23rd January, 2nd June, 13th July, 31st July and 30th December. Has the company violated the provisions of Section 285 of the Companies Act? What will be the position of the company if the last meeting which was scheduled to be held on the 30th December 1986 had to be adjourned for want of quorum? The adjourned meeting was, however, held on the 6th January 1987. Advise as the Secretary of the company to the Chief Executive.

Ans. : Section 285 of the Companies Act requires that a meeting of the Board of Directors of every company must be held at least once in three months and at least four such meetings shall be held in every year. The term "every three months" has been clarified by the Department of Company Affairs as 'three months taken together'.

In the first problem, during the first three months (January to March) meeting was held on 23rd January, second three months (April to June) on 2nd June, third three months (July to September) on 13th July and 31st July and last three months (October to December) on 30th December. So the requirements of Section 285 have been complied with.

In the second part of the problem, the meeting which was scheduled to be held in the last three months, i.e., October to December could not be held for want of quorum. According to Section 288(2) of the Companies Act, 1956, the provision of Section 285 shall not be deemed to have been contravened merely by reason of the fact that a meeting of the Board which had been duly called but could not be held for want of quorum. So, in the instant case also, the company has not violated any provision of Section 285.

Q. 9. "The transactions at a Board meeting, the notice of which was not sent to one of the directors". What will be the effect of the meeting?

Ans. : In terms of Section 296, notice of every Board meeting shall be given in writing to all the directors of the company for the time being in India. Any default makes the meeting invalid and resolution(s) passed at such a meeting is (are) inoperative. (Re : Parmeshwari Prasad Gupta versus Union of India).

Q. 10. What is the law relating to resolutions passed by circulation? What are the matters which should be considered only at Board meetings? (ICSI)

Ans. : According to Section 289 of the Companies Act, 1956, no resolution shall be deemed to have been duly passed by the Board or by a Committee thereof by circulation, unless the resolution has been circulated in draft, together with the necessary papers, if any, to all the directors, or to all the members of the committee, then in India (not being less in number than the quorum fixed for a meeting of the Board or Committee, as the case may be) and to all other directors or members at their usual addresses in India and has been approved by such of the directors as are then in India, or by a majority of such of them, as are entitled to vote on the resolution.

The Secretary is to arrange for recording the resolution so passed by circulation in the immediately next Board meeting.

The matters which should be considered only at a Board meeting by means of resolutions passed are enumerated below :

(a) to make calls on shareholders—Section 292(1)(a);

(b) to issue debentures—Section 292(1)(b);

(c) to borrow moneys otherwise than on debentures—Section 292(1)(c);

(d) to invest the funds of the company—Section 29(1)(d); and

(e) to make loans—Section 292(1)(e).

Some of these powers may be delegated to a committee of directors or to the managing director or the manager or any other principal officer of the company. [(Section 292(c), (d) and (e)].

It may be mentioned in this context that the resolution by circulation cannot, however, be passed by the Board in respect of the matters discussed above.

Q. 11. X Limited having rupees ten lakhs as paid-up capital and subscribed capital has a surplus fund amounting to rupees three and half lakhs. The Directors are of the opinion that the surplus fund will not be required for the company's business purposes for the next three years and, therefore, it should be invested in the shares of Y Ltd. Draft the necessary resolution for the Board Meeting to enable the company to do the same. Also give an outline of the procedure required to be followed for the purpose (ICSI).

Ans. : The resolution to be passed by the Board of Directors at its meeting is as follows :

"Resolved that out of the surplus funds of the Company a sum of Rs. 3,50,000/- which

may not be profitably utilised by the company for its business purposes in the next three years — be and is invested in the shares of Y Ltd. and that Shri Ratan Ray, Director of the Company, be and is hereby authorised to negotiate the deal and to execute Transfer Deed and other documents if necessary for the said purpose."

Legal Provisions : The following provisions of the Companies Act, 1956, may be borne in mind :

(a) The Memorandum and Articles of Association of the Company shall authorise the Directors to do so [Section 292(1)].

(b) The Board of Directors shall exercise the power to invest the funds of the company by means of a resolution [Section 292(1) (d)].

(c) The Power to invest in any shares and debentures of any other body corporate requires the unanimous consent of all the directors present at the Board Meeting and entitled to vote [Section 372(5)].

(d) The Board of Directors can thus invest up to 10% of the subscribed capital of the investee company provided that :

  (i) The aggregate of the investments so made by the Board in all other bodies corporate shall not exceed 30% of the subscribed capital of the investing company [Section 372(2)].

  (ii) The aggregate of the investments made in all other bodies corporate in the same group shall not exceed 20% of the subscribed capital of the investing company [Section 372(2)].

(e) Investment in excess of the aforesaid limit is permissible provided it is sanctioned by a resolution of the investing company in general meeting and it is approved by the Central Government [Section 372(4)].

Procedure : The following steps are required to be taken in this connection :

1. A certificate is to be obtained by the company from a Chartered Accountant or Consultant to the effect that the surplus funds may not be required for the company's business for the next three years or may not be profitably utilised by the company and the same may be invested in the shares of Y Ltd.

2. A resolution to the effect has to be passed by the Board of Directors at their meeting.

3. A resolution has to be passed in the general meeting.

4. Approval of the Central Government has to be obtained.

5. The Board of Directors will authorise one of the Directors to effect the transaction.

6. The Director so authorised is required to report the details of the transaction to the Board of Directors.

Q. 12. (a) The meetings of Board of Directors of ABC Ltd. were held on the following dates :

10th January 1986; 24th May 1986; 29th June 1986 and 14th December 1986. Explain whether the provisions of Section 285 of the Companies Act, 1956, are complied with.

(b) Does the Companies Act prohibit holding of directors' meetings elsewhere than at the registered office of a company?

(c) Can a Board Meeting be held on a public holiday?

(d) A director of a company being told that a meeting would be held next week said, 'I cannot be there'. No notice of meeting was sent to him. Is the meeting valid?

Ans. : (a) No. Refer to Section 285 of the Companies Act.

(b) No.

(c) Yes.

(d) No. Refer to Sec. 286 of the Companies Act.

Q. 13. Draft the proceedings of the first Board Meeting of a Public Limited Company.
(ICSI; C.U. 1994, 1990, 1968 and 1966; B.U. 1966)

Ans. :

Andrew Yule and Co. Limited

Minutes of the first Meeting of the Board of Directors of the Company held at its Registered Office, 8 Clive Row, Calcutta 700001, on Monday, 2nd September 2000, at 11 a.m.

Present :

Shri	C. Borde	Director
Shri	P. Umrigar	Director
Shri	P. Roy	Director
Shri	V. Manjarekar	Director
Shri	B. Bedi	Director
Shri	A. Baig	Director

In Attendance :

Shri C. Chandrasekhar, Secretary.

Shri S. Gutta, Solicitor.

1. **Chairman**

Shri C. Borde was elected Chairman of the Meeting.

2. **Incorporation of the Company and Appointment of directors**

Shri S. Gutta, Solicitor, produced before the meeting the Certificate of Incorporation dated the August 23rd, 2000 and reported that the directors present were named in the Articles of Association and they had signed the usual acceptance of office as well as applied for the necessary qualification shares.

3. **Appointment of Chairman**

"Resolved that Shri P. Umrigar be and is appointed the Chairman of the Board of Directors."

4. **Appointment of Secretary**

"Resolved that Shri C. Chandrasekhar be and is hereby appointed the Secretary of the Company on a monthly salary of Rs. 25,000/- (Rupees Twenty-five thousand only) plus the usual perquisites as applicable to the senior officers of the Company and the appointment to be terminable by three months' notice on either side and the solicitor be and is hereby instructed to prepare an agreement embodying the terms."

5. **Appointment of Auditors :** Resolved "That Messrs. Ray & Ray, Chartered Accountants, be and is hereby appointed auditors of the company on a remuneration of Rs. 57,500/- for the year *plus* out of pocket expenses."

6. **Appointment of Bankers :** Resolved "That the State Bank of India, Calcutta Main Branch, be and is hereby appointed the bankers of the company and any two directors of the company are authorised to operate the account jointly."

7. **Seal :** Resolved "That the seal of which an impression is affixed to these Minutes be and is hereby adopted as the official seal of the company and that the same be kept in a box under lock and key and that one key of the box be kept with the Chairman and other retained by the Secretary."

8. **Next Meeting :** The Secretary was directed to call the next Board Meeting on Friday, the 20th December 2000, at 3 p.m. at the Registered Office of the Company.

9. **Vote of Thanks :** The meeting terminated with a vote of thanks to the Chair.

Calcutta C. Borde
Dated the 22nd September 2000 Chairman

Q. 14. Draft the Minutes of a Board Meeting incorporating, inter alia, the following agenda items :

(i) to appoint Mr. X as Secretary;

(ii) to approve an agreement to take office premises on rent;

(iii) to allot 100 forfeited shares. (ICSI)

Or, Draft the minutes of proceedings of the meeting, not being the first meeting of the Board of Directors of Blue Bird Co. Ltd., taking five imaginary items of business which are transacted at the meeting. (C.U. 1987, 1981)

Ans. : Minutes of the Board Meeting of the Blue Bird Co. Ltd. held at the Registered Office of the Company on Thursday the 29th January 2000, at 2 p.m.

Present :

1. Shri	A. Acharya	—	Chairman
2. Shri	B. Bhusan	—	Director
3. Shri	C. Chaturvedi	—	Director
4. Shri	D. Debnath	—	Director
5. Shri	E. Eaphen	—	Director
6. Shri	F. Fernandez	—	Managing Director.

In Attendance :

Smt. B. Debnath, Chief Law Officer.

1. **Minutes of the Last Meeting :** The minutes of the last meeting held on 30th December 1999 were read, approved and signed by the Chairman.

2. **Appointment of Mr. X as Secretary :** It was resolved that Mr. X of Calcutta be and is hereby appointed Secretary of the Company at a consolidated salary of Rs. 18,000/- (Rupees Eighteen Thousand only) per month, the appointment to be subject to three months' notice on either side and that a formal agreement be drawn up accordingly.

3. **Rented Office Premises :** It was resolved that the office premises offered by Messrs. Talbot & Co. at Rs. 66.25 per square meter be taken on lease for 12 years and the draft agreement between the lessor and the company placed before the Board was approved and signed by Shri A. Acharya, Chairman, under the Common Seal of the Company.

4. **Allotment of 100 Forfeited Shares :** It was resolved that 100 equity shares of Rs. 100/- each originally registered in the name of Shri Mukul Das, Calcutta, and forfeited for non-payment of final call of Rs. 20/- each be and are hereby re-issued to Shri Bimalendu Bhattacharya, Calcutta, at Rs. 75/- per share.

5. **Filling Up Casual Vacancy :** It was resolved that Shri Amitava Mukherjee of Calcutta be and is hereby appointed a director of the company in place of Shri K. N. Dhar (since resigned) for the period for which Shri Dhar was elected, until the next Annual General Meeting.

6. **Next Meeting :** It was decided to hold the next meeting of the Board of Directors on Thursday, the 31st March 2000 at 11 a.m. at the Registered Office of the company.

7. **Vote of Thanks :** The meeting terminated with a vote of thanks to the Chair.

1 Lovers' Paradise
Calcutta 700001
The 8th February 2000

A. Acharya
Chairman

9

COMPANY MEETINGS (C)
STATUTORY MEETING

[**Contents** : Statutory Meeting—its objects, Company Secretary's Duties—Statutory Report & its contents—Notice & Agenda—Rights of Members in regard to Statutory Meeting.]

Q. 1. (a) What is a statutory meeting and what are its objects?

(b) Discuss the provisions of the Companies Act in regard to this meeting.

(c) What are the duties of the Company Secretary in relation to this meeting?

Ans. : *For (a) and (b), refer to page 142.*

(c) The duties of the Secretary may be discussed under the following three heads, viz., before the meeting, at the meeting and after the meeting :

Before the Meeting

(i) He is to prepare the statutory report on the prescribed form as per the provisions of the Act.

(ii) He has to get the financial items certified by the Auditors of the company.

(iii) He has to convene a Board Meeting and get the statutory report approved and signed by directors.

(iv) He has to arrange for printing of statutory report, notice, etc.

(v) He has to mail the notice to the members of the company at least 21 days before the meeting.

(vi) He has to file a duly certified copy of the statutory report with the Registrar of Companies.

(vii) He has to prepare the agenda of the meeting in consultation with the Chairman.

(viii) He has to prepare a list detailing the names, addresses and number of share(s) held by each of the members for inspection at the meeting.

(ix) He has to arrange for seating accommodation and items of stationery.

At the Meeting

(i) He has to ascertain or help the Chairman to ascertain the quorum.

(ii) He has to read the notice convening the meeting if and when instructed by the Chairman.

(iii) He has to read the statutory report when so directed by the Chairman.

(iv) He has to produce before the meeting the list of members.

(v) He has to render able assistance to the Chairman throughout the currency of the meeting.

(vi) He has to note down the proceedings of the meeting.

After the Meeting

(i) He has to prepare the draft minutes and place the same before the Chairman.

(ii) He has to get the minutes approved and signed by the Chairman within 30 days from the date of the meeting.

(iii) He has to take the necessary steps and ensure that the resolutions passed at the meeting be implemented.

(iv) He has to send the Minutes of the meeting to the Stock Exchange(s) if the company's shares are listed.

Q. 2. What is Statutory Meeting and what is the purpose? Enumerate the provisions of the Companies Act, 1956, in regard to a Statutory Meeting. (C.U. 1966, 1968)

Ans. : *Refer to pages 191-192.*

Q. 3. (a) What is a Statutory Meeting and what are the provisions of the Companies Act in relation thereto? (ICSI)

(b) Give a list of the principal contents of a Statutory Report. (C.U. 1999, 1983, 1964)

Ans. : *(a) Page 142.*

(b) Section 165(3) of the Companies Act, 1956 provides that a Statutory Report must contain the following particulars :

1. Total number of shares allotted (both fully paid-up and partly paid-up).

2. Total amount of cash received in respect of shares allotted for cash.

3. An abstract of receipts (viz., on account of allotment of shares) and payments (on account of preliminary expenses, commission, brokerage, etc.).

4. Names, addresses and occupations of Directors, Auditors and Secretary of the company.

5. Particulars of any contract which are to be submitted to the meeting for approval, together with modifications, if any.

6. Particulars of underwriting contracts (details of contracts carried out or not, with reasons).

7. Arrears, if any, due on calls from the directors, Managing Director, etc.

8. Particulars of any commission, brokerage paid or to be paid in connection with issue or sale of shares to any director/Managing Director/Manager.

Q. 4. (a) Draft a notice of the statutory meeting of a Public Limited Company.

(b) Draft a specimen agenda for the statutory meeting.

Ans. : (a)

Kusum Products Limited, Calcutta 700053

Notice of the Statutory Meeting

Notice is hereby given that in pursuance of Section 165 of the Companies Act, 1956, the statutory meeting of the company will be held at "Jeevan Deep", 1 Middleton Street (3rd Floor), Calcutta 700071 on Monday, the 31st January 2000, at 3 p.m. to consider the Statutory Report and to conduct any other business ought to be conducted at such meeting.

A copy of the Statutory Report is enclosed.

Registered office	By order of the Board
1 Middleton Street	S. N. Gargari
Calcutta 700071	Director
Dated the 7th January 2000	

Note :

1. A member entitled to attend and vote at the meeting is entitled to appoint proxy to attend and vote instead of himself and the proxy need not be a member of the company.

2. An explanatory statement, in pursuance of Section 173 of the Act, is forwarded herewith.

Agenda for the statutory meeting

1. The Chairman to ask the Secretary to read the notice of the meeting.

2. The Chairman to draw the attention of the members to the fact that the list detailing the names, descriptions, addresses of the members and the number of shares held by them is open for inspection.

3. To move that the Statutory Report be taken as read.

4. To invite discussion from the members with regard to the Statutory Report.

5. To propose that the modification of contract be approved.

6. To consider any other business with the permission of the Chairman.

Q. 5. (a) What are the rights of the members in regard to a statutory meeting?

(b) Draft a notice of the statutory meeting.

Ans. : (a) The rights of the members in a statutory meeting are enumerated below :

(i) **Right of discussion** : Section 165(7) provides that the members present can discuss any matter relating to the formation of the company or arising out of the statutory report whether previous notice has been given or not; but no resolution may be passed of which previous notice has not been given.

(ii) **Right of adjourning the meeting** : Section 165(8) provides for adjournment of statutory meeting. The meeting may adjourn from time to time and any resolution for which notice has been given may be passed. The adjourned meeting shall have the same powers as the original meeting.

(iii) **List of Members** : The members have the right to inspect the list of members.

(iv) **Winding-up of the company** : Any member may apply to the Court for winding-up of the company if the provisions of Section 165 are not duly complied with.

(b) *Page 193.*

Q. 6. What is a Statutory Report? What are the consequences of default in filing of Statutory Report? Draft a Statutory Report of XYZ Company Limited.

(C.U. 1999, 1982, 1966; B.U. 1963)

Ans. : Section 165 of the Companies Act, 1956, states the provisions regarding the statutory meeting and statutory report. Every public limited company must hold a general meeting of the members within a period of not less than one month and not more than six months from the date of commencement of business. This meeting which is the first meeting of the shareholders of a company and held once in the life-time of a company is known as the statutory meeting. A private company need not hold a statutory meeting or file a statutory report. The members discuss at this meeting the report prepared by the directors which is termed the statutory report. This report contains particulars as to the formation of the company. The report is certified to be correct by at least two of the directors one of whom must be the Managing Director, where there is one. The Board of Directors have to arrange for sending a copy of the report to each of the members at least twenty-one days before the date of the meeting. A copy of the report is required to be filed with the Registrar of Companies. This report is also certified by the auditors of the company so far as it relates to shares allotted, cash received in respect of these shares and the receipts and payments of the company.

Consequences of default : If the provisions of Section 165 are not complied with, every director or other officer of the company who is in default shall be punishable with fine which may extend to Rs. 500/- (Rupees Five Hundred only).

XYZ Company Limited

Statutory Report of the Directors

(Pursuant to Section 165 of the Companies Act, 1956)

Name of the Company	XYZ Company Limited
Presented by	Shri Aniruddha Ghosh, Secretary

Date of Notice for holding the statutory meeting	2.1.2000
Date and place of the statutory meeting	2.2.2000 at the Registered Office of the company at 8 Clive Row, Calcutta 700 001

The Board of Directors submits this statutory report to the members in pursuance of Section 165.

1. Shares allotted and cash received up to 1.1.2000 :

Number of Shares		**Nominal value of each Share**	**Cash received up to 1.1.2000**
		Rs.	Rs.
(a) Allotted subject to payment thereof in Cash :			
(i) Equity	5,000	10.00	25,000.00
(ii) Redeemable Preference Shares	—	—	—
(iii) Preference Shares other than Redeemable Preference shares	—	—	—
(b) Allotted as fully paid-up otherwise than in Cash and the considerration for which they have been allotted :			
(i) Equity	Nil	Nil	Nil
(ii) Equity	—	—	—
(iii) Equity	—	—	—
(c) Allotted as partly paid up to the extent of Rs. 5/- per share and the consideration for which they have been so allotted :			

Number of Shares		Nominal value of each Share	Cash received up to 1.1.2000
(i) Equity	Nil	Nil	Nil
(ii) Equity	—	—	—
(iii) Equity	—	—	—
(d) Allotted at a discount of Rs. Nil per share :			
(i) Equity :	Nil	Nil	Nil
(ii) Equity :	—	—	—
(iii) Equity :	—	—	—

2. Abstract of Receipts and Payments up to 1.1.2000 :

Receipts	Rs.	Payments	Rs.
Equity Shares	25,000	Preliminary Expenses	5,000
		Commission on Issue or Sale of Shares	2,000
		Capital Expenditure :	
		Land	15,000
		Balances :	
		at Bank	500
		in Hand	2,500
	25,000		25,000

3. Preliminary Expenses as estimated in the prospectus : Rs. 10,000.

4. Names, Addresses and Occupations of Directors, Auditors and Secretary :

Name	Address	Occupation	Particulars of any change since the date of Incorporation	Date of Change
A. Directors :				
1. Shri A. K. Sen	38 Unique Park Calcutta 700034	Merchant	Nil	Nil
2. Shri D. Chakraborty	420 B.T. Road Calcutta 700050	do	—	—
3. Shri Subrata Roy	15 Gariahat Road Calcutta 700019	do	—	—
B. Auditors :				
Messrs. Chakraborty, Nath & Co.	186 Harish Mukherjee Road Calcutta 700025	Auditor	—	—
C. Secretary :				
Shri D. R. Sharma	1 Central Park Calcutta 700032	Service	—	—
D. Manager :				
Shri Phalguni Chatterjee	30 Ballygunge Place Calcutta 700019	Service	—	—

5. Particulars of any contract which are to be submitted at the meeting : Nil.

6. Underwriting contracts (Details of contracts carried out or not with reasons) : Nil.

7. The arrears, if any, due on calls from Directors, Managing Directors and Manager.

8. Particulars of any commission, brokerage paid or to be paid in connection with the issue or sale of shares to any director, Managing Director.

We hereby certify that the above report is correct.

Sd/- A. K. Sen, Director

Dated, the 2nd January 2000 Sd/- D. Charkraborty, Director

We hereby certify as correct so much of the report as relates to the shares allotted by the company and to the cash received in respect of such shares and to the receipts and payments.

Sd/-Chakrabarty and Nath
Auditors

Dated, the 2nd January 2000

Q. 7. Draft the Minutes of the statutory meeting of Messrs. Deb Asish & Co. Ltd.

Ans. : Minutes of the Statutory Meeting of Messrs. Deb Asish & Co. Ltd. held on Thursday, 2nd January 2000 at the Registered Office of the Company at 2.30 p.m.

Present :

1.	Shri	S. D. Burman	—	Chairman
2.	Shri	Hemant Kumar	—	Director
3.	Shri	Manna De	—	Director
4.	Shri	Md. Rafi	—	Director
5.	Shri	Kishore Kumar	—	Director
6.	Shri	Mahendra Kapoor	—	Director
		and 153 shareholders.		

In Attendance :

Shri R. D. Burman, Secretary.

1. **Notice :** The Secretary read the notice convening the meeting.

2. **List of Members :** The Chairman informed the meeting that the list of members was on the table for inspection during the currency of the meeting.

3. **Statutory Report :** The Chairman took the Statutory Report as read with the permission of the members.

4. **Discussion :** The Chairman invited the members to raise any questions on any matter arising out of the Statutory Report. A number of questions were put by the members to the Chairman and he answered the questions to the entire satisfaction of the members.

5. **Vote of Thanks :** Shri Hemant Kumar proposed and Shri Kishore Kumar seconded a hearty vote of thanks to the Chairman for presiding at the meeting. The Chairman replied suitably to the vote of thanks and the meeting terminated.

Calcutta — S. D. Burman

Dated the 31st January 2000. — Chairman

9

COMPANY MEETINGS (D)
ANNUAL GENERAL MEETING

[**Contents** : Procedure for conducting AGM—Annual Return—Books of Account—Secretary's Duties Before, At & After AGM—Notice/Agenda—Filing of Accounts—Minutes.]

Q. 1. When should the first annual general meeting of a company be held? What are the statutory limits for holding subsequent annual general meetings? (C.U. 1980)

Ans. : *Refer to Ans. to Q. No. 1, page 142.*

Q. 2. Describe briefly the procedure/rules to be followed in conducting an Annual General Meeting of a company. (C.U. 1991)

Ans. : The procedure for conducting an annual general meeting is outlined below :

1. **Quorum :** Unless the Articles of Association of the company provide for a larger number, at least five members in the case of a public limited company and two members in the case of a private limited company form the quorum. The minimum number of five is, however, not applicable to companies under Section 43A, i.e., deemed public companies.

2. **Chairman :** Every meeting must have a Chairman — either permanent or elected — by the members present at the meeting.

3. **Voting :** Sections 177-185 provide for the rules of voting. In the first instance, all the resolutions should be decided by show of hands. Declaration of the results of voting by the Chairman is conclusive. If a poll is demanded by a certain number of persons and it relates to a resolution for adjournment of the meeting or election of the Chairman, it should be taken immediately. Otherwise, it may be taken any time within 48 hours of demand. The manner in which it should be regulated is decided by the Chairman. He appoints two scrutineers to scrutinise the ballot papers. In case of a tie, he can exercise his casting vote which is in addition to his usual vote as a member of the meeting.

4. **Election of Directors :** Section 256 of the Act provides that at each annual general meeting one-third of the directors liable to retire shall retire. They are, however, eligible for re-appointment and will be re-elected unless it is expressly resolved not to re-elect them or to appoint some other persons in their places. Separate resolutions need to be passed for appointment of individual directors. All persons, other than retiring directors, seeking election must give at least 14 days' notice to the company communicating their intention of nomination.

They should also file with the Registrar of Companies their consent to act as directors. The officers, employees, etc. of the company may be elected as directors by a special resolution with a special notice.

5. **Appointment of Auditors :** Sections 224, 224A and 225 deal with appointment of auditors. At each annual general meeting, a retiring auditor is automatically re-appointed, unless

(a) he is not qualified for re-appointment;

(b) he has given the company notice in writing of his unwillingness to be re-appointed;

(c) a resolution has been adopted appointing someone else in his place or providing expressly that he shall not be re-appointed;

(d) where notice has been given to appoint someone else in place of the retiring auditor but by reason of his death/incapacity/disqualification, he cannot be appointed.

According to Section 231, notice of all general meetings must be given to the auditors and they are entitled to attend any general meeting and speak on any matter which concerns them.

6. **Minutes :** The Minutes refer to the proceedings of a meeting. The Minutes must contain a fair and correct summary of the proceedings. The Chairman's discretion as to inclusion or otherwise of any item in the Minutes is final. Members are entitled to obtain copies of Minutes on payment of the requisite fees to the company.

7. **Filing of Accounts :** At the conclusion of the meeting, three copies of balance sheet and the profit and loss account duly signed by the director/authorised official of the company must be filed with the Registrar of Companies within 30 days of the meeting. If the meeting does not adopt the accounts, a statement to this effect together with the reasons therefor must be annexed to the accounts and filed with the Registrar.

Q. 3. Write short notes on : (a) Annual Return; (b) Annual Report.

Ans. : (a) Annual Return : In terms of the provisions of Section 159(1) of the Companies Act, 1956, every company having a share capital shall, within 60 days from the day on which each of the annual general meeting referred to in Section 166 is held, prepare and file with the Registrar a return containing the particulars specified in Part 1 of Schedule V, as they stood on that day, regarding :

(a) its registered office,

(b) the register of its members,

(c) the register of its debentureholders,

(d) its shares and debentures,

(e) its indebtedness,

(f) its members and debentureholders, past and present, and

(g) its directors, managing directors, managers and secretaries, past and present.

Where full particulars of past or present members were given in any of the two immediately preceding Returns, subsequent Returns may mention the changes in shareholding only. In terms of Section 161, the Return shall be signed both by a director and by the manager or secretary of the company, or where there is no manager or secretary, by two directors of the company, one of whom shall be the managing director where there is one.

(b) **Annual Report :** Section 217 of the Companies Act, 1956, states that there shall be attached to every balance sheet laid before a company, in general meeting, a report by its Board of Directors with respect to the state of the company's affairs, amounts proposed to be transferred to reserves, amount recommended for dividend etc. Large industrial houses, banks, financial institutions—especially whose shares are listed—usually print the annual reports for sending to their members. In short, an annual report is the combination of the Directors' Report and financial statements of the company together with Schedules/Annexures duly signed by the Directors as well as the Company Secretary and audited by the statutory auditors of the company. The Companies Act requires the companies to file with the Registrar of Companies three copies of the annual report duly certified by a Director and Company Secretary together with the requisite filing fee within 30 days from the date of the annual general meeting.

Q. 4. (a) What books of account are required to be kept by a Company? (b) Who are the persons who can inspect books of account? (c) Can a director take inspection of the books of account through an agent? (d) Can a shareholder inspect books of account? (ICSI)

Ans. : (a) Refer to Section 209(1) of the Companies Act, 1956. (b) Any director of the company, Registrar of Companies, officers authorised by the Central Government and every auditor of the company can inspect the books of account of the company. (c) The right of a director to inspect the books of account of the company cannot ordinarily be delegated to any other person. However, the Bombay High Court has held that a director has the right to take inspection of the books of account through an agent if the agent undertakes to disclose the information so obtained only to his principal, i.e., the director. (d) A shareholder has no statutory right of inspection of the books of account of the company.

Q. 5. What is the work that the Secretary has to do before, at and after an Annual General Meeting? (ICSI)

Or, Enumerate the steps to be taken by a Secretary before and after the Annual General Meeting of a company. (ICSI; N.B.U. 1976)

Or, Enumerate the secretarial work before the A.G.M. of a public limited company. (C.U. 1983)

Ans. : The work involved in the office of the Secretary in connection with an annual general meeting may be discussed under three heads, viz., (a) Before the meeting, (b) At or during the meeting and (c) After the meeting.

Before the Meeting

1. Preparation of agenda at his own responsibility or in consultation with Chairman.

2. Preparation of final accounts and collection of Auditors' Report relating to the accounts of the company.

3. Preparation or assistance in the preparation of the Chairman's speech.

4. Arrangement for printing of the final accounts, Directors' Report, Chairman's Speech, etc.

5. **Board Meeting :** Though the date for the meeting of the Board of Directors is fixed by the Chairman, it is the Company Secretary who usually convenes the meeting.

6. **Notice to the Members :** A printed copy of the annual accounts inclusive of notice and proxy form is required to be sent to shareholders/debentureholders and other persons at least 21 days before the date of the meeting.

7. **Closure of Books :** A notice of closing the Register of Members and Register Debenture-holders is sent to the press for publication.

8. **Annual Return :** He has to prepare the annual return for the purpose of filing with the Registrar.

9. **Proxies :** He has to scrutinise the proxies and record those in the proxy list which are in order.

10. **Polling :** He has to arrange for polling in case it is demanded and resorted to.

11. **Admission Cards** : Issuance of admission cards which ensures entry of the desirable persons at the meeting is arranged by him.

12. **Accommodation :** He should arrange for adequate accommodation for members, directors and other invited persons.

13. **Keeping Documents Ready :** Besides placing a copy each of the annual accounts, Register of Directors' shareholdings (Sec. 307), Directors' and Auditors' Reports, Chairman's speech, etc., the Secretary is to keep ready other books and documents which may be required during the currency of the meeting. These are Memorandum and Articles of Association, register of Members, Minutes Book, Proxy list with proxies lodged, etc.

At the Meeting

1. **Quorum :** Unless the quorum is formed within half-an-hour from the scheduled time, the meeting is adjourned. Commencement of the proceedings of a meeting is, therefore, possible only when there is a quorum.

2. **Keeping Documents Ready :** He should arrange for copies of Memorandum and Articles of Association, Final Accounts, Directors' and Auditors' Reports, Chairman's Speech. Besides, Register of Members, Minutes Book, proxies lodged together with the relative list should be made available by the Secretary.

3. **Attendance :** The number of members present is counted and recorded. He has to arrange for obtaining the signatures of the Chairman and the Directors in the Attendance Book.

4. **Stationery :** He has to arrange for items of stationery, viz., paper, pencil, etc. for use of the members.

5. **Reading the Notice of the Meeting :** The Chairman starts the proceedings of the meeting by way of asking the Secretary to read out the notice of the meeting and the latter does it.

6. **Reading the Directors' and Auditors' Reports :** In case the Directors' Report is not taken as read, the Secretary is required to read out the report. In absence of the auditors, the Secretary is asked to read the Auditors' Report.

7. **Taking the Notes of the Meeting :** He takes notes of the proceedings of the meeting which help him in preparing the minutes.

8. **Helping the Chairman :** He is to assist the Chairman in properly conducting the meeting.

After the Meeting

1. **Minutes :** On the basis of the notes taken by the Secretary and notes supplied to him by the Chairman, he is to prepare the minutes of the meeting.

2. **Implementation of the Resolutions :** He is to comply with the various instructions contained in the resolutions adopted at the meeting.

3. **Final Accounts :** Three copies of final accounts, duly signed by the authorised person, must be filed by him with the Registrar of Companies within 30 days from the date of conclusion of the meeting.

4. **Annual Return :** Within 60 days from the date of the meeting, every company must prepare its annual return and file the same with the Registrar of Companies.

5. **Advice to Auditors :** He has to advise the auditors of their appointment or re-appointment.

6. **Dividend Warrants and Payment of dividend :** The Secretary is to ensure that dividend warrants have been mailed to those who are entitled to get these. He should further note that the dividend is paid within a period of 42 days from the date of its declaration. He has to arrange for payment of dividend tax within 14 days from the date of declaration of dividend at the annual general meeting and deposit the amount with the Income-tax Authorities.

Q. 6. Draft the notice of an Annual General Meeting in which, besides ordinary business, special business will also be transacted. (V.U. 1987; C.U. 1997, 1987)

Or, Prepare a notice (including the agenda) convening the annual general meeting of Fox & Co. Ltd., in which only ordinary business are to be transacted.

(C.U. 1990, 1983, 1981)

Ans. :

Fox & Co. Ltd.

Notice is hereby given that the thirty-eighth Annual General Meeting of the members of the Company will be held at Halder House, 38 Unique Road, Calcutta 700001 on Friday the 16th July 2000 at 3 p.m. to transact the following business :

1. To consider and adopt the accounts of the Company for the year ended the 31st March 2000 and the Directors' and Auditors' Reports.

2. To declare Dividend.

3. To appoint a Director in place of Shri A. K. Sarkar who retires by rotation but being eligible offers himself for re-appointment.

4. To appoint Auditors to hold office until the conclusion of the next Annual General Meeting and to fix their remuneration but Messrs. Chakraborty Nath & Co., the retiring auditors, being eligible, offer themselves for re-appointment.

Special Business

5. To consider and if thought fit to pass the following resolution as an Ordinary Resolution, with or without modifications :

"Resolved that in supersession of the ordinary resolution with regard to the borrowing powers adopted at the last Annual General Meeting, the Directors be and are hereby authorised to borrow moneys (apart from temporary loans obtained from the Company's bankers in the ordinary course of business) for the Company up to the aggregate of the paid-up capital (Rs. 5 crores) and free reserves (Rs. 2 crores), i.e., Rs. 7 crores at any point of time."

By Order of the Board
Gautam Dey
Secretary

Registered Office :

6, Cliveghat Street
Calcutta 700001
Dated the 16th June 2000

Notes

1. A member entitled to attend and vote at the meeting is entitled to appoint a proxy to attend and vote instead of him and the proxy so appointed need not be a member of the Company.

2. Pursuant to Section 173(2) of the Companies Act, 1956, the Explanatory Statement in respect of the special business is enclosed.

Explanatory Statement

Consequent upon expansion of scale of operations of the Company and its embarking on a plan of expansion, the financial requirements are visualised to be in the region of Rs. 7 crore which is equal to the aggregate of paid-up capital and free reserves of the Company. Though, in terms of Section 293(1) (d) of the Companies Act, consent of the members is not required, it has been decided to report the matter to the members.

Q. 7. Notice is hereby given that the Twenty-Second Annual General Meeting of the Excalibre Enterprises Ltd. will be held on Sunday, the 31st May 1993 at 3 p.m. at its registered office, Calcutta, to transact the following business :

(i) to receive, consider and adopt annual accounts for the year ended the 31st March 1993;

(ii) to declare dividend;

(iii) to appoint directors in place of B. Debnath, S. Basu and D. Das Gupta, who retire by rotation;

(iv) to appoint a director in place of S. Ray Chaudhuri, who was appointed as an additional director of the company and holds office until the conclusion of the annual general meeting.

Dated Calcutta **Sd/-Secretary**
the 5th May 1993

Does the above notice comply with the provisions of the Companies Act, 1956? If not, find out the mistakes and omissions.

Ans. : The mistakes and omissions in the notice are enumerated below :

(a) Sunday is a 'public holiday' under Sec. 2(38) of the Negotiable Instruments Act, 1881, and in terms of Sec. 166(2) of the Companies Act, an annual general meeting must not be held on a 'public holiday'.

(b) Full address of the Registered Office where the meeting will be held has not been given.

(c) The words "annual accounts" should be replaced by "the Directors' Report, the audited balance sheet as at 31.3.93 and profit & loss account for the year ended 31.3.93."

(d) Appointment of directors in place of B. Debnath, S. Basu and D. Das Gupta should have been mentioned as separate items of business.

(e) Appointment of a director in place of S. Ray Chaudhuri is an item of special business and should have been mentioned in the notice as such. Further, the name of the person who is proposed to be the director in place of S. Ray Chaudhuri should have been mentioned.

(f) Since item (e) above comes under special business, an explanatory statement under Section 173(2) of the Companies Act should have been annexed to the notice.

(g) Appointment or re-appointment of auditor(s) has not been mentioned in the notice.

(h) The Secretary is not the competent person to convene the meeting. He should have quoted the authority, i.e., 'By order of the Board.'

(i) In terms of Section 171(1), twenty-one clear days' notice has not been given.

(j) According to the provisions of the Companies Act, ordinary business and special business should have been mentioned separately.

(k) The notice does not indicate anything regarding 'closing of books of account of the company'.

(l) The notice is silent about voting by proxy in terms of Section 176(2) of the Companies Act.

Q. 8. A public limited company having share capital was incorporated on the 8th March 2000 and the certificate for commencement of business was issued on the 30th April 2000. You have been asked by the Chief Executive of the Company to advise him on the following points :

(i) the last date on which the company must hold its first annual general meeting;

(ii) the earliest and the latest dates on which the company must hold its statutory meeting and

(iii) in case the company were registered without share capital, what would be your advices in (i) and (ii) above?

Ans. : (i) In terms of Section 166(1) of the Companies Act, every company must hold its first annual general meeting within 18 months from the date of incorporation. So the company must hold its first annual general meeting latest by the 7th September 2001.

(ii) In terms of Section 165(1), the statutory meeting must be held within a period of not less than one month and not more than six months from the date of commencement of business. As such, in the instant case, the company can hold the statutory meeting earliest on the 30th May 2000 and latest on the 29th October 2000.

(iii) According to Section 166(1), every company is required to hold its annual general meeting. Therefore, had the company been registered without share capital, it would still require to hold the annual general meeting. In terms of Section 165(1) of the Companies Act, only the companies limited by shares and the companies limited by guarantee and having share capital are required to hold statutory meeting. As, in the instant case, the company is registered without share capital, it is not required to hold the statutory meeting.

Q. 9. (a) XYZ Ltd. was registered on 1st July 1978. At the meeting of the Board of Directors held on 14th August 1978 the Board appointed P & Co. as the auditors.

Is this appointment valid? Give reasons.

(b) Under what circumstances can the Board make the appointment of auditors?

(c) If at the annual general meeting no auditors are appointed or reappointed, are the retiring auditors deemed to be automatically reappointed? If not, how can the vacancy be filled?

Ans. : (a) The appointment of the auditors by the Board of Directors of the company is not valid since the appointment of auditors in the instant case was made after one month from the date of registration of the company. [Sec. 224(5)]

(b) The Board can make the appointment of auditors :

(i) Within one month from the date of registration of the company. [Sec. 224(5)]; and

(ii) When there is any casual vacancy in the office of the auditor. [Sec. 224(6)]

(c) If the annual general meeting fails to appoint an auditor, a notice is required to be given by the company to the Central Government within a week. In the circumstances, the Government may appoint a person to fill the vacancy [Sec. 224]. The casual vacancy so caused may be filled by the Board of Directors. [Sec. 224(6)]

Q. 10. Draft the notice of 10th Annual General Meeting of XYZ Ltd. whose capital is held by general insurance companies to the extent of 15%, by Central Government to the extent of 5% and Maharashtra Government to the extent of 5%, considering the following items along with other usual items :

(a) appointment of S as wholetime director for a period of 5 years;

(b) appointment of X as a director in place of Y who had resigned after 9th AGM; and

(c) appointment of Z & Co. as the auditors.

Ans. : (a) Refer to Sec. 269; (b) Refer to Sec. 262; (c) Refer to Sec. 224A.

Q. 11. The Company of which you are the Secretary has adopted 31st March as its financial year. The last annual general meeting of the company was held on 30.9.1987 to approve the accounts for the year 1986-87. The audit of the accounts for the year 1987-88 has not been completed. Your directors intend to hold the annual general meeting on 30.9.1988 to transact the business other than the consideration of the accounts for the year 1987-88 and then adjourn the meeting to a later date for the purpose of adoption of the annual accounts for 1987-88.

Whether intended procedure would be in order? Comment on holding the adjourned meeting on 31.1.1989, if the audit is completed in December, 1988. (ICSI)

Ans. : *For the first part of the question, refer to ICSI Question Answer. No. 10 page 401.* In case the adjourned meeting is held on 31.1.1989, there will be violation of the provisions of Section 210(3) of the Companies Act, 1956, and the delinquent directors of the company will be liable for prosecution.

Q. 12. A limited company listed on Stock Exchange is having paid-up capital of rupees three crores and free reserves of rupees two crores. Draft notice for the annual general meeting of members in which borrowing powers of directors to be increased up to Rs. 7 crores. (ICSI)

Ans. : *Refer to pages 203-04 and Sections 293(1)(d), 173(1)(b) and 173(2).* Section 293(1)(d) states that with the consent of the Company in a general meeting, the borrowing powers of the Board of Directors can be increased beyond the aggregate of the paid-up capital of the company and its free reserves. In terms of the provision of Section 173(1)(b), the business under consideration has to be included in the notice as special business. Section 173(2) states that an Explanatory Statement, setting out all material facts concerning such business inclusive of nature of interest, if any, of the director, etc., has to be annexed to the notice.

Q. 13. The company of which you are the Secretary has October-September accounting year. The accounts for the year 1986-87 (1.10.86 to 30.9.87) were approved in the annual general meeting held on 31.3.1988. In view of the amendment in the Income-tax Act, 1961, the company wants its accounting year to be changed to financial year to be extended to 18 months from 1.10.87 to 31.3.89. Advise the company :

(i) Can it extend the financial year to 18 months and, if so, what are the formalities to be complied with?

(ii) Can it hold its next annual general meeting on 30.9.1989 to consider the accounts for the financial year 1987-89 (1.10.1987 to 31.3.1989)? (ICSI)

Ans. : (i) In terms of Section 210(4) of the Companies Act, 1956, the financial year of a company may be less or more than a calendar year but it shall not exceed fifteen months. As per the proviso to the said sub-section, the financial year may extend to eighteen months provided the Registrar of Companies accords his specific permission therefor.

(ii) In terms of Section 166(1) of the Companies Act, 1956, every company is required to hold its annual general meeting in each year. However, not more than fifteen months' time should elapse between two such meetings. The Registrar may, for any special reason, extend the time by three months. So the meeting must be held on or before 30.6.1989. But if the company desires the meeting to be held on 30.6.1989, it should obtain prior written approval from the Registrar of Companies.

Q. 14. Draft the proceedings of the Annual General Meeting of a Public Limited Company assuming that no special business was conducted thereat.

(C.U. 1999, 1996, 1965; ICSI)

Or, Draft the minutes of the 19th Annual General Meeting of the Peerless Paint Co. Ltd. in which only the ordinary business was transacted. (C.U. 1991, 1982, 1980)

Or, Give the specimen of the Minutes of the proceedings of the thirty-first Annual General Meeting of Beehive Co. Ltd. in which only ordinary business was transacted.

(V.U. 1988; C.U. 1980)

Ans. : Minutes of the third Annual General Meeting of the Peerless Paint Company Limited held on Monday, the 24th January 2000, at 2 p.m. at the Registered Office of the Company, 42 Chowringhee Road, Calcutta 700 071.

Present :

1.	Shri	A. Acharya	—	Chairman
2.	Shri	B. Bhattacharya	—	Director
3.	Shri	C. Chatterjee	—	Director
4.	Shri	D. Debnath	—	Director
5.	Shri	E. Eaphen	—	Director
6.	Shri	F. Ferguson	—	Director
7.	Shri	G. Ghosh	—	Director

and 200 shareholders.

In attendance :

Shri A. Kulkarni, Secretary.

Shri S. K. Kripalani, Auditor.

1. **Chairman's Statement :** In his statement, the Chairman briefly recapitulated the performance of the company during the year 1998-99 and reviewed the operations of the company during the current financial year.

2. **Notice of the Meeting :** The Secretary read out the notice convening the meeting.

3. **Adoption of the Directors' Report and Accounts :** The Chairman stated that as the Directors' Report and Accounts together with Auditor's Report have been in the hands of the members for quite some time, he would take the reports, etc. as read. He invited the members to speak on the Directors' Report and Accounts for the year ended the 31st October 1999 and the relative Auditor's Report. The questions were answered satisfactorily. The Chairman's motion was duly seconded and it was unanimously resolved "That the Directors' Report and the Statement of Accounts for the year ended the 31st October 1999 and the Auditor's Report thereon placed at the meeting be and are hereby approved and adopted."

4. **Declaration of Dividend :** The Chairman's proposal for declaration of dividend was duly seconded by Shri Ashok Kumar. Thereafter, it was unanimously resolved "That a dividend of Rs. 5/- per share on 30,000 Preference Shares and a dividend of Rs. 4/- per share on 5,00,000 Equity Shares, as recommended by the directors, be and are hereby declared and that the same be paid on the 28th February 2000 to those shareholders whose names appeared on the Register of Members as on the 30th January 2000."

5. **Appointment of Director :** The motion of Shri A. Acharya, Chairman, was seconded by Shri D. Bhattacharya (a shareholder) and it was resolved "That Shri C. Chatterjee, who retires by rotation but being eligible offers himself for re-appointment, be and is hereby appointed a Director of the Company."

6. **Appointment of Auditor :** The Chairman's motion was seconded by Shri Y. Yadab, a shareholder, and it was unanimously resolved "That Shri S. K. Kripalani, Chartered Accountant, the retiring auditor, be and is hereby re-appointed auditor of the Company on a remuneration of Rs. 57,500/- and is allowed to hold office from the conclusion of this meeting to the conclusion of the next Annual General Meeting."

7. **Vote of thanks :** Shri D. Ghosh, a member, proposed a vote of thanks to the Chairman who responded in suitable terms and terminated the Meeting.

Dated the 23rd February 2000

A. Acharya
Chairman

9

COMPANY MEETINGS (E) EXTRAORDINARY GENERAL MEETINGS

[**Contents** : EGM—Who can convene? Secretary's Duties—Notice/Agenda/Explanatory Statement—Resolution—Minutes.]

Q. 1. (a) What is an Extraordinary General Meeting? (b) Who may convene such meeting? (c) What are the Company Secretary's duties in relation to such a meeting?

Ans. : *(a) Refer to page 142.*

(b) An **Extraordinary General Meeting** may be called by—

(i) the Directors whenever they think fit on their own initiative. They are, however, required to pass a resolution in the Board Meeting for convening such a meeting. This power is usually provided in the Articles of Association of the company;

(ii) the Directors at the initiative of the requisitionists holding not less than one-tenth of the total voting rights with regard to the matter in question (Section 169);

(iii) the requisitionists themselves, within a period of three months from the date of depositing the requisition, having not less than one-tenth of the total voting right with regard to the matter in question, if the Directors fail to call the meeting within forty-five days from the date of requisition (Section 169);

(iv) the Company Law Board, either of its own motion or on the application of any Director or member of the company, who is entitled to vote at the meeting, if for any reason it is impracticable to call an extraordinary general meeting (Section 186).

(c) The duties of the Company Secretary in relation to such meetings may be discussed under the following three heads, viz., (1) Before the Meeting, (2) At the Meeting and (3) After the Meeting.

Before the Meeting

(i) He is to convene a Board Meeting in consultation with the Chairman to consider the matter of holding the Extraordinary Meeting.

(ii) He has to prepare the draft notice, resolution and explanatory statement for approval of the Board.

(iii) He has to arrange for printing of the notice, explanatory statement, etc.

(iv) He has to arrange for issuing the notice together with explanatory statement etc.

(v) He has to arrange for press publicity and has to send an intimation to the Stock Exchange.

(vi) He has to keep ready the attendance list of members.

(vii) He has to prepare a list of proxies and arrange for poll.

At the Meeting

(i) He has to ascertain or help the Chairman to ascertain the quorum.

(ii) He has to read the notice convening the meeting when directed by the Chairman.

(iii) He has to keep ready all the documents, statements, lists etc. which may be required at the meeting.

(iv) He has to assist the Chairman in conducting the meeting smoothly.

(v) He has to take down notes of the proceedings of the meeting.

After the Meeting

(i) He has to draft the minutes of the meeting and get them approved and signed by the Chairman in the next meeting of the Board of Directors.

(ii) He has to file the copies of special resolutions with the Registrar of Companies within thirty days of the meeting.

(iii) He has to file with the Registrar the changes, if any, in the Memorandum and Articles of Association of the company. He is to file the revised copies within three months.

(iv) He has to carry out the instructions of the meeting.

Q. 2. Draft the notice of an Extraordinary General Meeting of a Public Limited Company containing an agenda. (ICSI)

Ans. :

Brentford Electric Ltd.

Notice is hereby given that an Extraordinary General Meeting of the Company will be held at its Registered Office at 6 Koilaghata Street, Calcutta 700001, on Thursday, the 27th January 2000 at 4 p.m. to transact the following special business :

To consider and, if thought fit, to pass, with or without modifications the following resolution :

As a Special Resolution

"That pursuant to Section 314 of the Companies Act, 1956, consent of the Company be and is hereby accorded to Shri N. R. Bhartia, a Director of the company, for holding and continuing to hold the office or place of profit under the company as the Chief Executive of the Company or otherwise in any other capacity on the same terms including remuneration as are contained in the Service Agreement between the company and Shri Bhartia dated the 1st January 2000."

By order of the Board
Brentford Electric Ltd
P. K. Chatterjee
Secretary

Registered Office
6 Koilaghata Street
Calcutta 700001
Dated the 1st January 2000

Notes :

(i) Regarding proxy

(ii) Regarding Explanatory Statement under Section 173(2) of the Companies Act, 1956.

Q. 3. Draft the proceedings of an Extraordinary General Meeting of a Public Limited Company.

Ans. :

Carew & Co. Ltd.

Minutes of the Extraordinary General Meeting of the members of the company held at its Registered Office, 6 Bankshall Street, Calcutta 700001, on Thursday, the 27th January 2000, at 3 p.m.

Present :

Shri A. Aich	—	Chairman
Shri B. Bardhan	—	Director
Shri C. Chand	—	Director
Shri D. Dorai	—	Director
Shri E. Eaphen	—	Director
Shri F. Ferguson	—	Director
Shri G. Gargari	—	Director

and 101 members were present in person.

In attendance :

Shri S. Senapati	Secretary.
Shri A. Addy	Auditor.

1. **Quorum and Notice of the Meeting :** The Chairman declared that the Quorum was present and asked the Secretary to read out the notice convening the meeting. The Secretary read the notice.

2. **Alteration of the Articles of Association :** The following resolution was proposed as Extraordinary resolution of the Company and passed as such :

"That Clause 2 of the Articles of Association of the Company be amended to read as 1,20,000 equity shares in place of 1,00,000 equity shares."

3. **Issue of Bonus Shares :** Resolved "That subject to the approval of the concerned authorities and compliance with the provisions of the Act, 5,000 bonus shares be and are hereby issued to those members whose names figure in the company's books as at 31st December 1999 in the ratio of 1 : 5."

4. **Closure of the Meeting :** The Chairman declared that all the items of the agenda had been taken up.

5. **Vote of Thanks :** The meeting terminated with a vote of thanks to the Chair.

Dated the 26th February 2000

A. Aich
Chairman

Q. 4. A public limited company wishes to issue further shares within its authorised capital. However, it does not like to give any right or option to the shareholders and, therefore, likes to empower the directors of the company to dispose of the shares in any manner suitable to the interest of the company. Draft the notice of a general meeting of the company together with the agenda required for the purpose. Also mention the procedure for doing the same. (ICSI)

Ans. :

Notice

Notice is hereby given that an Extraordinary General Meeting of Messrs. D. Das & Co. Ltd. will be held at the Registered Office of the Company at 18/17A Fern Road, Calcutta 700019, on Monday, 15th February 2000 at 3 p.m. to transact the following business :

To consider and, if thought fit, to pass the following resolution with or without modification, as a special resolution :

"That 10,000 new Equity shares of the face value of Rs. 100/- each to be allotted by the company be offered to the public at par for subscription and in the event of some shares remaining unsubscribed, the same be offered to the existing shareholders pro rata."

By Order of the Board,
P. Adhikary
Secretary

Calcutta
January 16, 2000

Notes

1. The relative Explanatory Statement as required under Section 173(2) of the Companies Act, 1956, in respect of the above resolution is annexed to the notice in the form of a circular.

2. A member entitled to attend and vote is entitled to appoint a proxy or proxies to attend and vote instead of himself and the proxy or proxies need not be a member or members of the company.

Legal provisions

In terms of the provisions of Section 81 of the Companies Act, 1956, further shares shall be offered to the existing equity shareholders. But Section 1A of the Act, as amended in 1960, provides the circumstances under which the further shares may be offered to the outsiders :

(i) if a special resolution to that effect is passed by the company in a general meeting; or

(ii) if an ordinary resolution is passed to that effect, an application is made by the Board of Directors in this behalf to the Central Government and the Government is satisfied that the proposal is most beneficial to the company.

Procedure

(a) There must be a provision in the Articles of Association of the Company; otherwise, the Articles will have to be altered/amended suitably.

(b) To convene a meeting of the Board of Directors to consider the plan.

(c) Prior approval of the Securities and Exchange Board of India is to be obtained.

(d) Notice of Extraordinary General Meeting together with Explanatory Statement is to be forwarded to the members well in time.

(e) Passing of resolution—ordinary or special (as already discussed above).

(f) A copy each of the notice and resolution shall be filed with the Registrar of Companies within 30 days.

10

WINDING-UP OF COMPANIES

[**Contents** : Winding-up & its Types—Dissolution Order—Secretary's Duties in relation to Winding-up.]

Q. 1. What is Winding-up? Discuss the various modes of winding-up. What do you mean by Dissolution Order?

Ans. : A company is the creation of law and winding-up is a process which brings about the death or termination of the company. On winding-up, all the assets of the company are realised and the liabilities are paid-off. In the process, if there is a surplus after payment of creditors, the balance is due to the members for distribution. On the other hand, if there is a deficit, the members of the company are required to contribute to its assets to the extent of unpaid amount of share capital. Sections 425 to 600 of the Companies Act, 1956, govern winding-up of a company.

According to Section 425(1), the winding-up of a company may be either :

(a) by the Court; or
(b) voluntary; or
(c) subject to the supervision of the Court.

According to Section 481(1) of the Companies Act : "When the affairs of a company have been completely wound-up (or when the Court is of the opinion that the liquidator cannot proceed with the winding-up of a company for want of funds and assets or for any other reason whatsoever and it is just and reasonable in the circumstances of the case that an order of dissolution of the company should be made), the Court shall make an order that the company be dissolved from the date of the order, and the company shall be dissolved accordingly". The order of the Court is known as dissolution order. According to Section 481(2) : "a copy of the order shall, within thirty days from the date thereof, be forwarded by the liquidator to the Registrar who shall make in his books a minute of the dissolution of the company."

Q. 2. Discuss the duties of the Secretary in respect of compulsory winding-up of the company.

Ans. : The duties of the Company Secretary in regard to compulsory winding-up may be summed up as under :

(a) If the petition for winding-up is to be presented by the company itself, the Secretary is to prepare the scheme.

(b) A copy of the winding-up order duly passed by the Court is to be filed with the Registrar of Companies within thirty days of the order.

(c) He is to prepare or help the directors to prepare the Statement of Affairs of the company in the prescribed form for submission to the Official Liquidator. This statement is to be submitted within 21 days of the winding-up order or within such extended time as fixed by the Court or the Official Liquidator. This requires proper verification by the Secretary and/or Director/Manager of the company.

(d) During the currency of the winding-up, he is to ensure that all letters, invoices, etc. issued by the company contain a statement that the company is being wound-up.

(e) He is to provide all the information/particulars asked for by the Court during the currency of winding-up.

Q. 3. What are the duties of the Secretary in regard to voluntary winding-up by the members of the Company?

Ans. : The duties of the Secretary in regard to voluntary winding-up by the members of the company may be summed up as under :

(a) The Secretary will have to arrange for a meeting of the Board of Directors and the Directors are required to pass a resolution and file the declaration of solvency.

(b) He will have to see that the declaration is verified before it is filed with the Registrar and advertised in the newspaper (Sections 488 and 485).

(c) He will ensure that the declaration is made within five weeks immediately before the date of the passing of the resolution and it is accompanied by a report of the auditors of the company on its profit and loss account and it embodies a statement of the company's assets and liabilities as on the latest practicable date [Sec. 488(2)].

(d) He is to arrange for convening an Extraordinary General Meeting and ensure that a special resolution is passed thereat.

(e) He is to ensure that the resolution embodies the appointment of liquidator and his remuneration (Sec. 490).

(f) He is to see that the special resolution as well as notice of the appointment of the liquidator is filed with the Registrar.

(g) He is to ensure that the statement of affairs of the company, duly verified by an official of the company, is submitted in duplicate to the liquidator (Sec. 454).

(h) He is to see that a general meeting of the creditors is duly convened to fill up the vacancy caused by death, resignation, etc. of the liquidator (Sec. 506).

(i) He is to ensure that during the currency of the winding-up all letters, invoices, etc. issued by the company contain a statement that the company is being wound-up.

(j) On the application of the liquidator, the Court may require the Secretary to present himself before the Court for public examination and giving evidence (Sec. 519).

Q. 4. Describe the secretarial duties in regard to voluntary winding-up by the creditors of the company.

Ans. : The duties of the Secretary in regard to the creditors' voluntary winding-up may be summed up as under :

(a) The Secretary will have to arrange for two separate meetings—one of the members and the other of the creditors of the company. These meetings may be held on the same day or on two consecutive days. Notices for the meetings are to be issued at the same time. Advertisement in the Official Gazette as also in the newspaper is also necessary (Sec. 500).

(b) He is to see that the statement of affairs of the company and the list of creditors detailing the amount of their respective claims are duly prepared. The statement is to be presented at the creditors' meeting and one of the directors of the company is to be nominated to preside at the meeting.

(c) He is to see that the liquidator is duly appointed by the creditors and the company at their respective meetings. If the two meetings nominate two different persons as liquidators, the creditors' nominee shall be the liquidator (Sec. 502).

(d) He is to see that notice of resolutions passed by the creditors' meeting is given by the company to the Registrar within ten days of passing thereof (Sec. 501).

(e) He is to see that the statement of affairs of the company is duly verified by affidavit and submitted, in duplicate, to the liquidator within twenty-one days from the relevant date or as determined by the Court/liquidator (Sec. 454).

(f) He is to ensure that a copy of the special resolution for winding-up of the company is filed with the Registrar within thirty days of passing thereof [Sec. 192(1)].

(g) He is to see that after passing of resolution for voluntary winding-up, notice thereof is given within 14 days in the Official Gazette and local newspaper [Sec. 485(1)].

(h) He is to see that a general meeting of the creditors is duly convened and another liquidator nominated in case the office of the first liquidator falls vacant (Sec. 492).

(i) He is to ensure that during the currency of the winding-up all letter heads, invoices, etc. issued by the company contain a statement that it is being wound-up.

(j) On the application of the liquidator, the Court may require the Secretary to present himself before the Court for public examination and giving evidence (Sec. 519).

Q. 5. What are the duties of the Company Secretary in respect of winding-up under the supervision of the Court?

Ans. : During the currency of voluntary winding-up — whether by members or creditors—the liquidator or any creditor or contributory may apply to the Court for a supervision order. The Court may make an order that the voluntary winding-up shall continue but subject to the supervision of the Court and on such terms and conditions as the Court thinks just.

The duties of the Secretary in respect of this type of winding-up are similar to his duties in respect of voluntary winding-up by members/creditors. (For further details, reference may be made to Sections 522 to 527 of the Companies Act, 1956.)

11

MISCELLANEOUS

[**Contents** : Advertisement Inviting Public Deposits—Secretary's Duties & Responsibilities under the Companies Act—Guidelines for Issue of Fresh Share Capital—Provisions regarding Payment of dividend—Guidelines for Issue of Bonus Shares—Sources of Information.]

Q. 1. Draft an advertisement to be published in a daily newspaper inviting fixed deposits from the public, company's shareholders and employees.

Ans.

Jain & Raghaban Co. ltd.

Registered office : 1 Camac Street, Calcutta 700 016

Terms of Deposits :

1. Amounts are accepted in multiples of Rs. 1,000/- with a minimum of Rs. 2,000/-.

2. Interest on deposits will be calculated from the date of realisation of the cheque/draft and will be payable half-yearly. Interest on deposits will cease from the date of maturity.

Rate of Interest per Annum

Period	Amount Rs.	Rate of Interest to be reviewed when the ceiling on it is raised or removed by the Government	Maturity value Rs.
1st year	1,000	10%	1,400
2nd year	1,000	11%	1,500
3rd year	1,000	12%	1,500

3. Particulars as per the Companies (Acceptance of Deposits) Rules, 1975 are as under :

(a)	Name of the Company	: Jain & Raghaban Co. Ltd.
(b)	Date of incorporation	: 16th March 1950.
(c)	Business carried on by the Company	: Manufacturers of containers.
	Branches/Units	: The company has its establishments in Mumbai, Delhi and Ahmedabad.
(d)	Management	: The company is managed by the Managing Director, subject to the superintendence, control and direction of the Board of Directors.

(e) Names, addresses and occupations of the directors :

Name	Address	Occupation
1. Shri P. C. Sen	1 Lansdowne Terrace Calcutta 700026	Chartered Accountant
2. Shri B. K. Debnath	18/17A Fern Road Calcutta 700019	Cost Accountant
3. Shri R. Roy	50 Townshend Road Calcutta 700025	Engineer
4. Srri V. Subba Rao	22 Lake Place Calcutta 700029	Attorney
5. Smt. Bani Debnath	73 Lake Road Calcutta 700029	Director (Andrew Yule and Co. Ltd.)
6. Shri S. Bhattacharya	1 L. C. Road Calcutta 700014	Business Executive
7. Shri A. K. Bhattacharya	12B Park Street Calcutta 700016	Solicitor

(f) Profits and Dividends : (In lacs of Rupees)

	Profits		Dividends	
Financial Year ended	Before taxes	After taxes	Equity	Preference
31.3.97	39.84	27.90	9.45	2.49
31.3.98	30.84	11.34	6.30	1.66
31.3.99	41.38	10.29	3.15	1.66

(g) Other financial particulars as on 31.3.99 being the date of the last audited Balance Sheet of the Company :

		(In lacs of Rupees)
(i)	Paid-up share capital	100.00
(ii)	Free Reserves	58.00
(iii)	Deposits	Nil
(iv)	Loans — secured	80.00
(v)	Loans — unsecured	20.00
(vi)	Accumulated losses	Nil

(vii) Utilisation of deposits — to supplement fixed and working capital requirements of the company.

Necessary approval of the Government has already been obtained.

A copy of this advertisement, duly signed by all the Directors, has been filed with the Registrar of Companies, West Bengal, for registration.

Application forms are available from the Managers to the Scheme, SBI Capital Markets Ltd., 44 Shakespeare Sarani, Calcutta 700017, or at the Registered Office of the Company.

By Order of the Board of Directors

Dated, Calcutta
the 2nd January 2000

P. C. Sen
Managing Director

Q. 2. What are the duties and responsibilities to be shouldered by a Company Secretary directly or indirectly in accordance with the provisions of the Companies Act as amended up to 1988?

Ans. : A Company Secretary is involved in implementing the requirements of the Companies (Amendment) Act, 1988. The duties and responsibilities to be shouldered by a Secretary — directly and indirectly — are enumerated below :

Deemed Public Companies (Section 43A)—Section 43A of the Companies Act, 1956, provides for the circumstances under which private companies are automatically converted into public companies.

For further discussion, please refer to pages 13-14.

Public Deposits (Section 58A)

The new Section 58A provides for the rules regarding invitation and acceptance of public deposits. This empowers the Central Government to frame such rules and regulations as are considered necessary in consultation with the Reserve Bank of India. The Secretary's duties in this regard are :

(a) On or before the date of advertisement inviting deposits, the company shall file a copy thereof, duly signed by all the persons named therein as directors, to the concerned Registrar of Companies for registration.

(b) Such an advertisement can only be issued on the authority and in the name of the Board of Directors of the company. This should further state the circumstances under which the deposits will be accepted.

(c) The company should maintain proper registers of deposits, pay interest on deposits at the appropriate time and file the relative return with the Registrar of Companies.

Stock Exchange Enlistment : Section 73 states the prescribed time limit for enlistment with the Stock Exchange(s) provided, of course, there is specific mention in this regard in the prospectus.

The Secretary's duties in this regard are :

(a) In case the company's application for enlistment is rejected by the Stock Exchange, the Secretary may, with the consent of the Board of Directors, appeal to the Central Government.

(b) The Secretary has to bear in mind that non-payment of all moneys, in excess of the application money on shares allotted within 8 days, will make the company liable to pay interest @ 12% per annum.

Share Capital stands increased by an order under Section 81 (4) : On receipt of the order from the Central Government, the company must file with the Registrar a return in regard to increase of share capital within 30 days from the date of receipt of the order.

Inspection of Books of Account, etc. of Companies (New Section 209 A of the Amendment Act of 1974) : The person making inspection may make copies of books of account and other books and papers. He may put marks of identification on the books and papers in token of verification thereof. Every officer of the company must assist the inspector in the proper discharge of his duties. Any defaulting officer is liable to punishment by way of fine and/or imprisonment.

Directors' Report : According to new Sub-section (2A) of Section 217, the Directors' Report must include a list of persons detailing the names, designations, duties performed, qualification and experience who are in receipt of not less than 50,000/-* (inclusive of the value of perquisites) per month. the Secretary has to ensure that the provision of Section 217 is duly complied with.

Appointment of Auditors : Section 224A of the Amendment Act of 1974 provides the cases where auditor shall not be appointed except with the approval of the company by a special resolution. The Secretary is required to see whether his company comes under the purview of this Section. If so, he has to adopt the relative procedure.

Cost Audit : Section 233B provides for the rules of cost audit. The company shall provide the cost auditor with all facilities and assistance in the proper discharge of his duties. If default is made in compliance of the provisions of this Section, the company is liable to punishment.

---

*The amount has since been raised to not less than Rs. 50,000/- vide GSR No. 752(E) dated 12.03.1999.

Managing Director—Appointment and Reappointment : Section 269 as amended by the Amendment Act of 1988 gives wider powers to the Central Government inasmuch as it provides that the appointment and/or re-appointment of managing/whole-time director cannot be made without the Government approval. The company is to ensure compliance of this stipulation.

Appointment of Sole Selling Agents : Section 294A empowers the Central Government to prohibit, in certain cases, appointment of sole selling agents for a specified period of time.

Contract between a Director and the Company : A Company Secretary is required to see that the procedure outlined under Section 297 of the Act as well as its amendment in regard to the contracts between the directors and the company is complied with.

Government-appointed Directors : Section 408, as amended by the Amendment Act of 1988, empowers the Central Government to appoint directors when it considers necessary. The Secretary has to bear in mind the directives issued by the Government from time to time in this regard.

Foreign Company : In addition to compliance with the provisions of Section 592 to 602 of the Companies Act, 1956, the Secretary of a foreign company shall note the provisions of Sections 591(2) and 600 as amended by the Act of 1974.

Government Company : The provisions of Sections 619 and 619B of the Companies Act, 1956, have to be complied with by the Secretary of a Government Company.

Remuneration : Under the new Section 637A of the Amendment Act of 1974, the Central Government is empowered to impose administrative ceiling within the statutory ceiling fixed by the Act of 1956.

Q. 3. Discuss in detail what is dividend and what are the latest provisions in regard to it? (ICSI)

Ans. : *Refer to page 176.*

Legal provisions regarding dividend :

1. Section 93 of the Companies Act, 1956, provides that if the Articles of Association so authorise, dividends can be paid by the company in proportion to the amount paid-up on each share.

2. In terms of the provisions of Section 205, dividends can be declared or paid only out of :

   (a) the current/accumulated revenue profits of the company after providing for depreciation as required under Section 205(2).

   (b) capital profits, if realised and if authorised by the Articles.

   (c) moneys provided by the Central/State Government in pursuance of a guarantee given by that Government.

3. Section 205(2A) of the Act as amended by the Amendment Act of 1988 provides that no dividend shall be declared or paid by any company except out of the current profits arrived

at after providing for depreciation as required under Section 205(2) except after transfer of reserves not exceeding 10% of profits.

4. Section 205A(3) provides that, where, owing to inadequacy or absence of profits in any year, if any company proposes to declare dividend out of accumulated profits/reserves, declaration can only be made in accordance with the rules framed by the Central Government in this behalf.

5. Section 205(3) states that dividends shall be paid only in cash except where as per the provision of the Articles fully paid-up bonus shares are issued or partly paid-up shares are treated as fully-paid in adjustment of the dividends.

6. As per Section 205(5) (b), any dividend payable in cash may be paid by cheque or warrant.

7. Dividends shall be paid to the registered shareholders, their orders or bankers.

8. Dividends shall be paid or warrants issued within forty-two days from the date of declaration.

9. Section 205A further states that unpaid dividend shall be transferred within a period of forty-nine days from the date of declaration to a special account titling "Unpaid Dividend Account of..........................Company Limited/Private Limited" should be opened by the company in any scheduled bank.

10. Section 205A(5) states that the dividend unpaid or unclaimed for three years from the date of transfer as aforesaid, shall be transferred by the company to the general revenue account of the Central Government.

Q. 4. (a) State the conditions and procedure for the payment of interim dividend.

(b)(i) Can the decision for payment of interim dividend be revoked?

(ii) What is the time limit, if any, for payment of interim dividend? (ICSI)

Ans. : (a) *Refer to pages 224-25.*

(b) (i) An interim dividend is subject to the will of the Board of Directors of the company until it is actually paid. Hence, the decision to pay the interim dividend can be revoked.

(ii) Final dividend is required to be paid within 42 days from the date of declaration. However, payment of interim dividend does not become a liability of the company until and unless it is actually paid.

Q. 5. What are the popular sources from which a Secretary collects various types of information? Discuss how a Secretary makes use of the reference sources.

Ans. : A busy executive or an individual holding a responsible position in the society has very little time to spare to collect the information that he may need for his day-to-day affairs. He has, therefore, to bank on his personal Secretary for this purpose. A successful Secretary will have to guess in advance the type of information his boss may ask from him. He is supposed to be a widely-read person and his boss expects him (the Secretary) to be a "walking encyclopedia". He should know where to look for the required information and how to find out the same.

Some of the sources from which a Secretary collects various information are enumerated below :

1. **Dictionary :** The dictionary is a storehouse of various types of information. Besides, some special dictionaries are also available which are meant for different professional persons.

2. **Encyclopedia :** It is a book of information on any subject. The information is arranged in alphabetical order.

3. **Telephone Directory :** The names, addresses and telephone numbers of the subscribers are incorporated in a telephone directory in an alphabetical order. It is normally published once a year taking into consideration all the changes. It helps the Secretary to get the proper spelling of a name of an individual or firm, telephone numbers and addresses. It contains a classified section which details the names, addresses, phone numbers of a number of firms dealing in certain types of products/services.

4. **Yellow Pages :** It is like a telephone directory which contains names addresses, telephone numbers etc. of various persons, firms, companies, banks, insurance companies who deal in various products or render specialised services.

5. **City Directory :** A city directory generally contains information in two parts. In the first part, names of all streets and number of houses on each of the streets are entered alphabetically. This part is known as street directory. Ordinarily, a map of the city is found in it. The second part details in an alphabetical order the names, addresses, occupations, etc. of all important persons of the city. It is known as the directory of private residents.

6. **Atlas :** Maps of different countries of the world provide the Secretary with various information of geographical and political interest.

7. **Railway Time Table :** It contains timings of departure and arrival of various types of trains, names of stations, etc. in a particular zone. The Indian Bradshaw is a combination of Railway Guide and Time Table.

8. **Postal Guide :** It furnishes the rules, regulations and laws of the Postal Department.

9. **Shipping Guide :** It contains useful particulars regarding the routes, rate of freight, etc.

10. **Business Directories :** The Chambers of Commerce publish at periodical intervals business directories which contain the particulars of their members in an alphabetical order.

11. **Directories of Newspapers and Journals :** These directories give the detailed particulars of the various dailies and periodicals.

12. **Year Books :** These books contain details of various events and general information of the countries of the world. Hindusthan Year Book, Manorama Year Book, Competition Success Year Book etc. are a few examples.

13. **India :** In recent years, the Publications Department of the Government of India publishes this book which contains information of national importance. This book is published annually incorporating all the uptodate information and current events of national as well as international importance.

14. **Financial Journals :** These contain particulars of credit information about individuals, firms and companies. These journals may be published both by public sector undertakings or by the private sector undertakings. A number of dailies, e.g., The Economic Times, The Indian Financial Express, The Business Standard, etc. also provide financial information.

15. **Government Publications :** Both the Central and the State Governments issue quite a number of publications on various matters.

16. **Libraries :** Large offices normally collect various publications on the lines of their business in addition to general collections.

The following procedure may be adopted for finding out any information efficiently and quickly :

(i) to ascertain the nature of information being sought;

(ii) to ascertain the actual purpose of the information;

(iii) the proper and relevant source is to be approached;

(iv) for the secretaries having voluminous work of this nature, arrangements for cataloguing and indexing may be of much advantage;

(v) detailed reference of the source should be mentioned while collecting the information.

12

DRAFTING OF REPORTS AND CIRCULARS

[**Contents** : Report—Types, Form & Arrangement—Specimen Reports on : Costing System, Issue of Fresh Additional Capital, Need for Advertisement Campaign, Agitation by Workers, Defects in Routine Work, Insufficient Work, Fall in Production & Remedial Measures—Proceedings of a Board Meeting, Auditors'/Directors' Reports, Installation of Business Machines, Standardisation of Office Furniture/ Forms, Proposed Showroom, Long-standing Grievances of Office Staff, Economic Use of Stationery, Increase in Prices, Admission of a New Partner, Change of Address, Opening of a New Showroom, Import Restrictions, Termination of Services, Accident in Factory Premises, Reasons for losses, Proposed Three-Shift System of Working, Financial Position, Proposal for Amalgamation.]

Q. 1. What is a report and what are its types? **(N.B.U. 1977)**

Ans. : A report is the presentation of certain facts about some specific sphere of the business activities in an organised and systematic manner. It is prepared by the writer on completion of his investigation of the matter on which he will have to report. It may be prepared by an individual or by a Committee comprising a number of persons, and it is meant for a particular person or a group of persons. Ordinarily, it includes the opinion of the writer and his recommendation too; but a report may be without any opinion or recommendation. It may be oral or in writing. Written report is preferred to oral report because the former is more accurate, less expensive and a documentary evidence.

Types of Reports : A report may be grouped into either of the following two classes :

(a) Formal or informal.

(b) Routine or special.

Formal or Informal

A Formal Report, as the name suggests, is drafted in an approved or prescribed form and presented in the conventional procedure. This report is of informational type which presents the facts as they are. This report is either periodical or routine in nature.

An Informal Report, on the other hand, is not subject to any prescribed form or procedure. This report is analytical in nature and, normally, it contains the recommendations/opinions of the writer.

A Formal Report may be either of the following two types, viz. : (i) Statutory and

(ii) Non-Statutory. A statutory report is required to be prepared and submitted to the appropriate authority with a view to complying with the provisions of the statute. Examples are : statutory report of the statutory meeting, auditors' reports, directors' report to the shareholders in the annual general meeting etc.

Routine or Special

An ordinary report is a statement of facts designed to convey some information and it is prepared as a matter of routine. This report does not contain any opinion or recommendation of the writer. Examples are : report of the Board of Directors to the shareholders of the company in the annual general meeting, report of the auditors, etc.

Peculiar problems very often crop up in a business necessitating investigation by an individual or a committee. The results of the investigations or the findings of a detailed enquiry together with the reasoned recommendations of the writer are incorporated in the special report. Examples of special report are : report on results of special projects, report on opening of new branches or closing down a branch, report on taxation and legislation and effects thereof on the company's economy, etc.

Q. 2. What is meant by 'form and arrangement' of a report? List the guiding principles of writing a report. How does it differ from a circular?

Or, Outline the broad principles governing the preparation of reports.

(C.U. 1977, 1963, and B.U. 1964—Adapted)

Ans. : The form and arrangement of a report will be determined by the type of report to be prepared. An informal report is usually presented in the form of a letter and, as such, the features common to business letters are found in an informal report.

In preparing the formal report, the following arrangement may be used :

1. **Heading or Title or Caption :** A report should have a self-explanatory heading or title and it should mention the period to which it relates.

2. **Address :** The report should be addressed to those persons for whom it has been prepared.

3. **Contents :** Lengthy reports usually contain a list detailing the topics dealt with together with the serial number, page number, etc.

4. **Body of the Report :** The body contains the main part of the report and it may be subdivided into the following parts :

(i) Introduction—Terms of reference.

(ii) Results of investigation or finding with reference to the facts and figures, suitably paragraphed.

(iii) Conclusion.

(iv) Recommendations and the reasons therefor.

5. **Reference and Bibliography :** For further and detailed studies on the subject, readers of the report are referred to the various books, etc. which helped the writer to prepare the report.

6. **Signature :** Report should be signed and dated by the writer thereof.

Qualities of an Effective Report : There is no short-cut method or ready-made rule for writing a good report. Reports on the same subject matter prepared by different persons differ because of their different approach, temperament and style of writing. The following general principles may, however, be adopted for the purpose of preparing a good and effective report :

(a) Report is to be presented promptly; otherwise, the very purpose for which it is prepared will be defeated.

(b) It should be accurate. A wrong report may prompt the management to take wrong decision(s).

(c) It should be accurate and in a simple and clear language. Use of ambiguous words should be avoided as far as practicable.

(d) The facts, figures, findings and recommendations should be presented in a logical manner to make the report more effective.

(e) It should be impartial.

(f) It should be brief.

(g) Recommendations made should be based on facts and backed by reasoned arguments.

(h) Report prepared by an individual should be in the first person. But when it is prepared by a committee/sub-committee it should be in the third person.

Features of a circular

1. A circular is to be prepared very carefully so that all the information which is required to be conveyed finds place in it.

2. Its form should be pleasing and language should be courteous. Use of stereotyped phrases in the circular makes the readers allergic to it.

3. A circular may be printed or cyclostyled.

4. The signature of the persons sending the circulars makes these more effective to the recipients.

Q. 3. Write Short Notes on the following :

(a) Verbatim Report

(b) Summarised Report

(c) Privileged Report and

(d) Memorandum.

Ans. : (a) **Verbatim Report :** When the discussions or proceedings of a meeting are recorded word-by-word, the report is called a verbatim report. Examples are the proceedings in a Court of law or the Parliament or an Assembly.

(b) **Summarised Report :** As the name suggests, a summarised report is the summary of the proceedings of the meeting. This is sent to the shareholders and/or to the press for publication.

(c) **Privileged Report :** Some of the reports are immune (i.e., free) from legal action, but this immunity is a qualified one. These are known to be privileged reports inasmuch as the law grants privilege to these reports. The proceedings in a Court of law and Parliament and report of public meetings published in the newspapers are examples of privileged report.

The following conditions must be fulfilled in order to claim the 'Privilege' :

(i) It must be a fair and accurate report of the proceedings.

(ii) It must contain the statements which were made in the Court of law, in the Parliament or in the meeting.

(iii) It should be made in good faith.

(iv) It must not be malicious or defamatory.

(d) **Memorandum :** Memorandum, in short, can be said to be a sort of reminder in writing from any individual/trade union/society/Chamber of Commerce/Club/Government Department for an action. In recent times, a memorandum is very often submitted to the concerned authorities for ventilation of the grievances of the writers and putting forward their demands to the higher authorities.

Q. 4. Draft a report as the Secretary of a Company to its Board of Directors about the advantages of a good costing system. (C.U. 1962)

Ans.

Dated the 1st February 2001

The Board of Directors
Elite Engineering Company Limited
1 Middleton Street
Calcutta 700016

Re : Costing system

Dear Sirs

As desired, I submit herewith my report on the advantages to be derived from the introduction of a good costing system in our company.

Costing refers to the techniques and processes of ascertaining costs and cost accounting system refers to the application of costing and cost accounting principles, methods and techniques to the practice of cost control and the ascertainment of profitability. In short, it will enable an organisation to ascertain the cost of a product, process or contract. For this purpose, a number of books and records are required to be maintained.

The advantages which are expected to be derived from the introduction of costing system may be summed up as under :

(i) It helps to fix up selling price in such a way as to enable the company to earn the budgeted profit.

(ii) It locates the unprofitable activities, losses and inefficiencies occurring in the form of wastage of man-power, materials and machine facilities.

(iii) It reveals the cause for decrease or increase in profit.

(iv) It helps in the proper preparation of estimate in quoting prices.

(v) It helps the comparison in respect of costs of jobs, processes, etc. from period to period.

(vi) Cost comparison, in turn, helps cost control.

(vii) It facilitates launching of cost reduction programme which, in turn, leads to economy.

(viii) Costing system provides ready figures which are used by the Government, trade union, wage tribunals in connection with price fixation, price control, wage level fixation, etc.

(ix) It helps the management to define responsibilities properly and fix them on individuals.

(x) It facilitates quick valuation of inventories and preparation of periodical profit and loss accounts.

In view of the above, I am quite sure that introduction of costing system in our organisation will be of immense help.

Should you need and further clarifications/information, I shall provide you with the same.

Yours faithfully
Mantu Debnath
Secretary

Q. 5. As a Secretary of a Public Limited Company, draft a report for raising fresh additional capital contemplating to undertake new extensions and schemes of rationalisation. (ICSI)

Or, Draft a Secretarial Report for raising fresh additional capital for Jintan Ltd., Kanpur contemplating to undertake new extensions and schemes of rationalisation. (B.U. 1964, 1966)

Ans.

Dated the 1st February 2000

The Chairman
Jintan Limited
Kanpur

Re : Fresh additional capital

Dear Sir

As desired, I give below my report on the need for and avenues of raising fresh additional capital for our company.

The need for raising additional capital stems from the following facts :

1. Increasing demand for our cotton textile products cannot be met from our present scale of operations. Expansion of our mills by way of acquisition of more spindles and weaving machines seems essential. This entails investment of sizable amount of capital.

2. With a view to eliminating wasteful competition and organising the industry on healthy lines, schemes of rationalisation need immediate introduction in our organisation. This also involves huge capital investment.

3. Competition with the modern mills is sure to pose a problem to us. These mills will be able to produce and sell at lower rates. Unless we go in for modern and automatic machines, it is very likely that we will be out of the market within a span of a few years. This possibility can be ruled out if we can acquire a few automatic machines. This course of action involves sizable amount of capital investment.

4. In order to cater to the needs of our export market as well as to earn invaluable foreign exchange for the country, we must increase our production capacity and reduce the cost of production. To achieve these twin objects, we have no option but to undertake new extensions, schemes of rationalisation and methods of diversification of our products. This, too, involves sizable amount of capital investment.

The cost of this programme has been estimated to be Rs. 30 lakhs at a meeting of the Chiefs of Production, Engineering, Finance and Sales Divisions of our company. A copy each of their reports detailing the expenditure to be incurred, the pay back period of the cost and the rate of return on investment is enclosed. It will be observed from the reports that within a period of 5 years our company will be able to repay this debt in full.

Possible avenues of raising capital

1. A medium-term loan of Rs. 10 lakhs may be obtained from the Industrial Finance Corporation of India against the security of machines to be imported. Our project report is ready and the Corporation, after appraising the project report, will have no objection in granting us this loan.

2. A further sum of Rs. 10 lakhs may be procured by issuing 12% Redeemable Preference Shares of Rs. 100 each. From the enclosed cash-flow statement it will be observed that the company will be in a position to redeem these shares after 7 years.

3. The working capital of Rs. 5 lakhs may be procured from the State Bank of India—our bankers—against hypothecation of raw materials, stocks-in-process and finished goods.

4. The conditions obtaining in the share market are quite favourable and it appears that

fresh issue of 50,000 equity shares of Rs. 10/- each at par may be subscribed. In the circumstances, it appears judicious to go in for fresh issue also.

Yours faithfully
K. K. Dutta
Secretary

Q. 6. Draft a Report as a Secretary to the Board of Directors about the need for an immediate advertising campaign.

(C.U. 1991; B.U. 1963)

Ans.

Dated the 13th January 2000

The Chairman
Board of Directors
India Lever Limited
Calcutta

Re : Need for advertising campaign

Dear Sir

In pursuance of your directive, I have carefully conducted a thorough investigation into the causes of the declining sales of our " Palmolive Shaving Cream" and have to report as follows :

'Palmolive Shaving Cream' was introduced by us in the market in 1992 and it was widely accepted by the customers for its high quality and competitive price. Consequent upon its winning the confidence of the market, we had to step up production of this item to a considerable extent to cope with the increasing demand. Sale of this product increased by 200% as was revealed from our Trading Account during the year ended 31.3.98. 25% of the total sales of the company was contributed by this product. This product, for the first time, suffered a set-back during the year ended 31.3.99 when sale of "Palmolive Shaving Cream" dropped to 50% of what was sold in 1997-1998.

The decline in sales may be attributed to the following reasons :

1. Growing competition in the market from quite a number of newly established firms. Some of the competitors are marketing the products even at lower prices.

2. Even though we enjoy a goodwill in the all-India market, we have not at all tried to better the quality during the last eight years.

3. Some of the firms offer attractive gifts, prizes, etc., which have enabled them to get an entry into the market.

4. From 1.4.99, the commission to salesmen as well as to the agents has been reduced by 50%. The salesmen are dissatisfied and they take very limited interest in retaining our custom. The agents contend that they are offered better terms by the other firms and that is why they push the products of our rival firms.

5. During the last five years, we have spent very little on advertisement of this product.

In view of the above, I feel that to arrest the declining sales as well as to regain the lost market, we should immediately launch an extensive all-India advertising campaign. The cost to be incurred is estimated at Rs. 12 lakhs and the benefits to be derived from this must more than offset the cost within a period of two years only.

Yours faithfully

Biresh Guha

Secretary

Q. 7. Draft a report to the directors of your company on the agitation of the workmen for a higher percentage of bonus and threatened strike by workmen. (C.U. 1988, 1970)

Ans.

Dated 1st February 2000

To

The Board of Directors

Shaw Wallace and Co. Ltd.

1 Bankshall Street

Calcutta 700001

Re : Agitation of the workmen

Dear Sirs

As desired by you, I submit hereunder my report on the agitation of the workmen for a higher percentage of bonus and threatened strike.

A thorough investigation into the matter prompts me to make the following observations :

Firstly, the principal grievance of the workers is due to the fact that they do not get reasonable amount of bonus from the company. They have demanded bonus equivalent to four months' basic pay for the year ended 31.3.99. During the year ended 31.3.98, they were paid bonus equivalent to 1½ months' basic pay. Bonus paid by us to the workers appears to be on the low side as compared to what is paid by other firms of our standard in the industry. We may assure the workers' union that the company is agreeable to consider their demand for bonus in terms of the provisions of the Bonus Act.

Secondly, the scale of pay offered by us to the workers is lower than the scale offered by other companies of our standard. I feel that the workers' union be assured that this aspect will also be considered by the company sympathetically.

Thirdly, I feel the need for introducing incentive system of wage payment which will benefit the workers and the company as well.

Fourthly, in addition to the existing privilege leave and casual leave, I feel that the workers be allowed sick leave of 20 days a year with full pay.

If we communicate our stand to the Workers' Union, I am sure that the union will not go for the threatened strike as from the 1st March 2000.

On receipt of your advice, I propose to negotiate with the representatives of the Workers' Union.

Yours faithfully
B. Bhatnagar
Secretary

Q. 8. You have recently joined A. B. C. Co. Ltd. as a Secretary. Write a report to the Managing Director on the defects in routine work of the company's office.

(C.U. 1995, 1994; B.U. 1962)

Ans.

Dated, the 25th January 2000

The Managing Director
A B C Co. Ltd.
41A Baghbazar Street
Calcutta 700003

Re : Defects in our routine work

Dear Sir

I have to report the following defects in our routine work which have come to my knowledge after I took up the new assignment :

1. **Attendance and departure :** Though our working hours are from 10 a.m. to 5 p.m. on weekdays and 10 a.m. to 2 p.m. on Saturdays, quite a number of staff—especially the juniors—attend office even at 11 a.m. and leave office before the scheduled hours of departure! This is not only a sheer indiscipline but also deters the smooth flow of work. Besides, this is the cause of displeasure amongst those members of the staff who attend office punctually and leave it even after the stipulated hours. I suggest that the departmental managers be requested to evince more interest on this critical point. The attendance registers should be kept in the chambers of the managers and the staff members should be advised to sign in the registers in the presence of the respective managers.

2. **Overtime in Accounts Departments :** Overtime is a regular phenomenon in the Accounts Department inasmuch as 50% of the staff are required to overstay to clear the backlog! A discreet enquiry in this regard reveals that the department is not at all understaffed but the members of the staff deliberately keep their work pending in anticipation of getting overtime allowance! The Accounts Manager is used to sanction overtime without examining the actual needs and the volume of work. I suggest that the Accounts Manager be requested to properly supervise the work of his department — both during the office hours and overtime. Though the practice cannot be stopped overnight, a considerable amount of money being spent for payment of avoidable overtime can thus be saved.

3. **Mailing Section :** This appears to be the most neglected section. Its staff comprise new hands and some 'condemned' persons. It is observed that both the supervisor and his staff

take very little interest in the work. Incoming mail is not properly opened in the presence of the supervisor and, many a time, cheques and enclosures to letters are reported to be missing. Details of outgoing letters are also not entered properly. I suggest that the supervisor be strictly advised of the methods to be adopted by him for proper handling of his work.

4. **Filing and Indexing :** The supervisor looking after the filing and indexing has very little knowledge of the method of indexing followed by us. Besides, he does not appear to be acquainted with the methods and procedure of filing! I feel that he should be advised of the modern computerised methods and procedures to be adopted by him to carry on his departmental work smoothly.

5. **Internal Check :** In view of the fact that a number of frauds were committed by the employees of our Accounts Department, I feel that a punctilious system of internal check be introduced in our office as early as possible. I suggest that some of the members of the staff be transferred to different sections of the same department.

I hope that the above suggestions — as and when implemented — are sure to improve the efficiency of the office and better our image in the eyes of the outsiders.

Yours faithfully
A. Das
Secretary

Q. 9. Draft a report as the Secretary of Messers National Rubber Company Limited to its Chairman on the grounds of alleged insufficient output of work by the clerical staff/ workers.

Dated the 1st February 2000

The Chairman
National Rubber Co. Ltd.
43A J. L. Nehru Road
Calcutta 700071

Re : Insufficient work by the staff

Dear Sir

As directed, I have made an investigation into the grounds which are leading our employees to render insufficient work. The investigation includes a number of personal interviews with the members of the staff and random inspections.

I have to make the following observations in this regard :

1. **Allocation of work :** The present system of allocation of work is not at all satisfactory inasmuch as placement of men has not been made on the basis of their qualifications, experience and practical training. While some of the employees remain overburdened with increasing work, quite a good number of them do not even have a full day's work! As a remedial measure, I suggest that allotment of work be made on a scientific, rational and realistic basis.

2. **Lack of co-ordination and co-operation :** Lack of co-ordination between the different departments and lack of co-operation amongst the staff deter the smooth flow of the

work. I suggest that the employees at different levels be sufficiently impressed upon of the impelling need for co-ordination and co-operation.

3. **Promotion Policy :** The promotion policy which is in vogue is subjective inasmuch as the management's main consideration is the observations of the reporting officials. This has always been a source of dissatisfaction among the employees. I suggest that a suitable promotion policy be evolved in which the qualifications, experience, practical training, performance, seniority, etc. will be also considered.

4. **Closure of the Guwahati Branch :** The recent closure of our Guwahati Branch has made our people panicky. They are under the impression that the company is going to close down a few more Branch offices due to curtailment in the volume of our business. I suggest that a circular be issued detailing the circumstances under which we had to close down our Guwahati Branch and the conditions now obtaining.

5. **Lack of supervision :** Lack of proper supervision is resulting in most of the workers going slow. I suggest that the situation can be remedied if the supervisors are called in a meeting in which they will be impressed upon of the need for proper and adequate supervision.

Should you require any further information or clarifications, I shall supply you with the same.

Yours faithfully
D. Debnath
Secretary

Q. 10. You have been asked by the Board of Directors of the company where you are working as Secretary, to enquire into the causes of the steep fall in production of the company and to suggest remedial measures. (C.U. 1996, 1983)

Ans.

Dated the 1st February 2000
Calcutta

The Chairman
Excalibre Industries Ltd.
38 B.B.D. Bagh
Calcutta 700001

Dear Sir

Re : Causes of steep fall in production and remedial measures therefor

As instructed, I have made a thorough investigation in the matter and ascertained the possible reasons for steep fall in production of the company. The reasons and the remedial measures therefor to set right the position are given below for your kind consideration :

(a) **Attendance :** Majority of the workers do not report in time for their duties and they leave the factory premises well before the scheduled working hours. This leads to huge loss of man-hours and production. The manager of the time office and the departmental managers/engineers must also evince more interest in enforcing the rules of attendance. The timings of attendance and departure of the workers must be recorded on their respective cards in presence of a responsible officer. This will automatically put a check on late attendance and early departure which, in turn, will increase the company's production.

(b) **Lack of Co-ordination :** Lack of co-ordination between the production department, purchase department and stores department and the departmental managers is very much apparent. All of them are functioning according to their own assumptions for which it has not been possible to reach the corporate goal. I, therefore, suggest that a meeting of all the departmental managers be immediately arranged under the chairmanship of the Managing Director of the company to make them understand the impelling need for co-ordination. This will not only increase our production but also save a lot of avoidable expense.

(c) **Appointment of Foremen :** The foremen appointed during the last three years are neither technically qualified nor sufficiently experienced. Naturally, they are not very clear about the role they are expected to play in the management of the workers. Naturally, they do not have the necessary expertise to guide the labour force. The labourers, in turn, do not care for the foremen and they do whatever they like to do! I would, therefore, suggest that our Works Manager be requested to train-up the foremen — both theoretically and on-the-job — for at least one month. This will equip the foremen properly and they would be confident in guiding the labourers in the right direction. Needless to say, the ultimate result will be higher production and better profit.

Thanking you,

Yours faithfully
Purnendu Maity
Secretary

Q. 11. You are a Company Secretary. Write a letter to a Director giving a short account of the proceedings of the Board Meeting in which he was absent.

(B.U. 1962)

Ans.

Marshall and Co. Ltd.

1 B.B.D. Bagh
Calcutta 700001
24th January 2000

Shri P. C. Sen
1 Lansdowne Terrace
Calcutta 700026

Dear Sir,

As desired, I give hereunder a short account of the proceedings of the last meeting of the Board of Directors which was held at the Registered Office of the company on the 20th January 2000 at 2 P.M.

All the directors—save and except you—were present at the meeting which was presided over by Shri S. K. Gupta.

The minutes of the last meeting held on the 3rd December 1999 were read, confirmed and signed by the Chairman.

A few cases of forfeiture and transfer of shares were placed before the Board for its approval.

It was resolved by the Board that the final call of Rs. 5/- due on 10,000 equity shares be made by issuing notice to the shareholders.

It was further resolved by the Board that the Industrial Credit and Investment Corporation of India Ltd. be approached for import of Heidelberg Automatic Printing Machine worth Rs. 91,00,000/- from Germany for the company's printing division.

It was further resolved that the State Bank of India, Commercial Branch, Calcutta, be approached for a working capital loan of Rs. 32,00,000/- against hypothecation of raw materials, work-in-progress and finished goods of our Factory No. 1.

The date of the next Board Meeting was fixed on 16th March 2000.

Thanking you,

Yours faithfully
Salil Banerjee
Secretary

Q.12. Draft the Memorandum of Association of an Engineering Company showing, amongst others, one paragraph dealing with principal object of the company. Use imaginary particulars relating to signatories thereto.

(C.U. 1964)

Ans. : Memorandum of Association of the Britannia Engineering Co. Ltd. (A company limited by shares).

1. The name of the company is "The Britannia Engineering Company Limited."
2. The registered office of the company will be situated in the State of West Bengal.
3. The objects for which the company is established are :
   (a) To carry on business as manufacturers, assemblers, repairers and converters of all kinds of plant, machinery and equipment.
   (b) To carry on business as design and engineering consultants in all its respective branches.
   (c) To act as consultants on all matters and problems of administration, organisation, management, production, marketing, distribution, purchasing, etc.
   (d) To carry on business as exporters and importers, wholesale and retail traders of engineering equipment, plant and machinery, etc.
   (e) To carry on any other business incidental to the attainment of the above objects.
4. The liability of the members is limited.
5. The Share Capital of the company is Rs. 25,00,000/- divided into 25,000 equity shares of Rs. 100/- each.

6. We, the persons whose names and addresses are subscribed, are desirous of being formed into a company in pursuance of this Memorandum of Association and we, respectively, agree to take the number of shares in the capital of the company set opposite our respective names :

Names, Addresses and Descriptions of Subscribers	Number of Shares taken by each Subscriber	Witness
1. A. Acharya, Merchant 1 Unique Park, Calcutta 38	100	V. Vakharia 1 Middleton St. Calcutta 1
2. B. Banerjee, Merchant 1 Sunny Park, Calcutta 34	100	do
3. C. Chandrani, Merchant 1 Fern Road, Calcutta 10	100	do
4. D. Debnath, Merchant S. N. Roy Rd., Calcutta 38	100	do
5. E. Eapen, Merchant 620 Jodhpur Park, Calcutta 31	100	do
6. F. Ferguson, Merchant 1 Park St., Calcutta	50	do
7. G. Guha Roy, Merchant 1 K.S. Roy Road, Calcutta 1	50	do

Q. 13. Give a specimen of the Auditors' Report to the Shareholders in an Annual General Meeting of a Public Limited Compnay.

Ans.

AUDITORS' REPORT

To
The Shareholders of
Discount and Finance House of India Limited

We have audited the attached Balance Sheet of DISCOUNT AND FINANCE HOUSE OF INDIA LIMITED as on 31st March 2000 and also the Profit and Loss Account of the Company for the year ended on that date annexed thereto and report that :

1. As required by the Manufacturing and Other Companies (Auditors' Report) Order, 1988, issued by the Government of India in terms of Section 227 (4A) of the Companies Act, 1956, we give in the Annexure a Statement on the matters specified in paragraphs 4 and 5 of the said Order.

2. Further to our comments in the Annexture referred to in paragraph (1) above :

(a) We have obtained all the information and explanations which, to the best of our knowledge and belief, were necessary for the purpose of our audit;

(b) In our opinion proper books of account have been kept by the Company as required by law so far as it appears from our examination of those books;

(c) The Balance Sheet and Profit and Loss Account referred to in this report are in agreement with the books of account;

(d) In our opinion and to the best of our information and according to the explanations given to us, the said accounts drawn in accordance with the significant accounting policies and read with the notes thereon forming part of the accounts, give the information required by the Companies Act, 1956, in the manner so required and give a true and fair view :

(i) In the case of the Balance Sheet, of the state of affairs of the Company as at 31st March 2000, and

(ii) In the case of the Profit and Loss Account, of the Profit of the Company for the year ended on that date.

For Dhar & Co.
Chartered Accountants
Mahaprabhu Dhar
Partner

Mumbai
Dated 23rd July 2000

Q. 14. What is a Directors' Report? Give a specimen of the Directors' Report to the Members of a Public Limited Company. (C.U. 1999)

Ans. : According to the provision of Section 217(1) of the Companies Act, 1956, there shall be attached to every balance sheet laid before a company in general meeting, a report by its Board of Directors with respect to :

(a) the state of the company's affairs;

(b) the amount, if any, which it proposes to carry in such balance sheet;

(c) the amount, if any, which it recommends should be paid by way of dividend;

(d) material changes and commitments, if any, affecting the financial position of the company which have occurred between the end of the financial year of the company to which the balance sheet relates and the date of the report.

Directors' Report to the Members

The directors have pleasure in submitting their Annual Report together with the audited accounts for the period from 1st April 1998 to 31st March 1999.

	31.3.99	31.3.98
	(In lakhs of Rs.)	
Sales	11,900	10,000
Profit before taxation	600	500
Provision for taxation	380	310
Profit after taxation	220	190
Contingencies reserve withdrawn	5	10
Surplus available	225	200
Which sum the Directors have transferred to :		
Development Rebate Reserve	5	10
Capital Reserve	2	—
Interim Dividend	60	60
General Reserve	158	130

Turnover : Increase in Sales revenue was due to an excellent export performance and an increase in domestic consumption.

Dividend : An interim dividend of Rs. 2/- per share, amounting to Rs. 60/- lakhs, was paid in December 1999.

Provision for taxation : As against Rs. 310 lakhs provided for during the previous year, a sum of Rs. 380 lakhs has been provided for taxation for the current year.

Diversification : Our application for a Letter of Intent for setting up a leather factory awaits the approval of the Government of India.

Memorandum and Articles of Association : To enable the company to embark upon a programme of diversification, changes are being proposed to the objects clause of the Memorandum. This has already been included in the Notice of the Annual General Meeting as an item of special business.

Directors : Shri B. Vaidya and Shri S. Santalia retire from the Board by rotation and, being eligible, offer themselves for reappointment.

Auditors : Messrs. Roy and Roy Co., Chartered Accountants, 6, Church Lane, Calcutta 700001, retire and have expressed their willingness to continue in office, if reappointed.

Staff : The Directors express their appreciation to the employees at all levels for their continued support in the year 1998-99.

Dated
Lipton House
1 B.B.D. Bag
Calcutta 700001
The 24th July 2000

On behalf of the Board
D. Sona
Chairman and Managing Director

Q. 15. What is a Directors' Report? Draft a short Directors' Report of the Pioneer Sports Ltd. regarding the company's state of affairs for the year 1963-64.

Or, What is the Directors' Report? Draft a short Report of the Hind Trading Co. Ltd. using imaginary figures and other details regarding the company. (C.U. 1962)

Ans. : Write on the basis of the Answer to the previous question.

Q. 16. Draft a brief report for submission to the Chairman of a large public body on the pros and cons of introduction of a mechanised accounting system.(C.U. 1972, 1969, 1965)

Or, Prepare a draft report for consideration of the Board of Directors of your company about the advantages expected from mechanisation of office work. (C.U. 1982)

Or, As the Secretary of a company prepare draft of a report for consideration of Board of Directors giving a proposal for mechanisation of the office referring to its advantages from the point of view of the company and its employees. (C.U. 1980)

Or, As the Secretary of a developing business, draft a report addressed to Chief Manager stating the advantages of installation of a computerised accounting system in the firm.

(C.U. 1998)

Ans.

ABC Company Limited

1 Connaught Place
New Delhi 110001
Dated the 1st February 2000

The Chairman
Board of Directors
ABC Company Limited
1 Connaught Place
New Delhi 110001

Re : Installation of Business Machines

Dear Sir

As per your instructions, I have carefully considered the proposal for mechanisation of the office and I submit my report thereon.

Advantages to the Company

1. The main advantage is speed. Invoices and bills for customers will be prepared quickly.
2. Reduction in clerical expenditure in the long run.
3. It ensures accuracy.
4. It helps to attain improved managerial control.

Advantages to the employees

1. Improvement of the image of the organisation arouses in the minds of the employees a sense of belonging.
2. Better machines and equipment inspire the employees to work better and harder.
3. Improvement in the quality of work makes the employees contented.

Advantages to the outside public

1. The machines help the customers/parties to minimise the loss of time and quicker service is ensured.
2. Accuracy of the various calculations is ensured.

Disadvantages

1. Cost of installation of the machines is high.
2. Opposition from trade unions.
3. Dearth of skilled persons to operate the machines.
4. Possibility of redundancy of staff.

During the last five years, the volume of business in our office has increased manifold. Some of the Departmental Managers have been asking for additional hands to cope with their increased work. Though overtime work has been a regular feature in the Accounts Department, it has never been a solution to the problem of increasing arrears of work. Customers have been complaining for some time past about errors in the bills sent to them for payment. This causes frequent frictions between the supervising and clerical staff.

In this context, it may be mentioned that I have had some preliminary discussions with the leaders of the trade union. They would have no objection to the installation of office machines provided none of their members is declared redundant. The possibility of surplus staff can be ruled out in the event of judicious reshuffling of the staff between the departments, as also curtailment of new appointments — except for dire need.

In the above perspective, I consider that mechanisation of our office will be beneficial for the growth and prosperity of our company. This will also satisfy our innumerable customers and well-wishers. My recommendation, therefore, goes in favour of mechanisation.

Awaiting your further instructions,

Yours faithfully
Malay Shah
Secretary

Q. 17. Draft a report for submission to the Board of Directors of a Company about the desirability or otherwise of standardisation of office furniture, forms and stationery.

(B.U. 1967; C.U. 1968, 1966)

Ans.

Bestobell India Limited

11 Camac Street
Calcutta 700016
Dated the 5th January 2000

The Chairman
Board of Directors
Bestobell India Limited
9A Camac Street
Calcutta 700017

Re : Standardisation of office furniture, forms and stationery

Dear Sir

As instructed by you, I have carefully considered the feasibility of standardising furniture, forms and stationery in our office. A survey of ten leading companies in this regard prompts me to comment that nine of them have taken recourse to standardisation.

The advantages which accrue to this system may be summed up under the following two heads :

Office furniture

1. Standardisation facilitates benefits of bulk purchase.
2. Replacement of stocks becomes easy.
3. Space available may be utilised in the most economic way.
4. It helps to develop a sense of equality and fair treatment amongst the various cadres of staff.

Forms and Stationery

1. Forms are designed in such a way as to contain the maximum relevant information and these can be easily understood and quickly analysed by those for whom these are meant.
2. Enormous time and a lot of money can be saved by proper use of well-designed forms.
3. Use of standard forms and stationery increases the efficiency of the employees.
4. Use of proper forms helps to systematise most of the office routines.

In view of the above, I am inclined to take a favourable view of the above proposal. I, however, await your final instructions in the matter.

Yours faithfully
R. Singhania
Secretary

Q. 18. Draft a report for submission to the Board of Directors about the location of a new showroom proposed to be opened by a Company. (C.U. 1998, 1964)

Ans.

Haralalka Stores Private Limited

Regd. Office :
50 College Street
Calcutta 700013
02.01.2000

The Chairman
Board of Directors
Haralalka Stores Pvt. Ltd.
38 College Street
Calcutta 700012

Re : Report on the location of our new showroom

Dear Sir

As desired, I have inspected the premises at 3 Chowringhee Square, the site for our new showroom, and have to report as under :

1. The place is centrally located and, as such, it would be convenient for all the people of Calcutta, irrespective of their residential areas.

2. The place is well-connected with vehicular traffic and the customers desirous of paying visits to our shop will not experience any difficulty for transport.

3. The building is quite commodious and would enable us to start a few new departments and the customers will be able to get all their items under one roof.

4. Seating accommodation — which is presently inadequate—will be quite sufficient in the proposed building.

5. The space available within the compound may be utilised to park the cars of the visitors, officers, and our delivery vans also.

6. The rent of Rs. 6 per square meter appears to be moderate considering the importance of the area.

7. It may now be possible for us to instal the latest computers for accounting in all the departments. This will ensure better and quicker service as also enhance the prestige of our company.

In the light of the above, I suggest that the site for new showroom will be suitable for us. I, however, await final instructions from you.

Yours faithfully
C. Bhatia
Secretary

Q. 19. As the secretary of a large manufacturing concern, draft a suitable report for consideration by the Board of Directors on the opening of a stall in the ensuing Calcutta Industrial Fair.

(C.U. 1990)

Ans.

2nd January 2000

The Board of Directors
Larsen & Toubro Ltd.
1 Shakespeare Sarani
Calcutta 700001

Dear Sirs,

Re : Opening of a Stall in Calcutta Industrial Fair

We have been approached, as in the previous years, by the authorities of the Calcutta Industrial Fair (CIF) which is scheduled to be held on and from 1st February 2000 and continue up to the 21st February. I have carefully examined the offer of the CIF and have the following observations to make for your kind consideration :

(i) Almost all the major all-India manufacturing concerns of repute, inclusive of the multinationals, will participate in the fair.

(ii) About 1,00,000 people — inclusive of manufacturers, buyers, sellers and export houses — are expected to visit the fair daily.

(iii) Booking a stall and making it equipped with our range of products—specially the latest ones—will be an ideal medium of advertisement and is sure to boost up sales considerably.

2. In this context, I would like to mention that the sales effected through the stall during the financial year ended 31.3.1998 and 31.3.1999 were 7% and 11% of the Company's total sales for the respective years.

3. In the light of the above and the fact that the charges to be incurred for booking a stall of 1,500 sq. ft. will be a mere Rs. 20,000/- only, I am inclined to take a favourable view of the request of CIF authorities and recommend accordingly.

I propose to proceed further in the matter on receipt of your approval/instruction.

Thanking you

Yours faithfully
Trisul Halder
Company Secretary

Enclosure : Offer letter of CIF

Q. 20. Prepare the draft of a report to be sumbitted to the Board of Directors of your company on certain long-standing grievances of the office-staff, e.g., lack of adequate accommodation, poor lighting, insufficient ventilation and unhygienic surroundings and recommending measures to be taken to remove the grievances. (V.U. 1987; C.U. 1981)

Ans.

1 B.B.D. Bagh
Calcutta 700001
2.2.2000

The Board of Directors
Excalibre Enterprises Ltd.
38 B.B.D. Bagh
Calcutta 700001

Re : Report on long-standing grievances of the office staff

Dear Sirs

As instructed, I submit my report hereunder on the long-standing grievances of our office staff. I have also suggested the remedial measures which may be adopted to set right the position and make the staff contented :

(a) **Lack of adequate accommodation :** During the last three years, staff strength has increased by about 25% and they have to share the same accommodation/space amongst themselves. The position has, of late, been so bad that two or three members have to share one table for their work! This not only disturbs the smooth flow of work but hampers the productivity. Besides, the staff feel very much discontented. If our office is shifted to a more spacious building, the problem can be solved immediately.

(b) **Poor Lighting :** The building being a very old one, the lighting arrangement is also old-fashioned. The amount of natural light is very insignificant. The staff members—especially of the Drawing and Designing Department—really experience much difficulty to perform their work. I, therefore, suggest that until shifting of our office to a new premise, all the old-fashioned bulbs be replaced by fluorescent tubes.

(c) **Insufficient Ventilation :** The arrangement for ventilation in the existing premises is insufficient. This tells upon the health of the employees which, in turn, affects the output of work—both qualitatively and quantitatively. I would, therefore, suggest that pending shifting to a new premises, a number of ventilators in each room be constructed as early as possible.

(d) **Unhygienic Surroundings :** Office environment and surroundings largely influence the work of the staff—both from the points of view of quality and quantity. Pending shifting to a new premises, the files and records staggered here and there may be kept in the stationery room and the entire floor may be white-washed/colour-washed.

Yours faithfully
S. Basu
Secretary

Q. 21. Draft an Office Circular emphasising the need for economising expenditure on uses of paper, stationery and stores which are not only costly but also scarce, impressing that it is as much in the interest of the Company and its employees as of the nation.

(C.U. 1974)

Ans.

Indo-Asahi Glass Company Limited

Circular No. GEN/420

12, Sudder Street
Calcutta 700016
13th January 2000

Re : Economic use of office stationery

Dear Colleagues

You are perhaps aware that the expenditure incurred by the Company on account of stationery during the year ended 31.10.99 has increased by nearly 75% compared to what was incurred in the previous year.

The possible reasons for this increase may be summed up as under :

(i) Carelessness in the use of the stationery items is the most important cause of waste and hence the increased expenditure. Expensive letter-heads are often used as strung slips (scratch papers)! Pencils and erasers are discarded even when usable!

(ii) Overstocking by quite a number of our employees has resulted in deterioration in quality of some of the items and some of them have proved unusable.

(iii) Unauthorised removal of stationery by a section of the employees.

You will appreciate that increased expenditure results in lesser profit of the company. This, in turn, entitles the employees to get lesser bonus. From the viewpoints of national economy, the wastage on account of increasing expenditure of stationery is much criticised.

In view of the above, the following suggestions, if adopted, may go a long way to arrest the increasing expenditure on stationery :

(i) A need-based approach to use and handling of stationery by all the categories of staff is a must.

(ii) More attention on the part of all of us will arouse cost-consciousness amongst us.

(iii) Requisitions for stationery should be routed through the Departmental Heads and the supplies will be made on the 1st and 16th of each month. In the event of any of these dates being a holiday, the next available working day will be the scheduled date for issue of office stationery.

(iv) Letter-heads and other printed forms should not be used for drafting letters or as a scribbling pad.

(v) Shorthand pencils and typewriting erasers (viz. Vandite, which is German make) should not be supplied to employees other than stenographers and typists.

Hope the above suggestions will receive your careful consideration.

Yours faithfully
B. Dattaram
Secretary

Q. 22. Draft a circular on behalf of an Engineering Concern to be issued to all customers informing unavoidable price increase for its products and stocks and spares due to rise in costs and levy of additional regulatory excise duties. (C.U. 1998, 1972)

Ans.

India Fan Industries Ltd.

10 Biren Roy Road
Calcutta 700008

Circular No. 121/9300 20th January 2000

Re : Increase in prices of India Fans

Dear Sir/Madam

Your are perhaps aware that prices of all factors of production have been rising in such a way that despite our best endeavours we are not in a position to offer our brands at the existing prices. Besides, to further aggravate the position, the Government has proposed to levy additional excise duties to the tune of 10%. Consequently, we have been compelled to price our products at 20% to 25% more than current prices with effect from September 1, 2000.

You will appreciate that in arriving at the above prices we have even to reduce our existing profit margins.

In the light of the above, we hope we will get the same patronage as we have been getting from you.

Thanking you in anticipation of your continued goodwill,

Yours faithfully
for India Fan Industries
K. Kamalaksha
Sales Manager

Q. 23. Draft a circular informing customers and others of admission of a new partner in place of an old partner who has died, the firm continuing business with greater vigour and expecting larger business. (C.U. 1971)

Ans.

Calcutta Chemicals

29 Broad Street
Calcutta 700019
2nd January 2000

Dear Sir/Madam

We very much regret to announce the sudden demise of our partner, Shri S. Bhattacharya, on 25th December 1999. We have inducted his only son, Shri K. Bhattacharya, as a partner of our firm. Shri K. Bhattacharya was in the employ of Messrs. Imperial Chemical Industries Ltd. as the Chief Chemical Engineer. He left his job and has joined us with effect from today. His professional qualifications and vast experience with Messrs. Imperial Chemical Industries Limited will be an asset to us.

According to the new scheme of diversification, we shall shortly be able to provide you with a few more varieties of quality products. We expect to offer these products probably at cheaper rates.

In the light of the above, we hope we will be favoured with your continued patronage.

Thanking you,

Yours faithfully
for Calcutta Chemicals
Deb Ashish
Partner

Q. 24. Draft a circular letter to the customers of your Company about the change of address of the Head Office emphasising that the new place will be to the customers' advantage. **(C.U. 1970)**

Ans.

Elite Department Stores Limited

Regd. Office :
1B Asuthosh Mukherjee Road
Calcutta 700020
7th January 2000

Dear Sir/Madam

Re : Change of Address

It gives us immense pleasure in announcing that owing to continuous expansion of our business, it has become absolutely necessary to shift our office to a more commodious building. The present premises in which we started our business proves inadequate for the growing needs of our large number of customers. Besides, our office is not situated centrally.

The proposed building at 16 J. N. Road, where we will be operating with effect from 23.01.2000, has a number of advantages. It is centrally located and well-communicated with vehicular traffic. This will thus help the people of Calcutta and suburban areas to visit our shop with ease. The space within the premises will enable us to start a few more departments and thus satisfy your various demands. Seating accommodation, which is still now inadequate in most of the departments, will be improved. Free movement of the customers and visitors will also be amply facilitated. It will now be possible for us to instal computers in all the departments and this will ensure better and quicker service to our innumerable customers. There is enough space within the compound to park your cars and our delivery vans.

Hope to have the same patronage as we have been having from you.

Thanking you,

Yours faithfully
S.K. Mitra
Director (Commercial)

Q. 25. Draft a circular letter to customers or dealers announcing the opening of a new Showroom or Branch.

Ans.

Haralalka Stores Private Limited

Regd. Office :
206 Bidhan Sarani
Calcutta 700006
2nd January 2000

To
Shri/Shrimati ....
....

Re : Opening of a New Showroom

Dear Sir/Madam

It gives us immense pleasure to announce that as from the 1st February 2000, we are going to open our new showroom at 3 Chowringhee Approach. Enormous increase in the volume of our business during the last few years and continuous pressure from our customers from south and central Calcutta set us seriously considering for opening of another showroom. Now it has been possible for us to give the plan a concrete shape by way of opening the showroom. The showroom has the following advantages :

(i) Enough space to house all the departments in a planned way.

(ii) Facilities of all kinds of transport owing to situational advantages.

(iii) Availability of enough parking space.

(iv) Provision of godowns within the same building.

(v) Possibility of installation of computers.

The showroom will be headed by Shri D. De, one of our very efficient Sales Managers. We hope to have your patronage as before.

Thanking you,

Yours faithfully
R. Sundaram
Sales Manager

Q. 26. Draft a circular letter by a dealer in foreign calculating machines to all customers advising them of his inability to maintain supplies in future due to import restrictions. **(C.U. 1965)**

Ans.

International Comptometer Machines Ltd.

Regd. Office :
10 Bentinck Street
Calcutta 700001
1st February 2000

Circular No. ....

Import Restrictions
Stoppage in supply of imported machines

Dear Sir(s)

Consequent upon the Government of India imposing restrictions on the import of calculating machines, we are compelled to communicate our present inability in executing the orders placed by you. This step has been taken by the Government to tide over the crisis of foreign exchange which the country has been facing during the last few months. We are in correspondence with the Government and we have been given to understand that this ban on import might be withdrawn towards the end of the current year. If it proves to be true, we shall be able to start regular supply sometime in April 2000.

In the circumstances, may we request you to please bear the situation with us which is completely beyond our control.

Yours faithfully
S. N. Garg
Managing Director

Q. 27. Draft a circular letter to all customers of a firm advising them about termination of the services of a travelling salesman (authorised to accept orders and collect bills) and appointment of a new representative in his place. **(C.U. 1963)**

Ans.

ICI (India) Limited

Regd. Office :
30 Chowringhee Approach
1st January 2000

Circular

To ________________________________

____

now obtaining. A thorough investigation was undertaken by a Committee of the Board of Directors and, based on the report of the Committee, we have to lay before you the following facts for your information and consideration :

(a) **Closure of Guwahati and other Branches :** As a sequel to the political disturbances, we had to close the offices which normally used to account for 25% to 35% of our total business. The staff thus rendered surplus have been transferred to our other offices. The possibility of reopening the Branches in the near future appears to be quite bleak.

(b) **Export Market :** The principal importers of our products, viz., Malaysian countries, have developed their own industries. Our endeavours to explore the possibilities of exporting to other countries are yet to be successful.

(c) **Import of Raw Materials :** Consequent upon our retreat from the foreign market, the Director of Foreign Trade is now allowing us only to import such materials which we are entitled against export. The substitute materials, which are indigenously available, are not of good quality and the prices thereof are more than double the imported variety.

(d) **Double-shift Working :** Due to non-availability of adequate raw materials as well as orders from indentors, we have been compelled to run all our factories on double-shift basis instead of triple-shift basis. The burden of fixed overhead remaining at more or less the previous level, the operations of the company, despite our best endeavours, are proving uneconomic.

We are making every endeavour to tide over the difficulties and a number of remedial measures have already been taken on various fronts. The outcome of our efforts will surely be communicated to you at the appropriate time.

Yours faithfully
Bani Haldar
Chairman

Q. 30. As the Works Manager of a Company, draft a concise report to the Board of Directors of the Company advocating introduction of a three-shift system in the Company's factories. (ICSI)

Ans.

1 Temple Road
Puri 752001
16th January 2000

The Board of Directors
Unique Manufacturing Co. Ltd.
Puri 752001
Orissa

Re : Three-shift system in the Company's factories

Dear Sirs

As desired at the last Board Meeting, I submit my report on the three-shift system of working in the Company's factories as under :

(a) **Capacity :** With the existing complement of plant and machinery, our production may be increased by about 50% if we work on three-shift system instead of two-shift.

(b) **Demand :** The demand for our products—both in the home and the foreign markets—is quite encouraging. The entire production may be marketed at the ruling price without any difficulty. A confirmatory statement from our Sales Manager is enclosed for your perusal.

(c) **Capital :** At the moment, no fixed assets need to be purchased. The requirement of additional working capital is estimated to be in the region of Rs. 30 lacs and the amount can be arranged by way of working capital loan from our existing bankers. A statement from our Chief Financial Adviser confirming this is attached herewith.

(d) **Labour :** The standard of living being very low and population very high, labour will be available at cheap rate.

(e) **Incidence of Cost :** Most of the fixed costs remaining at the same levels, it is expected that overall cost of production will reduce by at least 25%. The view of our Cost Accountant contains in the enclosed statement.

(f) **Profitability :** The overall profitability is estimated to increase to 20% from 10%.

All considered, I recommended three-shift working in all our factories.

Yours faithfully
Kumar Halder
Works Manager

Enclosures : As above

Q. 31. Draft a report of a Committee appointed to investigate the financial position of a company with recommendations as to the future policy. (ICSI)

Ans.

Date : 12th January 2000

The Board of Directors
Weak Company Limited
1 Strong Road
Cuttack

Re : Report on the financial position

Dear Sirs

As desired by you at the last Board Meeting, we have thoroughly investigated the financial position of the company and have to lay before you the following facts for your consideration and necessary action :

(a) **Nationalisation of Coal Industry :** Consequent upon nationalisation of Coal Industry, the Bengal Coal Ltd. and the National Coal Co. Ltd. have been taken over by the Government. The contribution of these two companies towards our overall profit was always above 75%.

(b) **Loss in Export Market :** Last year we sent a consignment of tea worth Rs. 1 crore to London. But the entire consignment was sent back by the indentor on the ground of sub-standard quality. The direct loss occasioned to us on this score veers around Rs. 10 lakhs and the indirect loss is irreparable, i.e., loss of market once for all.

(c) **Competition in Local Market :** As regards the cosmetic products and battery, we had been reigning more or less like a monopolist. But now that a number of competitors have emerged, we have been compelled to resort to price reduction. This has resulted in further erosion of profit.

(d) **Strikes, Lock-outs and Closure :** Due to labour troubles, as many as four of our factories are closed — either as a result of strike or lock-out. Besides, two of our factories located in Patna and Shillong have suspended manufacturing operations as a sequel to political disturbances.

The following **remedial measures** may be suggested for immediate adoption with a view to arresting the declining profit/increasing loss :

(a) The conditions now obtaining in the share market are quite favourable and it is expected that 1,00,000 equity shares of Rs. 100/- at par will be fully subscribed. Out of this, a sum of Rs. 80 lakhs may be utilised to purchase two tea gardens in Assam and the balance may be utilised towards replacement of worn-out plant and machinery of our Cuttack unit.

(b) Negotiations with an American buyer for sale of our Patna unit are under progress and a somewhat lower price may be offered with a view to expeditious finalisation of the deal.

(c) Production of battery and cosmetics may be increased which will bring down the per unit cost of production of each of the items. In such a situation, we may even lower our sale prices which will increase sales volume and, in turn, the profits.

(d) Negotiations with the representatives of the labour unions reveal that if we agree to offer some marginal benefits, the outstanding issues will be resolved. Regarding the surplus staff, they may be usefully deployed in our expansion projects.

Should you, however, require any further information/clarifications, we will provide you with the same.

Yours faithfully
Anutosh Chakraborty
T. C. Bhattacharya
S. K. Talukdar
B. Debnath

Members, Committee of Directors

Q. 32. As Secretary of a Joint Stock Company, draft a circular letter to the shareholders containing proposals for amalgamation with another company. (ICSI)

Ans.

The Weak Company Limited
Regd. office : 1 Strong Avenue
Calcutta 700001

Circular Date : 16.10.2000

To
All the Shareholders of the Company

Re : Proposal for Amalgamation

Dear Sir/Madam

We forward herewith a notice convening an Extraordinary General Meeting in connection with voluntary liquidation of the company, appointment of official liquidator and approval of the draft scheme of amalgamation of the company with The Strong Company Limited.

In this context, the following points need special mention which have prompted the Board of Directors to recommend this course of action :

(a) Our company has been making loss for the last few years and, as such, has been compelled to stop payment of dividend for the last two consecutive years.

(b) The cut-throat and unhealthy competition obtaining in the market is too difficult for us to tackle.

(c) Consequent upon our retreat from the international market, the possibility of our revival, unaided, in the near future is also very bleak.

In view of the above and the fact that the interest of our shareholders will not be jeopardised in any way by this merger, the Directors have recommended the above course of action.

A copy of the draft scheme and a proxy form are enclosed.

Yours faithfully
Bani Debnath
Secretary

Enclosures : Two

13

CORRESPONDENCE

[**Contents** : Commercial Correspondence—Definition & Style, Essential Features—Specimen letters : Application for Employment, Advertisement inviting Applications for Employment—Letters of Introduction & Letters of Credit, Status Enquiry, Letters of Offer, Acceptance & Order—Confirmation, Execution, Refusal and Cancellation of Orders—Correspondence with Banks—Correspondence with Insurance Companies—Letters of Agency—Correspondence with Government Departments—Secretarial Correspondence—Letters to Editors — Miscellaneous.]

Q. 1. What do you mean by the term 'Commercial Correspondence'? Why is it preferred to other media of communications? What do you mean by the style of commercial correspondence?

Ans. : 'Commercial Correspondence' can be said to be a potent means of "communication of information on matters of trade and commerce". It is also known as business letter. The main purpose of writing such a letter is to bring the buyer and seller of a product or service into close contact. A commercial correspondence may be between two persons, two organisations, or one person and an organisation. It has been aptly said that the commercial correspondence is a "silent ambassador."

Other media of communication are personal contacts, telephonic conversations, contacts through sales representatives etc. But correspondence is considered as the most effective medium of communication from the viewpoints of economy, safety and suitability. Besides, business letters can be produced as evidence in the courts of law in case of necessity.

Letters can broadly be divided into two categories, — personal letters and business letters. The personal letters are quite informal and the language used is flowing and homely. Business letters, on the other hand, are written for some specific purpose(s). The language used here is precise and formal. The style of writing letters is a quality peculiar to the individual and the factors which determine and influence this quality are education, training, experience and way of thinking of the person concerned. The desirable qualities for a good style of writing are **simplicity**, **clarity**, **sincerity**, **courtesy** and **conciseness**.

Q. 2. State the essential features of a commercial correspondence or a business letter. What do you understand by the term "Form and arrangement of a letter"?

Ans. : The essential qualities or features of a good business letter are :

(a) **Sincerity :** The person writing the business letters must be sincere in his work. He must try to be original and give the stamp of his personality in his writing as far as possible, write in his own words and in his own way.

(b) **Simplicity :** Letters should be written as simply as possible. Long sentences and high-sounding words and expressions in roundabout ways should be avoided.

(c) **Style :** The letter-writer must be able to convey the message to the recipient in clear and unambiguous terms. The sentences should be grammatically correct and properly worded.

(d) **Clarity :** The letter-writer must be able to convey the message to the recipient in clear and unambiguous terms. The sentences should say what he means and mean what he says.

(e) **Conciseness :** Letters should be brief and to the point. This quality can be achieved by the writer if he has extensive vocabulary and mastery over the subject. It should, however, be remembered that brevity or conciseness must not be resorted to at the cost of clarity.

(f) **Courtesy :** The letter-writer must be courteous and sympathetic. A courteous letter not only improves the image of the organisation but also makes a lot of friends. This, in turn, helps the organisation to secure good business.

(g) **Completeness :** The letter should be complete in all respects so that the recipient gets the message properly and is not required to write back for further clarifications. The writer must know what he is to write and for whom it is meant.

(h) **Form and Arrangement :** The letter must, as far as possible, conform to the conventional form and arrangement. A letter comprises : (i) Heading, (ii) Inside Address, (iii) Salutation, (iv) Body and (v) Complimentary close.

APPLICATION & APPOINTMENT LETTERS

Q. 3. An application for the Personal Assistant to Company Secretary. (C.U. 1969)

Ans. :

The Personnel Manager

Indian Tobacco Ltd.

Chowringhee Road

Calcutta 700016

Re : Recruitment of a Personal Assistant to the Company Secretary

Dear Sir

With reference to your advertisement in The Statesman of 31st December 1999, I would like to offer myself as a candidate for the above post in your much-esteemed and ever-expanding organisation.

As regards academic attainments, I passed the School Final Examination of the Board of Secondary Education, West Bengal, in 1970 and was placed in the First Division. Thereafter, I passed the Pre-University Examination in 1971 from Prafulla Chandra College, being placed in the First Division. I passed the B.Com. (Hons.) Examination from the same College in 1974 and was placed in the Second Class.

I passed the Diploma Examinations in Shorthand and Type-writing in 1975 with a speed of 120 words and 50 words per minute, respectively. I am now fifty-one and possess a good physique.

As to my experience, I have been in the employ of Messrs. Andrew Yule & Company Ltd. since 2-1-76. I joined the Company as a Stenographer to their Secretary and in 1981 I was promoted to the post of Personal Secretary to the Managing Director of the Company. During my 24 years' stay with the Company, I have got plenty of opportunities of learning the routine secretarial work.

Consequent upon disposal of some of the major units, the volume of business previously handled by the Company has been reduced to half. As a result, the scope of my further advancement and promotion appears to be quite limited. Hence, I am looking for a change. A certificate from my present employer is enclosed.

In view of the above, I shall be obliged if you kindly consider my candidature for the post and call me for an interview.

Thanking you in anticipation,

Yours faithfully
Tapan Mukherjee

Address :
18/17A Fern Road, Calcutta 700019
Dated the 1st January 2000

Q. 4. Draft an advertisement inviting applications for the post of the Secretary of a Club. (C.U. 1968)

Ans.

12th January 2000

Mohun Bagan Athletic Club
Calcutta 700001

Applications are invited by the President of the above club for the post of a Secretary. The candidates must be Graduates of any Indian university and should have not less than 10 years' experience of which 5 years must be as Secretary/Assistant Secretary of any reputed sports club. The desired age group is 35-40 years. Salary will be commensurate with qualifications and experience. Those drawing less than Rs. 10,000/- per month need not apply. Please apply within a fortnight giving names of two persons to whom references, if required, may be made as to your antecedents.

Q. 5. Draft an application for the post of a Company Secretary or a Private Secretary. (C.U. 1962)

Or, Draft an application for the post of Deputy Secretary of a public company which has been recently advertised. (C.U. 1981)

Ans.

The Managing Director
Andrew Yule and Co. Ltd.
8 Clive Row
Calcutta 700001

Re : Application for the post of a Company Secretary

Dear Sir

With reference to your advertisement in The Statesman of date, I would like to offer myself as a candidate for the above post in your much-esteemed and ever-expanding organisation.

A resumé of my particulars is appended for favour of your kind perusal and sympathetic consideration :

Name	: S. K. Debanth
Address	: 10 Chandra Mandal Lane, Calcutta 700026.
Date of birth	: 1.2.1947
Educational Qualifications	: Passed the M.Com. Examination from the Calcutta University in 1969 and was placed in the Second Class. Passed the B.A. (Special) Examination from the same University in 1970.
Professional Qualifications	: Passed the Final Examination of the Institute of Company Secretaries of India in 1972 and obtained its Associateship in 1974. Passed the LL.B. Examination from the University of Calcutta in 1970, being placed in the Second Class. Passed the Final Examination of the Indian Institute of Bankers in 1970. Passed the Final Examination of the Institute of Cost and Works Accountants of India in 1974 and obtained its Associateship in 1975.
Experience	: About five years' experience in the State Bank of India from 2.1.69 as a Junior Officer. After leaving the Bank, I joined Messrs. Karamchand Thapar Ltd. on the 3rd March 1974 as its Assistant Secretary and was promoted to Dy. Secretary on 3.3.1988. During my twentyfive years' stay with this company, I had to act as the Secretary during the absence of the permanent incumbent.

Reasons for
Change : For the last few years, there has been a declining trend in the volume of business handled by the company. Consequently, scope of my further prospects in the company is very much limited. Hence this application.

Present
Emoluments : Rs. 17,500/- per month, plus attractive perquisites.

Reference : Shri N. K. Bose, President, Institute of Company Secretaries of India, 1 Rani Jhansi Road, New Delhi 110055.

Thanking you in anticipation of your consideration,

Yours faithfully

Dated the 1st February 2000 S.K. Debnath

Q. 6. Draft a letter offering an appointment to an individual in the post of a Company Secretary in Messrs. Andrew Yule & Co. Ltd.

Ans.

Andrew Yule & Co. Ltd.

Shri D. Dasgupta, A.C.S.
229 Rash Behari Avenue
Calcutta 700019
No. PER/2001/2000

Yule House
8 Clive Row
Calcutta 700001
January 20, 2000

Re : Company Secretary

Dear Sir

With reference to your application dated the 24th December 1999 and subsequent interview, we are pleased to offer you employment as our Company Secretary. The terms and conditions of the appointment are embodied in the Memorandum which was handed over to you at the time of last interview. If you are agreeable to accept the employment, may we request you to join us as early as possible, but in any case not later than two months?

Thanking you,

Yours faithfully
for Andrew Yule & Co. Ltd.
P. R. Roy
Chief, Administration & Personnel

OFFICE ACCOMMODATION

Q. 7. Draft an advertisement offering office accommodation in a multi-storied building nearing completion. **(C.U. 1967)**

Ans.

Cox & Pollock Pvt. Ltd.

Registered office :
10 Rowdon Street
Calcutta 700016
Phone 244-4488 (3 Lines)
Dated the 1st February 2000

The Editor
The Statesman
Chowringhee Square
Calcutta 700001

Dear Sir

We shall be glad if you will please arrange to publish the enclosed advertisement in the 'Office Accommodation' column of your esteemed daily dated the 3rd February 2000.

The relative bill may please be forwarded to us for payment in the usual manner.

Thanking you,

Yours faithfully
for Cox & Pollock Pvt. Ltd.
Amar Banerjee
Director

Enclosure : One

Advertisement for Publication

A multi-storied building equipped with automatic lifts, 24-hours' water supply, underground car parking space, etc. is nearing completion in Park Street area. Each floor has a covered space of 1,500 square feet and will be available from 01.03.2000 at a monthly rental of Rs. 9/75P per square foot. Suitable for banks and showrooms. Offers in sealed covers with detailed particulars along with the Bank reference may please be made to Messrs. Cox & Pollock Pvt. Limited, 10 Rowdon Street, Calcutta 700016, within a fortnight from the date of this advertisement.

LETTERS OF INTRODUCTION AND LETTERS OF CREDIT

Q. 8. Draft a letter recommending a business friend for advice and guidance.

Ans.

Unique Traders

1 Unique Park
Calcutta 700034
3rd January 2000

Messrs, Batliboi & Co.
1 Backbay Reclamation
Bombay 400021

Re : Letter of Introduction

Dear Sirs

This is to introduce Shri L. Purohit, bearer of this letter, who is our Chief Sales Organiser for whole of North Bengal. He is leaving Calcutta today for an extensive tour of North Bengal in connection with popularising our products. We shall be glad if you will kindly extend your valuable advice with regard to our prospective customers to Shri Purohit.

In this connection, should Shri Purohit require any money, we open a credit to him to the extent of Rs. 50,000/- (Rupees Fifty Thousand only) with any of the undernoted firms. The money should be advanced to him only against receipt in duplicate bearing Shri Purohit's signature, one of which will be retained by you and the other forwarded to us. You may cover yourself for the money so paid together with incidental expenses by placing the amount to the debit of our account with you. This letter will remain in force up to 15th March 2000.

We shall keep ourselves ready to reciprocate similar service in case of your need.

Thanking you,

Yours faithfully
for Indian Glasses
D. Das
Partner

Specimen signature of
Shri L. Purohit

To : 1. Messrs. Raju and Co., Siliguri, W.B.

2. Messrs. Chatterjee and Sons, Station Road, Jalpaiguri.

3. Messrs. Sen Brothers, Cooch Behar.

Q. 9. Draft a letter of recommendation as the Director of Messrs. Castiplast Co. Private Limited to another employer.

Ans.

Castiplast Co. Pvt. Ltd.

No. CCPL/GEN/421

1 Love lane
Calcutta 700001
13th January 2000

Messrs. Modi Electronics Ltd.
2 Clive Row
Calcutta 700001

Re : Letter of Introduction

Dear Sirs,

We take the opportunity of introducing to you Shri Nara Narayan Naha, the bearer of this letter, who is our Chief Sales Supervisor for the whole of Assam. In view of the chaotic conditions now obtaining in Assam, we are left with no alternative but to close down our Regional Office in Guwahati. As such, we recommend him for a similar post in your company.

Shri Naha joined us as a Sales Trainee in 1990. He now holds a key position in our Sales Department. He has come up to this position because of his sincerity, intelligence, drive and honesty. He is capable of shouldering any responsibility which is entrusted to him. He comes of a respectable family and bears a good moral character.

In the light of the above, we can safely recommend him for any suitable post in your company. We shall highly appreciate your help to Shri Naha in the matter.

Thanking you,

Yours faithfully
for Castiplast Co. Pvt. Ltd.
R. Karmakar
Director

LETTERS OF ENQUIRY

Q. 10 & 11. Draft an enquiry to be issued to approved suppliers of stationery articles to be issued in an office. (C.U. 1999, 1964)

Ans.

Tribeni Tissues Ltd.

Regd. Office :
6 Middleton Street
Calcutta 700071
Dated the 5th January 2000

Messrs. Eveready Stationers
161/1 Biplabi Rashbehari Bose Road
Calcutta 700001

Enquiry for Stationery Articles

Dear Sirs

We shall be glad if you will please arrange to furnish us with your quotation for supply of the undernoted items of stationery. The quotation should be sent in a sealed cover within a fortnight from the date of this letter.

1. 1,000 Reams Double Demy White Print Paper (Weight 17 kgs).
2. 2,000 bottles (size —5 litre) Ink (Royal Blue).
3. Black Carbon Paper (13" x 8") —100 boxes.
4. Vandite Typewriting Eraser—100 numbers.
5. Envelopes—white (a) size 9" x 4" and (b) 6" x 3".
6. Gems clip (Standard size)—100 Boxes.
7. Pin (Standard size)—100 boxes.

If your rates prove to be really competitive, we may place a substantial order of repetitive nature with you.

Thanking you,

Yours faithfully
for Tribeni Tissues Ltd.
Dulal Kumar Das
Secretary

Q. 12. Draft an enquiry for the supply of uniforms to peons and bearers of a large commercial establishment. (C.U. 1968)

Ans.

Brooke Bond India Limited

Regd. Office :
12 Shakespeare Sarani
Calcutta 700017
Dated the 1st February 2000

No. BB/GEN/75/201

Messrs. Eveready Stores Private Limited

31F Vijay Nagar

Delhi 110009

Sub : Supply of Uniform — Enquiry

Dear Sirs

We shall appreciate your submitting to us your quotation for supply of the following items of uniform for use of our Class IV staff :

Coarse Quality Black-coloured
Woollen full-pants (trousers) 500 pieces
Woollen full shirts 500 pieces
(Specifications for the items are enclosed)

Your quotation should reach us within a period of three weeks from the date of this letter. As the items are meant for coming winter, your supplies should reach us latest by the end of September, 2000 in the event of our placing the order with you.

Please treat this letter as very urgent and send your quotation in a sealed cover marked 'Quotation for Uniform'.

Thanking you,

Yours faithfully
For Brooke Bond India Limited
S. K. Chatterjee
Chief Purchase Officer

Enclosure : Specifications of Uniform

TRADE/STATUS ENQUIRIES

Q. 13. Draft a letter of enquiry concerning the status of a firm.

Ans.

India Trading Company

3 Mangoe Lane
Calcutta 700001
1st February 2000

Messrs. Textile Corporation
Colaba
Mumbai 400005

Dear Sirs

We have received an order worth Rs. 10,00,000/- (Rupees ten lakhs only) from a firm of your city whose particulars are given in the enclosed slip. As the firm is quite unknown to us, we desire to ensure about their credit-worthiness and reputation before establishing any business relations. We would deem it a favour if you will kindly arrange to furnish us with a report on the firm. We assure that any information supplied by you will be treated in the strictest confidence and we shall be glad to reciprocate with similar service should such an occasion arise.

Thanking you,

Yours faithfully
for India Trading Company
N. D. Bhowmick
Partner

Messrs, Elite Traders
Colaba, Mumbai 400005

Q. 14. Draft a reply to a letter of enquiry conveying favourable information.
(V.U. 1987)

Ans.

Electornics Corporation

Colaba, Mumbai 400005
10th March, 2000

The Spectrum Electronics
75/57 S. N. Roy Road
Calcutta 700038

Credit Report

Dear Sirs

With reference to your letter of the 1st March 2000, concerning the financial status of Messrs. Elite Electronics, we have to advise that the firm, which is a proprietary concern, enjoys good credit in the local market. Shri A. Agarwala, the proprietor of the firm, is a highly respectable and experienced businessman. As far as we know, he can be relied upon to honour his commitments. But, as you are aware, chances of sudden reverses in the fortune of a business cannot be ruled out.

The information supplied to you is without any responsibility and obligation on our part.

Yours faithfully
for Electornics Corporation
D. Gutta
Partner

Q. 15. Draft a reply to a letter of enquiry conveying unfavourable information.
(V.U. 1987)

Ans.

Electronics Corporation

Colaba, Mumbai 400005
13th January 2000

The Spectrum Electronics
75/57 S. N. Roy Road
Calcutta 700038

Re : Credit Report

Dear Sirs

With reference to your letter of the 1st January 2000, concerning the financial status of Messrs. Elite Electronics, we regret that we cannot give you the assurance you seek regarding the firm. It is a fact that once it was a reputed firm of the city, but, consequent upon death of one of its partners, Shri M. M. Mittal, the rosy picture has completely changed to a gloomy one. We have had several dealings with it during the last year and most of the payments from it are still outstanding. Its present financial position is not at all sound. Besides, during the current year, the firm is reported to have suffered a huge loss on an export deal.

In the circumstances, we cannot recommend any credit transactions with it.

We shall appreciate your treating the information as strictly confidential.

Yours faithfully
for Electronics Corporation
D. Debnath
Partner

LETTERS OF OFFER, ACCEPTANCE AND ORDER

Q. 16. Draft a letter of offer to a retailer.

Ans.

The People's Pharmaceuticals

39 Broad Street
Calcutta 700019
1st March 2000

Messrs. Elite Stores
Jalpaiguri
West Bengal

Re : 'Clean-well' — Liquid Cleaning Soap

Dear Sirs

We have pleasure in sending you today a sample packet of 'Clean-well' which has recently been introduced by us in the market. The product is the result of a number of years' tireless efforts of our highly qualified research staff.

We forward herewith a few copies of our leaflets so that you can distribute the same for the purpose of advertisement. It will be observed from the leaflets that the various qualities associated with the product are really unique. We also enclose a few copies of the price lists and you will appreciate that the prices quoted are really competitive.

As per our terms, you will be allowed two months' credit and discount of 20% on catalogue price.

Thanking you and looking forward to a mutually beneficial business relation we remain,

Yours faithfully
for The People's Pharmaceuticals
Ratan Roy
Managing Partner

Enclosures : As above

Q. 17. A letter to the Managing Director recommending acceptance of a quotation though it is a bit higher than other quotations giving convincing reasons for your recommendations. (C.U. 1970)

Ans.

The Managing Director
Debnath Enterprises Ltd.
38 B.B.D Bag
Calcutta 700001

Regd. Office :
3 Middleton Street
Calcutta 700071
Date : 02.01.2000

Re : Acceptance of Quotation
Purchase of Office Stationery

Dear Sir

With reference to the above, I have carefully examined all the quotations received from various parties. Though the lowest quotation has been offered by Messrs. India Trading Co., I consider the offer from Messrs. Eastern Stationers (P) Ltd., (even if a bit higher), may be accepted by us on the following grounds :

(i) Messrs Eastern Stationers (P) Ltd. is a renowned concern and is known to honour its commitments.

(ii) Some of the items of stationery which are manufactured/supplied by it are surely of better quality than those offered by Messrs. India Trading Company.

(iii) The former's credit terms are also more liberal inasmuch as payment may be deferred up to 6 months from the date of delivery.

In view of the above, my recommendation goes in favour of the Eastern Stationers (P) Ltd. I, however, await your instructions in the matter.

Yours faithfully
S. Natarajan
Purchase Manager

Q. 18. Draft a suitable reply to an offer.

Or, Draft a letter for placing orders for cleansing soap of different qualities.

Ans.

Elite Stores

Station Road
Jalpaiguri
West Bengal
January 2, 2000

The People's Stationers
39 Broad Street
Calcutta 700019

Re : Order No. ES/399/92

Dear Sirs,

With reference to your letter of the 1st January, we are pleased to place with you the following order for your immediate execution :

Serial No.	Item	Quantity
1.	'Clean-well' — Major	100 Packets
2.	do — Economy	50 Packets
3.	do — Special	30 Packets

Please confirm your acceptance by return of post and advise us as to the date by which the consignment will reach us.

Thanking you,

Yours faithfully
for Elite Stores
Bidyut Mukherjee
Proprietor

Q. 19. Draft a letter placing an order with Messrs. Robinson & Co. Ltd., Bombay, for supply of 1,000 T.V. sets, stressing upon them that if the order is not executed within 60 days, the order will be treated as cancelled. (C.U. 1983)

Ans.

Spectrum Electronics

75/57 S. N. Roy Road
Calcutta 700038
February 2, 2000

Messrs. Robinson & Co. Ltd.
Ballard Estate
Mumbai

Subject : **Supply of 1,000 T.V. sets**

Dears Sirs

With reference to your quotation dated the 24th January 2000, we are pleased to place with you an order for supply of 1,000 black-and-white standard 'Robin' brand T.V. sets.

The goods must be securely packed and comprehensively insured before despatch. Please note that the consignment must reach Calcutta within 60 days from the date of this letter as the goods are meant for the festive season.

In case of your failure to comply with this stipulation regarding time of delivery, we will be constrained to cancel the order.

You may send your bill together with the documents to our bankers, State Bank of India, Chowringhee Branch, Calcutta 700071, for payment.

Please confirm your acceptance within 15 days hereof and advise us as to the date by which the consignment is expected in Calcutta.

Yours faithfully
for Spectrum Electronics
Bani Debnath
Partner

CONFIRMATION, EXECUTION, REFUSAL OR CANCELLATION OF ORDERS

Q. 20. Draft a letter acknowledging receipt of order, advising despatch and requesting early remittance.

Ans.

J. R. Batliboi & Company

23 Ganesh Ch. Avenue
Calcutta 700013
14th January 2000

Messrs. Tiger Lily Press
40/ H Raja Santosh Road
Calcutta 700027

Your Order No. TLP/121/75 dated 31.12.1999

Dear Sirs

While thanking you very much for your valued order for supply of a Heidelberg Automatic Platen Machine, we have to advise that the same has already been sent to you. We have entrusted the work of installing the machine in your factory to two of our senior technicians. We hope that the installation work will be over within three days and the machine will be ready for commercial run.

In this connection, we forward herewith our Bill No. JRB/MISC/77/555 dated the 12th January 2000 for Rs. 1,23,777/50 P. and shall appreciate your arranging for its early payment.

Assuring you of our best services,

Yours faithfully
for J. R. Batliboi & Company
P. Maity
Sales Manager

Q. 21. You have received a good order for such goods which are not in your stock. Draft a suitable reply to the indentor tactfully offering substitutes.

Ans.

Hind Trading Company

2 Clive Row
Calcutta 700001
21st January 2000

Messrs. Lux Traders
73 Unique Park
Calcutta 700034

Re : Your Order No. LS/120 for 1,000 pieces of Malay Soap

Dear Sirs

Thank you very much for your order dated the 15th January 2000. Unfortunately, we do not have any stock of this brand currently. Due to some unavoidable reasons, it may not be possible for us to produce this brand in the near future. In the circumstances, we can offer you a substitute— 'Janata Brand'— which is equally good, if not better than, 'Malay Brand'. The price of this brand is Rs. 9.75 per piece, less usual discount. We hope that this brand too will also be equally popular within a short time. We send you herewith a few pieces of this soap as samples.

We await your valued order for this brand.

Yours faithfully
for Hind Trading Company
Nataraj Gupta
Proprietor

Q. 22. You have received an order from a firm of Patna where you have exclusive agent. Draft a letter tactfully refusing the order on technical ground.

Ans.

Gupta Lighthouse Private Limited

Registered office :
111 Netaji Subhas Road
Calcutta 700001
31st January 2000

Messrs. M. L. Halder & Co.
Station Road
Patna

Your Order No. MHL/120/69

Dear Sirs

Thank you very much for your above order and your keen interest in our goods. We, however, regret our inability to accept the order for our direct exceution as we have already given our exclusive agency for the state of Bihar to Messrs. Ahluwalia & Sons, Budh Marg, Patna 1.

In the circumstances, we are forwarding your order to Messrs. Ahluwalia & Sons who will surely contact you in the matter shortly.

Should you experience any difficulty in obtaining the goods, we shall appreciate your contacting us without any hesitation.

Thanking you,

Yours faithfully
for Gupta Lighthouse Pvt. Ltd.
P. K. Chakraborty
Sales Manager

Q. 23. Draft a letter cancelling your order for woollen garments due to inordinate delay in supply.

Ans.

Wool House

Al, New Market
Calcutta 700016
3rd January 2000.

Messrs. Srinivasan Woollen Mills Ltd.
Station Road
Amritsar

Re : Our Order No. WH/111 dated 04.05.1999

Dear Sirs

We have to advise that the above order was placed with you about eight months ago. You perhaps remember that one of the stipulations of the order was that the goods should be supplied latest by the 31st October 1999. During this interlude, we have neither received the goods nor heard anything from you explaining the reasons for the inordinate delay. Due to persistent pressure from our customers, we had no alternative but to procure the goods from other sources.

In the circumstances, we are compelled to cancel our above order.

Yours faithfully
for Wool House
Bejoy K. Modi
Proprietor

CLAIMS, COMPLAINTS AND ADJUSTMENTS

Q. 24. Draft a letter from a manufacturer to a dealer suitably making out the points : third reminder; default; breach of dealership contract; further supplies being stopped; quality complaint may be settled on arbitration; immediate payment with interest for business continuance. (Assume form and names as may appear realistic).

(C.U. 1991, 1974)

Ans.

Hindusthan Lever Limited

Regd. Office :
1 Brabourne Road
Calcutta 700001
Dated 12.02.2000

Messrs. North Bengal Stores
Station Road
Jalpaiguri
West Bengal

Re : Breach of Dealership Contract

Dear Sirs

Further to our letters dated the 15.01.2000 and 31.01.2000 asking for settlement of your account, we regret to point out that you have neither sent any remittance nor cared to reply. According to the terms and conditions of dealership, you were to remit the payment for supplies made to you by 30.11.99. We would have stopped subsequent supplies but, in view of your past dealings with us, we did not take recourse to this drastic action and have supplied you in December also.

You will quite agree that you have contravened the terms of dealership. In the circumstances, before cancelling the dealership, we offer you another opportunity to set the position right. Now you will have to arrange for payment of all dues inclusive of interest which works out to Rs. 90,550/- within ten days from the date of this letter. On receipt of your payment, we will, however, be prepared to settle your complaint as to quality of the product by way of arbitration.

In the event of your failure to comply with our instructions, we would be constrained to cancel the dealership and take necessary steps to enforce our payment.

Please treat this letter as very urgent.

Yours faithfully
for Hindusthan Lever Limited
D. Debnath
Sales Manager

Q. 25. Draft a representation to the General Manager, South Eastern Railways, for waiving demurrage for the period of strike by Railway employees. (C.U. 1974)

Ans.

Gupta Lighthouse Company

1 Netaji Subhas Raod
Calcutta 700001
10th January 2000

The General Manager
South Eastern Railway
16 Strand Road
Calcutta 700001

Re : R.R. No. 00011 Dated 01.01.2000 —Waiver of Demurrage

Dear Sir

We would like to bring to your kind notice that a consignment of electrical goods was booked by our Cuttack Office on 1st January 2000 under the captioned RR number and the same arrived at Howrah Station on the 2nd January 2000. On receipt of the advice, we sent our men to collect the goods on the 3rd January 2000. But as the Railwaymen were on strike from the 3rd January, delivery could not be taken. A perusal of your advertisement which came out in today's Statesman makes us to believe that your normal working will resume shortly.

As a matter of rule, we are required to pay demurrage for the period from 3rd January to the date of actual delivery; but payment of demurrage by a small firm like ours is surely a heavy burden. Besides, the delay in taking delivery stemmed from the fact that the Railwaymen went on strike which was, you would no doubt agree, no fault of ours.

In the circumstances, we shall deem it a great favour if you will kindly arrange to waive the demurrage that we are supposed to pay.

We await your early and favourable reply.

Yours faithfully
for Gupta Lighthouse Co.,
B. M. Bhide
Proprietor

Q. 26. A letter from a manufacturer-customer regretting failure of his supplier of some critical materials to supply in time and claiming compensation for the loss sustained in making local purchase at higher prices. (C.U. 1972)

Ans.

Chemical Engineering Co. Limited

Regd. Office :
1 Prince Anwar Shah Road
Calcutta 700033
2nd January 2000

Messrs Indian Chemical Industries Ltd.
30 Mount Road
Madras 600001

For kind attention of Shri A. K. Sen, Sales Manager

Dear Sirs

Re : Delay in Supply of Caustic Soda

Will you please refer to our order No. CECL/99/10 dated 30.11.99 for supply of 10 tonnes of caustic soda and your letter of acceptance dated 15.12.99? As per our instruction and your assurance, you were to supply the above item latest by the 31.12.99. Subsequently, we entered into an export contract with Messrs. Mitsubishi Co., Japan, and, accordingly, shipping space was booked. We had to compensate the Shipping Company for cancellation of our booking of the shipping space as we did not get the material from you and, consequently, could not stick to our production schedule and export programme. Besides, our factory, having a labour strength of 2,000, would have been closed had we not purchased the material from a local manufacturer. You may recollect that you undertook to supply the material @ Rs. 1,500/- per tonne; whereas we had to purchase it @ Rs. 1,650/- per tonne!

In the circumstances, we have no option but to cancel the order and ask for compensation of the loss (Rs. 150/- × 10 tonnes = Rs. 1,500/- sustained by us for your fault. We shall be glad if you will please arrange for payment of Rs. 1,500/- within a fortnight from the date of this letter. Otherwise, we will be left with no alternative but to take recourse to legal action.

Yours faithfully
for Chemical Engg. Company Ltd.
V. Subba Rao
Director (Commercial)

Q. 27. A claim to be made on Railways for shortage found in consignment and for which a short certificate had been obtained at the time of delivery. (C.U. 1977, 1973)

Ans.

Caxton and Company Pvt. Ltd.

Registered Office :
1B Ashutosh Mukherjee Road
Calcutta 700020
Date 02.01.2000

The Superintendent (Claims)
South Eastern Railways
16 Strand Road
Calcutta 700001

Re : Claim on account of shortage of goods under R.R No. 0012 dated 20.12.1999 from Puri to Howrah

Dear Sir

With reference to above, we have to advise that 1,000 cases containing printed cartons were despatched by our Puri Branch Office under the above-noted Railway Receipt (R.R.) but, while taking delivery, only 950 cases were handed over to us by your Goods Office. We were, however, given a certificate to this effect duly signed by the Station Superintendent, Howrah. We forward herewith the short certificate in original to justify our claim. Besides, an invoice for Rs. 50,000/- being the value of 50 cases @ Rs. 1,000/-, is enclosed.

In this connection, we have to state that the goods in question are urgently required for delivery to Messrs. Union Carbide Ltd. In the circumstances, unless we receive the cases within a forthnight, we would have no option but to request you to pay the amount of Rs. 50,000/- at your earliest as compensation.

Thanking you,

Yours faithfully
for Caxton & Company Pvt. Ltd.
K.P. Nath
Secretary

Enclosures : Two

Q. 28. Draft a letter to a supplier complaining about the quality of materials supplied and asking for suitable remedy. (C.U. 1967)

Or, Draft a letter to a supplier complaining about inferior quality of goods supplied and asking for suitable remedy. (C.U. 1997, 1980)

Ans.

B. C. Maity and Company

94 Premchand Baral Street
Calcutta 700012
2nd January 2000

Messrs. Gillanders Arbuthnot & Co. Ltd.
Gillander House
1 Netaji Subhas Road
Calcutta 700001

Re : Supply of inferior quality of tea
Our Order No. BCM/74-75 dated 20.12.1999

Dear Sirs

We acknowledge with thanks receipt of your consignment containing 100 chest of Dooars Pekoe Tea (Broken) on the 30th December, 1999. In this connection, we regret to point out that the quality supplied by you appears to be of second grade whereas the quality ordered for by us was of first grade.

In the circumstances, we have to advise that this quality can be accepted by us provided, of course, you allow us a discount of 20% on the price quoted by you. Alternatively, we would have no option but to return the chests at your cost. Meanwhile, we are holding the goods at your risk and responsibility.

If the first option is acceptable to you, we will be pleased to place with you our original order for immediate execution.

We await your immediate advice in the matter.

Yours faithfully
for B. C. Maity and Company
J.K. Kanjilal
Partner

Q. 29. A letter to a supplier complaining about shortage in quantity and inferior quality of materials supplied and claiming suitable remedy. **(C.U. 1988, 1967)**

Ans.

Makaibari Tea Company Pvt. Ltd.

Registered Office :
4/1 Madan Street
Calcutta 700013
5th January 2000

The Bengal Dooars Tea Company Limited
Station Road
Jalpaiguri
West Bengal

Supply of tea against our order No. MTC/100 dated 25.12.1999 — Shortage in quantity and inferior quality of tea

Dear Sirs

While acknowledging receipt of your consignment No. BDT/SI/75 dated 1st January 2000 for 50 chests of Dooars Broken Pekoe Tea, we thank you very much for your expeditious execution of our above order. In this context, we have to point out that the quality supplied to us is undoubtedly inferior to that of the sample forwarded to us along with your quotation. You will surely appreciate that, under the circumstances, we cannot pay you for the supply at the rate previously agreed upon by us. So we are constrained to inform you that, unless you allow us a discount of 20% on the quoted price, we will have no option but to return the goods at your cost.

Please advise us by return as to what you would like us to do in respect of this supply.

Moreover, as per agreement, each chest was to contain 1,000 kgs of tea. Though you have billed for 50,000 kgs. (50 Chests × 1,000 kgs), we have actually received 49,500 kgs. Out of the total number of boxes, two boxes were seriously damaged due to rough handling in the course of transit and this appears to have resulted in the loss of 500 kgs of tea.

We return herewith your bill which may please be resubmitted to us for payment making proportionate deduction for loss of 500 kgs of tea.

Please treat this letter as extremely urgent.

Yours faithfully
Nishan Halder
Purchase Manager

Enclosure : As above

Q. 30. Write a letter of complaint into consideration of the following points :

(a) goods are of inferior quality

(b) shortage in weight.

Ans.

Moonlight Printers

1 S. P. Mukherjee Road
Calcutta-700026
January 14, 2000

Messrs. Seal and Co.
13 Moti Seal Street
Calcutta 700013

Sub. : Order No. CAX/20/75/dated 15.12.1999

Dear Sirs

Thank you very much for your prompt despatch of consignment containing 100 drums of varnish and 10 drums of thinner.

But, we regret to point out that the qualities supplied by you largely differ from the samples which prompted us to place the order with you. The varnish and thinner appear to be too thick and these are sure to render our printing faulty and uneconomical. In the circumstances, we can accept the materials only in the event of your allowing us 10% discount off the invoice price; otherwise, we would have no option but to retain them at the sole risk and responsibility of yours.

In this connection, we have to point out that 10 drums of varnish are found to be short of weight by 1 kg each. The shortage, you will surely appreciate, is too heavy to be ignored. We shall, therefore, request you to kindly send us a credit note in respect of the shortage in question.

Yours faithfully
for Moonlight Printers
Sona Dantewala
Proprietor

Q. 31. Draft a suitable reply to the above letter (or a specimen letter for adjustment).

Ans.

Seal and Company

13 Moti Seal Street
Calcutta 700013
Date : January 7, 2000.

The Moonlight Printers
1 S. P. Mukherjee Road
Calcutta 700026

Re : Complaint

Dear Sirs

We acknowledge receipt of your letter of the 1st January and note contents with regret. This is perhaps for the first time that we had to receive a complaint from you. On receipt of your letter, we had conducted a detailed investigation into the matter and our findings are given below :

(i) The consignment in question was meant for another indentor. Due to oversight, wrong label was pasted and the materials were consigned to you.

(ii) Regarding shortage in weight in some of the drums, we have to point out that due to your urgency we had to procure quite a few drums from another local supplier. In a hurry, we could not check up the weight of the drums and consigned them as they were received. We have already taken up the matter with the supplier seriously.

In the circumstances, we would request you to accept the materials and pay for the quantity actually determined by you less an allowance of 15%.

Incidentally, while apologising for this unfortunate mistake, we assure you of our best endeavours to prevent recurrence of this type of event.

We once again regret the inconvenience caused to you.

Yours faithfully
for Seal and Company
D. Debnath
Partner

Q. 32. A letter to a supplier cancelling an order due to failure to supply within the period specified in the order and reserving the right to claim payment of difference in price, if any, arising out of purchase from other sources. (C.U. 1996, 1989, 1969)

Ans.

Samp Enterprises

11 Basanta Bose Road
Calcutta 700026
Phone : 4757310
November 15, 1999

Messrs. Wool House Pvt. Ltd.
Ludhiana
Punjab

Re : Cancellation of our order No. SE/100/1993 dated the 1st August 1999 for supply of 1,000 pieces of woollen garments

Dear Sirs

Would you refer to our above order wherein it was specifically stated that goods in question should reach us latest by the 15th October 1999, so as to enable us to sell in the Puja Market? Now the market for winter too is almost over. Meanwhile, we had sent to you as many as three telegrams — none of which has been replied to by you! We had, therefore, to make local purchase at higher prices to keep our commitments. The excess payment so made by us is being calculated by our Accounts Department.

Under the circumstances, we shall appreciate your treating the order as cancelled and arranging for payment to us the excess amount which we have paid for your fault. The relative bill will be forwarded to you within a week for payment.

Yours faithfully
for Samp Enterprises
P. Maity
Proprietor

Q. 33. Messrs. Dutta and Company Ltd. of Calcutta placed an order with the Peerless Paint Co. Ltd. of Mumbai for supply of paints. The materials ordered were not supplied by the latter on due date; nor had they sent any reply to reminders given by the former.

Draft (a) a letter on behalf of Messrs. Dutta & Co. Ltd. giving notice of cancellation of the order unless the materials are delivered within fifteen days from the date of issue of the letter, and

(b) the reply of the Peerless Paint Co. Ltd. informing that the materials ordered had already been despatched. (C.U. 1995, 1982)

Ans. (a)

Dutta & Co. Ltd.

75/57 S. N. Roy Road
Calcutta 700038
6th March 2000

The Chief Executive
Peerless Paint Co. Ltd.
Sassoon Dock, Colaba
Mumbai 400005

Re : Supply of Paints

Dear Sir

Please refer to our order No. DCL/1110 dated the 20th November 1999 and reminder No. DCL/R/3009 dated the 28th December 1999.

2. You will surely recall that one of the most important conditions of our order was 'to supply the goods within 30 days from the date of order'. On expiry of this period, we had sent a reminder to you on the 28th December 1999 requesting immediate delivery. We were very much disappointed when our reminder too did not evoke any response from you. This is not expected from a company of your repute. As a result of non-delivery of the goods by you, we are losing our goodwill and image to our valued customers.

3. In the above circumstances, unless the goods are delivered within fifteen days hereof, we would be left with no option but to ask you to treat our order as cancelled.

Please treat the letter as extremely urgent and send your confirmation, or otherwise, by telephone/fax/express telegram.

Yours faithfully
for Dutta & Co. Ltd.
Sunayana Halder
Chief Executive

(b) Reply to the above letter

Peerless Paint Co. Ltd.

Sassoon Dock
Colaba, Mumbai 400005
2nd January 2000

The Chief Executive
Dutta & Co. Ltd.
75/57 S. N. Roy Road
Calcutta 700038

Re : Supply of Paints

Dear Sir

With reference to your letter of the 1st instant, we confirm having sent the following telegram to you on date :

"GOODS DESPATCHED ON SECOND JANUARY DELAY REGRETTED. LETTER FOLLOWS."

We sincerely regret our inability to supply the goods ordered by you in time. This is mainly because of the fact that all on a sudden the workers and other employees of our factory at Pune went on strike as we could not settle their wage revision immediately. We discussed the issue with the representatives of their union and wanted some time, but they were adamant and went on strike as from the 31st October 1999. The factory started working again as from the 25th December only. As, during the period of strike, tension was high around the factory premises, we did not dare enter our office. This, precisely, is the reason for your not getting the supply in time as well as any reply to your reminder.

Hope we have been able to clarify the position. You will kindly appreciate that the delay in supply was unavoidable and completely beyond our control. We, however, assure you of our best services at all times.

Yours faithfully
for Peerless Paints Co. Ltd.
Sumana Halder
Chief Executive

Q. 34. Draft a reminder to be issued to debtors of a firm drawing their attention to outstanding dues and requesting early settlement thereof, with particular reference to credit terms allowed to them. (C.U. 1964)

Ans.

Dipak Shilpa Sarjan

Reminder

29 Purna Das Road
Calcutta 700029
1st February 2000

Messrs. ....
....
....

Re : Your order No. 1XN dated 1.2.99 and
Our Invoice No. DSS/1947/520 dated 16.2.99 for Rs. 20,000/-

Dear Sirs

In the course of a routine scrutiny, it appears from our records that payment of the above invoice by you is already overdue and it is still outstanding in our books. This has, perhaps, been overlooked at your end. We shall be thankful if you will please look into the matter and arrange for payment at the earliest.

In this context, we have to state that our accounting year closes on the 31st March, and your kind cooperation in the matter will help us to prepare and compile our accounts quickly If you propose payment within a fortnight, you may deduct 10% as discount allowed to you and make the remittance accordingly.

Yours faithfully
for Dipak Shilpa Sarjan
Dipak Mitra
Partner

Q. 35. On behalf of the proprietor of a Textile Mill, write a letter to a stockist asking him as to why the goods ordered by him have not been lifted so far, explaining the consequences. (ICSI)

Ans.

Janata Textile Mills

1 Unique Road
Ahmedabad 1
26th February 2000

Ref. JIM/101/0/92
Messrs. Agarwala Textile Company
1 Armenian Street
Calcutta 700007

Re : Your Order No. 38/1999 dated 5.8.99
for100 bales of standard A-1 shirting

Dear Sirs

Your would recall that the captioned goods which were ordered by you on the 5th August 1999 were to be lifted latest by the 30th September, 1999. You have not done so till date. During the interlude, two reminders were sent advising you to lift the stock without any further loss of time. It is quite surprising as to why you have not even cared to reply to the letters.

In this connection, you are doubtless aware that our products have always been enjoying a very good market and — consequent upon export of our products last year — the demand has increased manifold. You will surely appreciate that it is your long and valuable association which has compelled us not to strike off your name from the list of our stockists. Needless to say, once we strike off from the list the name is never inserted/restored on any ground whatsoever.

In the circumstances, we give you another opportunity of lifting the stock within a fortnight hereof failing which we will be compelled to strike off your name from our list of stockists.

Yours faithfully
for Janata Textile Mills
J. K. Kanjilal
Sales Manager

Q. 36. One of the dealers of your product has suggested a reduction in the price of your product with a view to meeting the competition of rival manufacturers. As a Secretary of the manufacturing company, write a tactful reply stating why you cannot accept the dealer's suggestion. (ICSI)

Ans.

Limelight Toilet Soap Manufacturing Co. Ltd.

Regd. Office :
1 Connaught Place
New Delhi 110001
24th January 2000

Messrs. Bani Trading Company
32 Chittaranjan Avenue
Calcutta 700072

Re : Reduction in Price of 'Lyrill'

Dear Sirs

While acknowledging receipt of your letter of the 20th instant, we thank you very much for your valuable suggestion.

In this connection, we have to make the following observations :

(a) A break-up of the product cost reveals that in fixing the sale price we have kept a profit margin of 2% on cost of production. You are perhaps aware that we usually retain a profit of 10% to 15% on total cost of production.

(b) On the production front, no further cost reduction appears to be feasible immediately as measures for cost reduction have already been taken.

(c) A company of our status should not take recourse to price reduction without any cogent reason.

In view of the above, we would request you to take the following measures to tackle the situation :

(a) The consumers should be convinced that it is the quality which determines the price and, qualitywise, ours is undoubtedly the best available in the market.

(b) Our product lasts longer vis-a-vis other brands and the loss of scent due to use is also, comparatively, far less.

(c) Material content of our product is more as compared with other toilet soaps in the comparable price range as weight indicated on our brand is exlusive of packing materials unlike in the cases of other competitive brands.

Hope we have been able to explain the position to your entire satisfaction.

Yours faithfully
C. Bhatia
Secretary

Q. 37. Write a letter to X Transport Company, Mumbai, complaining that over a week ago you despatched a packet that has not reached its destination and asking for immediate attention to the matter. State to whom the package was addressed, where and when, and give a description. (ICSI)

Ans.

Caxton & Co. Ltd.

1B Ashutosh Mukherjee Road
Calcutta 700020
1st March 2000

Messrs. X Transport Company
120 Backbay Reclamation
Mumbai 400021

Your T.R. No. STC/40 dated 22.2.2000 :
Non-receipt of packet containing cover-pages of a book

Dear Sirs

With reference to above, I am surprised that the captioned packet which was personally handed over by me on 22.2.2000 to your Manager, City Office, Mumbai, has not reached Calcutta till date. In view of the urgency, special freight was paid to you. On my return to Calcutta, I came to know about it from the Manager of Publications to whom the packet was addressed. Now that the session for colleges is in full swing in West Bengal and the demand has reached its peak, we are not in a position to market the book but for the covers contained in the said packet.

In the circumstances, we are sure that you will appreciate our difficulties and pay immediate attention to the matter and ensure its immediate despatch. Meanwhile, please arrange to send a telegram/fax advising us as to the fate of the packet.

Yours faithfully
for Caxton & Co. Ltd.
Arun Ghosh
Managing Director

Q. 38. Your customer has placed an order with you for radios, but has now cancelled it. Write a letter to him persuading him to replace the order. (ICSI)

Ans.

Universal Radio Corporation

38 Chandni Chawk Street
Calcutta 700013
3rd March 2000

Ref. URC/0/94
Shri C. I. Grover
P-640 New Alipore
Calcutta 700053

Re : Your Order dated the 1st January 2000
for Janata Radio

Dear Sir

We are really taken aback to receive your letter of the 1st March 2000 advising us to treat your captioned order as cancelled. We believe that there is every reason for your being displeased with us due to the inordinate delay in sending you the radio. The delay stems from two facts. Firstly, due to a strike by the transport operators in Mumbai, the manufacturers could not send the consignments as per the agreed schedule of supply. Secondly, we were given to understand that the manufacturers would market Janata (Special) Radio by the 1st week of March at the same price at which they were selling the Janata Radio. Now that we have received the first consignment of the new brand consisting of 100 radios, we propose to send you one as soon as you are pleased to place the order with us once again.

In this connection, we once again regret the unwarranted delay and the inconvenience caused to you.

Assuring you of our best services at all times

Yours faithfully
for Universal Radio Corporation
Priyabrata Ghosh
Sales Manager

Q. 39. A manufacuring compnay which has agreed to deliver certain goods finds it difficult to give delivery within the specified time. Write a letter requesting extension of time. (ICSI)

Ans.

Indian Carbon Manufacturing Co. Ltd.

Registered Office :
1 Ashoke Avenue
Calcutta 700001
1.4.1999

Ref. IC/94/40

The Stockwell Stores Company
38 Begumpet
Hyderabad 500016

Your Order No. SSC/1999 for supply of Dry Cell Battery

Dear Sirs

With reference to your captioned order, we very much regret our inability to execute the same within the stipulated time consequent upon a recent directive issued by the Government. Accordingly, all the manufacturers of battery must earmark not less than 25% of their production during the period from 1st March to 30th April 1999 for export. In view of this, it would not be possible for us to execute your order before the end of June 1999.

You will appreciate that the circumstances are completely beyond our control and we have no alternative but to request you to bear this with us for the present.

In view of the conditions now obtaining, we request you to please advise us by return the extension of time as to supply of the goods in question.

Thanking you in anticipation of your favourable reply,

Yours faithfully
for Indian Carbon Manufacturing Co. Ltd.
Saroj Banerjee
Sales Manager

Q. 40. Draft a letter from a manufacturing company in Calcutta to its wholesale dealer in Bombay making out the points : orders cannot be executed according to schedule of delivery due to irregular power supply; no compensation claim entertainable for factors beyond control; contracted price to be maintained on confirming acceptance of full ordered quantity when supplied. (C.U. 1975)

Ans.

Rana Containers Ltd.

Registered Office :
57 V.I.P. Road
Calcutta 700054
20th November 1999

The Bombay Pharmaceuticals Ltd.
Fort
Mumbai 400001

Supply of Containers : Your Order No. 57/2995 dated 11.9.99

Dear Sirs

Please refer to your above order and our letter dated the 21st October 1999 confirming execution of your order by the end of November 1999.

You are doubtless aware of the power crisis the State of West Bengal has been passing through. The position has suddenly worsened from the second week of October — just after we had confirmed execution of your captioned order. Now it has been so acute that we hardly get adequate power to work for even twelve hours a day! Consequently, the volume of production has drastically come down to barely 50% of our usual production. This has thrown us completely out of gear and, despite our best endeavours, we are not in a position to stick to our production and delivery schedules. The State Government has recently communicated its inability to improve the position before January 2000. As the situation is completely beyond our control, we have no alternative but to request you to kindly bear with us.

In the circumstances, we can execute your order subject to the following additional conditions :

(i) Supplies will be made during March-April 2000.

(ii) We will not be liable to entertain you compensation claim, if any, for such factors which will be totally beyond our control.

(iii) The contract price must be maintained on confirming acceptance of full ordered quantity when supplied.

Please now advise us by return whether you are agreeable to accept the revised terms and conditions as outlined above.

We shall proceed further in the matter on hearing from you.

Yours faithfully
for Rana Containers Ltd.
H. R. Kamath
Director (Marketing)

Q. 41. POB Co. Ltd. could not pay their creditors XYZ Co. Ltd. Rs. 10,000 on the stipulated date, 14th March 2000. Draft a letter on behalf of POB Co. Ltd. requesting for extension of time by a month. **(V.U. 1991)**

Ans.

POB Co. Ltd.

Registered Office :
24 Park Street
Calcutta 700016
24th March 2000

The Managing Director
XYZ Co. Ltd.
Nestlés Apartment 3 'B'
Pandurang Budhkar Marg
Mumbai 400025

Dear Sir

Sub. : Payment of Outstanding Bill

We sincerely regret our inability to pay your bill for Rs. 10,000/- on or before the stipulated date of 14th March 2000. This is mainly because of the fact that all on a sudden the workers and employees of our factory as well as office went on strike from 1st March pending settlement of their wage/salary revision without giving any notice. As tension around the factory was high, we did not dare enter our office. However, following withdrawal of the strike by the workmen/employees, we started normal working as from 20th March.

2. In the circumstance, we would request you to allow us extension of time by a month. We, however, assure that we would send our cheque for Rs. 10,000/- to you latest by 10th of April.

Looking forward to your kind understanding of our predicament,

Yours faithfully
for POB Co. Ltd.
Mridul Datta
Managing Director

Q. 42. Draft a letter to a Bank from the Managing Director of a new Company enclosing requisite documents/papers required for opening a Current Account and asking for a cheque book. **(C.U. 1963)**

Ans.

Clipper Belt Lacer Company Pvt. Ltd.

Registered Office :
10 Townshend Road
Calcutta 700025
1st February 2000

Ref. No. Clip/Bank/75/103

The Branch Manager
State Bank of India
Bhowanipore
Calcutta 700025

Sub. : Opening of a Current Account

Dear Sir

We are desirous of opening a current account with you and forward herewith the following documents/papers for your necessary action :

(i) A copy of the Memorandum and Articles of Association of the Company.

(ii) A certified true copy of the Resolution of the meeting of the Board of Directors of the Company authorising opening of a current account with you.

(iii) A certified copy of the Certificate of Incorporation issued by the Registrar of Companies, West Bengal.

(iv) Current account opening form duly filled in.

(v) A specimen signature card bearing the signatures of the persons authorised to operate the account.

(vi) A pay-in-slip duly filled in together with a sum of Rs. 13,000/- as the amount of initial deposit.

We shall be glad if you will please arrange to open a current account in the name of our company, issue a cheque book of 100 pages (order cheques), and hand over the same to the bearer whose signature is attested hereunder.

Yours faithfully
for Clipper Belt Lacer Co. (P) Ltd.
Noor Mohammad
Managing Director

Signature of Sri M. Basu (bearer)

Q. 43. A letter to the Company's Bankers asking them to make enquiries as to the financial standing of a firm with whom the Company wishes to enter into business contract.
(C.U. 1999, 1970)

Ans.

D. G. Industries (P) Ltd.

Registered Office :
28 Ganesh Ch. Avenue
Calcutta 700013
16th March 2000

The Branch Manager
State Bank of India
Bhowanipore
Calcutta 700025

Re : Credit Report on Messrs. Cosmos Pharmaceuticals Company
82 Janpat, New Delhi

Dear Sir

We have got an order from the captioned firm for supply of various sizes of containers worth Rs. 11 lakhs. We do not have any knowledge about the standing and credit-worthiness of the firm. We may have to allow credit terms to them. Therefore, before establishing any business relations with them, we would request you to kindly obtain the firm's credit report from their bankers, Punjab National Bank, Janapat, New Delhi. On receipt of your advice, we will proceed further in the matter.

Thanking you,

Yours faithfully
for D. G. Industries (P) Ltd.
S. K. Sen
Managing Director

Q. 44. You want to start a small-scale industry in a semi-urban area. Address a letter to a Nationalised Bank in that area with a request to provide you with a loan of Rs. 20,000/- which you require as your initial capital to start the business. (C.U. 1990)

Ans.

2nd February 2000

The Branch Manager
State Bank of India
Memari Branch
Dist. : Burdwan (W.B.)

Dear Sir

Re : Application for a Bank Loan

This is for your kind information that I am an inhabitant of this locality. I am keen on setting up a small industrial unit for manufacturing bulbs and seek your financial assistance of Rs. 20,000/- as initial capital to start the business. I enclose a xerox copy of the scheme which has been approved by the District Industries Centre, Burdwan. It will be observed from the scheme that a composite loan of Rs. 20,000/- (Rs. 10,000/- for working capital and Rs. 10,000/- for term loan) will be necessary in the first phase of production.

I submit below, in brief, some relevant particulars for you kind perusal :

Name	:	Ganesh Chandra Das
Address	:	'Daspara', Memari Station Road, Memari, Burdwan
Age/Date of Birth	:	39 years/1.5.61
Educational Qualification	:	Passed B.Sc. with Physics, Chemistry and Mathematics from Burdwan University (copy of certificate enclosed).
Experience	:	About 5 years' experience in a leading bulb manufacturing concern as an apprentice and a technician (xerox copy of certificate enclosed).
Description of Project	:	Manufacturing of bulbs at the above address. Production per week consisting of 6 working days : 500 bulbs. Cost of raw materials per unit Rs. 2/50, cost of labour per unit Rs. 2.00, other expenses per unit Re. 0.50. Total cost of production per unit : Rs. 5. Entire production of bulbs will be sold in the Memari market and its surrounding places.

2. In this context, as one month's stock has to be maintained on regular basis for smooth supply to the market and machines as well as equipments have to be purchased, a composite loan of Rs. 20,000 from the Bank will be required, as computed below :

For build-up of one month's stock	
(500 bulbs/week for 4 weeks @ Rs. 5/- per unit)	Rs. 10,000/-
Cost of machines and equipment	Rs. 10,000/-
	Rs. 20,000/-

3. In view of the above, I shall be obliged if you will kindly sanction in my favour a composite loan of Rs. 20,000/- under your usual terms and conditions to enable me to set up the unit.

Should you require any further particulars, I will be glad to provide you with the same.

Thanking you,

Yours faithfully

Enclosures : As above

Ganesh Chandra Das

Q. 45. A letter to the Bank for increasing the overdraft limit to cover increase in prices of stock and expansion in business. (C.U. 1975, 1973)

Ans.

D. G. Industries Private Ltd.

Registered Office :
23 Ganesh Chandra Avenue
Calcutta 700013
24th January 2000

The Branch Manager
State Bank of India
Bhowanipore Branch
Calcutta 700025

Re : Increase in Overdraft Limit from Rs. 20 lakhs to Rs. 40 lakhs

Dear Sir

You are doubtless aware that the prices of raw materials and other components are rising by leaps and bounds. During the last few months, the average price increase is approximately 50% ! This has put our company to great difficulties, specially in the matter of procurement of materials. Working capital available does not permit us to purchase raw materials required to maintain the existing level of production uninterrupted. Moreover, we have embarked upon an expansion programme which necessitates an additional investment of Rs. 10 lakhs towards procurement of stocks.

In the light of the above, we would request you to kindly enhance our overdraft limit from Rs. 20 lakhs to Rs. 40 lakhs.

We forward herewith a copy of the Company's balance sheet as at 31.10.99 and a copy of the Scheme of Expansion passed by the Small Industries Service Institute.

In this connection, if you so require, we are agreeable to furnish any other securities available with us in addition to hypothecation of stocks.

Thanking you,

Yours faithfully
for D. G. Industries Pvt. Ltd.
B. Dutta Gupta
Managing Director

Enclosures : Two

Q. 46. Write to the Secretary of a limited company whose account has been overdrawn without advice to you—the company's Bankers. You wish to retain the connection and have accordingly honoured the cheques on presentation. (ICSI)

Ans.

State Bank of India

Puri
Orissa
March 16, 2000

No. ADV/C-38

The Secretary
Bijoy Marine Products Ltd.
Puri Marine Drive
Puri 752001

Re : Your Current Account No. 01190091351

Dear Sir

We have to advise that, consequent upon payment of your two cheques for Rs. 55,001/- and Rs. 38/40 today drawn in favour of the Reserve Bank of India and the Oriental Fire & General Insurance Co. Ltd., your current account has been rendered irregular to the tune of Rs. 4,321/38. As a matter of practice, we do not honour any cheques without previous arrangements therefor, but in your case we have taken a different stand in view of your highly satisfactory dealings with us. In the circumstances, we would request you to replenish sufficient funds in your account with a view to regularising the position.

Incidentally, may we request you to call at this office to have a discussion with the undersigned in case you need some credit facilities on a continuing basis?

Yours faithfully
Udayan Chakraborty
Manager

Q. 47. Your Company had deposited an outstation cheque for Rs. 25,000/- on 5th March and had issued a cheque for Rs. 20,000/- in favour of a creditor on the following day. The Bank had dishonoured the cheque.

Draft (a) a letter to the bank enquiring about the reason of dishonour of the cheque and (b) the reply of the bank to your letter referred to under (a) above. (C.U. 1982)

Ans. (a)

Carbon India Ltd.

Registered Office :
162/1/2 Lake Gardens
Calcutta 700045
16th March 2000

The Manager
State Bank of India
Lake Gardens Branch
Calcutta 700045

Re : Dishonour of Cheque

Dear Sir

We are suprised to know from one of our valued creditors to whom we issued a cheque bearing No. AB/9 862000 for Rs. 20,000/- drawn on you that you had returned the cheque on 10.3.2000 with the objection "Not arranged for". As per our records, we had a credit balance of Rs. 19,000/- on the 5th of March and we deposited a cheque for Rs. 25,000/- drawn on your Burdwan Branch for credit to our account on that date. Following return of the cheque, we are in an embarrassing position vis-a-vis our valued creditor. We are afraid that because of this untoward incident we may not get any credit from the party in future for no fault of ours.

In view of what has been stated above, we would request you to please look into the matter and send your reply as early as possible.

Yours faithfully
for Carbon India Ltd.
Raju Garg
Director (Finance)

(b) Reply to the above letter

State Bank of India, Lake Gardens, Calcutta 700045

18th March 2000

The Director (Finance)
Carbon India Ltd.
162/1/2 Lake Gardens
Calcutta 700045

Re : Dishonour of Cheque

Dear Sir

With reference to your letter of the 16th March, we very much regret the inconvenience caused to you for dishonour of the cheque in question. We have carefully checked our records and fully agree with your statement regarding the credit balance and deposit of an outstation cheque for Rs. 25,000 as on 5th March. You are, doubtless, aware that it takes about a week to get the clearance of the outstation cheques. Therefore, the sum of Rs. 25,000/- could not be credited to your account the next day and the account on the date of return of the cheque showed a credit balance Rs. 19,000/- only.

Hope the reason for return of your cheque is now quite clear to you.

Assuring you of our best of services at all future dealings

Yours faithfully
B.S. Sadasiv
Manager

Q. 48. (a) Draft a letter to your banker requesting them to grant your company a loan of Rupees twenty five lakhs for which your company is ready to pledge plant and machineries worth Rupees fifty lakhs which have been recently purchased and installed.

(b) Draft a reply from your banker to letter (a) above agreeing to lend your company the amount asked for which shall be repaid in five annual instalments commencing from the first day of November 1987 and interest shall be paid @ 10% per annum. (C.U. 1984)

Ans. (a)

Progressive Engineering Co. Ltd.

Registered Office : 11 Strand Road
Calcutta 700001
Date : 16.3.2000

The Dy. General Manager (Advances)
State Bank of India
Commercial Branch
24 Park Street
Calcutta 700016

Application for a term loan of Rs. 25 lakhs

Dear Sir

You are surely aware that we have been maintaining a current account with you since a decade which, on an average, shows a credit balance of Rs. 30 lakhs. Of late, we have purchased new machinery to the tune of Rs. 50 lakhs and installed them at our Narendrapore works. The machines have been purchased from the Hindustan Machine Tools Ltd., and the relative challans, bills, vouchers and money receipts are with us. Following the purchase of the machinery, we are experiencing acute shortage of working capital.

In the circumstances stated above, we would request you to please sanction a medium term loan of Rs. 25 lakhs only, repayable in twenty monthly instalments of Rs. 1,25,000/-. The interest — as and when due — will also be paid by us. In this connection, we enclose a copy each of our company's balance sheets as at 31.10.97, 31.10.98, 31.10.99 together with the relative profit & loss accounts for your kind perusal. We also enclose a copy of each of the proforma projected balance sheets as at 31.10.2000 and 31.10.2001, funds-flow statements for the said two years and loan application form duly filled in. We also forward herewith a copy of the project report on our diversification scheme prepared by the noted consultants, Messrs. S. R. Batliboi & Co.

As security for the proposed loans, the machinery will be pledged with you and all the directors of the company will extend their guarantees — both in their official and personal capacities.

In view of what has been stated above, we would request you to please accord your sanction as early as possible.

Thanking you,

Yours faithfully
for Progressive Engg. Co. Ltd.
Subha Halder
Managing Director

(b) Reply to letter (a) above

State Bank of India
24 Park Street
Calcutta 700016
No. ADV/MTL/12345
31st March 2000

The Managing Director
Progressive Engineering Co. Ltd.
11 Strand road
Calcutta 700001

Medium Term Loan of Rs. 25 lakhs

Dear Sir

We acknowledge receipt of your letter dated the 16th March together with enclosures.

Though as a matter of principle and convention we do not sanction any loan to any party for the machinery already purchased by it, we have considered your application altogether on a different footing. It has, however, finally been possible for us to sanction the loan in your favour under the following terms and conditions :

(a) Limit—Rs. 25 lakhs.

(b) Margin—50% of the cost of machinery.

(c) Security—(i) Pledge of machinery for which the loan has been sanctioned and the other machines also. (ii) Hypothecation charge on all other current assets. (iii) Personal guarantees of the whole-time directors of the company.

(d) Interest—15.5% per annum. The rate will be suitably adjusted with the increase or decrease in the State Bank of India Advance Rate.

(e) Repayment—The loan should be repaid in five equal monthly instalments of Rs. 5 lakhs each and the first instalment will fall due for payment after seven months from the date of disbursement of the loan.

(f) Insurance—All the items of machinery of the company must be comprehensively insured against the risks of fire, strike, riot, burglary and flood and the policy should be in the joint names of the Bank and the company.

(g) Inspection—The officials of the Bank, as well as those from the Reserve Bank of India, will be at liberty to inspect the factory and registered office of the company. The books of account must be made available to them for inspection too.

If you agree to the above terms and conditions, please return the duplicate copy of this letter duly signed by the Managing Director and the whole-time directors of the company in token of your acceptance. Please also collect from us the security document forms for stamping and execution.

Yours faithfully
Rani Halder
Dy. General Manager

Q. 49. Draft a letter to an Insurance Company intimating destruction of insured goods and property worth Rs. 3 lakhs by fire and requesting immediate action for survey and settlement of the claim. (C.U. 1978, 1974)

Or, Draft a letter to your insurers intimating destruction of insured goods worth Rs. 2 lakhs by a fire in your godown and requesting an early survey and settlement of the claim. (C.U. 1994, 1991, 1988, 1983)

Ans.

Arim Icecream Industries

39 Borad Street
Calcutta 700019
2nd January 2000

The General Manager
Oriental Fire and General Insurance Co.
4 Lyons Range
Calcutta 700001

Fire Policy No. 42000/1999

Dear Sir

We have to advise that a fire broke out in the warehouse of our factory premises on the 31st December, 1999 at midnight. The night watchman reported the incident of fire to the police and fire-brigade as soon as he came to see the flame. The fire caused severe damage to our entire stocks which were kept in the warehouse. The loss is to the tune of Rs. 3 lakhs. The books of account and most of other records have, fortunately, been saved.

In the circumstances, we shall be glad if you will please depute your surveyor to undertake a thorough inspection and forward to us a copy of the claim form to enable us to lodge our claim.

We will appreciate your taking an early action in the matter.

Yours faithfully
H. Das
Proprietor

Q. 50. Draft an advice to an insurance company about damage caused to an incoming consignment covered by a Marine Policy issued by them requesting early settlement of the claim. (C.U. 1965)

Ans.

Indian Spices Limited

Registered Office :
1 Strand Road
Calcutta 700001
1st February 2000

Messrs. National Insurance Company Limited
4 Lyons Range
Calcutta 700001

Re : Marine Insurance Policy No. MIP/101—Claim

Dear Sirs

We have just now received an intimation from our London Agent that S.S. Mahalakshmi which was carrying the consignment of spices for us had met with an accident on its way to Liverpool. This has caused major damage to the ship and the cargo meant for us has been reported to be totally destroyed. This shipment is under the cover of your insurance. In accordance with the terms and conditions of the policy, we hereby lodge our claim for Rs. 25,000/- which is the estimated loss suffered by us.

In view of the above, we shall be glad if you will kindly arrange for an early settlement of our claim.

Yours faithfully
for Indian Spices Limited
S.K. Bhadra
Law Officer

LETTERS OF AGENCY

Q. 51. Draft a letter seeking an agency of a firm which is not represented in your district. (C.U. 1996, 1991, 1987)

Ans.

The Very Well Stores

Paradise Place
Jalpaiguri
2nd January 2000

The Lux Toilet Company
38 Unique Park
Calcutta 700034

Re : Application for Agency

Dear Sirs

You are perhaps aware of the possibilities of your various products in our district. We have no hesitation to comment that a commission agent of our standard — backed by a well-designed advertising campaign — is sure to make a successful outlet of your products.

In this context, in view of our long experience and valuable connections, we are sure to render you the service that you actually need. Our showrooms situated in the heart of the town are commodious and offer excellent facilities for displaying your products.

As regards our terms, we charge 15% commission on sales and need reimbursement of any incidental expenses incurred for displaying the goods. Should you require any credit report of ours, you may refer to our banker — State Bank of India, Jalpaiguri.

Hope you will entrust us with the representation of your firm.

Thanking you,

Yours faithfully
for The Very Well Stores
B. Dastur
Proprietor

Q. 52. Draft a letter offering agency.

Or, Draft a letter offering an agency for supply of your products to a businessman of Jalpaiguri. (C.U. 1981)

Ans.

Lux Toilet Company

38 Unique Park
Calcutta 700034
23rd July 2000

The Very Well Stores
Paradise Place
P.O. & Dist. Jalpaiguri
West Bengal

Re : Offer of Agency

Dear Sirs

With reference to your letter of the 1st July, we have pleasure in appointing you as our agent for the district of Jalpaiguri as from the 1st August 2000 on the following terms and conditions :

(i) You will be allowed an ordinary commission of 10% and a del credere commission of 2½% on sales.

(ii) We can cover you to the extent of Rs. 1,500/- per month towards your advertising and miscellaneous expenses — in case the turnover does not fall below Rs. 55,000/- per month.

(iii) You will have to remit the sale proceeds in the first week of every month together with a statement of sales effected during the previous month.

(iv) You can allow credit to your customers for a period not exceeding two months.

In this connection, we forward herewith some papers for your signature and return.

Yours faithfully
for Lux Toilet Company
Debasish Debnath
Proprietor

Enclosures :

Q. 53. Draft an announcement about the appointment of sole selling agent for a company's products covering a particular territory. (C.U. 1968)

Ans.

Hind Cycles Private Limited

Registered Office :
Circular No. 7 Hare Street
Calcutta 700001
4th January 2000

Re : Appointment of Messrs. North Bengal Cycle Stores, Jalpaiguri, as sole Selling Agents for all the districts of North Bengal

Dear Sirs

We are pleased to announce the appointment of Messrs. North Bengal Cycles Stores, P.O. and District Jalpaiguri, as our Sole Selling Agent for all the districts under North Bengal with effect from 1st June 2000. We are aware of your experiencing a lot of difficulties in obtaining supply of cycles and/or their accessories direct from our office. More often than not, obtention of supply in this way entails both loss of time and avoidable cost. To put an end to the insurmountable difficulties faced by our valued customers, the above step has been taken by us. Messrs. North Bengal Cycle Stores will be having quite adequate stocks of cycles and their spare parts to cope with your demand.

In the circumstances, we will appreciate your placing all orders for cycles and their spare parts with the captioned firm.

Thanking you,

Yours faithfully
for Hind Cycles Private Limited
Bidyut Mukherjee
Chief Sales Manager

Q. 54. A letter from Renowned Battery Manufacturers Ltd., Calcutta, regretting inability to immediately appoint an applicant as its approved retail dealer but assuring consideration in future when production improves. (C.U. 1972)

Ans.

Renowned Battery Manufacturers Ltd.

Registered Office :
1 Middleton Street
Calcutta 700016
1st March 2000

No. RBM/Agency/1994/1
Messrs. Battery Distributors
Berhampore
Dist. Murshidabad
West Bengal.

Sub : Agency

Dear Sirs

With reference to your letter of the 25th February 2000, we cannot but appreciate your interest in our products. We very much regret in communicating our inability to offer you our dealership for the district of Murshidabad at the moment. We have, however, empanelled your name for future consideration. We hope to gear up our production by 50% within a period of six months when we shall possibly be in a position to offer you our retail dealership.

Thanking you,

Yours faithfully
D. Debnath
Sales Manager

Q. 55. A letter to be addressed to a few firms in Dubai introducing your firm as an established exporter of handloom goods and handicrafts of Eastern India and desirous of appointing reputed agents in Dubai. (Supply imaginary particulars assuming yourself as a Calcutta firm exporting to several Middle-East countries.) (C.U. 1976)

Ans.

Eastern Arts & Crafts
Limited
1 B.B.D. Bag
Calcutta 700001
2nd January 2000

Messrs Shaff & Sons, Dubai
Messrs Islam Traders, Dubai
Messrs Gulf Crafts & Curios, Dubai
Messrs Ghulam & Co. Dubai

Handloom Goods & Handicrafts of Eastern India

Dear Sirs

We take the opportunity of introducing the fragile beauty and breath-taking charm of Indian handicrafts and handloom products to your great land. We are an organisation established a quarter century ago and have the proud distinction of being the pioneers in merchandizing and indeed promoting handicrafts and handloom products — especially of the eastern part of India where we are based. Today, we have six direct retail outlets in the United Kingdom (U. K.) and the Continent and thrice the number as agents/representatives located all over the world. We have recently opened a branch office in Cairo to cater to the unprecedented demand for our products in the North African and Middle-East countries.

Our products, bearing the stamp of hard work and skill of Indian craftsmen, have the unmistakable authenticity of Indian handicrafts. It is the marriage of artistic grace with modern taste and are not mere objects of art. Craft-pieces are not manufactured on assembly lines but in the staid country-homes of the regional craftsmen. This is precisely the reason why the products marketed by us have established their identity all over the world and lately in Saudi Arabia, Kuwait, Iraq and Doha.

We enclose for your perusal an introductory booklet but emphasize that it is by no means an exhaustive catalog of our product range. We hope you will give us the opportunity of presenting samples of our wares for your inspection. We also enclose a schedule of the usual terms of trade which we engage in.

We seek your trading acquaintance and hope that it blossoms into a long and fruitful commercial relationship.

Thanking you,

Yours faithfully
for Eastern Arts & Crafts Ltd.
N. Srinivasan
Director (Marketing)

Enclosures : As given

Q. 56. A letter from a Calcutta manufacturer to its Siliguri Agent expressing concern about the fall in sales of their products in the last two quarters in comparison with the last year and inviting suggestions for boosting sales. (C.U. 1976)

Ans.

Waco Pumps (India) Ltd.

1 N.S. Road
Calcutta 700001
24th January 2000

The Siliguri Pumps & Accessories Private Ltd.
Upper Road
Siliguri
West Bengal

Re : Fall in Sales

Dear Sirs

We are in receipt of your trading statement for the quarter ended the 31st December, 1999 and are indeed concerned to observe the downward trend in sales and off-take as compared to the previous two quarters, as well as the figures for the corresponding time period last year. The trend is all the more perplexing when viewed in the light of the increase in the overall sales figure for our range of pumps and accessories and the average 10% growth rate in turnover that we have achieved in the last two years. Indeed, nine out of our ten regional distributors in the three Eastern States have reported increased sales and off-take volumes in the last quarter.

In the circumstances, and in view of your vast experience in marketing of pumps and your close proximity to the customers, we shall be very glad if you will please send us your analysis of the sales trend, the market and other related issues together with your suggestions/ recommendations in the matter. These will enable us to effect a better understanding of the problem and take the necessary remedial measures to put your district sales on the growth chart again.

Yours faithfully
for Waco Pumps (India) Ltd.
Abhay Kulkarni
Sales Manager

Q. 57. Draft a letter to your agents in Madras drawing their attention to the steep fall in sales during the last two quarters and asking for a report on the causes of fall in sales. (C.U. 1983)

Ans. : Write on the lines of the Answer to the previous question-answer.

Q. 58. Draft a letter in reply to the above letter (Q. 56) informing that the decline in sales during the last two quarters has been due to emergence of a strong competitor of Mumbai who is selling the same articles at a price 5 per cent less than the price quoted by your company and also due to the fact that a large number of customers are dissatisfied because of the inordinate delay in supplying the articles ordered for. (C.U. 1983)

Ans.

Well Electronics Enterprise

38 Mount Road
Chennai 600001
Date 01.01.2000

The Chief Sales Executive
Specturm Electronics
75/57 S. N. Roy Road
Calcutta 700038

Re : Reasons for decline in sales

Dear Sir,

Please refer to your letter No. Sono/Sales/106 dated the 25th December 1999 on the above subject.

On receipt of your letter under reply, we deputed three of our senior sales supervisors to conduct a detailed survey so as to ascertain the reasons for decline in sales of your products. They visited the main business centres in the city of Chennai and its sub-urban areas for the purpose. Based on their reports and the information available with us at this office, the possible reasons for decline in sales of your products may be enumerated as under :

(a) **Competition :** There has emerged a strong competitor from Mumbai who manufactures the same types of products. Though its products are not superior to that of yours, the covers/boxes supplied by that firm are very attractive. Besides, to popularise the products, the manufacturer has made arrangements for free gifts to the buyers of its products.

(b) **Price :** The prices of our competitor's products are, on an average, 5% less as compared to yours. It is understood from reliable sources that it will very soon increase the prices of the products by 5% to 7%.

(c) **Delay in Supply :** According to the present practice, our customers have to wait for at least one month to get the articles they want to buy. On receipt of the orders together with 10% advance, we mail them to you for despatch of the articles and we deliver the goods to the indentor only on receipt from you. As against this system, our competitor has appointed a local distributor who caters to the needs of the agents immediately.

If you can take the remedial measures — as suggested in paragraphs 2(a) and (c) above — we are sure that your products will again be increasingly demanded and our sales will automatically pick up.

Yours faithfully
for Well Electronics Enterprise
A. B. Chaturbedi
Partner

CORRESPONDENCE WITH GOVERNMENT DEPTS.

Q. 59. A letter from a firm to the Post-Master General, W. Bengal Circle, complaining against continuous wrong deliveries of letters and postal articles and return of registered articles by the local post-office in spite of repeated representations to the Branch Post-Master personally. (C.U. 1972)

Ans.

Noakhali Machine Tools Company

P.O. Narendrapur
Dist. 24-Parganas (South)
West Bengal
Date : 02.01.2000

The Post-Master General
West Bengal Circle
B.B.D. Bag
Calcutta 700001

Re : Wrong Deliveries of Postal Articles

Dear Sir

We would like to draw your kind attention to the fact that since your new Post-Master assumed charge of Narendrapur Post Office, many firms and individuals of our locality are not getting their mail in time. A number of articles/letters meant for some people have been delivered to some other people. There are a few instances in which even "Registered Letters" addressed to us have been returned with the remark "Not Known"! It would not be out of place to mention that we are a much reputed firm in Narendrapur. You can well appreciate the difficulties we have to experience due to wrong delivery and non-delivery of mail, etc.

We wrote a few letters to the Post-Master, Narendrapur, requesting him to take such action as would prevent recurrence of similar events and set right the position. Subsequently, we met him personally several times — but this too has elicited no results.

In the circumstances, we have no option but to request you to kindly enquire into the matter and take proper steps so as to prevent recurrence of such wrong deliveries and consequent harassment and loss to those availing your postal service.

Thanking you,

Yours faithfully
for Noakhali Machine Tools Co.
D. Sona
Works Manager

Q. 60. A representation on behalf of Chamber of Commerce to the Ministry of Finance, Government of India, pointing out the possible difficulties to be faced by industry due to the imposition of additional customs and excise duties by supplementary budget proposals made in Parliament and asking for suitable relief. (C.U. 1966)

Ans.

Indian Chamber of Commerce

India Exchange Building
Indian Exchange Place
Calcutta 700001
The 3rd January 2000

The Secretary
Ministry of Finance
Government of India
Parliament Street
New Delhi 110001

**Supplementary Budget Proposals :
Imposition of additional customs and excise duties**

Dear Sir

While referring to the supplementary budget proposals placed by the Finance Minister before the Parliament during the last week, we have to make the following observations :

1. One of the principal functions of this Chamber is to help its members in all possible ways to increase exports of the country and thus enable our country to earn valuable foreign exchange. The proposed levy will not act as a fillip to boost up our export but, on the contrary, it will be a deterring factor to increasing export.

2. The prices of our products in the international market are already on the high side and the proposed imposition of additional customs and excise duties will further worsen our position.

3. The proposed imposition will also adversely affect our trade and commerce. Due to increasing trend in prices of manufactured goods, consumers are already experiencing much difficulty and any further burden thereon will surely deteriorate the situation.

In view of the above, we shall be glad if you will kindly reconsider the matter and arrange to exempt the export-oriented industries from the purview of the imposition of additional customs and excise duties.

Thanking you,

Yours faithfully
D.K. Deb
Secretary

Q. 61. Draft a letter to the Chief Controller of the Imports requesting revalidation of an import licence on the basis of some valid grounds/justifying the extension applied for. (C.U. 1963)

Ans.

Chemicals (India) Limited

Registered Office :
20 Camac Street
Calcutta 700016
24th December 1999

The Director of Foreign Trade
4 Esplanade (East)
Calcutta 700001

Sub : Revalidation of Import Licence No. P/S/177981/R/ML/C/55-56/37/111

Dear Sir

We have to advise that the captioned licence was issued to us on 2.12.98 for import of Parachloronitrobenzene up to c.i.f. value of Rs. 100 lakhs as the material is not indigenously available.

Accordingly, our banker, State Bank of India, Calcutta, opened a credit on the Grindlays Bank, London, favouring Messrs. Imperial Chemical to help us carry on our production smoothly. Due to some unavoidable reasons, the suppliers could not effect the shipment within the scheduled time. Of late, we have been informed by them that they would ship the material by 25th January 2000. Incidentally, the validity period of the licence in question expires on 31.12.99.

In view of the above, we shall be glad if you will kindly extend the validity period of the licence by another twelve months and thus enable us to obtain the material and continue production as well as keep our hundreds of employees on the roll.

Thanking you,

Yours faithfully
for Chemicals (India) Limited
R. Marwaha
Managing Director

Q. 62. A letter to General Manager, Calcutta Telephones, claiming preferential treatment in the matter of installation of Telex (teleprinter) unit on the basis of satisfactory export performance and enclosing a Bank Certificate relating to value of export during the previous year. (C.U. 1969)

Ans.

Gillander Arbuthnot and Co. Ltd.

Gillander House
N. S. Road
Calcutta 700001
2nd January 2000

The General Manager
Calcutta Telephones
Telephone Bhavan
Calcutta 700001

Re : Installation of Telex (Teleprinter) Unit

Dear Sir

You are perhaps aware that we are one of the largest exporters of tea. During the period from 1.4.1998 to 31.3.1999 we have earned total foreign exchange worth Rs. 50 crores. We bank with State Bank of India, N. S. Road Branch, Calcutta, and we enclose a certificate from our banker in support of our statement. During the current year, we expect at least 50% more earning than what we did in the last year.

In this connection, we have to state that our Branch Offices are located in New Delhi and Mumbai. We are required to make frequent contacts with our Branch offices and but for telex in our offices we have been experiencing a lot of difficulties. This creates a bottleneck in our performance which, in turn, adversely affects our export performance.

In view of the above, we shall be glad if you will kindly treat our case preferentially and arrange to instal telex in our offices at the earliest.

Yours faithfully
for Gillander Arbuthnot and Co. Ltd.
K. Kumar
Managing Director

Enclosure : Banker's Certificate.

Q. 63. A letter from the Government of West Bengal (say, Chief Secretary) to all Chambers and Associations expressing its anxiety on uptrend in prices and inviting suggestions on measures which may be taken to curb speculation and hoarding for profiteering. (C.U. 1976)

Ans.

Government of West Bengal
Writers' Buildings
Calcutta 700001
Date : 02.01.2000

From
The Chief Secretary
Government of West Bengal
Writers' Buildings
Calcutta 700001

To

All Chambers of Commerce/Trade Associations

Re : Uptrend in Prices

Dears Sirs

As you are aware, the last two months have seen a general uptrend in the price level of essential commodities causing considerable hardships to the common man. The consumer price index has risen by six points during the last two months. Even after adjustments for seasonal fluctuations, the price level stands at an ominously high level as compared to the corresponding period last year.

The Government of West Bengal is seriously concerned about the situation and it is felt that substantial grounds may be gained by curbing speculative trading and hoarding of stocks for which, it needs hardly be emphasised, the co-operation of the people, the Chambers of Commerce and the Trade Associations is of paramount importance.

The Government would welcome your suggestions and proposals in respect of steps and measures to be adopted for curbing profiteering in essential commodities by unscrupulous traders.

Yours faithfully
J. K. Kanjilal
Chief Secretary

SECRETARIAL CORRESPONDENCE

Q. 64. Draft a reply to a shareholder explaining the reasons for fall in the market price of shares.

Ans.

Jardine Handerson Limited

Registered Office :
4 Clive Row
Calcutta 700001
Date : 1.3.2000

Shri Debashish Debnath
10 Chandra Mandal Lane
Calcutta 700026

Re : Fall in Market Price of Shares

Dear Sir

While thanking you for your letter, we very much appreciate the interest evinced by you in our company.

The fall in the market price of the company's shares stems from the following facts :

(i) Prevalence of slump conditions in the market.

(ii) Jute industry is adversely affected for sluggish demand.

(iii) Unstable political conditions have also adversely affected the speculative activities.

In this connection, we can assure you that this state of affairs is not going to continue indefinitely and there is no real ground which can prompt you to take an alarmist view.

Yours faithfully
Dustam Desai
Secretary

Q. 65. Draft a circular letter to shareholders of Messrs. Caxton & Co. Limited for issuance of bonus shares.

Ans.

Caxton and Company Limited

Registered Office :
1-B Ashutosh Mukherjee Road
Calcutta 700020
1st March 2000

To
All Shareholders
....
....

Dear Sir/Madam

Re : Issue of Bonus Shares

I have been directed by the Board of Directors to advise you of their resolution for issue of 5,000 bonus shares of Rs. 10/- each. This was adopted by them at their meeting held on the 17th December 1999.

In view of the increasing business handled by the company and consequent steady progress, time appears to be the most opportune when we can strengthen our equity base. The Securities & Exchange Board of India has already been approached for necessary permission for issuance of bonus shares.

We forward herewith a copy of the notice convening the Extraordinary General Meeting together with the relative resolution for your necessary action. We also enclose a proxy form for your use in case you cannot be present in person at the meeting.

Yours faithfully
Mantu Debnath
Secretary

Q. 66. A letter to a renowned business leader conveying on behalf of the Chairman of the Board of Directors an invitation to him to join the Board of your Company.(C.U. 1970)

Ans.

Sahu and Jain Limited

11 Clive Row
Calcutta 700001
1st February 2000

Shri A. K. Sen
21 B.B.D. Bagh
Calcutta 700001

Dear Sir

Re : An invitation to join the Board of Directors

I have been directed by our Board of Directors to invite you to please join the company's Board as Additional Director. This is as a sequel to the resolution adopted by the Directors at their Board Meeting held on 31.1.2000. It may be mentioned that consequent upon the sudden death of Shri S. K. Tatadia, Director, the vacancy has arisen and I take the opportunity of inviting you to join the Board as early as possible.

Though you are well aware of our company, I forward herewith a copy each of the following documents/papers for your ready reference :

(i) Memorandum and Articles of Association.

(ii) Balance Sheet and Profit and Loss Account together with the relative schedules for the last three years.

(iii) A new scheme for diversification of the company's products awaiting implementation.

We shall be glad if you will kindly accept the offer and communicate your assent to us.

Thanking you and looking forward to your valuable cooperation,

Yours faithfully
J. Bose
Secretary

Enclosures : Three

Q. 67. Draft a reply by the Secretary of a Public Limited Company to one of the shareholders complaining about the low rate of dividend recommended by the Board of Directors and enquiring about prospects of future working and dividends. (C.U. 1963)

Or, As a Secretary of a company write a suitable reply to a shareholder who has enquired about the likelihood of higher dividends in the coming year. (C.U. 1980)

Ans.

Indian Mica Industries Limited

Registered Office :
4 Clive Row
Calcutta 700001
3rd January 2000

Shri Ram Ratan Ram
41 Ballygunje Place
Calcutta 700019

Dear Sir

Re : Low Rate of Dividend

While acknowledging receipt of your letter of the 3rd January, we thank you very much for the keen interest shown by you by way of enquiring about the low rate of dividend paid by the company for the year ended 31.10.99.

With the presumption that you have glanced through the audited accounts of the company for the year ended 31.10.99, we can safely conclude that the financial position of the company is as sound as it was.

The low rate of dividend recommended by the Board of Directors stems from the following facts :

1. The mine at Giridi—which is undoubtedly the biggest unit of the company—was under strike for eight months in 1998. This has resulted in reduction of our annual overall production by 30%.

2. Another mine located at Jharia faced an epidemic. 90% of the labour left their jobs and this mine hardly produced anything during the six months during the last financial year. This too reduced our overall production by 10%.

You will surely appreciate that it is the lesser production which has made an inroad into the profitability of the company. The Board of Directors considered that declaration of lower rate of dividend was better than to fall back upon the reserves of the company to maintain uniformity in the rate of dividend.

As both the mines have started normal operations, we expect to raise our production to the original level, if not surpass it soon. In this perspective, we hope to restore the normal dividend in the next year, if not raise it.

Yours faithfully,
B. B. Bose
Secretary

Q. 68. A shareholder seeks your advice as he wishes to buy some more shares of the company. As the Secretary of the company, write a suitable reply. (ICSI)

Ans.

Blank & Co. Ltd.

Shri Raj Halder
Sea Beach
Puri
Orissa

Registered Office :
1 Backbay Reclamation
Mumbai 400021
March 16, 2000

Re : Future prospects of the company

Dear Sir

This refers to your letter No. RH/200 of the 7th March. I very much regret my inability to supply you with the information you seek. You will surely appreciate that by virtue of my holding the office of Secretary, I am prevented from divulging any information which may be detrimental to the interests of the other shareholders. In this context, I may suggest you to go through the company's annual accounts and Directors' Reports for the last 2/3 years. This is sure to help you form an idea about the future prospects of the company.

Yours faithfully
for Blank & Co. Ltd.
Samir Dastagir
Secretary

LETTERS TO EDITOR

Q. 69. Draft a letter to the Editor of a Newspaper, including a draft advertisement for recruitment of a stenographer, for publication. (C.U. 1965)

Ans.

Carter Hydraulic Power Limited

Registered Office :
69 Block E
New Alipore
Calcutta 700053
2nd January 2000

The Editor
The Statesman
Calcutta 700001

Re : Publication of Advertisement

Dear Sir

We forward herewith a copy of the advertisement for publication under the "Situations Vacant" column of your issue of the 7th January 2000. The relative bill may please be sent to us for payment.

Thanking you,

Yours faithfully
K. K. Dutta
Secretary

Copy of Advertisement

Wanted an experienced Stenographer (computer literate) by an international manufacturing company for its Calcutta Office. Candidates must be Graduates of any recognised university, having speed of 120 words per minute in shorthand and 50 words per minute in typewriting. They should have pleasing personality and should be able to correspond independently. Experience in an engineering company is desirable but not essential. Salary and perquisites are negotiable but should not be less than Rs. 8,000/- month. Write with bio-data, salary expected and a recent passport size photograph (which may not be returned) to Box No. 1200, The Statesman, Calcutta 700001, within a week from the date of publication.

Q. 70. A letter to the Editor of a daily Newspaper ventilating risk and damage to men and machinery resulting from unscheduled shedding of power supply to the factory.

(C.U. 1973)

Ans.

Cablex Engg. Co.
Workers' Association
1 Lee Road
Calcutta 700020
14th January 2000

The Editor
The Statesman
Calcutta 700001

Dear Sir

Re : Unscheduled load-shedding

We shall be grateful if you will kindly publish the following paragraphs in your esteemed daily to draw the attention of the authorities concerned to the above matter :

In recent years, the city of Calcutta and its suburbs are experiencing a lot of difficulties due to load-shedding. During the latter part of 1999, the Government introduced rationing of electricity and, when unavoidable circumstances would arise, shedding of power would be made according to a programme communicated to the consumers in advance.

Unscheduled load-shedding is attendant with the risk and damage to men and machinery. Factory workers are to handle various types of machines and operations of some of them require much attention. Workers are required to feed the machines and sudden stoppage of the machines due to load-shedding may endanger the lives of the operatives and put the machines out of gear. It may so happen that even incurring considerable amount of expenditure will not bring the machines back to normal working condition. The usual precautions adopted by the workers and operatives prove futile when unscheduled load-shedding comes into play.

In the above perspective, we shall be glad if the Government takes up the matter with the Calcutta Electric Supply Corpn. Ltd./State Electricity Board to implement rationing of electricity which will minimise unscheduled load-shedding. This, in turn, will help workers and operatives to escape avoidable hazards and the owners of the machines will be able to save some avoidable expenditure, harassment, and needless discomfort.

Yours faithfully
B. Mazumder
Secretary, Workers' Assocn.
Cables Engg. Co. Ltd.

Q. 71. Letter to Editor of a Daily Newspaper to ventilate the difficulties experienced by you in your business due to bad telephone service.

Ans.

Indian Trading Company

3 Mangoe Lane
Calcutta 700001
Date : 02.01.2000

No. ITC/VEN/101
The Editor
The Statesman
Calcutta 700001

Dear Sir

We shall be glad if you please arrange to publish the following few paragraphs in your much-esteemed daily to ebable us to ventilate our grievances due to bad telephone service.

Thanking you,

Yours faithfully
D. K. Debnath
Manager

Bad Telephone Service

Telephone is a very important and easy medium of communication. It costs very little to make a call but enables the caller to collect valuable information within a very short time. It helps a businessman to conduct business smoothly and solve various problems. In recent times, on an average 30% to 40% of the total numbers remain out of order and the position worsens during the rainy season. Despite several requests, the mechanics of the service department do not visit the spots. On some occasions, they do not hesitate to ask for bribes before taking up the repairing work.

Cross-connection is another regular feature of the Calcutta Telephones. This results in unnecessary loss of time, energy and money—a botheration indeed. It may be mentioned that the ladies attending Dial Nos. 196, 197, 198, 199, etc. care very little to reply to the calls. You will appreciate while rental for telephones is increasing, the quality of service rendered by the Telephone Department is deteriorating day by day.

In the circumstances, we would like to draw the attention of the concerned authorities to our grievances and request them to adopt suitable steps to set right the position.

Yours faithfully
Debashish Deb
Partner

Q. 72. Write a letter to the Editor of a leading newspaper expressing your views on devaluation of English in School/College/University education.

Ans.

Ranishri
Sea Beach
Puri 752001
01.01.2000

The Editor
The Statesman
Calcutta 700001

Dear Sir

I shall be highly obliged if you will kindly arrange to publish the following few paragraphs in your much-esteemed daily to enable me to draw the attention of the authorities concerned.

Thanking you,

Yours faithfully
Raj Halder

Re : Spreading education at the cost of abolishing English and higher education as well

The Government of West Bengal and the University of Calcutta have started the all-round campaign of taking education at the doorsteps of masses living in villages which are, so to say, the edifice on which the civilisation of the cities and towns has thrived. If it is really the case, the movement — though initiated at a very late stage — cannot but be appreciated. But in the name of spreading education, they are going to side-track English, if not abolish it altogether! They do not have the courage to pronounce that higher education is not universal, it is meant for a few selective people. They opine that it is the vernacular which is the best medium of learning. But, needless to say, the framers of the rules are used to send their children to English-medium Schools/Colleges!

To further worsen the situation, the University of Calcutta has proposed to make English and Bengali optional in undergraduate courses because the study of languages proves—in their parlance — "burdensome and wasteful". In the process, a total English gap in our academic life is sure to persist with a root of permanence. Consequently, this will constrict the higher education for want of required books in the vernacular medium and employment opportunities in other States in the country and abroad. What has not been possible over a period of more than 50 years since our independence, how do the Government and the University dare contemplate to achieve overnight?

If our students are compelled to fall back upon vernacular medium, they will be thrown into the insularity of a region known as West Bengal both for education and for employment.

May we request the concerned authorities to reconsider their views once again before their recommendations are implemented?

Yours faithfully.
Raj Halder

14

MODEL QUESTIONS WITH ANSWERS

Secretarial Practice & Office Procedure

(Pass & Honours)

A. Secretarial Functions

Q. 1. Define 'Secretary'. **(C.U. 1998, 1988, 1981)**

Ans. Page 1.

Q.2. Is it compulsory for a Co-operative Society to appoint a full-time Secretary? **(C.U. 1981)**

Ans. : The Co-operative Societies Act, 1912, and the Bengal Co-operative Societies Act, 1940, have not made it compulsory to appoint a full-time Secretary. However, the deciding factor in this regard will be the volume of work being handled by the society. Therefore, the appointment of a full-time or part-time paid Secretary depends on the volume of work and not as per requirement of the Act. However, the Bye-laws of the Society provide that if the working capital of the Society exceeds Rs. 5 lakhs, a full-time paid Secretary must be appointed.

Q. 3. What is the difference between the status of a Private Secretary and a Personal Assistant? **(C.U. 1989, 1981)**

Ans. : Page 7.

Q. 4. Is there any difference between an 'Occupation' and a 'Profession'? **(C.U. 1989, 1981)**

Ans. : According to the Webster's Dictionary, the term 'occupation' means "the principal business of one's life" or "an activity in which one engages" himself to earn his livelihood. A 'profession', on the other hand, according to the Webster's Dictionary, is "a calling requiring specialised knowledge and long and intensive academic preparation". Though both the terms are loosely used, there is indeed a difference between the two.

Q. 5. Define a 'Profession'. **(C.U. 1981)**

Ans. : Please write the 'Profession' part from Q/A. No. 4, page 321.

Q. 6. Is Company Secretaryship a 'Profession' in India? (C.U. 1981)

Ans. : The term 'Profession' has been defined in the Webster's Dictionary as "a calling requiring specialised knowledge and long and intensive academic preparation". The secretaryship satisfies all the characteristics that are required of a profession. It has also won the legal and public recognition as a 'profession'.

Q. 7. Who appoints the first Secretary of a Company? (C.U. 1981)

Ans. : Page 25.

Q. 8. Can a Law Graduate be appointed the Secretary of a Public Company?(C.U. 1981)

Ans. : According to the Companies (Appointment and Qualifications of Secretary) Rules, 1988, as amended on 13th April 1993, vide Govt. Notification No. G.S.R. 372(E), a degree in law of any recognised university in India is one of the approved qualifications to be a company secretary in a company having paid-up share capital of less than Rs. 50 lakhs.

Q. 9. Who can be appointed the Secretary of a Company having a paid-up share capital of Rs. 50 lakhs? (C.U. 1981)

Ans. : According to Rule 2(1) of the Companies (Appointment and Qualifications of Secretary) (Amendment) Rules, 1993, a company having paid-up share capital of Rs. 50 lakhs or more must appoint a member of the Institute of Company Secretaries of India as its Company Secretary.

Q. 10. A Company has only two directors. Can any one of them be appointed Secretary of the Company? (C.U. 1991, 1981)

Ans. : According to Section 252 of the Companies Act, 1956, a public limited company must have three directors and a private limited company at least two directors. A director having the prescribed qualifications may be appointed as the Company Secretary also. But if there are only two directors in a Company, none of them can be appointed as its Secretary.

Q. 11. What are the statutory duties of a Company Secretary? (C.U. 1981)

Ans. : Page 30.

Q. 12. "A Secretary is a mere servant of the Company". "A Secretary is an officer of the Company with extensive duties and responsibilities."—Which of these two statements is corrent and why? (C.U. 1981)

Ans. : Page 30.

B. Office Procedure

Q. 13. The 'Office' performs a valuable service function. How? (C.U. 1989, 1981)

Ans. : The activities of a modern business enterprise are multifarious and the work of co-ordinating these activities is one of the important functions of an efficient office. The other important functions are (i) collection of data (ii) processing of data and posting of entries (iii) communication through letters, circulars, notices etc. and (iv) reporting matters to the proper levels of management to foster the growth of business. So it is true that 'Office' performs a valuable service function. 'Office' is also known as the nerve centre of the business enterprise.

Q. 14. Why is the 'Office' called the 'hub' of the business organisation? **(C.U. 1990, 1981)**

Ans. : The term 'hub' has been defined in the Webster's dictionary as "the central part of a wheel or propeller or the centre of activity". The office of any organisation can be called the 'hub' of the business organisation as the office is like the mainspring of a watch or the central part of a wheel of a car or a propeller.

Q. 15. Define 'Office-layout'. **(C.U. 1981)**

Ans. : Page 52.

Q. 16. 'Office rooms should have natural lighting as far as practicable'. Is there any alternative to natural lighting? **(C.U. 1982 & 1981)**

Ans. : Natural light is undoubtedly the best light; but it is always not possible to get natural light, e.g., after sunset, in cloudy days, etc. To keep the workflow continuous, modern offices have to arrange for artificial light despite the fact that natural light will be available during the daytime. In recent years, most of the States in India have been facing problems of power-cuts (load-shedding). So with a view to tackling this problem, arrangements for artificial light by installing generators and invertors are made by most of the modern offices.

Q. 17. What is 'Colour Conditioning'? **(C.U. 1988, 1981)**

Ans. : The term 'Colour Conditioning' may be defined as use of colours most effectively and efficiently so that the employees working in an organisation are in a position to render their best services. This, in turn, increases productivity and profitability of the business enterprise.

Q. 18. There are four methods of dictating letters. What are these? **(C.U. 1999, 1990, 1988, 1981)**

Ans. : The four methods of dictating letters in any modern organisation may be enumerated as under :

(a) Dictating to a stenographer;

(b) Dictating to a machine-writing stenographer;

(c) Dictating to a Dictaphone;

(d) Dictating to the typist direct by the executive.

Q. 19. What is the difference between 'Post-Book' and 'Book Post'? **(C.U. 1991, 1989)**

Ans. : A 'Post-Book' records the details of the letters/covers despatched by any organisation together with the amounts of stamps affixed on them. This book is an evidence of the outgoing mail. A 'Book Post', on the other hand, is an uncovered packet/unsealed envelope whose both ends/one end are/is open. This enables the postal authorities to examine the contents of the packet, if necessary. Book Post requires less postage stamp as compared to the registered/ordinary post.

Q. 20. A Post Box and a Post Bag serve the same purpose. Do you agree?
(V.U. 1988; C.U. 1991, 1989, 1984, 1981)

Ans. : All the communications addressed to the hirer of a Post Box (excluding registered letters/parcels, telegrams, money orders etc.) are kept in the relative box. A post bag is a special type of bag which is hired by any business house from the nearby post office for safe delivery of inward and outward mail from and to post office. All the incoming mail addressed to the hirer is kept inside the bag which remains locked. While the post box is mainly used for incoming mail, the post bag can be used both for incoming and outgoing mail.

Q. 21. What is a 'Typing Pool'? **(V.U. 1988; C.U. 1988, 1984, 1982)**

Ans. : When the services of all the typists in an organisation are placed in a common pool, it is known as a "Typing Pool" or "Typists' Pool". The pool works under the direct control and supervision of a specialised officer. This is an example of centralised service and has, therefore, the advantages of the centralised services, e.g., (a) more even distribution of work (b) minimisation of idle time (c) improved supervision of work and comparison of work done by different typists (d) minimisation of interruption to work as the 'pool' is normally housed in a corner of the office. The demerits of this system are (a) loss of personal contacts between the officers and the typists (b) chances of deterioration in the quality of work because of monotony.

Q. 22. For what types of business is the Alphabetical Classification of Files best suited?
(C.U. 1984, 1981)

Ans. : 'Alphabetical' Classification means classification of the files/folders according to the first letters of the names of the correspondents. The working of this method is similar to the working of a dictionary or a telephone directory. This is most suitable when the names of the correspondents are important. Besides, this is very useful for correspondence filing, contracts, staff records, etc.

Q. 23. "The Bound Book Index" has been replaced by other methods of Indexing. Name the other methods. **(C.U. 1988, 1981)**

Ans. : To obviate the difficulties experienced in a bound book index, other improved methods of indexing have been evolved. These are (a) loose-leaf book index (b) card index (c) visible index (d) fixed index and (e) vowel index. The most suitable system for any type of records will largely depend on the requirements of the individual filing system.

Q. 24. Define a 'Form'. **(C.U. 1981)**

Ans. : Page 76.

Q. 25. What is 'Continuous Stationery'? **(C.U. 1984, 1982)**

Ans. : Page 102.

Q. 26. Under what circumstances is 'Duplicating' used as a substitute for 'Printing'? **(C.U. 1981)**

Ans. : In large organisations where volume of work is more, printing machines can be installed for the purpose of printing of different forms. The main deciding factor in this regard is the volume of work of the concerned organisation. In short, when the number of copies required are beyond the capacity of the typewriter but not so much as would justify installation of printing machines, use of duplicating machines is recommended. Use of personal computers may also be advantageous in such a situation.

Q. 27. Name three machines for copying letters without repeating the original process of preparing the letters. **(C.U. 1982, 1984, 1981)**

Ans. : The names of a few machines for copying letters without repeating the original process are (a) Typewriter (b) Photostat and (c) Mimeograph (d) Personal computers.

Q. 28. In what way is the Franking Machine a labour-saving device? **(C.U. 1990, 1984, 1981)**

Ans. : A franking machine is a labour-saving machine inasmuch as it works at a high speed and affixes stamps on the outgoing mail. Since much of the labour required to paste stamps on the outgoing mail is saved, a franking machine is called a labour-saving device. An added advantage of this machine is that the user may incorporate a slogan or an advertisement on the envelope/cover. Such a machine can be purchased or hired from the Department of Posts.

C. Meetings

Q. 29. Name three basic requisites of a valid meeting. **(C.U. 1982, 1981)**

Ans. : The three basic requisites or requirements of a valid meeting are : (a) It must be properly convened (i.e., called) by the authorised person. (b) Proper notice of the meeting must be given to the members/persons/parties who are entitled to attend it. (c) A meeting must be properly constituted — it should have a chairman and the quorum.

Q. 30. 'A meeting becomes unlawful if it is held for an unlawful purpose.' Under what other circumstances can a meeting become unlawful? **(C.U. 1982, 1981)**

Ans. : Page 144.

Q. 31. A meeting is going to be held in a public park. Will it be a unlawful meeting? **(V.U. 1988; C.U. 1981)**

Ans. : A public park comes within the definition of a 'public place'. A meeting in a public place — if held without the permission of the appropriate authority — will be an unlawful meeting. If, however, the prior permission is obtained, the meeting will be a lawful one.

Q. 32. What rules should a Chairman follow in conducting the meeting of a private body? **(C.U. 1981)**

Ans. : Write the main points as given in Ans. to Q. No. 15, Pages 150-151.

Q. 33. What is meant by 'proper length of notice'? (C.U. 1982, 1981)

Ans. : Page 147.

Q. 34. What is 'Clear days' Notice? (C.U. 1982, 1981)

Ans. : Page 176.

Q. 35. What should be the contents of a valid notice of a meeting? (C.U. 1981)

Ans. : Page 145.

Q. 36. What is meant by 'Continuous Quorum'? (C.U. 1984, 1981)

Ans. : Page 162.

Q. 37. A meeting starts with a quorum of members, but subsequently the attendance falls below quorum. Can the meeting continue and transact valid business? (C.U. 1981)

Ans. : Page162.

Q. 38. When can the Chairman adjourn a meeting? (C.U. 1982, 1981)

Ans. : Page 151.

Q. 39. Who is a Chairman pro tem? (V.U. 1988; C.U. 1998, 1981)

Ans. : The term 'pro tem' (abbreviation of 'pro tempore') means 'for the time being'. In absence of the designated chairman, one of the members attending the meeting is elected as the chairman 'pro tem'. If the designated chairman arrives during the currency of the meeting, the chairman pro tem will vacate the Chair. If, however, the designated chairman requests the chairman pro tem to continue, the latter may continue to conduct the meeting till the end.

Q. 40. The Chairman of a meeting has two votes under the rules. What are these two votes and when can the second vote be used? (C.U. 1999, 1981)

Ans. : Page 151.

Q. 41. When can a member speak twice on the same primary motion? (C.U. 1981)

Ans. : Page 153.

Q. 42. X moves a motion before a meeting and Y seconds it. Can X withdraw the motion after seconding? (C.U. 1981)

Ans. : As soon as the motion is seconded by Y, the motion is put before the meeting for consideration. Thereafter, the motion cannot be withdrawn by X, the mover, without the consent of the meeting.

Q. 43. The wording of a motion should be in the 'affirmative'. When can the wording of a motion be in the 'negative'? (C.U. 1981)

Ans. : As a matter of convention, a motion should be in the affirmative and it should start with the word 'That'. However, wordings of a few formal motions may be in the negative.

Q. 44. Define a Substantive Motion. **(C.U. 1984, 1982, 1981)**

Ans. : Page 177.

Q. 45. A member who has spoken once on the main motion wants to move an amendment which seeks to negative the main motion. Can he do it? **(C.U. 1981)**

Ans. : An amendment to a motion to be valid must be moved by any member other than the mover. Therefore, the mover in the instant problem cannot move an amendment on the motion. An amendment — to be valid — must be in the affirmative. So, in the instant problem, the member cannot "move an amendment which seeks to negative the main motion."

Q. 46. Distinguish between a 'Motion' and a 'Resolution'. **(C.U. 1981)**

Ans. : Page 152.

Q. 47. During discussion on a motion a member moves a 'Previous Question' motion. What will happen to the original motion if the Previous Question is lost? **(C.U. 1984, 1981)**

Ans. : If and when the 'Previous Question' motion is lost, it is the Chairman who can order for votes to be taken on the original motion.

Q. 48. What is the purpose of moving the 'Next Business' motion? **(C.U. 1981)**

Ans. : Page 168.

Q. 49. What is a 'Point of Order'? **(C.U. 1984, 1981)**

Ans. : Page 168.

Q. 50. For what purpose is the Ballot method of voting used? **(C.U. 1981)**

Ans. : Page 160.

Q. 51. If a 'Poll' is properly demanded, when must the Chairman take the Poll? **(C.U. 1984, 1982, 1981)**

Ans. : Page 160.

Q. 52. In how many ways can a Proxy be revoked? **(C.U. 1981)**

Ans. : Page 166.

Q. 53. What method of voting will be best suited to a Public Company with a large number of shareholders who want to cast their votes in person or by proxy? **(C.U. 1981)**

Ans. : Voting by 'Poll' will be the most suitable to the company meetings with large attendance. This method of voting helps the company to get rid of the unqualified persons from taking part in the discussion.

Q. 54. What is meant by Qualified Privilege? **(C.U. 1981)**

Ans. : Page 170.

Q. 55. Under what circumstances will a defamatory statement enjoy Absolute Privilege? (C.U. 1981)

Ans. : Page 170.

Q. 56. A witness in a criminal case makes a statement in the Court which the defendant considers to be defamatory. Can the witness claim privileges? (C.U. 1981)

Ans. : The witness, in the instant case, enjoys absolute privilege, since the statements made by a judge, advocate, juryman, witness and a party in the course of and/or in connection with any judicial proceedings in a Court of law are permitted absolute privilege.

Q. 57. A meeting has been adjourned by the Chairman, but no date has been fixed for the adjourned meeting. Is fresh notice necessary for the adjourned meeting?(C.U. 1981)

Ans. : An adjourned meeting is the continuation of the original meeting. The meeting at which adjournment is decided normally fixes the date, time and place for the adjourned meeting and no notice of adjournment is necessary if it is held within 30 days from the date of adjournment. But if the meeting is adjourned sine die (i.e., indefinitely), fresh notice needs to be served.

Q. 58. Distinguish between 'Minutes' and 'Proceedings' of a meeting. (C.U. 1981)

Ans. : Minutes are the written records of the business transacted at a meeting. The term 'Proceedings' means detailed report of the meeting, e.g., right from the names of the persons who attended the meeting to all the happenings up to the closure of the meeting. As such, minutes differ from report. While minutes refer to what was done, proceedings refers to what was said.

Q. 59. What is meant by 'Minutes of Decision'? (C.U. 1981)

Ans. : Page 175.

Q. 60. A director of a company lives outside India. Is it obligatory to send him notices of Company meetings? (C.U. 1981)

Ans. : In terms of Section 286(1) of the Companies Act, the notice of a Board Meeting must be given to all the directors who are present in India at their usual addresses. It is, therefore, not obligatory on the part of the company to send notice to the director living outside India.

Q. 61. What is the time limit for holding a Statutory Meeting? (C.U. 1981)

Ans. : According to Section 165 of the Companies Act, every public limited company having share capital, except unlimited companies, is required to hold a statutory meeting within a period of not less than one month and not more than six months from the date of commencement of business.

Q. 62. What is the time limit for holding a subsequent Annual General Meeting of a Company? (C.U. 1981)

Ans. : Page 140.

Q. 63. What are the provisions of the Companies Act regarding holding of Board Meeting? (C.U. 1981)

Ans. : Section 285 provides that such meeting should be held at least once in every three months and four times in a year. Section 286 provides that, in absence of quorum, the meeting is automatically adjourned. Section 289 provides for the rules of circulating the resolution to the directors.

Q. 64. What penalty is provided in the Companies Act for default in holding Annual General Meetings? (C.U. 1981)

Ans. : According to Section 168 of the Companies Act, if the company defaults in complying with the provisions of Sections 166 and 167, the company and its officers will be liable to a maximum fine of Rs. 5,000/- and for continuing default, a further sum of Rs. 250/- per day.

Q. 65. Can a Company Meeting be held on any day at any place and at any time? (C.U. 1981)

Ans. : Page 176.

Q. 66. The first Annual General Meeting of a Company was held on 15th November 1980. The financial year expires on 30th September of each year. The Company wants to hold the next Annual General Meeting on 10th February 1982. Will such a meeting be legally valid? (C.U. 1982, 1981)

Ans. : As per the provision of Section 166 of the Companies Act, ordinarily, not more than 15 months should elapse between the two annual general meetings. In the instant case, the next annual general meeting can be validly held on any day up to the 14th February 1982.

Q. 67. When can a Company Meeting be held with a one-member quorum? (C.U. 1998, 1991, 1989, 1981)

Ans. : Page 163.

Q. 68. What is the quorum for a Shareholders' meeting of a Public Company under the Companies Act? Can the Articles increase it? (C.U. 1981)

Ans. : Section 174(1) of the Companies Act provides that unless the Articles prescribe for a larger number, five members, personally present, shall be the quorum for a shareholders' meeting of a public limited company. The Articles of Association may, however, provide for a larger number for the purpose of quorum.

Q. 69. What is the time limit for writing the Minutes of a Board Meeting? (C.U. 1999, 1981)

Ans. : The minutes of the Board Meeting or Committee thereof must be signed within a period of 30 days from the date of the meeting by the Chairman of that meeting or the next succeeding meeting.

Q. 70. What kind of resolution will be necessary if a Company wants to (a) alter the name of the Company and (b) appoint an Auditor other than the retiring Auditor? **(C.U. 1981)**

Ans. : (a) Under Section 189(2), alteration of the name of the Company requires a special resolution. (b) Under Section 225 of the Companies Act, a resolution requiring special notice is required to appoint an auditor other than the retiring auditor.

Q. 71. Can a member of a Company claim privilege in speeches made in a Company Meeting? **(C.U. 1981)**

Ans. : Page 170.

D. Secretarial Practice

Q. 72. Why is it necessary to prepare Precis of business correspondence? **(C.U. 1990, 1987, 1981)**

Ans. : "A precis is a succinct (i.e., concise) digest of essential facts contained in any piece of printed, written or spoken matter". Modern age is the day of 'management by exception'. Busy executives hardly find any time to go through the minute details of the business affairs. Therefore, all papers are placed before them in precise form or 'precis' which saves the executives' invaluable time.

Q. 73. What is the purpose of writing a Trade Circular? **(C.U. 1990, 1982, 1981)**

Ans. : Business houses are very often required to convey some information, particulars or changes to their customers, dealers, friends, well-wishers and the general public. This is done by way of a communication which is known as the trade circular. The form of circular should be pleasant and the language lucid as well as courteous.

Q. 74. Distinguish between a 'Circular' and a 'Notice'. **(C.U. 1988, 1981)**

Ans. : A circular is a means of conveying some information, particulars, data to the customers, dealers, agents, patrons, well-wishers of any business house and to the public in general. A notice, on the other hand, is an intimation to the members and other persons who are entitled to attend the meeting about the time, date, place and nature of business to be transacted thereat.

Q. 75. For what purposes would you use informal resolutions? **(C.U. 1981)**

Ans. : Informal resolutions are used when some informal matters are discussed and, ultimately, the decision of the meeting is recorded. For example, to express sympathy, condolence etc. informal resolutions are passed. As the term 'informal resolutions' suggests, these resolutions do not follow any standard form.

Q. 76. What are Privileged Reports? **(C.U. 1981)**

Ans. : Page 231.

Q. 77. What is a Statutory Report of a Company? **(C.U. 1981)**

Ans. : Page 194.

Q. 78. What is an Ad hoc Committee?

Ans. : The term 'Ad hoc' means 'for the particular purpose'. So an 'Ad hoc' Committee means a committee to which a specific job is given. The Committee dissolves as soon as the job is completed.

Q. 79. What does the 'Heading' of a commercial letter usually include? (C.U. 1981)

Ans. : The 'Heading' or caption of a commercial letter ordinarily includes the name of the firm/company, its full postal address, telegraphic address, e-mail address, telephone number(s), fax number and telex number. More often than not, it includes the names of the products manufactured/services rendered by it and the year of its establishment.

Q. 80. What is the purpose of having a 'Telegraphic Address'? (C.U. 1981)

Ans. : Page 69.

Q. 81. What complimentary close should be used with the salutations (a) Sir, (b) Dear Sir and (c) Gentlemen?

Ans. : (a) Yours faithfully, (b) Yours faithfully, and (c) Yours truly.

Q. 82. What is a 'Postscript'? (C.U. 1988, 1981)

Ans. : The dictionary meaning of the term 'Postscript' is a note or a series of notes appended to a completed letter, article or book. After the letter or report is formally closed and signed by the writer, some more points need to be added. These are handwritten/type-written after the word 'Postscript'. The abbreviation of Postscript is "P.S.".

Q. 83. What is the difference between a 'General Offer' and a 'Specific Offer'? (C.U. 1988)

Ans. : An offer involves the making of a proposal. The person who makes the offer or the proposal is known as the offeror or the promissor/proposer and the other person to whom it is made is the offeree. When the offer is made to the public in general, it is known as a general offer. On the other hand, when the offer is made to a person or a group of persons, it is known as the specific offer.

Q. 84. What do you mean by 'Quotation' as used in business transactions? (C.U. 1989, 1981)

Ans. : The term 'Quotation' has been defined in J. L. Hanson's "A Dictionary of Economics and Commerce" as "A statement of prices. A purchaser may ask his supplier for a quotation for a particular order. When such a quotation is given, it applies only to that particular transaction." Besides price, the quotation contains detailed specifications of the goods, terms of payment etc. The term 'Quotation' is also known as the 'Proforma Invoice'.

Q. 85. Under what circumstances can a customer claim compensation or adjustment from a supplier? (C.U. 1981)

Ans. : A customer can claim compensation or adjustment in the following circumstances : (a) When the quality and quantity of goods supplied are not as per the contract.

(b) When the goods supplied are damaged ones. And (c) When the goods are supplied much later than the scheduled time. After mutual agreement, compensation or adjustment is normally made either by the buyer or the seller against some previous or future bills.

Q. 86. Who is a Commission Agent? (C.U. 1981)

Ans. : A commission agent is more or less like a broker. He secures buyers for sellers — and the vice versa — in return for a commission on the sale. He may — or may not — have the goods in his possession.

Q. 87. What is a Status Enquiry? (C.U. 1991, 1989, 1981)

Ans. : A status enquiry is made by the supplier of goods/services to commercial banks, business friends, credit information agencies about the creditworthiness and reputation of the prospective buyers. Ordinarily, the supplier approaches its banker to obtain the status report on the prospective buyer. The banker of the supplier then approaches the banker of the buyer for the status report. On receipt of the report, the supplier's banker passes on the required information to the supplier.

Q. 88. Who exercises the operational control on the company?

Ans. : Operational control on the company is exercised by : (a) Shareholders in general meeting, (b) Board of Directors and (c) Executives of the company, e.g. managing director, whole-time director, manager, company secretary.

Q. 89. What are the sources of the corporate powers?

Ans. : The sources from which the corporate powers are derived are (a) The Memorandum of Association, (b) The Articles of Association and (c) Any other statutes providing for corporate powers, e.g., Companies Act, 1956.

Q. 90. What are the organs under the "Company Law Administration"?

Ans. : The various organs of the "Company Law Administration" are (a) Department of Company Affairs in the Ministry of Law, Justice and Company Affairs, Government of India; (b) Regional Directors located in Mumbai, Calcutta, Chennai and Kanpur; (c) Registrar of Companies; and (d) Company Law Board, which is a quasi-judicial body.

Q. 91. What are the occasions or the possible reasons for adjournment of a meeting?

Ans. : An adjournment of a meeting may be caused by : (a) Failure to form the quorum; (b) Failure to maintain or keep up the quorum; (c) Failure to collect the necessary information/data/particulars before the meeting; (d) If and when the members present decide/resolve to adjourn the meeting; (e) Chairman's action to adjourn the meeting.

Q. 92. Is it necessary to give fresh notice to hold an adjourned meeting?

Ans. : As the adjourned meeting is continuation of the original meeting, no fresh notice is necessary if the meeting is held within 30 days from the date of adjournment. If a meeting is adjourned sine die (i.e., indefinitely), fresh notice will be necessary. An adjourned meeting can validly transact only those business which could not be transacted at the original meeting.

Q. 93. Can an Annual General Meeting or an adjourned Annual General Meeting be held on a public holiday?

Ans. : In terms of the provisions of Section 166 of the Companies Act, an annual general meeting cannot be held on a public holiday. An adjourned annual general meeting should also not be held on a public holiday. However, the Department of Company Affairs has clarified that the provision of Section 166(2) will not be contravened if the adjourned meeting comes to be held on a public holiday just as a coincidence.

Q. 94. What is revocation of proxy? (C.U. 1999, 1988)

Ans. : When the member having appointed the proxy personally attends the meeting and votes thereat, there is revocation of proxy. A proxy is also revoked as soon as the company receives notice of revocation by way of death, insanity etc. of the member.

Q. 95. Name the types of companies which are not required to hold statutory meeting.

Ans. : In terms of the provisions of Section 165 of the Companies Act, public company limited by shares and every public company limited by guarantee and having share capital are required to hold statutory meeting. Therefore, a private company and a company limited by guarantee and not having a share capital are not required to hold statutory meeting.

Q. 96. Can a meeting be held with a shorter notice? (C.U. 1999)

Ans. : A clear twenty-one days' notice is required to be given to those who are entitled to get it and attend general meeting. An annual general meeting with shorter notice may be validly held if all the members entitled to vote thereat agree to it. Other meetings with shorter notice can be held lawfully if the members holding 95% of the paid-up capital of the company agree to it. A Board Meeting can be held with a shorter notice.

Q. 97. What is a 'Public Holiday'?

Ans. : In accordance with the provision of Section 2(38) of the Companies Act, "Public Holiday" means a public holiday within the meaning of Section 25 of the Negotiable Instruments Act, 1881. Public holiday includes Sundays and other days as declared by the Central Government by way of notification in the Official Gazette. 30th September and 31st March are declared holidays for the limited purpose of half-yearly and yearly closing in banks. So Section 166 of the Companies Act does not consider these two days as public holidays.

Q. 98. When is a meeting dissolved and not adjourned?

Ans. : If there is no quorum within half an hour from the time fixed for the meeting called on the requisition of members, the meeting will be dissolved and not adjourned.

Q. 99. Who can inspect the Minutes of the Board Meeting?

Ans. : The following persons are entitled to inspect the Minutes of the Board meetings : (a) All the directors of the company; (b) Auditors of the company (for the purpose of audit only); (c) The Investigating Officers in the course of their investigation into the affairs of the company. (d) Officers from the office of the Comptroller and Auditor-General of India, in respect of the Government companies under Section 619 of the Companies Act, 1956.

Q. 100. State the minimum and maximum number of directors a company is required to have.

Ans. : According to Section 252 of the Companies Act, the minimum number of directors for a public company, deemed public company and any other company/private company is 3, 2 and 2, respectively. The Articles of Association of the Company prescribe the maximum number of directors which a company may have on the Board. A public company or a private company subsidiary to a public company ordinarily can have 12 directors at the most. This number may, however, be increased with the specific approval of the Central Government.

Q. 101. Explain whether a director holding 40% shares can be appointed a scrutineer to scrutinise the votes at the poll.

Ans. : In terms of Section 184 of the Companies Act, the Chairman of the meeting can appoint two scrutineers one of whom must be a member of the company. The term 'member', however, does not include any employee or officer of the company. So the director holding 40% shares can be appointed a scrutineer provided the other scrutineer to be appointed is a member of the company.

Q. 102. A director was informed by the Company over telephone about a Board Meeting on a particular date. The director said "I cannot be there"; no notice in writing was sent to him thereafter. Is the meeting valid?

Ans. : According to Section 286 of the Companies Act, notice of every Board meeting has to be sent to all the directors in writing. It is immaterial whether any director has communicated his unwillingness or inability to attend the meeting. So the meeting in question is in contravention of the provision of Section 286 and, as such, it is not valid.

Q. 103. Can a non-member become the Chairman of a company?

Ans. : Ordinarily, an outsider can neither attend a meeting nor can he/she preside thereat. If, however, the Articles of Association of the Company provide that the directors need not acquire any qualification share(s), a non-member can act as Chairman. A nominee-director or salaried director may act as a chairman.

Q. 104. Is it necessary for a company registered without share capital to hold : (a) annual general meeting and (b) statutory meeting?

Ans. : According to Section 166 of the Companies Act, every company with or without share capital must hold annual general meetings. According to Section 165(1) of the Act, the companies limited by shares and the companies limited by guarantee and having share capital are required to hold the statutory meeting. So, in the instant case, the company registered without share capital need not hold the statutory meeting.

Q. 105. Shri Kamal Krishna Kankaria—an M. Com. of a recognised Indian university—was appointed Company Secretary of Messrs. Jardine Henderson Ltd. on 31.8.76.

At that time the Company's paid-up share capital was Rs. 20 lakhs which was increased to Rs. 60 lakhs on 30.11.1994. Can Shri Kankaria still continue in the post of the Company Secretary?

Ans. : According to Section 383A of the Companies Act, in the case of a company having a paid-up capital of rupees fifty lakhs or more, the membership of the Institute of Company Secretaries of India is the requisite qualification. As Shri Kankaria does not possess the requisite qualification, he cannot be allowed to continue in the post of Company Secretary.

Q. 106. Can a director of the company be appointed a Company Secretary?(C.U. 1990)

Ans. : A director of the company can be appointed a Company Secretary if the following two requirements of the Companies Act are complied with : (a) the company must have more than two directors; and (b) the director to be appointed as secretary must have the 'prescribed qualifications' as required under the Companies (Appointment & Qualifications of Secretary) Rules, 1988, as amended in 1993.

Q. 107. There was the required quorum when the meeting started. Subsequently, the attendance fell short of quorum. Will the business transacted thereafter be valid? What will be your answer when it is a (i) General Meeting and (ii) Board Meeting? (C.U. 1988)

Ans. : According to Regulation 49(1) of Table A, quorum is necessary only to start the meeting but it is silent as to whether quorum should be present throughout the currency of the meeting. A similar ruling was given in Re : Hartley Baird Ltd. case which states that the quorum is necessary only to start the meeting. But the quorum must be present throughout the currency of the Board Meeting (Re : Henderson vs Louttit). So, in the instant case, the business transacted in the General Meeting will be valid and those transacted in the Board Meeting will be invalid.

Q. 108. Name the three most important documents with which a company is concerned.

Ans. : A company is concerned with the following most important documents : (a) Memorandum of Association, (b) Articles of Association and (c) Prospectus.

Q. 109. What do you mean by statistical books and statutory books of a company? Give examples. (C.U. 1991)

Ans. : The Companies Act requires a company to maintain several types of books and registers. Statistical books refer to the books of account and some related registers. Statutory books refer to those books and registers which are required to comply with the legal requirements. Some examples of statutory books are : registers of members, registers of directors, minutes book, register of mortgages and charges, register of directors' shareholdings.

Q. 110. Who can inspect the proxies?

Ans. : According to Section 176(7) of the Companies Act, every member who is entitled to vote at a meeting is also entitled to inspect the proxies. He has, however, to give not less than three days' notice in writing to the company communicating his intention to inspect the proxies. The inspection can be made in the usual office hours of the company during the period beginning 24 hours before the scheduled time of the meeting and the conclusion thereof.

Q. 111. How can a Company Secretary be dismissed? (C.U. 1999)

Ans. : As the Company Secretary is an employee of the company, his dismissal or removal is governed by the general law applicable to master and servant. The terms and conditions of his appointment normally include a clause regarding his suspension and/or removal. Depending on the nature of his offence, he may be dismissed with or without notice by the Board of Directors/Managing Director of the Company.

Q. 112. Is it obligatory on the Chairman to order for taking poll immediately on demand?

Ans. : The Chairman has to order for taking poll immediately on demand in the following circumstances :(a) On a question of adjournment (Section 180 of the Companies Act); and (b) On election of the Chairman [Section 175(2) of the Companies Act]. According to Section 180(2), a poll demanded on any other question may be ordered to be taken by the Chairman any time within 48 hours from the time of demand.

Q. 113. How will the following persons be counted for the purpose of quorum : (a) Chairman, (b) proxy-holder, (c) Preference share-holder, (d) joint shareholder, (e) public trustee, (f) legal representative, (g) authorised representatives of a body corporate, (h) an employee/officer of the company holding 10% of the total equity capital, (i) lady member, (j) a member of the company who is also representing a company member?

Ans. : Page 164.

Q. 114. Who are entitled to receive notice of annual general meeting?

Ans. : The following persons are entitled to receive notice of annual general meeting (a) every member of the company; (b) legal representative (successor) of the deceased, member; (c) Official assignee/receiver consequent upon insolvency of the member; and, (d) the auditors of the company.

Q. 115. Can the auditor of the company vote on any question before the general meeting of the company?

Ans. : Though the auditor is entitled to receive notice of the meeting and can attend it, he cannot vote thereat. He can speak only on questions relating to the accounts of the company.

Q. 116. Notice of a general meeting was given to those who were entitled to receive it. It subsequently transpired that there was accidental omission to give notice to O, a member of the company. N, another member, reportedly did not receive the notice. Will the proceedings of the meeting be valid?

Ans. : In terms of Section 172(3) of the Companies Act, 1956, the accidental omission to give notice to, or the non-receipt of notice by any member or other person to whom it should be given, shall not invalidate the proceedings of the meeting.

Q. 117. What is the provision of company law relating to signing of Directors' Report?

Ans. : Ordinarily, the Chairman of the Board is authorised by the Board of Directors of the company to sign the Directors' Report. If he is not so authorised, the report should be signed by the Manager or Secretary, if any, and at least by two Directors of the company — one of whom shall be the Managing Director, if any, of the company.

Q. 118. When and to whom the Directors' Report is required to be sent?

Ans. : The Directors' Report has to be sent to every member of the company, auditors, and other eligible persons at least 21 clear days before the date of the annual general meeting of the company.

Q. 119. When is it not necessary to give notice of a meeting?

Ans. : In the following circumstances, notice of a meeting need not be given (a) When the members present at a meeting decide about their next meeting; (b) The Board of Directors or Committees thereof may decide to meet on fixed dates or at specified intervals of time; and (c) When a meeting is adjourned for want of quorum to the next week, same day, same time and same place automatically.

Q. 120. "Sometimes all the members or directors constitute the quorum." Is the statement correct?

Ans. : In the following circumstances, presence of all the members/directors is necessary to form the quorum : (a) At a Board Meeting of a private company having two directors only, presence of both the directors is necessary to form the quorum, (b) At a general meeting of a private company having only two shareholders, presence of both of them is necessary for the quorum. So the statement is correct.

Q. 121. On what grounds can a Chairman reject an amendment to a motion?

Ans. : The Chairman of a meeting can reject an amendment on the following grounds : (a) if it negatives the original motion; (b) if it is ultra vires or beyond the scope of the meeting; (c) if it is not relevant to the original motion; (d) if it is inconsistent with the decision already taken in the meeting; (e) if it is an amendment to an amendment; and (f) if it is proposed as a formal or dilatory motion.

Q. 122. "One of the duties of the directors is to attend Board Meetings." —Elucidate.

Ans. : Though the directors are not bound to attend all the Board Meetings, they should try to attend them as far as possible. If any director absents himself from three consecutive Board Meetings or from all the Board Meetings held during a period of three months — whichever is longer—without leave of absence from the Board, the office of the director shall automatically become vacant.

Q. 123. Should a Co-operative Society appoint a full-time Secretary?

Ans. : The Co-operative Societies Act, 1912, provides that every co-operative society must appoint a Secretary for its day-to-day operations. There is, however, no mention as to whether the Secretary will be a whole-timer or a part-timer. It may, therefore, be said that it is the volume of work of the society which should decide this issue. However, the Bye-laws of the society provide that if the working capital of the Society exceeds Rs. 5 lakhs, a full-time paid Secretary must be appointed.

Q. 124. What is the maximum time-limit by which Minutes of the meetings have to be prepared? (C.U. 1999)

Ans. : The Companies Act, 1956, provides that the Minutes of the meeting—whether general or Board—must be prepared and signed within 30 days from the date of its conclusion.

Q. 125. A motion is moved by M and seconded by S. Thereafter, M wants to withdraw the motion. Is it permissible?

Ans. : As soon as the motion is seconded, it is a proposal placed before the meeting for consideration. Therefore, withdrawal of the motion by M at this stage is not permissible.

Q. 126. Can a Chairman allow the mover of a motion to speak twice on the same motion?

Ans. : The mover of a motion is ordinarily not allowed to speak twice on the same motion. But the Chairman can allow him to speak for the second time if the meeting wants some clarifications on the original motion.

Q. 127. Who can appoint a Company Secretary?

Ans. : Page 25.

Q. 128. Why is the Secretary called the liaison officer of the Company?

Ans. : The main function of any liaison officer is to keep liaison or link with various authorities within and outside the organisation for smooth running of the company in which he is employed. Similarly, a company secretary has to liaise between the Board of Directors, officers, staff members, shareholders and other persons who call on the company. It has, therefore, been aptly said that the Company Secretary is the liaison officer of the Company.

Q. 129. Who is responsible for issuing and signing the notice of a meeting?

Ans. : The appropriate authority for issuing a notice is the Board of Directors of the Company. However, the Board may authorise any Director or the Company Secretary to issue the notice on behalf of the Board. In such a case, the Director/Secretary should quote the authority in the notice. In special circumstances, the Central Government, Company Law Board and requisitionists (members) are the appropriate authorities for calling the meeting.

Q. 130. Who conducts the meetings of a company and signs the minutes of the meetings?

Ans. : The Chairman is a person who presides over and conducts the proceedings of a meeting. The minutes of the meetings—whether general or Board—must be signed within 30 days from the date of the meeting by the Chairman. While the minutes of the general meeting must be signed by the Chairman of that meeting, the minutes of the Board meeting can be signed by the Chairman of that meeting or the next meeting.

Q. 131. What is the basic difference between the Secretary of a Co-operative Society and the Secretary of a Club?

Ans. : According to the Co-operative Societies Act, 1912, a Co-operative Society must have a Secretary to discharge its various functions. There is no such enactment which requires a club to have a secretary. But, according to convention, a club normally has a secretary. While the secretary of a co-operative society is appointed by its managing committee, the secretary of a club is elected by its members.

Q. 132. When would you consider yourself qualified for becoming a Company Secretary?

Ans. : A company having paid-up share capital of Rs. 50 lakhs or more must employ such a person as its Secretary who is an Associate or Fellow Member of the Institute of Company Secretaries of India. For other companies, any one or more of the qualifications as prescribed by the Companies (Appointment & Qualifications of Secretary) Rules, 1988, as amended in April 1993, will make a person eligible for appointment as Company Secretary.

Q. 133. A Secretary is looked upon as a link-man in any organisation. Why?

Ans. : Page 26.

Q. 134. Show the prime distinction between a proposition and a resolution.

Ans. : A proposition, proposal or motion is placed before the meeting for discussion. The motion, with or without amendment, may or may not be accepted by the meeting. If and when the motion is accepted by the meeting, it is known as resolution. A resolution ultimately finds place in the minutes.

Q. 135. "A resolution is a motion but a motion is not a resolution"—Is the statement correct?

Ans. : The statement is correct. Write Ans. to Q. No. 132.

Q. 136. Could you reproduce the exact definition of a Company Secretary as provided by the Companies Act, 1956?

Ans. : Page 23.

Q. 137. A Company Secretary has to maintain secrecy. Is the statement correct?

Ans. : The Company Secretary attends ex-officio the Board Meetings which are confidential in nature. He should, therefore, ensure secrecy about the matters discussed at such meetings. Moreover, as per contractual liability, he cannot reveal trade secrets which he comes to know in the course of his employment in the company.

Q. 138. A notice of a meeting without agenda is said to be faulty and hence invalid. Why?

Ans. : It is customary with all organisations including the companies to send the agenda along with the notice of a meeting to their members. The term 'agenda' implies 'things to be done or business to be transacted' at a meeting. Section 172(1) of the Companies Act requires every notice of a meeting to contain "a statement of the business to be transacted thereat". In other words, the statement of the business to be transacted at a meeting is known as agenda. So agenda forms an essential part of the notice and without agenda the notice is faulty and invalid.

Q. 139. Who are the appointing authorities of the Secretary of (a) a company, (b) a co-operative society and (c) an embassy?

Ans. : The appointing authorities of the Secretary of a company, cooperative society and an embassy are the Board of Directors of the company, the Managing Committee of the Co-operative Society and the Embassy of the Diplomatic Mission, respectively. The Secretary of the Embassy assists the Ambassador/High Commissioner/Consul of the concerned country.

Q. 140. "In the case of a public company, a proxy has no right to speak in the meeting unless otherwise provided by...". Complete the sentence.

Ans. : "In the case of .... provided by the Articles of Association of the company."

Q. 141. Mention the kinds of meetings a Company Secretary has to deal with.

Ans. : A Company Secretary has to deal with the general meetings and Board Meetings. The term 'general meeting' includes the annual general meeting, extraordinary general meeting and statutory meeting. Board Meetings include the meetings of the Committees of the Directors.

Q. 142. What do you understand by the statutory duty of a Company Secretary? (Better, if you can answer the question in one sentence.)

Ans. : As the principal officer of the company, the Company Secretary has to comply with the requirements of the various Acts (i.e., Statutes) like the Companies Act, Income-tax Act, Stamp Act, Monopolies & Restrictive Trade Practices Act, Foreign Exchange Regulation Act, Sales Tax Act which have a bearing on the activities of the company.

Q. 143. When are the phrases "The Aye's have it" and "The No's have it" used in a meeting?

Ans. : Page 159.

Q. 144. From which Latin word is the term "Secretary" derived and what is its meaning?

Ans. : Page 1.

Q. 145. Is it legally necessary for a company having paid-up share capital of Rs. 20 lakhs to have a Secretary?

Ans. : It is not legally necessary to appoint Company Secretary in a company having paid-up share capital of less than Rs. 50 lakhs and a company having no share capital.

Q. 146. What should be "quorum" of a Board Meeting of a company? (C.U. 1988, 1983)

Ans. : In terms of Section 287(2) of the Companies Act, one-third of the total strength of the Board of Directors of the company (any fraction to be rounded-off as one) or two, whichever is higher, will form the quorum. The directors forming the quorum must be non-interested directors.

Q. 147. Should a meeting of the Parliament be called a Public Meeting? Give reasons for your answer. **(C.U. 1983)**

Ans. : A meeting of the Parliament is a private meeting and not a public one. A private meeting can be attended by the members of that organisation only and the public are not allowed any entry thereat. Meetings of the Parliament can be attended by the members of the Parliament only and, as such, it is a private meeting.

Q. 148. Can one person form the quorum of a meeting? **(C.U. 1983)**

Ans. : Page 163.

Q. 149. The Annual General Meeting of a company was to be held on 31st October, 1982. The notice convening the meeting was dated 12th October 1982. Is the notice valid? **(C.U. 1983)**

Ans. : In terms of Section 171 of the Companies Act, not less than 21 clear days' notice is necessary to make the notice and the meeting valid. In calculating the clear days, the date of serving the notice and the date on which the meeting is scheduled to be held are excluded. So the instant notice is not valid. However, if all the members entitled to the notice and vote at the meeting agree to a shorter notice, the notice may be valid.

Q. 150. When can a person claim "Absolute Privilege of Speech"? **(C.U. 1983)**

Ans. : Page 170.

Q. 151. Are 'Adjournment' and 'Postponement' synonymous? **(C.U. 1983)**

Ans. : Though the terms are loosely used, they are not synonymous. While 'adjournment' refers to discontinuation of a meeting for some reason(s) for holding it on a future date, 'postponement' means deferment of the meeting.

Q. 152. Votes were taken on a 'motion'. There was equality of votes 'In favour' and 'Against' the motion. How can a decision be taken in this case? **(C.U. 1999, 1983)**

Ans. : If the Articles of Association so provide, the Chairman is entitled to his casting vote which is in addition to his usual vote as a member of the company. In the given problem, there is a 'tie' and the Chairman can use his casting vote either in favour or against the motion to take a decision.

Q. 153. One member is persistently obstructing the proceedings of the meeting. What should the Chairman of the meeting do on such occasion? **(C.U. 1983)**

Ans. : Page 151.

Q. 154. Define Guillotine Closure.

Ans. : Page 178.

Q. 155. Define Kangaroo Closure (in relation to a meeting). **(C.U. 1983)**

Ans. : Page 178.

Q. 156. What is 'Loophole Agendum'?

Ans. : The term 'agenda' implies "things to be done" or "business to be transacted" at a meeting. The term agendum is the singular form of agenda. The term 'Loophole Agendum' means "any other business". Usually the last item of the agenda reads as "Any other business" or 'Loophole Agendum'.

Q. 157. What is a "Rider"?

Ans. : A 'Rider' is added at the end of a motion as a suggestion or recommendation. In this connection, an agendum also adds words at the end of a motion; but this is not in the form of a suggestion/recommendation.

Q. 158. The first Annual General Meeting of a company was held on 15th November 1980. The financial year expires on 30th September each year. The company wants to hold the next Annual General Meeting on 10th February 1982. Will such a meeting be legally valid? (C.U. 1983)

Ans. : Section 166 of the Companies Act provides that the difference between two annual general meetings shall not be more than 15 months. Section 210(3) provides that the annual general meeting should be held within 6 months from the financial year-ending. In the instant case, both the requirements of the Act will be complied if the meeting is held on 10th February 1982. Hence, the meeting will be legally valid.

Q. 159. Can the auditor of the company be a director of that company?

Ans. : In terms of Section 226(2) (b) of the Companies Act, the auditor of the company cannot be a director of that company.

Q. 160. (a) Total strength of the Board of Directors of your company is ten :

(i) How many directors are liable to retire by rotation in the next annual general meeting?

(ii) What will be the quorum of the Board Meeting?

(b) In order to pass the resolutions what is the minimum number of directors who must consent in favour of each of the following items, assuming that all the 10 directors of your company are present at the meeting :

(i) Approval of a contract to be entered into with a private limited company in which Mr. D, a director of your company, is Managing Director.

(ii) Appointment of Mr. Das as Managing Director of your company.

(iii) Approval of balance sheet and profit & loss account of the company.

(iv) Investment in shares of other body corporates. (I.C.S.I)

Ans. : (a) (i) Section 256(1) states that one-third of total directors will retire every year at every annual general meeting. If their number is not three or multiple of three then the number nearest to one-third will have to retire. So three directors will retire in the instant problem. (ii) In terms of Section 287(ii), one-third of the total strength (any fraction to be rounded-off as one) will be the quorum. (b) (i) D being interested, there remains only 9 directors. So 5 will form the majority. (ii) Since D is already a Managing Director, unanimous resolution is necessary in terms of Section 316. (iii) 6 out of 10 directors must consent in favour. (iv) If the proposed investment falls within the limit prescribed by Section 372(2), unanimous resolution of the Board is necessary. Otherwise, investment requires the approval of the shareholders in a general meeting and the Central Government also.

Q. 161. (a) Who is authorised to sign a Board's Report? (b) Explain whether you will include the following names in the statement of employees under Board's report covering company's financial year ending 31st December 1983; (i) Mr. 'X'—whose remuneration has been raised from Rs. 2,800/- to Rs. 3,200/- per month effective from 1st October 1983. (ii) Mr. 'Y'—who was drawing a monthly remuneration of Rs. 3,000/- resigned on 31st January 1983, (iii) Mr. 'Z'—who was drawing a monthly remuneration of Rs. 1,000/- sought voluntary retirement on 31st March 1983, and was paid Rs. 15,000/- as leave encashment and ex-gratia compensation. (I.C.S.I.)

Ans. : (a) If so authorised by the Board, the Chairman can sign the report on behalf of the Board. Otherwise, two directors, one of whom shall be the Managing Director of the company, shall sign the report (Sections 215 and 217). (b) In terms of Section 217(2A), the Directors' Report shall, inter alia, include the names of such employees who, if employed throughout the financial year, would have earned not less than Rs. 36,000/- per annum. If any person was employed for a part of the year and in receipt of remuneration at a rate which works out to Rs. 3,000/- per month*, his name will also be included in the list. (ii) Y's name shall be included in the list. (iii) Z's name shall not be included. The gratuity relates not only to the current year but also the earlier years.

Q. 162. As Secretary of a public limited company, how would you deal with each of the following situations : (a) At a Board Meeting : (i) All directors except one are interested in a resolution. (ii) Due to resignation of one director out of a total of three, the strength of the Board has fallen below the minimum required under law, (b) At a General Meeting : (i) Only one person, authorised representative of five shareholding companies, is present at the meeting. (ii) Name of a shareholder is proposed at the meeting for appointment as director in place of a director retiring by rotation whose resolution for reappointment has not been passed. (ICSI)

Ans. : (a) (i) The Articles of Association may provide for appointment of additional director. The item will be placed before the Board after such appointment. (ii) According to the provision of Section 187, there cannot be a meeting with one person. The Articles provide for co-option of additional directors. The item will be placed before the Board after such co-option. (b) (i) As Section 187 requires presence of five members in person, there cannot be a meeting with one person. (ii) This cannot be considered at the annual general meeting inasmuch as there is lack of proper and adequate notice as required under Section 257.

*Raised to Rs. 6,000/- w.e.f. 15.6.88 and to Rs. 12,000/- w.e.f. 18.9.90, to Rs. 25,000/- w.e.f. 17.10.94. and Rs. 50,000/- w.e.f.' 12.3.1999 vide GSR 704(E) dated 12.3.1999.

Q. 163. Advise the legal position : (a) Directors A and B are going abroad : (i) Mr. A desires that during his stay abroad, notice of Board meetings be served on him at his London address. (ii) Mr. B desires that no notice be sent to him during next three months. (b) Previous meeting of the Board of Directors was held on 1st October 1983. Due to non-availability of majority of directors in India, the Chairman proposes to hold the next meeting : (i) On 31st March 1984 in India, or (ii) On 31st December 1983 in London, where majority of directors may be present. (ICSI)

Ans. : (a) (i) Section 286 of the Act requires that notice should be sent to the usual address of the director in India. So no notice to the director's London address should be sent. (ii) The Act requires that notice shall be sent to the director in spite of his request. (b) (i) In terms of Section 285, holding of the meeting on 31st March will be valid. (ii) In terms of Section 301(5), the meeting may be held in London provided the prior permission of the Reserve Bank of India is obtained and the books/ registers are made available at the meeting.

Q. 164. Advise on the following situations : (a) The only director present at the annual general meeting of a public limited company is not willing to act as Chairman of the meeting. (b) Notice of a general meeting was found not sent to a member holding 100 equity shares. The name and address of the said member printed by the computer on a separate sheet was inadvertently taken for a blank paper by the staff employed for the purpose. (c) Within half an hour from the time appointed for a general meeting of a public company convened by the Board, the quorum was not present. What is the consequence? Would the position be different if it was a requisitioned meeting? (ISCI)

Ans. : (a) As per Regulation 52 of the Articles of Association of the company, members present can appoint a Chairman. If the members thereafter elect another person as Chairman, he shall be the Chairman for the rest of the meeting. (b) Under Section 172(3) of the Companies Act, accidental omission to give notice to any member will not violate the proceedings of the meeting. (c) In the first case, the meeting will be adjourned in terms of Section 174(4) and, in the latter case, the meeting stands cancelled.

Q. 165. The total strength of the Board of Directors of a company is ten. Six directors were present at a Board meeting and two of them were found to be interested in a few items of business. (a) What do you understand by the term 'total strength'? (b) What is the quorum in this case and why? (c) What steps would you, as Secretary, take to see that the provisions of Section 300 are complied with? (ICSI)

Ans. : (a) The term 'total strength' means the total strength of the Board of Directors of the company minus the number of directors whose place(s) may remain vacant. (b) In terms of Section 287(2), one-third of the total strength, any fraction to be rounded-off to one, is the quorum. So, in the instant problem, one-third of 10 directors works out to 3⅓ which will be rounded off to 4. So four directors will form the quorum. (c) Section 300 of the Companies Act debars an interested director from taking part in the discussion or voting on any matter in which he is directly or indirectly interested. The Company Secretary must ensure that the interested directors do not participate in the discussion.

Q. 166. At the Annual General Meeting of A. Ltd. when the motion for appointment of a director was put to vote, the Chairman was surprised at the employee-members raising their hands "against the motion" and out-numbering the hands raised "for the motion". He did not, therefore, declare the results. As Secretary, advise on each of the following points treating them separately : (a) Two members each holding one-twelfth of the total equity shares demand a poll. (b) 10 holders of equity shares present by proxy demand a poll. (c) 5 holders of cumulative preference shares on which dividend has not been paid for one year preceding the meeting demand a poll. (d) The Chairman himself wants to order a poll without waiting for a valid demand for poll. (e) The employee-members relented and wanted to support the resolution. (ICSI)

Ans. : (a) In terms of Section 179 of the Companies Act, the Chairman will have to grant poll. (b) In terms of Section 179, the Chairman will have to grant poll. (c) In terms of Section 179(1)(d), Poll cannot be granted by the Chairman. (d) In terms of Section 179(1), it is valid. (e) This is not tantamount to a valid demand for poll and decision on show of hands cannot be altered. The Chairman, if not satisfied, can demand a poll on his own motion.

Q. 167. Advise the legal position : (a) Regarding right to attend the general meeting : (i) If two proxies, both appointed by same member with an interval of a day, are present at the meeting; (ii) if, after appointing the proxy, a member himself is also present at the meeting; (iii) if a person produces the proxy at the time of the meeting. (b) Regarding right to inspect proxies : (i) by a proxy, at the time of meeting, during business hours, after giving one week's notice; (ii) by a member, at the time of meeting, during business hours, after giving 48 hours' notice; (iii) by a member, at the time of meeting, which has continued beyond business hours, after giving one week's notice. (ICSI)

Ans. : (a) (i) Appointment of a fresh proxy revokes the earlier one. (ii) The presence of the appointer of proxy does not revoke the right of the proxy to vote unless the appointer votes personally. (Knight vs Bulkeley). (b) (i) In terms of Section 176(7), this is not permissible. (ii) Section 176(7) of the Companies Act provides that the members can inspect proxy forms twenty-four hours before the meeting if they have given a notice for this purpose three days in advance of the meeting. So the members' request will not be entertained. (iii) In terms of Section 176(7), the member's request will not be acceded to.

Q. 168. Complete the following : (i) Appointment of an auditor in a company in which not less than twentyfive per cent of the subscribed share capital is held by Government company shall be made by...... (ii) The Minutes of the proceedings of a company meeting can be signed by........ and in case of general meetings by ....(iii) A preference shareholder has a right to vote at a general meeting only when....... and a proxy has a right to vote at a general meeting only when.......(iv) A general meeting of a public limited company may be called after giving shorter notice than twentyone days if consent is accorded thereto in case of annual general meeting by ....and in case of any other general meeting by ....(v) A company may close the register of its members after giving not less than ...... days' previous notice by ...... (ICSI)

Ans. : (i) ...... by a special resolution (Section 224A). (ii) .....by the chairman of that meeting or the successive meeting......by the Chairman of that meeting. (iii) .....his interest is affected and .....when there is a poll. (iv) .....in case of annual general meeting by all members and .....by members holding not less than 95% of the paid-up share capital and entitled to vote thereat. (v) .....not less than seven days' previous notice by advertisement in some newspapers with appropriate circulation.

Q. 169. As Secretary of a public limited company, what would be your advice regarding the validity of quorum under each of the following situations : (a) At a Board Meeting where, out of seven directors, three are present and : (i) one director is interested in a particular item of agenda; and (ii) to catch the flight, one director leaves the meeting before completion of last item on the agenda. (b) At the General Meeting where, out of seven members, five are present and (i) four members are interested in a particular item of business; and (ii) in order to break the quorum, one member leaves the meeting before completion of last item of business. (ICSI)

Ans. : (a) (i) Under Sec. 287(2), if the Articles do not fix the quorum, at least two disinterested directors or one-third of the total strength of the Board (any fraction to be rounded-off as one) whichever is higher, shall be the quorum. So, in the instant case, three directors will form the quorum. (ii) According to Regulation 49 of Table A, the quorum need not be present throughout the meeting. A similar ruling was given in Re : Hartley Baird Ltd. case. But, as per Henderson vs Louttit case, the quorum must be present throughout the currency of the meeting. (b) (i) According to Section 174, quorum of effective (i.e., dis-interested) members must be present when the questions are being discussed for decisions. Therefore, in the instant case, there is no quorum and any decision, if arrived at, will be a nullity. (ii) According to Regulation 49 of Table A and the ruling given in Hartley Baird Ltd. case, the quorum need not be present throughout the meeting. In the instant case, the member leaves the meeting with an intention to break the quorum. According to the American Encyclopedia Dictionary of Business "if any shareholders withdraw for breaking a quorum, because of whim, caprice or other mala fide motives, the proceedings of the meeting will not be vitiated for want of quorum."

Q. 170. C, the Chairman of the company, was not present within fifteen minutes after the appointed time of 4-45 p.m. of the annual general meeting; D, the only director present, was elected as the Chairman of the meeting. Under D's chairmanship, C arrived and sat along with other members. How would you deal with the following points raised by the members challenging the validity of the meeting and the proceedings thereat : (a) proper Chairman C is not in the chair; (b) meeting has actually commenced after the business hours at 5-02 p.m.; (c) notice was not received by one of the shareholders as his envelope containing the notice had got mixed up with similar empty envelopes; (d) the notice and the auditor's report should be read instead of taking them as read. (ICSI)

Ans. : (a) D is the chairman pro tem (i.e., temporary) and, as such, if so required by the meeting or the permanent chairman, D will have to vacate the chair. (b) In terms of Section

166 of the Companies Act, the annual general meeting must be held within the "business hours". The term "business hours" ordinarily means the time between 10 A.M. to 5 P.M. So there has been violation of the provision of Section 166. (c) In terms of Section 172(3), accidental omission to give notice to any member will not invalidate the proceedings of the meeting. (d) In terms of Section 230 of the Companies Act, the auditor's report is read before the company in general meeting and is open to inspection by any member of the company.

Q. 171. What are the main documents/papers which should be kept ready by the Secretary at the general meeting?

Ans. : The documents are : (a) Memorandum of Association (b) Articles of Association (c) Audited balance sheet (d) Notice of the meeting (e) Proxies lodged (f) Register of Members etc.

Q. 172. What are the ways in which the main motions can be interrupted?

Ans. : Page 153.

Q. 173. What do you mean by the sense of the meeting or what are the different methods of voting?

Ans. : Page 159.

Q. 174. How does a Secretary collect various types of information?

Ans. : Page 225.

Q. 175. Mention the methods of becoming a member of a company.

Ans. : A person can become a member of a company in one of the following ways : (a) By signing the Memorandum of Association (b) By getting shares by inheritance, i.e., transmission of shares (c) By the 'Principle of Estoppel'.

Q. 176. How can a director be removed from the office ?

Ans. : A director can be removed from his office by the (a) shareholders (b) Court and (c) Central Government.

Q. 177. What is a dividend?

Ans. : Page 176.

Q. 178. Who can call an extra-ordinary general meeting?

Ans. : An extra-ordinary general meeting may be called by the (a) Directors on the basis of the resolution (b) Directors on requisition (c) The requisitionists (d) Company Law Board.

Q. 179. What do you mean by the term 'Transmission of shares'?

Ans. : Page 46.

Q. 180. What is a defunct company?

Ans. : A company which is not carrying on business or is not in operation is called a defunct company.

Q. 181. Explain the term 'Walk-out'. (C.U. 1976)

Ans. : According to a "A Dictionary of Economics and Commerce" 'walk-out' is a colloquial term for a strike. In the meetings of the Parliament/Assembly when the motion of the opposition party is not allowed to be moved by the Speaker or is rejected by him outright, the aggrieved members usually prefer to 'walk-out' rather than staying back as silent spectators. In the case of company meetings, the same move is taken by the aggrieved members when the Chairman does not pay heed to their proposal/motion.

Q. 182. Explain the term 'Dissenting Note'.

Ans. : In a Board Meeting, it sometimes happens that a resolution is passed with majority of the directors voting in its favour and one or two voting thereagainst. Those voting against the resolution are known as the dissenting directors and they may cause the meeting to get their dissent noted in the Minutes of the meeting. This is known as 'Dissenting Note'.

Q. 183. What are the resolutions that cannot be passed by the directors by circulation? (ICSI)

Ans. : Page 186.

Q. 184. Is is essential for the resolution passed by circulation to be confirmed at the next Board Meeting? (ICSI)

Ans. : Yes. Refer to page 186 also.

Q. 185. A notice convening a general meeting has been issued by the directors. They decide afterwards that there was no necessity to hold the meeting. Can the directors now send another notice cancelling the general meeting already convened? (ICSI)

Ans. : Unless the Articles of Association of the Company specifically provide for this type of cancellation of meeting, a properly called meeting cannot be cancelled or postponed by a subsequent notice.

Q. 186. Can a director claim to have a copy of the Minutes of the Board Meeting?

Ans. : A director can claim to have a copy of the Minutes of the Board Meeting. When a director cannot attend a meeting, he usually asks for a copy of the Minutes of that meeting which enables him to know the outcome of the meeting.

Q. 187. Is it necessary that a resolution be seconded so as to be considered by the general meeting? (C.U. 1998)

Ans. : A motion is said to be 'before the meeting' if and when it is seconded. The motion, when adopted by the meeting, is known to be a resolution. Therefore, the question of seconding a resolution does not arise.

Q. 188. Indicate the type of meeting—Board, Shareholders, Miscellaneous—at which the following items of business can be transacted : (i) to re-elect a director; (ii) to alter the Articles of Association; (iii) to adopt Statutory Report; (iv) to recommend dividend; (v) to appoint a new trustee for debentureholders. (ICSI)

Ans. : (i) Annual General Meeting; (ii) General meeting; (iii) Statutory Meeting; (iv) Board Meeting; (v) Debentureholders' Meeting i.e., (Miscellaneous).

Q. 189. Can a person be appointed a managing director of a company without first being appointed a director?

Ans. : In terms of Section 2(26) of the Companies Act, 1956, only a director of the company can be appointed a managing director of the company.

Q. 190. Will a person, representing one company under Section 187 of the Companies Act, 1956, in addition to representing himself as a member in a general meeting of a company, be counted as two persons for the purpose of quorum?

Ans. : In terms of Section 187(1) and (2) and 187A of the Companies Act, 1956, he will be counted as two persons for the purpose of quorum.

Q. 191. Can an adjourned annual general meeting (which has been adjourned for want of quorum) be held on a public holiday?

Ans. : An annual general meeting which has been adjourned for want of quorum to a public holiday may be validly held.

Q. 192. Is the Chairman bound to answer all the questions raised by the members on items of agenda in the annual general meeting?

Ans. : The chairman is supposed to answer all the relevant questions emanating from the items of business as given in the agenda.

Q.193. Is it obligatory on the part of the Chairman to record all the discussions at the annual general meeting in the minutes?

Ans. : The Chairman exercises an absolute discretion regarding inclusion or non-inclusion of any matter in the Minutes which he may consider to be defamatory of any person, irrelevant or immaterial to the proceedings or detrimental to the interest of the company.

Q. 194. A director of a company whose articles require the holding of share qualification has held the shares within the prescribed time, but did not get the shares registered in his name within two months of his appointment. Is this in order?

Ans. : In terms of Section 270 of the Companies Act, 1956, there has been a violation and, as such, this is not in order.

Q. 195. The Articles of Association of a company provide for sitting fee of Rs. 250/- per meeting. The Company wishes to enhance it to Rs. 500/- per meeting. Is it possible?

Ans. : In terms of the provision of Section 310 of the Companies Act, 1956, and the Government Notification No GSR. 58 (E) dated 17.01.2000 issued by the Dept. of Company Affairs, the maximum sitting fee can be Rs. 5,000/-. However, the increase in fee has to be recommended by the Board and, accordingly, the Articles have to be amended by the general body meeting.

Q. 196. A notice for an annual general meeting was posted to the members. Besides ordinary business, only one special business of appointing the sole selling agents was to be discussed. The explanatory statement attached to the notice simply stated that the agreement to be executed with the sole selling agents would be available for inspection at the registered office of the company. Would you consider the business transacted at the meeting as valid?

Ans. : In terms of Section 173(2) of the Companies Act, 1956, in case of a special business there must be annexed to the notice a statement mentioning all material facts concerning that item of business. In the instant case, the explanatory statement does not contain all the material facts and, as such, the business transacted at the meeting is invalid.

Q. 197. Some libellous and scandalous questions on the accounts of the company were answered at the meeting by the Chairman. These question-answeres did not find any place in the Minutes of the meeting. Is the position all right?

Ans. : According to Section 193(5) of the Companies Act, the Chairman has the authority of such non-inclusion. So the position is quite in order.

Q. 198. A proxy, properly executed by one of the joint shareholders, was lodged 48 hours before the commencement of an adjourned annual general meeting of a public company. Is it valid?

Ans. : According to Regulations 57 and 61 of Table A of Schedule to the Companies Act, 1956, such a proxy is valid.

Q. 199. In a Board Meeting, all the directors except one are interested persons. What is the consequence?

Ans. : Section 300 of the Companies Act debars the interested directors from voting at a Board Meeting. So in the instant case, there will not be any quorum to transact the business.

Q. 200. At a general meeting of a company 30 shareholders were present, 18 voted for a special resolution, 4 voted against and 8 did not vote at all. As no poll was demanded, the Chairman declared the resolution to be carried. Is this a valid resolution?

Ans. : The resolution is valid inasmuch as more than three-fourths of the shareholders voted in favour of the proposal. Those who abstained from voting would not be counted for the purpose.

Q. 201. A casual vacancy in the Board was filled by the Board of Directors of the company under Section 262 and as per the provision of the Articles of Association. The person so appointed vacated his office and the Board again filled the vacancy by appointing another person as director. Is the action of the Board valid?

Ans. : In terms of the provisions of Section 262 of the Companies Act, 1956, the action of the Board in regard to filling the vacancy for the second time is not valid.

Office Procedure

Q. 202. Should every organisation have a registered office? **(C.U. 1991)**

Ans. : The organisation which is registered under any Act must have its registered office. Companies, registered partnership firms and societies must have their registered offices to enable the Registrar of Companies/Firms/Societies to communicate with them. Other organisations are not required to have their registered offices.

Q. 203. In modern times, an office is often termed as a Service Department. Why? (C.U. 1991)

Ans. : The activities of a business enterprise are varied and numerous. The work of co-ordinating these activities and rendering assistance in the preparation of various matters are the functions of an efficient office. The various functions of the office are, therefore, like rendering services. That is why an office is termed as service department.

Q. 204. Mention at least five main departments of a large commercial office. (C.U. 1998)

Ans. : A large commercial office has a number of departments headed by the departmental managers. Each of the departments has separate functions. Some of the more important departments in such an office are : (a) Personnel and Administration; (b) Purchase; (c) Sales; (d) Accounts; and (e) Secretarial.

Q. 205. Mention at least four essential features of a business letter. (C.U. 1990; V.U. 1988)

Ans. : The essential features of a business letter are as follows : (a) Clarity, i.e., the language shall be clear; (b) Conciseness, i.e., should be brief and to the point : (c) Complete, i.e., complete in all respects and (d) Courtesy—A letter is said to be a silent ambassador of the business house. Drafting of letters is an art and the letters should be drafted with such care that they can convey the required meassage to the reader(s)/recipient(s).

Q. 206. Give the full names for PBX, PABX, EDP, MRTP Act, FERA. (C.U. 1984)

Ans. : (a) Private Branch Exchange (b) Private Automatic Branch Exchange (c) Electronic Data Processing (d) Monopolies & Restrictive Trade Practices Act (e) Foreign Exchange Regulation Act.

Q. 207. "Office equipments are often termed as labour-saving devices even though they save time and cost of running operations".—Is the statement correct?

Ans. : Office equipments are called labour-saving devices because they save considerable amount of manual labour. These machines save a lot of time and cost of running operations as well. Use of these machines improves the efficiency and betters the image of the organisation. So these machines save not only manual labour but also operational costs.

Q. 208. What is the difference between a telegram and a phonogram?

Ans. : Telegraphic meassage can be sent by an individual/firm/company etc. by filling in the standard form of the Department of Posts and paying the prescribed charge which depends on the number of words used. The same meassage can be conveyed by the sender to the Department for onward transmission to the addressee over the telephone by dialling a particular number. In other words, when the telegraphic meassage is sent by the sender over telephone, it is known as phonogram. The charge for phonogram is included in the telephone bill.

Q. 209. Give two basic advantages of a centralised correspondence system in an office.

Ans. : Two of the basic advantages derived from centralised correspondence system are : (a) Specialisation of the employees increases their efficiency and enhances the image of the organisation. (b) Avoidance of duplication of work results in cost reduction and increases the profitability of the organisation.

Q. 210. Define Office Forms. (C.U. 1983)

Ans. : Page 76.

Q. 211. Mention different methods of 'filing' and state which one of them will be suitable for a concern for maintaining personnel files. (C.U. 1983)

Ans. : Ordinarily, the methods of filing are : (a) Horizontal, (b) Vertical and (c) Lateral. A concern maintaining personnel files may use alphabetical classification.

Q. 212. Mention four important points which should be borne in mind in preparing the layout of an office. (C.U. 1983)

Ans. : The person preparing the layout of an office must bear in mind the following points : (a) Accessibility to customers; (b) Accessibility to banks, post-office, railway station, bus terminus; (c) Proximity of the office to its factory, warehouse, sales office, etc. (d) Availability of personnel locally, as far as possible.

Q. 213. State the advantages of 'Microfilming'. (C.U. 1983)

Ans. : The advantages of microfilming are as follows : (a) Safe preservation of records; (b) Photographs may be obtained promptly and accurately.

Q. 214. Mention four basic advantages of a 'Loose-leaf Register'. (C.U. 1990, 1983)

Ans. : Page 102.

Q. 215. Name three labour-saving devices which are usually maintained in a business undertaking. (C.U. 1998, 1983)

Ans. : A business house commonly uses typewriters, duplicators (e.g., hectograph) and calculators as labour-saving devices. Depending on the size of the organisation and the volume of business handled by it, the types of labour-saving devices are ascertained.

Q. 216. Define 'Telegraphic Address'. (C.U. 1990, 1983)

Ans. : Page 69.

Q. 217. Which one of the salutations—Sir, Dear Sir, Gentleman — will you prefer in addressing a Minister and what should be the complimentary close in such case? (C.U. 1983)

Ans. : In addressing a Minister, the salutation should be 'Sir' and the complimentary close should be 'Yours faithfully'.

Q. 218. Who is a Del Credere Agent? **(C.U. 1991, 1983)**

Ans. : According to "A Dictionary of Economics and Commerce" by G. L. Hanson, a Del Credere Agent is "An agent who, in return for a higher rate of commission, guarantees that his principal will receive payment for the goods he has sold on his behalf."

Q. 219. What do you mean by "Attendance Records"?

Ans. : Page 356.

Q. 220. What is xerography?

Ans. : Xerography is the process of electrical photography which uses ordinary paper. This process does not involve any chemical treatment. The impressions on the original are reproduced on the ordinary paper by electrostatic charges. This process is ordinarily known as 'xerox'.

Q. 221. What is radio-telephony?

Ans. : Radio telephones are very useful when frequent contacts between the headquarters and a number of moving vehicles are necessary. The system which is known as radio-telephony can be introduced with the prior permission of the Postal Authorities and the Department of Telecommunications.

Q. 222. What do you mean by P.A.Y.E.?

Ans. : P.A.Y.E. stands for Pay As You Earn. This is a system of collection of income-tax introduced for the first time in the year 1944 in the United Kingdom.

Q. 223. What do you mean by the term "psychromatics"?

Ans. : Colourful decoration not only beautifies the appearance of the office but also helps the employees working there to render their best services. They undoubtedly feel psychologically better-off to be sincere in their work. The study of the inter-relation of colour and its effect on the employees working in the colourfully decorated rooms/halls is known as "psychromatics".

Q. 224. What is a 'Recorded Delivery'?

Ans. : The post-offices provided 'Recorded Delivery' service of inland postal articles and this service was less expensive as compared to registered post. The post office delivering such letters to the addressee kept a record of posting and delivery. Such a letter was delivered to the addressee or his authorised representative only after acknowledgement on a piece of paper of the concerned post-office. This is not in vogue now.

Q. 225. What do you mean by 'Cablegram'?

Ans. : A 'cablegram', as the name suggests, is a telegram or meassage telegraphed by submarine cable.

Q. 226. What do you know about 'Radio-telegrams'?

Ans. : A radio-telegram is a meassage telegraphed by wireless. Radio-telegrams are usually used for sending meassage to ships at sea.

Q. 227. What is the function/duty of an 'Audio-Typist'?

Ans. : The term 'audio' is derived from the Latin word '*audire*' which means 'to hear'. Unlike the ordinary typists who type from the manuscript or documents/matters supplied to them, the 'Audio-Typists' type letters, documents etc. after hearing the recordings. The busy executives dictate the matters at their spare time which are recorded into dictating machines. The Audio-Typists play back the disc containing dictation on the transcribing machine at such a speed at which they can type.

Q. 228. Define Office Manual. **(C.U. 1984)**

Ans. : Page 65.

Q. 229. How do 'lighting and ventilation' affect efficiency of employees of an office? **(C.U. 1984)**

Ans. : Page 54.

Q. 230. Discuss the usefulness of 'Dictaphone'. **(C.U. 1984)**

Ans. : Page 75.

Q. 231. Define office forms.

Ans. : Page 76.

Q. 232. What are the modern methods of filing?

Ans. : Page 85.

Q. 233. What are the main advantages of mechanisation of office work?

Ans. : The principal advantages of mechanisation of office work are : (a) Saving in labour, time and labour cost; (b) Greater efficiency which leads to productivity; (c) Reduction in cost and increase in profit; (d) Better communication with the constituents/public; (e) Availability of accurate and uptodate records, (f) Better service to the constituents/public creates a good image of the organisation.

Q. 234. What are the important copiers or copying machines in the modern offices?

Ans. : Page 94.

Q. 235. What is a Trunk Call?

Ans. : Page 105.

Q. 236. What is a 'Press Communique'?

Ans. : Page 171.

Q. 237. Name some of the basic advantages of a 'Loose-leaf Register'.

Ans. : Page 102.

Q. 238. What is meant by 'Flow of Work'?

Ans. : Page 58.

Q. 239. What are the common difficulties which stand in the way of getting the ideal flow of work in the office?

Ans. : Page 58.

Q. 240. What are the services available from the Department of Posts?

Ans. : Page 72.

Q. 241. Mention the popular sources from which the Secretary collects various types of information.

Ans. : Mention the headings only from pages 226-29.

Q. 242. What is an 'Enclosure'?

Ans. : Enclosure is that which is enclosed to a letter. More often than not, invoice, bill, cheque, challan etc. are sent along with the letter as enclosures. 'Enclo.', 'Enc.' or 'Encl.' is used as the abbreviation of the term 'Enclosure'. This word is typed or hand-written at the bottom left-hand corner of the letter.

Q. 243. What are the characteristics of a good report?

Ans. : Page 230.

Q. 244. How does a Secretary collect various types of information for his employer?

Ans. : Page 225.

Q. 245. What do you mean by a 'Postal Guide'?

Ans. : Page 69.

Q. 246. What are the machines used in the mailing department of a modern office?

Ans. : Page 98.

Q. 247. What is Log Book?

Ans. : Page 102.

Q. 248. Name some of the machines used in the Accounts Department of a modern office.

Ans. : Page 96.

Q. 249. Name some of the duplicating machines and copying machines.

Ans. : Page 94.

Q. 250. What do you mean by private office?

Ans. : A private office is an enclosed area which is exclusively used by a high official, or an official whose work demands high level of concentration or frequent interviews of private and confidential nature. In other words, private offices should be provided to the top executives.

Q. 251. What is the difference in status of a Personal Assistant, Confidential Assistant and Private Secretary?

Ans. : Pages 2 and 7.

Q. 252. What do you mean by the term 'Attendance Records'? (C.U. 1975)

Ans. : The Attendance Records are kept by an organisation for the purpose of noting the details of time of arrival and departure, leave, unauthorised absence of the employees in any organisation. Maintenance of such records helps the organisation to calculate the salaries and wages properly. Signing the attendance register by the employees with time of arrival and departure is a measure of discipline.

Q. 253. What is the usefulness of a 'Receptionist'? (C.U. 1975)

Ans. : The receptionist receives the visitors on behalf of the organisation in which she or he is employed. In office administration, the usefulness of a receptionist is : (a) Visitors —when received — feel themselves as very important persons, (b) They, after being interviewed, are directed to the concerned officers. (c) Time of the visitors is thus saved and the image of the organisation is bettered.

Q. 254. How is Office Procedure related to Secretarial Practice? (C.U. 1999, 1986)

Ans. : According to N. C. Deyner, the term 'Office Procedure' is used to describe office systems and such procedure is made up of a number of operations. On the other hand, Secretarial Practice relates to performance of different types of office work. Therefore, a scientific office procedure helps to perform secretarial work more efficiently. Office procedure is thus related to secretarial practice.

Short Questions on Local Self-government (Panchayati Raj) with Answers

Q. 255. How is a Zilla Parishad Secretary appointed?

Ans. : The first Secretary of a Zilla Parishad is appointed by the concerned State Government. The subsequent appointments are usually made by the concerned Zilla Parishad.

Q. 256. What is the tenure of office of a Zilla Parishad?

Ans. : While the first Secretary of a Zilla Parishad holds office for a period of four years, the subsequent Secretaries hold office for five years.

Q. 257. What is the qualification of the Secretary of a Zilla Parishad Secretary?

Ans. : A Zilla Parishad Secretary must be a senior W.B.C.S. officer.

Q. 258. Can a Zilla Parishad Secretary be removed?

Ans. : A Zilla Parishad Secretary cannot be removed but he can be transferred by the Directorate of Panchayat on the recommendation of the District Magistrate.

Q. 259. Who is the Executive Officer of a Zilla Parishad?

Ans. : The District Magistrate is the Executive Officer of a Zilla Parishad.

Q. 260. Who are the members of a Zilla Parishad?

Ans. : Sabhapatis of the Panchayat Samitis of the districts, two elected representatives from each of the Blocks and MPs as well as MLAs of the district are the members of a Zilla Parishad.

Q. 261. Who is the head of a Zilla Parishad?

Ans. : Sabhadhipati is the head of a Zilla Parishad.

Q. 262. What is the tenure of office of the members of a Zilla Parishad?

Ans. : Tenure of office of the members of a Zilla Parishad is five years.

Q. 263. Who can convene a meeting of a Zilla Parishad?

Ans. : Meetings of a Zilla Parishad are convened by the Sabhadhipati.

Q. 264. What is the frequency of holding Zilla Parishad meetings and what is the minimum number of meetings a Zilla Parishad shall hold in a year?

Ans. : A Zilla Parishad is statutorily required to hold a meeting in each quarter. As such, it should hold at least four meetings in a year.

Q. 265. Who is the principal officer of the Corporation?

Ans. : According to Section 39 (i) of the Calcutta Municipal Corporation Act, 1988, the Municipal Commissioner is the principal officer of the Corporation.

Q. 266. What are the designations of the elected representatives of the Municipalities and Corporation?

Ans. : The elected members of the Municipalities and Corporation are designated as Commissioners and Councillors, respectively.

Q. 267. How is the Secretary of a Municipal Corporation appointed?

Ans. : A Municipal Corporation Secretary is appointed by the Managing/Executive Committee of the Corporation or by the State Government. He may be elected on honorary basis or appointed as a salaried employee.

Q. 268. How many members are there in the Calcutta Corporation?

Ans. : There are altogether 141 elected members who are known as Councillors. The Councillors elect amongst themselves one as the Chief Executive Officer of the Calcutta Metropolitan Development Authority, one as the Chairman of Board of Trustees of the Calcutta Improvement Trust and seven as Aldermen.

Q. 269. Who elect the Mayor and the Chairman of Calcutta Municipal Corporation and how long do they hold office?

Ans. : The Councillors of the Corporation elect among themselves the Mayor and the Chairman — usually for a period of five years.

Q. 270. How can the Mayor and the Chairman be removed?

Ans. : They can be removed by the Councillors by a resolution passed by majority of them at a duly convened special meeting.

Q. 271. Who convenes Municipal Corporation meetings and who presides at them?

Ans. : The Chairman of the Corporation convenes and chairs the Municipal Corporation meetings.

Q. 272. When should notice of Corporation meeting be sent to the Councillors and what is the quorum for such a meeting?

Ans. : Notice shall be issued to the Councillors at least 72 hours before the time fixed for the meeting. The quorum for the Corporation meetings is 1/5th or 20% of the total number of members of the Corporation.

Q. 273. Who convenes and chairs Gram Panchayat meetings?

Ans. : Gram Panchayat meetings are convened and chaired by 'Sarpanch' or 'Pradhan' of the 'gram' (i.e. village).

Q. 274. How many Gram Panchayat meetings shall be held in a year and how many days' notice is necessary?

Ans. : At least one meeting in a month and twelve such meetings in a year shall be held. Seven clear days' notice containing the agenda has to be sent to all the members of the 'gram'.

Q. 275. What is the quorum for a Gram Panchayat meeting?

Ans. : The quorum for a Gram Panchayat meeting is 1/4th or 25% of the total number of members.

Q. 276. What is the minimum educational qualification and what is the age limit for appointment as a Gram Panchayat Secretary?

Ans. : The candidate must have passed the School Final or Secondary or equivalent examination of the Board and the qualifying age should be between 18 to 35 years.

Q. 277. How long do the members of Gram Panchayat hold office?

Ans. : The members of Gram Panchayat hold office for a period of five years.

Q. 278. What should be the qualification of a Panchayat Samiti Secretary? Can he be removed?

Ans. : He shall be a W.B.C.S. officer or he may be appointed through departmental promotion. He may be transferred by the Directorate of Panchayat but he cannot be removed from his service.

Q. 279. What is the minimum as well as the maximum number of elected members in a Gram Sabha?

Ans. : In a Gram Sabha, while the minimum number of elected members is 7, the maximum number is 25.

Q. 280. Who are the members of a Panchayat Samiti?

Ans. : The members of a Panchayat Samiti are the Sarpanchs of all villages under the Samiti, MPs and MLAs belonging to the area and the concerned Block Development Officer.

INSTITUTE OF COMPANY SECRETARIES OF INDIA

IINTERMEDIATE EXAMINATION

Company Law & Practice : Company Administration & Meetings

Q. 1. The company secretary of a company having share capital of more than Rs. 50 lakhs resigned and left the company. The company has not appointed his successor. Meanwhile, it has started incurring losses. Its sales have declined and financial position became weak. Can it be a valid reason for not appointing a whole-time secretary? How long can the company delay the appointment? What penalty can be imposed? Will the liability extend to all the directors or only to the managing director?

Ans. : According to Section 383 A of the Companies Act, 1956, read with the Gazette Notification dated 29.11.88, the company cannot delay the appointment of a company secretary who will replace the earlier incumbent.

Acceptance or rejection of the plea of incurring losses is up to the discretion of the court which will try the offence of the company.

The quantum of penalty as specified in Section 383 A is Rs. 50/- per day for the period of default.

The managing director, whole-time director, manager, if any, or any director so specified will be the officer-in-default.

Q. 2. (a) Explain the statutory provisions with regard to the following points in the context of an annual general meeting :

(i) length and contents of notice;

(ii) time and place of meeting; and

(iii) persons entitled to receive notice.

(b) The auditor of a company complains that he was not given notice of a recently held general meeting of the company. The secretary of the company contends that as no part of the business of that meeting concerned the auditor, no notice was required to be given to him.

(i) Do you agree with the contention of the secretary?

(ii) If the auditor attends a general meeting, can he participate in the meeting?

Ans. : (a) Refer to page 145.

(b) (i) I do not agree with the secretary. The auditor is entitled to receive the notice.

(ii) The auditor is entitled to attend and speak at the general meeting on any part of the business which concerns him as an auditor (Section 231).

Q. 3. (a) Explain the provisions of the Companies Act, 1956, relating to unpaid and unclaimed dividend and its payment.

(b) When can payment of dividend be kept in abeyance and how can such dividend be withdrawn by the transferee?

Ans. : (a) Section 205 A of the Companies Act, 1956, read with the Companies Unpaid Dividend (Transfer to General Revenue Account of the Central Government) Rules, 1978, dwells upon unpaid and unclaimed dividend and its payments. (Refer to Section 205 A and the above rules for further details).

(b) Refer to Sections 206 A, 205 A and 205 B of the Companies Act, 1956.

Q. 4. Draft specimen resolutions for transacting the following items indicating the kind of meeting at which the resolution is to be passed and the type of resolution required :

(a) To remit debt of Rs. 5,000/- due by a director.

(b) To change the name of the company.

(c) To employ a director's relative at a monthly remuneration of Rs. 13,000/-.

(d) To change the financial year from 31st December to 31st March.

Ans. : (a) Kind of meeting—General meeting; Resolution—ordinary. "Resolved that in pursuance of the provisions of Section 293 (1) (b) of the Companies Act, 1956, consent of the company be and is hereby accorded to the Board for remission of debt of Rs. 5,000/- due by Shri A. N. Daw, Director of the Company."

(b) Kind of meeting—General meeting; Resolution—special resolution. Refer to page 21.

(c) Kind of meeting—general; type of resolution-special resolution. "Resolved that the consent of the company be and is hereby accorded under Section 314(1) of the Companies Act, 1956, to the appointment of Shri Anjan Kumar Aich, a relative of Shri Ranjit Kumar Dutta, a director of the company, as Dy. Finance Manager in the company at a total monthly remuneration of Rs. 13,000/-."

(d) Kind of meeting—Board meeting; Type of Resolution—Resolution by majority of directors present and entitled to vote at the meeting. "Resolved that the company's financial year which corresponds to the year ending 31st December, be changed to 31st March and in terms of Section 210 of the Act for the change the next annual accounts be prepared for the fifteen months ending 31st March, and thereafter the annual accounts be prepared for twelve months ending 31st March every year."

Q. 5. Distinguish between 'Managing Director' and 'Manager'. What are their disqualifications?

Ans. : Refer to Section 2 (26) and 2(24) of the Companies Act, 1956, for definitions of the terms. For disqualifications, refer to Sections 267, 274 and 585 of the Companies Act, 1956.

Q. 6. Inspection of books of account and other books and papers of the company is authorised under Section 209 A of the Companies Act, while investigation can be ordered under Section 235 or 237 or 239 of the Act.

Ans. : Refer to Sections 209A, 235, 237, 239 and 247 of the Companies Act, 1956.

Q. 7. Draft a specimen of directors' report.

Ans. : Refer to pages 242-43.

Q. 8. Comment on the following :

(a) Quorum need not be present throughout the Board meeting.

(b) One-man meeting.

(c) The transactions at a Board meeting, the notice of which was not sent to one of the directors.

(d) Annual general meeting of a public company was scheduled to be held on 15.12.1989. Mr. X, a shareholder, issued two proxies in favour of Mr. A and Mr. B. The proxy in favour of B was lodged on 12.12.1989 and the one in favour of Mr. A was lodged on 15.12.1989. The company rejected the proxy in favour of Mr. B as the proxy in favour of Mr. B was dated 12.12.1989 and that in favour of Mr. A was dated 13.12.1989.

(ICSI)

Ans. : (a) Page 162 (b) Page 163 (c) Page 186 (d) Pages 330 & 410.

Q. 9. (a) State the conditions and procedure for the payment of interim dividend.

(b) (i) Can the decision for payment of interim dividend be revoked?

(ii) What is the time limit, if any, for payment of interim dividend?

Ans. : (a) Refer to pages 176- 77.

Q. 10. The company of which you are the secretary has October-September accounting year. The accounts for the year 1986-87 (1.10.86 to 30.9.87) were approved in the annual general meeting held on 31.3.1983. In view of the amendment in the Income-tax Act, 1961, the company wants its accounting year to be changed to financial year to be extended to 18 months from 1.10.87 to 31.3.89. Advise the company :

(i) Can it extend the financial year to 18 months and, if so, what are the formalities to be complied with?

(ii) Can it hold its next annual general meeting on 30.9.1989 to consider the accounts for the financial year 1987-89 (1.10.1987 to 31.3.1989)?

Ans. : (i) In terms of Section 210(4) of the Companies Act, 1956, the financial year of a company may be less or more than a calendar year but it shall not exceed fifteen months. As per the proviso to the said sub-section, the financial year may extend to eighteen months provided the Registrar of Companies accords his specific permission therefor.

(ii) In terms of Section 166(1) of the Companies Act, 1956, every company is required to hold its annual general meeting in each year. However, not more than fifteen months time should elapse between two such meetings. The Registrar may, for any special reason, extend the time by three months. So the meeting must be held on or before 30.6.1989. But if the company desires the meeting to be held on 30.6.1989, it should obtain prior written approval from the Registrar of Companies.

Q. 11. Draft a notice of an annual general meeting scheduled to be held on 27.2.1990 of X Ltd. in which 25% of the subscribed capital is held by Life Insurance Corporation of India. Include in the notice a resolution authorising the Board of Directors to borrow in excess of the paid-up capital and free reserves.

Ans. : Refer to Sections 269, 262 & 224A of the Companies Act, 1956.

Q. 12. (a) Define 'Quorum'. What is the quorum for a general meeting and a Board Meeting? What course of action should be adopted when the quorum is not complete at a general meeting?

(b) Under what circumstances can one person form the quorum for a general meeting?

Ans. : (a) Page 162 (b) Page 163.

Q. 13. (a) State the resolutions and agreements which are required to be filed by a company with the Registrar of Companies.

(b) What are the details which have to be included in the register of directors' shareholdings? Who can inspect the register and require a copy thereof and when?

Ans. : (a) Page 158 (b) Pages 158-59.

Q. 14. Explain the law relating to authentication, circulation, adoption and filing of the annual accounts.

Ans. : Refer to Section 215 (for authentication of Accounts), 219 (for circulation of annual accounts), 210 (for adoption of annual accounts) and 220 (for filing of annual accounts) of the Companies Act, 1956.

Q. 15. Draft resolutions on the following matters and state the meeting at which the same should be passed :

(a) Investment in shares of bodies corporate under the same management;

(b) Disposal of an undertaking;

(c) Adoption of common seal;

(d) Appointment of the first auditor.

Ans. : (a) "Resolved that pursuant to Section 372(2) of the Companies Act, 1956, the company does hereby invest a sum of Rs. 20 lakhs and Rs. 50 lakhs in the equity shares of ABC Ltd. and XYZ Ltd., respectively, (under the same management as this company)". "Further resolved that Shri K. P. Roy, Director of the Company, be and is hereby authorised to sign and execute the necessary documents in this regard." Kind of Meeting—Board Meeting.

(b) "Resolved that in pursuance of the provisions of Section 293(1) (a) of the Companies Act, consent be and is hereby accorded to the Board of Directors of the Company to dispose of the whole or substantially the whole of the undertaking for such consideration and on such terms as the directors consider beneficial to the company." Kind of Meeting—General Meeting.

(c) "Resolved that the proposed seal of the company submitted to the company and a specimen of which is affixed in the margin, be and is hereby adopted as the common seal of the company and that the said seal be kept in the custody of Shri Prabir Kumar Mukherjee, Secretary of the Company." Kind of Meeting—Board Meeting.

(d) "Resolved that Messrs. Chakraborty & Nath, Chartered Accountants, be and are hereby appointed auditors of the company until the conclusion of the first annual general meeting on an annual remuneration of Rs. 45,000/- plus out-of-pocket expenses." Kind of Meeting—Board Meeting.

Q. 16. (a) What is a statutory meeting? When and how is it held?

(b) State the contents of the statutory report.

Ans. : (a) Page 140 (b) Page 194.

Q. 17. (a) Describe the provisions of the Companies Act, 1956 regarding compulsory appointment of a secretary.

(b) Explain the role of a company secretary in the functioning of a company.

Ans. : Refer to pages 23-24 and 32-33.

Q. 18. (a) What is the maximum number of directors who can be appointed in a public company on non-rotational basis, i.e., not subject to retirement in an annual general meeting? How is the appointment of such directors regulated in a private company?

(b) What are the restrictions on the powers of the Board of directors of a company? Can members in general meeting change a decision taken by the Board? What powers can be exercised by the Board only at its meetings?

Ans. : Page 183.

Q. 19. (a) Distinguish between :

(i) ordinary business and special business; and

(ii) ordinary resolution and special resolution.

(b) What points should be kept in view by the secretary in drafting notice for a meeting in which special business is to be transacted?

Ans. : (a) Pages 161, 154-56 (b) Pages 145-46.

Q. 20. (a) What is dividend?

(b) Can all companies declare dividend?

(c) Can dividend be declared out of capital?

(d) What provisions and rules have to be observed by a company before declaring dividend?

Ans. : (a) Page 176.

(b) All companies, barring those registered under Section 25 of the Companies Act, can declare dividend subject to the provisions of the Act;

(c) Refer to Section 205 of the Companies Act;

(d) Refer to Section 205 of the Companies Act, 1956.

Q. 21. (a) What books and papers of a company can be inspected by an officer authorised to carry out inspection under Section 209A(1)(ii) of the Companies Act, 1956?

(b) What registers of a company can be inspected by its members?

(c) State the circumstances on the basis of which Central Government may order investigation into the affairs of a company.

Ans. : (a) The officer is authorised to inspect ledger, cash book, journal and vouchers and other books and papers which include deeds, writings and documents.

(b) Register of investment held in company's name, register of charges, register of members/debenture-holders, foreign register of members, general meetings minute book, register of contracts in which directors are interested, register of directors' shareholdings, register of directors, register of loans, register of investments etc. can be inspected by its members.

(c) Refer to Sections 235 and 237 of the Companies Act, 1956.

Q. 22. Write notes on :

(a) Adjournment;

(b) Public holiday;

(c) Voting by poll;

(d) Minutes of general meetings.

Ans. : (a) Page 168 (b) Page 333 (c) Page 160 (d) Pages 209 & 213.

Q. 23. Draft specimen resolutions for transacting the following items indicating the kind of meeting at which each resolution is to be passed and type of resolution required :

(a) to appoint an additional director;

(b) to open a bank account giving authority to the managing director and officers to operate the account singly and/or jointly;

(c) to dispose of an undertaking of the company; and (d) to appoint a sole selling agent.

Ans. : (a) Kind of meeting—Board meeting : Resolution by simple majority : "Resolved that in pursuance of Article No. 80 of the Articles of Association of the company Shri Malay Kanti Halder be and is hereby appointed an additional director of the company who will hold office up to the date of the next annual general meeting."

(b) Kind of meeting —Board meeting : Resolution by simple majority. "Resolved that a current account of the company be opened with State Bank of India, Chowringhee Branch, Calcutta, to be operated upon by the Managing Director, Company Secretary and Chief Finance Manager jointly by any two of them." "Further resolved that the specimen signatures of the said officers be sent to the said bank duly verified by any of the directors of the company."

(c) Refer to page 402.

(d) Kind of meeting—General meeting.

Resolution — Ordinary resolution; special resolution will be necessary if the paid-up capital of the company is Rs. 50 lakhs and above.

"Resolved that pursuant to the provisions of Sections 294 and 294AA of the Companies Act, 1956 and subject to the approval of the Central Government, the company hereby appoints Messrs. Elite Engineering Co. as its sole selling agent for the district of Puri, Orissa, for a period of five years on the terms and conditions as set out in the draft agreement submitted to and approved by the meeting."

Q. 24. The Company of which you are the secretary has adopted 31st March as its financial year. The last annual general meeting of the company was held on 30.9.1987 to approve the accounts for the year 1986-87. The audit of the accounts for the year 1987-88 has not been completed. Your directors intend to hold the annual general meeting on 30.9.1988 to transact the business other than the consideration of the accounts for the year 1987-88 and to adjourn the meeting to a later date for the purpose of adoption of the annual accounts for 1987-88. Whether intended procedure would be in order? Comment on holding the adjourned meeting on 31.1.1989, if the audit is completed in December 1988.

Ans. : Refer to pages 207-208 and 401.

Q. 25. Draft resolutions for transacting the following business stating the kind of meeting at which each resolution is passed and the type of resolution required :

(a) To appoint an alternate director;

(b) To appoint an auditor in place of retiring auditor;

(c) To incorporate an article in the articles of association that the managing director and whole-time director shall not be liable to retire by rotation;

(d) Maintenance of register of members in the same city other than the place of the registered office of the company.

Ans. : (a) Meeting—Board of Directors : Resolution—Board resolution to be passed by simple majority.

(b) Kind of meeting — annual general meeting : Resolution—Ordinary resolution with special notice. Refer to Q/Ans. 15 (d), page 402.

(c) Kind of meeting—general; Resolution—special resolution.

"Resolved that the Articles of the company be altered by inserting Clause No. 10A as under : Pursuant to the provisions of Sections 255 and 256 of the Companies Act, the managing director and whole-time director of the company shall not be liable to retire by rotation."

(d) Kind of meeting—general meeting : Resolution—Special resolution.

"Resolved that in pursuance of the provisions of Section 163 of the Companies Act, 1956, the Register of Members of the company be maintained at 16K Fern Road, Calcutta 700019, instead of registered office of the company."

Q. 26. Explain the term 'Secretary' and elucidate his role as a co-ordinator.

Ans. : Refer to pages 23 and 28-29.

Q. 27. (a) What is the procedure for appointment of an auditor of a company in which 25% of the subscribed capital is held by Life Insurance Corporation of India?

(b) State the procedure for appointment of an auditor in a casual vacancy.

(c) State the provisions of law relating to the appointment of a cost auditor.

Ans. : Q/Ans. No. 10, page 207.

(c) Section 233 B of the Companies Act, 1956, empowers the Central Government to direct that an audit of cost account of a company should be considered by a cost accountant. A cost auditor is appointed by the Board of directors of the company with the previous approval of the Central Government. Refer to Sections 209 (1) (d) and 233B of the Companies Act, 1956, also.

Q. 28. (a) Draft a notice of an annual general meeting of a company to be held in July 1989 to transact the business ordinarily considered in such meetings and to authorise the Board of directors to borrow in excess of the paid-up capital of the company and its free reserves.

(b) At a general meeting of a company, 13 shareholders were present, six voted for a special resolution, five abstained from voting and two voted against. Should the Chairman declare the resolution as passed?

Ans. : (a) Refer to Q/Ans. No. 10, page 207.

(b) In terms of Section 189(2)(c), a special resolution will be declared to have been carried out if the votes cast in its favour are not less than three times the votes cast against it. Therefore, the question of number of members present at the meeting is immaterial or irrelevant. So in the instant case, the chairman should declare the resolution as passed.

Q. 29. (a) Define professional misconduct in relation to practising company secretaries.

(b) State briefly the procedure to be followed in making enquiries relating to misconduct of a company secretary in practice.

Ans. : (a) Refer to Section 22 of the Company Secretaries Act, 1980, and relevant schedules to the Act.

(b) Refer to Section 21 of the Company Secretaries Act, 1980.

Q. 30. (a) Explain 'adjournment', 'postponment' and 'dissolution' in relation to a company meeting.

(b) What is the effect of adjournment as regards notice, business and proxies?

Ans. : Q/Ans. No. 46, pages 169-70 and 333.

Q. 31. (a) What documents of a subsidiary company are prescribed to be annexed to the balance sheet of its holding company?

(b) State the contents of the directors' report required to be attached to balance sheet laid before an annual general meeting.

Ans. : (a) Refer to Section 210 (b) Page 242.

Q. 32. Write short notes on the following;

(a) Passing of resolution by circulation.

(b) Maintenance of minutes books in loose-leaf binders.

(iii) Register of contracts of companies and firms in which directors are interested.

(d) Register of renewed and duplicate share certificates.

Ans. : (a) Page 186 (b) Page 176.

(c) Refer to Section 301 of the Companies Act, 1956.

(d) In terms of Rule 7(2) of the Companies (Issue of Share Certificates) Rules, 1960, particulars of all share certificates issued in exchange for those which are sub-divided or consolidated or in replacement of those which are defaced, torn or old or worn-out or lost or destroyed, shall be entered in the Register of Renewed and Duplicate Certificates, with suitable remarks under authentication of the Company Secretary or any other officer duly authorised by the Board of Directors of the company.

Q. 33. Discuss the legal position of a company secretary and state his main functions.

Ans. : Pages 32-33.

Q. 34. State in relation to a public company

(a) When additional directors can be appointed and for what period?

(b) When an alternate director can be appointed and for what period?

(c) How the office of a director is filled in case of casual vacancy and for what period?

(d) Can directors be appointed by proportional representation?

Ans. : (a) Refer to Section 260 of the Companies Act, 1956;

(b) Refer to Section 313;

(c) Refer to Section 262;

(d) Refer to Section 265 of the Companies Act, 1956.

Q. 35. (a) State the provisions of the Companies Act, 1956, regarding the recording and signing of minutes of the proceedings of Board Meetings.

(b) What matters must be contained in the minutes of a Board Meeting?

(c) Can a director insist that his dissent be recorded in the minutes of Board meeting on a particular decision?

Ans. : Refer to pages 172-74.

Q. 36. Draft resolutions in respect of any four items of the agenda for the Board meeting :

(a) Appointment of Mr. A, ACS, as secretary of the company.

(b) Appointment of Mr. B., technical adviser, as managing director of the company.

(c) Payment of interim dividend.

(d) Appointment of cost auditors pursuant to Section 233 B of the Companies Act, 1956.

(e) Appointment of tax auditors pursuant to Section 44-AB of the Income-tax Act, 1961.

Ans. : Pages 188-89.

(c) "Resolved that an interim dividend of 8% on the paid-up share capital of the company be declared and paid out of the profits of the company for the year ending 31st March 1991 to those shareholders whose names appear in the Register of Members as on 30th March 1991, to those shareholders whose names appear in the Register of Members as on 30th September, 1990, subject to deduction of income tax as per the provisions of the Income-tax Act."

"Further resolved that the Register of Members be closed from 24.7.1991 to 31.7.1991, both days inclusive."

(d) and (e) Pages 188-89.

Q. 37. (a) What books of account are required to be kept by a Company?

(b) Who are the persons who can inspect books of account?

(c) Can a director take inspection of the books of account through an agent?

(d) Can a shareholder inspect books of account?

Ans. : Page 201.

Q. 38. (a) What do you understand by an office or place of profit held by a director under the company?

(b) What are the restrictions of the Companies Act, 1956, in respect of a director holding an office or place of profit under the company?

(c) Whether these restrictions apply if a relative of a director of a private company is appointed as managing director of a private company on a monthly salary of Rs. 3,500/-?

Ans. : (a) Refer to Section 314 of the Companies Act, 1956.

(b) Refer to Section 314(1) of the Act

(c) Refer to Section 314 (1B) of the Act.

Q. 39. As the secretary of a public company you have been asked to prepare a draft of the Board's report to be attached to company's annual accounts. State the matters statutorily required to be included in such a report.

Ans. : Page 242.

Q. 40. Write short notes on any four :

(a) Managing director;

(b) Explanatory Statement;

(c) Register of Members;

(d) Annual Return;

(e) Statutory Report.

Ans. : (a) Refer to Section 2(26) of the Companies Act, 1956.

(b) Refer to page 177.

(c) Refer to Section 150 of the Companies Act and Rule 7 of the Companies (Issue of Share Certificates) Rules, 1960;

(d) Page 200 (e) Page 194.

Q. 41. (a) Fill in the blanks :

(i) In the case of every company a meeting of its Board of Directors shall be held at least once in every———months and at least———such meetings shall be held in a year.

(ii) A general meeting of a company may be called after issuing shorter notice than twenty-one days if consent is accorded thereto in the case of annual general meeting by———and in the case of any other general meeting by—.

(iii) At any general meeting, a resolution put to vote of the meeting shall unless a———is demanded be decided on a——.

(iv) A company may, after giving not less than——previous notice by advertisement in some newspaper circulating in the district in which the registered office of the company is situate close the register of members for any period not exceeding——at any one time.

(v) A preference shareholder shall have a right to vote on resolutions placed before the company which affect the——attached to preference share and on every resolution placed before the company at any meeting if the——— due on such remain unpaid for a specified period.

(b) Outline the statutory duties of a company secretary under the Companies Act, 1956.

Ans. : (a)

(i) three.......four.

(ii) all the members entitled to vote thereat.......95% of the members entitled to vote thereat

(iii) poll.......show of hands

(iv) seven days......thirty days

(v) rights......dividend

(b) Pages 26-27.

Q. 42. Explain the duties of company secretary before, during and after annual general meeting of a public company whose shares are listed on a recognised stock exchange.

Ans. : Pages 30-31.

Q. 43. What do you mean by "poll"? Who can demand a poll and when? Is there any time limit for taking poll and, if so, what? Briefly explain the manner of taking poll and declaration of results on voting by poll.

Ans. : Pages 160-61.

Q. 44. (a) What is the procedure for passing a resolution by circulation?

(b) What are the matters in respect of which a resolution by circulation cannot be passed?

(c) A company has five directors. Two of them have gone abroad. A resolution is to be passed by circulation. It was approved by two of the directors then in India while the third director then in India voted against. What would be the fate of the resolution?

Hints : (a) Refer to Section 289 and page 186.

(b) Refer to Section 292 and page 186.

(c) Majority of directors then in India is three and all of them must approve the resolution. So, in the problem, the resolution is not passed.

Q. 45. (a) Discuss the provisions relating to length of the notice for the Board meetings. Who can issue the notice of a Board Meeting?

(b) Can first Board Meeting of a public limited company be held on a public holiday?

Hints : (a) Refer to Section 286 and pages 179-80.

(b) Page 176.

Q. 46. State the legal position as regards the following :

(a) Maintaining the minutes of meetings in loose-leaf form.

(b) The right of a non-member chairman to exercise casting vote.

(c) Due to torrential rain and consequent flooding of the roads, none of the members was able to attend the annual general meeting on a particular day.

(d) A member who after validly appointing a proxy arrives at the general meeting himself.

Hints : (a) Refer to Section 193(1) and page 176.

(b) Refer to Regulation 54 of Table A and page 334.

(c) In terms of Section 174(4), the meeting would automatically get adjourned.

(d) If the member votes prior to his proxy, the proxy is automatically revoked. Refer to Section 176 also.

Q. 47. (a) What is the minimum and the maximum number of directors a company must have?

(b) What matters are required to be approved by a resolution at a Board Meeting with the consent of all the directors present at the meeting?

(c) What are the acts which the Board of Directors cannot do without the consent of the company at a general meeting?

Hints : (a) Refer to Sections 252 and 259 of the Companies Act.

(b) Refer to Sections 316(2), 372(2) and 386(2) of the Companies Act.

(c) Refer to Sections 293 and 314 of the Companies Act.

Q. 48. State briefly the rights of the concerned parties in regard to the following :

(a) of a member to inspect the proxies;

(b) of a member to inspect the minutes of the Board meeting;

(c) of a director to appoint a proxy to attend the Board meeting;

(d) of a director to get a copy of the minutes of the Board meeting;

(e) of a corporate member to be represented at a general meeting;

(f) of an auditor to get copies of the minutes of the Board meeting;

(g) of a person having a fixed deposit with the company to receive a copy of the annual report and accounts;

(h) of a preference shareholder to get the notice of the annual general meeting.

Hints : (a) Refer to Section 176(7).

(b) The members can inspect the minutes of the general meeting but not the Board meetings.

(c) A director cannot appoint a proxy in terms of Section 312 of the Act.

(d) Though there is no such legal provision, as a matter of convention, copies of minutes of the Board meetings are usually sent to the directors.

(e) A corporate member can be represented in a general meeting vide Section 187 of the Act.

(f) In terms of Section 227, an auditor can inspect the books of account and minutes of all the meetings, but he is not entitled to get a copy of the Board meeting.

(g) Yes. Refer to Section 219(2).

(h) Yes. Refer to Section 172.

Q. 49. Write short notes on

(a) Public holiday and holding of a general meeting,

(b) Clear days' notice,

(c) Disinterested quorum at Board meetings,

(d) Resolutions requiring registration.

Hints : (a) Page 333 and 176 (b) Page 147 (c) Page 162

(d) Refer to Section 192 of the Companies Act.

Q. 50. Draft resolutions for transacting the following items, indicating the kind of meeting at which each resolution is passed and the type of resolution required :

(a) change of name by the company;

(b) convening the annual general meeting;

(c) adoption of statutory report; and

(d) adoption of annual accounts.

Ans. : Pages 16-17.

Q. 51. (a) Explain the provisions of Section 166 of the Companies Act, 1956, with regard to holding of an annual general meeting.

(b) Financial year of a company ends on 31st December. Third annual general meeting of the company was held on 25th March 1983. Examine the validity of its :

(i) Fourth annual general meeting held on 28th June 1984;

(ii) Fifth annual general meeting to be held on 1st July 1985.

Ans. : (a) Page 199.

(b) (i) Since the time gap between the third and the fourth meeting is more than 15 months, holding of the meeting on 28th June will contravene the provision of Section 166(1) of the Companies Act.

(ii) Though, in terms of Section 166, the time gap between two annual general meetings may be 15 months, Section 210 requires the final accounts to be placed before the meeting within 6 months from the date of closing of the accounts. So the meeting must be held on or before 30th June and not on 1st July.

Q. 52. (a) State the procedure for passing a resolution by circulation.

(b) Two out of five directors of a company have gone abroad. Out of the remaining directors in India, two have signed in favour and one has signed against a resolution sent by circulation. What is the fate of the resolution?

Ans. : (a) Page 186 and Section 289 of the Companies Act.

(b) The resolution has not been passed since majority of the directors (3 out of 5) have not voted in favour of the resolution.

Q. 53. (a) Can a person who is not a shareholder become—

(i) a chairman of the Board?

(ii) a chairman of a general meeting?

(b) Can a person who is not a director become

(i) a chairman of the Board?

(ii) a chairman of a general meeting?

Ans. : (a) (i) When the Articles of Association of a company do not specifically provide for holding of qualification shares, any person whether a shareholder or not can be appointed as a director of the company.

(ii) In the instant problem, a person who is not a shareholder cannot be the chairman of a general meeting (Regulation 52 of Table A).

(b) (i) A person who is not a director cannot be the chairman of the Board (Regulation 76 of Table A).

(ii) A shareholder who is not a director of the company can be the chairman of a general meeting. (Regulation 52 of Table A of Schedule A to the Companies Act, 1956).

Q. 54. Advise the legal position :

(a) Regarding a member's right

(i) to have a copy of the minutes of a general meeting;

(ii) to inspect the minutes of the Board meeting in which a resolution was passed in respect of a contract in which chairman was interested.

(b) Regarding director's right

(i) to have a copy of the minutes of a Board meeting, though he is not a working director;

(ii) to receive notice of a general meeting, though he is not a member.

Ans. : (a)

(i) Yes. [Section 196(2)].

(ii) Ordinarily, a member has no such right. But as an exception to the Rule under Section 301, the member can inspect the minutes.

(b) (i) Though a director has the right to inspect the minutes book of a Board meeting, he cannot get extract of the minutes if the Articles do not specifically provide for this.

(ii) According to Section 172, a non-member director is not entitled to receive the notice of general meeting.

Q. 55. In respect of Board and general meetings of a company, advise legal position regarding :

(a) keeping of minutes in loose leaves;

(b) signing of minutes;

(c) confirmation of minutes; and

(d) minutes as evidence.

Ans. : (a) Refer to Section 193(1B) of the Companies Act and page 176.

(b) Refer to Section 193(1A) of the Act and page 338.

(c) Minutes of a Board meeting are usually confirmed at the next Board meeting. However, as a matter of practice, the minutes of general meetings are not confirmed.

(d) Minutes of general meetings and Board meetings properly kept as required under Section 193 shall be an acceptable evidence (Section 194).

Q. 56. Draft a notice of annual general meeting of PQR Ltd., Chennai, with special business to appoint M/s. ABC Ltd., Mumbai, as their sole selling agent.

Ans. : Pages 205-06.

Q. 57. (a) Explain the term "secretary" under the Companies Act, 1956. Is it compulsory for every company to appoint a secretary?

(b) What are the qualifications prescribed for appointment of secretary of a company having a paid-up capital of rupees fifty lakhs and above? What difference would it make if the paid-up share capital is less than rupees fifty lakhs?

(c) Is it necessary to submit any return to the Registrar of Companies for appointment of a secretary?

Ans. : (a) Pages 23-24 (b) Pages 24-25.

(c) Particulars of the Secretary are required to be submitted to the Registrar of Companies in Form No. 32 (in duplicate) within 30 days from the date of his appointment.

Q. 58. Write short notes on any three of the following :

(a) Amendment of motions.

(b) Substantive motion.

(c) Refer back to committee.

(d) Point of order.

Ans. : (a) Page 153 (b) Page 177 (c) Page 169 (d) Page 168.

Q. 59. Complete the following :

(a) A public limited company incorporated on 1st September 1985 and having got a certificate for commencement of business on 31st October 1985 must hold its statutory meeting by——and its first annual general meeting by——

(b) For appointing an auditor a person other than the retiring auditor, a special notice to the company must be given by——member(s) not less than.....days before the annual general meeting.

(c) Appointment of an auditor in a company in which not less than 25% of the subscribed share capital is held by a public financial institution is——business and an explanatory statement——required to be attached to the notice calling the meeting.

(d) The directions, that even one member of the company present in person or by proxy shall be deemed to constitute a meeting, can be given by——in case of an annual general meeting and by——in case of extra-ordinary general meeting.

(e) In a company having seven directors, the quorum of the Board meeting shall be——; and——directors shall be liable to retire by rotation.

Ans. : (a) 30th April 1986, but not on or before 30th November 1985,.....on or before 28th February 1987.

(b) one; 14

(c) ordinary;.....is not.....

(d) Central Government;.......Company Law Board.

(e) Three;......two......

Q. 60. (a) ABC Leasing Co. Ltd. held four Board Meetings during the calendar year 1985 : on 19th January, 29th April, 26th June and 3rd October. Is there any violation of the provisions of the Companies Act, 1956?

(b) Will your answer to (a) above be different if the Board meeting scheduled to be held on 26th June had to be adjourned for want of quorum and was held in the next week, i.e., on 3rd July?

(c) What would have been the position if the Board meeting on 3rd October was an adjourned meeting against the original meeting which was scheduled to be held on 26th September and was adjourned for want of quorum?

(d) If the Board meeting scheduled to be be held on Saturday, 19th January, could not be held for want of quorum, on what date the adjourned meeting would have been held?

Ans. : (a) In terms of Section 285 of the Companies Act 1956, a Board meeting should be held once in every three months and at least four such meetings should be held in a calendar year. In the instant case, no Board meeting was held during the quarter July to September and, as such, there has been a violation of the provisions of Section 285.

(b) There has been no violation of the provisions of Section 285 of the Companies Act.

(c) There has been no violation of the provisions of Section 285 of the Companies Act. Please refer to Section 288 of the Act also.

(d) In terms of the provisions of Section 288(1), the adjourned Board meeting should be held on the same day in the next week, at the same time and place. In case the day is a public holiday, the meeting will be held on the succeeding day. In the instant case, the meeting should have been held on 26th January. But since the 26th January (Saturday) is a public holiday and the succeeding day is Sunday, the meeting should be held on Monday, the 28th January.

Q. 61. (a) The annual general meeting of Doomwell Ltd. was held on 31st March 1984, where the accounts for the financial year ending 30th September 1983 were adopted. The next annual general meeting was to be held on 30th June 1985 with the permission of the Registrar of Companies but due to non-finalisation of the accounts for the year ending 30th September 1984, on account of strike, the meeting was adjourned indefinitely and is not likely to be held in the immediate future. State

- **(i) by what time the company is liable to file copies of balance sheet as on 30th September 1984 with the Registrar under Section 220 of the Companies Act?**
- **(ii) whether there will be contravention of Section 210 of the Companies Act, 1956 for not laying the balance sheet and the profit and loss a/c before the annual general meeting in time?**

(b) The general meeting of M/s. Circumvent Ltd. was held on 16th December 1985. The Secretary, after drafting the minutes, has suddenly left the country to attend an urgent business conference and is likely to return to India only after 45 days. The chairman, who presided over the meeting, expired on 28th December 1985 without signing the minutes. Advise the company as to what course of action is to be taken for causing and signing of minutes of the company held on 16th December 1985.

(c) Mr. Foreigner had been appointed as a director in the last general meeting. Due to personal reasons he resigned from the directorship. The Board filled up the casual vacancy by appointing Mr. Sick in his place. On account of prolonged illness, Mr. Sick expired within few days of his becoming director. The Board wishes to fill up the casual vacancy by appointing Mr. Health in the place of Mr. Sick in the forthcoming Board meeting. Advise the Board suitably.

Ans. : (a) (i) Under Section 220 of the Companies Act, copies of balance sheet and profit & loss account etc. should be filed with the Registrar of Companies within 30 days from the date of annual general meeting. In the instant case, copies of balance sheet should have been filed on or before 30th July 1985 (within 30 days from 30th June 1985). Here the company could not finalise the annual accounts and as such, the question of filing them with the Registrar does not arise. So, the company has contravened the provisions of Section 210 and Section 220.

(a) (ii) The company has violated the provision of Section 210 as it has failed to lay the balance sheet and profit & loss a/c before the meeting.

(b) Section 193 provides that the minutes of a general meeting should be signed by the chairman of that meeting within 30 days from the date of the meeting. It further provides that in case of death or incapacitation, the Board will authorise one of the directors to sign the minutes. In the instant case, a Board Meeting should be held which will authorise one of the directors to sign the minutes within the statutory time limit of 30 days.

(c) When the Board fills in a casual vacancy by appointing a person and that person vacates his office, the resulting vacancy cannot be treated as casual vacancy. So, in the instant case, the Board can appoint Mr. Health as additional director and not as a director in the casual vacancy.

Q. 62. (a) Explain the provisions relating to service of documents on company, on Registrar of Companies and on members by the company.

(b) Mr. Smart, as a member, has advised M/s. Careless Ltd. well in time to send all documents to him at his registered address by registered post only and deposited necessary sum to defray the expenses. The company by oversight sent the notice of its extraordinary general meeting to him by ordinary post. Mr. Smart did not attend the meeting. State whether the company has effectively served the notice to Mr. Smart? Can Mr. Smart invalidate the proceedings of the meeting on this ground?

Ans. : (a) Refer to Sections 51-53 of the Companies Act, 1956.

(b) According to Section 53(2), notice may be sent by ordinary post. However, in the instant case, Mr. Smart had deposited the necessary sum of money and wanted the notice etc. to be sent to him by registered post. So, the service of notice by the company has not been proper and effective. Mr. smart can invalidate the proceedings of the meeting if he can prove mala fide on the part of the company in issuing the notice to him by ordinary post instead of registered post. Reference may please be made to Section 172.

Q. 63. Examine the validity of the following :

(a) M, a member, appointed P as his proxy in the forms set out in Schedule IX of the Companies Act, 1956. The company did not permit P to attend the meeting on the ground that the special requirements for the instrument in the Articles have not been fulfilled.

(b) X, a director of ABC Ltd., wishes to appoint Y as his proxy to attend the ensuing Board meeting proposed to be held on 6th January 1986.

(c) D, a non-member, has been appointed as a director. He has later become chairman of the Board. The Articles of the company provide that the chairman of the Board shall preside at every general meeting. In an annual general meeting, when D presided over the meeting, M, a member, objected to his chairmanship on the ground that D is not a member of the company.

(d) R and S have been appointed as directors on the same date. R is aged 55 years, S is aged 60 years. In the next annual general meeting, one director is liable for retirement by rotation by virtue of Section 256 of the Companies Act, 1956. R and S being holding offices for the longest period, the consultant has advised S to retire as he is senior to R in age.

Ans. : (a) In terms of Section 176(6) of the Companies Act, 1956, the company should have permitted P to attend the meeting.

(b) The Companies Act does not have any provision for appointment of a proxy by a director to attend a Board meeting.

(c) If the Articles do not require qualification shares for a director, a non-member can be appointed a chairman of the Board meeting. Refer to Regulation 50 of Table A of Schedule I to the Act.

(d) Section 256(2) provides for retirement of those directors who have been longest in the office. In the instant case, since both the directors have joined on the same day, retirement will be decided by draw of lots. So, the consultant's advice is not correct.

Q. 64. (a) Examine the validity of the following clauses which B. Pvt. Ltd. proposes to incorporate in its Articles of Association :

(i) Annual general meeting shall be called after giving shorter notice than that provided in the Companies Act, if consent is accorded by majority of the members entitled to vote thereat.

(ii) The quorum for general meetings shall be three members including proxies present thereat.

(b) Advise whether appointment of company secretary in the following cases is in order :

(i) B, an M.Com., is serving as a company secretary in ABC Ltd. whose paid-up capital is more than Rs. 25 lakhs from 1.1.1974. By virtue of his vast experience in the secretarial department, another company MNO Ltd., whose paid-up capital is more than Rs. 50 lakhs, wishes to appoint him as its company secretary.

(ii) The Board of D Pvt. Ltd., having a paid-up capital of Rs. 25 lakhs, consists of two directors A and B. A possesses the membership of the Institute of Company Secretaries of India. The company desires to appoint him as a company secretary also.

Ans. : (a) (i) The proposed provision in the Articles of the private company is valid in terms of Section 170(1) (ii) read with Section 171 of the Act.

(ii) The proposed provision in the Articles is valid in terms of Section 174(1) of the Act. It should however be noted that out of three persons present, two must be members personally present.

(b) (i) Since B does not possess the prescribed qualifications, he cannot be appointed as the company secretary of MNO Ltd. [Sections 2(45) and 383A].

(ii) When a private company has two directors only, none of them can be appointed as its company secretary. So, appointment of A as secretary will be in contravention of Section 383A.

Q. 65. What do you understand by the term "Quorum"? What is the quorum for the general meetings? Discuss the legal position when the quorum is incomplete at a general meeting. Can one person form the quorum of a general meeting?

Ans. : Pages 162-63.

Q. 66. Draft specimen resolutions for transacting any four of the following items, indicating the kind of meeting at which each resolution is passed and the type of resolution required :

(a) Appointment of auditors and fixation of their remuneration in respect of a company 30% of the subscribed capital of which is jointly held by Life Insurance Corporation, Unit Trust of India, National Insurance Company Ltd. and State Bank of India.

(b) Appointment of a director who was earlier appointed by the Board of Directors as an additional director.

(c) Adoption of the common seal.

(d) Borrowing in excess of paid-up capital and free reserves.

(e) Opening of a dividend account with a scheduled bank.

Ans. : (a) Annual general meeting : Special resolution (Section 224A).

(b) Annual general meeting : ordinary resolution.

(c) The resolution has to be passed in a Board Meeting.

(d) General meeting : ordinary resolution.

(e) The resolution needs to be passed at a meeting of the Board of Directors. For specimen resolutions, refer to pages 186-87 and 189.

Q. 67. Distinguish between :

(a) Adjournment and postponement,

(b) Motion and resolution,

(c) Ordinary business and special business,

(d) Deliberative vote and casting vote.

Ans. : (a) Page 168 (b) Page 152 (c) Page 161 (d) Page 151.

Q. 68. Draft specimen resolutions for transacting the following items, indicating the kind of meeting at which each resolution is passed :

(a) Shifting of the registered office of the company from Jammu to Srinagar.

(b) Keeping of books of account at a place other than the registered office.

(c) Approval to payment of interim dividend.

(d) Keeping of 'register of members' at a place other than the registered office.

Hints : (a) Refer to Pages 16-18 and Section 146 of the Companies Act. Special resolution needs to be passed at a general meeting of the company.

(b) Refer to page 201 and Section 209(1) of the Companies Act. A resolution to be passed by the Board of Directors of the Company is necessary for the purpose.

(c) Refer to page 176 and Regulation 86 of Table A. A Board resolution has to be passed for the purpose.

(d) Refer to page 46 and Section 163(1) of the Companies Act. A special resolution needs to be passed at a general meeting.

Q. 69. (a) When is the explanatory statement required to be annexed to the notice calling the general meeting of a company and what are the details to be set out therein?

(b) Is an explanatory statement required to be annexed for the following items :

(i) appointment of auditors by special resolution as required under Section 224A of the Companies Act, 1956; and

(ii) appointment by ordinary resolution at an annual general meeting of a director co-opted by the Board of Directors as an additional director.

Hints : (a) Refer to Section 173(1) and (2) of the Companies Act. The explanatory statement must contain a statement of the material facts of all the items of the agenda to be discussed at the meeting. The explanatory statement should also clearly mention the nature of concern or interest of the managerial personnel.

(b) (i) In terms of Section 173(1) (a) of the Companies Act, appointment of auditors which is an ordinary business does not require any explanatory statement.

(b) (ii) In terms of Section 173(1) (a) of the Companies Act, appointment of a director, other than those retiring by rotation, is an item of special business and as such, an explanatory statement is essential.

Q. 70. Examine the powers of the Chairman under the following situations :

(a) On a resolution when put to vote :

(i) there is a tie. The articles are silent on Chairman's right of casting vote. Can the Chairman exercise a casting vote and declare the resolution as passed ?

(ii) the Chairman counts ten votes in favour and eleven against the resolution. Can the Chairman cast his own vote which he had not exercised earlier in favour of the resolution and also the casting vote which the Articles authorise and declare the resolution as passed ? (b) In a meeting which has become disorderly : (i) the Chairman ejects the disorderly persons; (ii) the Chairman adjourns the meeting, though the majority is not in favour.

Hints : (a) (i) Refer to page 151, and Regulation 54 of Table A of Schedule I of the Companies Act. Since the Articles are silent on the Chairman's right of casting vote, the Chairman, in the instant problem, cannot exercise the casting vote and declare the resolution as passed.

(a) (ii) The Chairman can use the casting vote if the Articles so provide and only when there is a tie. The instant problem is not a case of tie and, as such, the question of the Chairman's casting vote does not arise. Further, the Chairman can use his own vote as a member only at the time of poll and not at the time of counting. So he cannot declare the resolution as passed.

(b) (i) It is well within the powers of the chairman to eject the disorderly persons.

(b) (ii) The Articles of Association of the Company may empower the Chairman to adjourn a meeting. If, however, the Chairman attempts to adjourn a duly convened and properly constituted meeting improperly and unjustifiably, the meeting may elect another person to transact the remaining business.

Q. 71. As a Chairman of the meeting :

(a) Would you allow a poll to be taken in each of the following situations when seven persons having voting rights are present and a poll is demanded by

(i) one proxy holder, in case of a private limited company;

(ii) four members present in person, in case of a public limited company;

(iii) a member holding one-twentieth of the total voting power in case of a company having no share capital.

(b) Up to what time can you order a poll to be taken, if demanded, on the following matters :

(i) election of the Chairman himself;

(ii) election of directors;

(iii) adoption of accounts.

Hints : (a) (i) In terms of Section 179(1) (b) of the Companies Act, as the demand for poll is in order, the Chairman will have to allow it.

(ii) In terms of Section 179(1) (a) of the Companies Act, poll must be demanded by at least five persons having rights to vote and present in person or by proxy. The Chairman should not allow the poll as because the demand for it has been made by four persons instead of the stipulated minimum of five persons.

(iii) In terms of Section 179(1) (c), demand for a poll must be made by member or members having not less than one-tenth of the total voting power. So in the instant problem, the demand should be disallowed by the Chairman.

(b) (i) According to Section 175(2), demand for a poll on the election of a Chairman should be met forthwith.

(b)(ii) & (iii) In terms of Section 180 (2), the poll demanded shall be taken at such time not being later than forty-eight hours from the time when the demand was made, as the chairman may direct.

Q. 72. (a) Subsequent to the issue of notice for annual general meeting, the scheduled day for holding the meeting is declared by the Central Government as a public holiday. Even otherwise, the day did not suit the chairman and he desires to hold the meeting later. Whether the meeting can be postponed for a month by giving a further notice?

(b) If an annual general meeting cannot be held on a public holiday whether it will be held on the next working day or on the same day in the next week?

(c) If an annual general meeting can be held on a public holiday, whether a resolution can be passed thereat for its adjournment for thirty days so that no fresh notice need be given?

Hints : (a) In terms of Section 2(38) of the Companies Act, if the proposed date of the meeting is declared as a public holiday subsequent to the date of issue of the notice by the company, the meeting should be held undisturbed. So the meeting must be held. Further, the chairman cannot postpone the meeting on the ground that 'the day did not suit' him. If necessary, the meeting may elect another Chairman.

(b) In terms of Section 166(2), an annual general meeting cannot be held on a day which is declared as a public holiday. However, in terms of Section 2(38), if the proposed date of the meeting is declared a public holiday subsequent to the date of the issue of the notice, the meeting can be held as scheduled. So the question of holding the meeting 'on the next working day or on the same day in the next week' does not arise at all.

(c) In the instant problem, the meeting can be held on a public holiday in terms of Section 2(38). Though the Chairman is empowered to adjourn a meeting, he cannot do so without valid reasons. No notice for adjourned meeting needs to be served if it is held within thirty days from the date of adjournment.

Q. 73. Examine whether the following clauses relating to meetings can be legally incorporated in the Articles of Association :

(a) In case of a public company :

- **(i) quorum of the general meetings as fifty members;**
- **(ii) quorum of the Board Meetings as one-half of the total strength;**
- **(iii) thirty days' clear notice for calling a general meeting.**

(b) In case of a private limited company :

- **(i) minimum strength of Board as three directors;**
- **(ii) life-time appointment of all of its directors without any provision for retirement by rotation;**
- **(iii) seven days' clear notice for calling a general meeting.**

Hints : (a) (i) In terms of Section 174(1) of the Companies Act, the Articles of Association of the Company may provide for larger number than five persons for the purpose of the quorum.

(a) (ii) According to Section 287(2) of the Act, the quorum for a meeting of the Board of Directors of a company shall be one-third of its total strength (any fraction to be rounded-off as one), or two directors, whichever is higher. So, the proposed clause cannot be legally incorporated in the Articles.

(a) (iii) In terms of Section 171, "a general meeting of a company may be called by giving not less than twenty-one days' notice in writing". Section 170(2) of the Act permits 'adaptations and modifications' of the provision of Section 171. Hence, the clause can be legally incorporated.

(b) (i) According to Section to Section 252(2) of the Companies Act, the minimum number of directors, in case of a private company, is two. So the proposed clause cannot legally be incorporated in the Article.

(b) (ii) Section 156 of the Act, which deals with ascertainment of directors retiring by rotation and filling of vacancies, does not apply to private companies. As such, the proposed clause is valid in the eyes of law.

(b) (iii) Section 171, which deals with length of notice for calling meeting is not applicable to private companies. Further, Section 170(1)(ii) of the Act permits the private companies to make their own regulations as regards length of notice. Here, the proposed clause is valid.

Q. 74. Draft a notice of Extraordinary General Meeting of a company authorised by the Board, being held for obtaining approval to the appointment of and remuneration including perquisites payable to the Executive Director together with the necessary explanatory statement.

Hints : Refer to page 212.

Q. 75. Comment on the following :

(a) A motion of point of order is the most potent and easiest of all dilatory motions.

(b) A pro-tempo Chairman, i.e., a Chairman who takes over in the middle of a meeting at the request of regular Chairman, has also the same powers as enjoyed by the Chairman including the casting vote.

(c) A director who does not hold any shares in the company can attend and participate in a General Meeting of a company.

(d) A Chair must exercise his casting vote in case of equality of votes, otherwise he will not be fulfilling his obligations or functions as Chairman.

Hints : (a) A point of order motion may be brought by any member without any notice. As soon as this motion is raised, the Chairman of the meeting has to give his ruling forthwith. When he gives his ruling, discussion on the main motion is diverted. So, the statement is fully correct.

(b) Since a pro-tempo Chairman is also a chairman, he enjoys all the powers enjoyed by a chairman. Rules 50 to 52 of Table A of the Schedule to the Companies Act corroborate the statement given in the question. So, the statement is correct.

(c) Though the Companies Act is silent on this score, the statement is correct.

(d) Use of casting vote by the chairman fully depends on his discretion. So, the statement is not correct.

Q. 76. Distinguish between :

(a) Trustee and Public Trustee,

(b) Proxy and Representative,

(c) Ordinary Business and Special Business,

(d) Motion and Substantive motion.

Hints : (a) A trustee is a person on whom the legal ownership/possession of the trust property is vested for the interests of the beneficiary/beneficiaries. A Public Trustee is an official appointed by the Government of India in terms of Section 153A of the Companies Act. As the the name suggests, he has to discharge the duties in the interest of the public.

(b) Proxy—Page 165. A representative is a person who represents any body corporate bodies and exercises all the rights of the shareholders of the company.

(c) Page 161 (d) Pages 152 and 179.

Q. 77. Draft specimen resolutions for transacting any four of the following business. Indicate against each resolution the nature of meeting where the respective business is transacted under normal circumstances. Also give explanatory statement where applicable :

(a) Change of accounting year;

(b) Adoption of common seal;

(c) Borrowing in excess of paid-up capital and free reserves;

(d) Declaration of annual dividend;

(e) Removal of auditor before expiry of his term.

Hints : Page 157.

Q. 78. State the different methods of appointment of directors. Who is disqualified from being appointed a director?

Hints : Pages 188, 188, 209, 188, and 188.

Q. 79. What requirements of law will you, as a company secretary, observe in relation to the holding of the statutory meeting? Mention the contents of the statutory report and state who should certify the same.

Hints : Pages 140 and 194.

Q. 80. What is a 'resolution'? Distinguish between

(a) Special and ordinary resolutions;

(b) Enumerate four items for which a special resolution is required;

(c) Enumerate four resolutions which require special notice;

(d) What resolution can be passed by circulation amongst directors?

Hints : Pages 156 and 188.

Q. 81. Complete any four of the following :

(a) Appointment of an auditor in a company in which not less than twenty per cent of the subscribed capital is held by Government Company shall be made by——

(b) The minutes of the proceedings of a company meeting can be signed in case of Board Meeting by——and in case of general meeting by——

(c) A preference shareholder has a right to vote at a general meeting only when——and a proxy has a right to vote at a general meeting only when——

(d) A general meeting of a public limited company may be called after giving shorter notice than twenty-one days if consent is accorded thereto in case of an annual general meeting by——and in case of other general meeting by——

Ans. : Pages 345-46.

Q. 82. Advise the legal position :

(a) Regarding the right to attend the general meeting :

(i) if two proxies both appointed by same member with an interval of a day are present at the meeting;

(ii) if, after appointing the proxy, a member himself is also present at the meeting;

(iii) if a person produces the proxy at the time of the meeting.

(b) Regarding the right to inspect proxies :

(i) by a proxy at the time of meeting, during business hours after giving 48 hours' notice;

(ii) by a member, at the time of the meeting, during business hours, after giving a week's notice;

(iii) by a member at the time of the meeting, which has continued beyond business hours, after giving one week's notice.

Ans. : Page 345.

Q. 83. As Secretary of a public limited company what would be your advices regarding the validity of quorum under each of the following situations :

(a) (i) one director is interested in a particular item of agenda and

(ii) to catch the flight one director leaves the meeting before completion of last item on the agenda.

(b) At the general meeting where out of seven members five are present and;

(i) four members are interested in a particular item of business; and

(ii) In order to break the quorum, one member leaves the meeting before completion of the last item of business.

Ans. : Page 346.

Q. 84. Draft the minutes of the Board Meeting convened to consider annual accounts, directors' report, etc.

Hints : Pages 189-190.

Q. 85. C, the Chairman of the company, was not present within fifteen minutes after the appointed time of 4-45 p.m. of the annual general meeting; D, the only director present, was elected as the Chairman of the meeting. Ten minutes after the commencement of the meeting under D's chairmanship, C arrived and sat along with other members. How would you deal with the following points raised by the members challenging the validity of the meeting and the proceedings thereat :

(a) Proper Chairman C is not in the chair;

(b) Meeting has actually commenced after the business hours at 5-02 p.m.

(c) Notice was not received by one of the shareholders as his envelope containing the notice had got mixed up with similar empty envelopes;

(d) the notice and the auditors' report should be read instead of taking the same as read.

Ans. : Q/Ans. No. 168, pages 346-47.

Q. 86. (a) Total strength of the Board of Directors of your company is ten.

(i) How many directors are liable to retire by rotation in the next annual general meeting?

(ii) What will be the quorum of the Board Meeting?

(b) In order to pass the resolutions what is the minimum number of directors who must consent in favour of each of the following items assuming that all the 10 directors of your company are present at the meeting :

(i) Approval of a contract to be entered into with a private limited company in which Mr. D, a director of your company, is the Managing Director.

(ii) Appointment of Mr. D as the Managing Director of your company also.

(iii) Approval of balance sheet and profit and loss account of the company.

(iv) Investment in shares of other body corporates.

Hints : Pages 342-43.

Q. 87. (a) Who is authorised to sign a Board's Report? Explain whether you will include the following names in the statement of employees under the Board's report covering company's financial year ending 31st December 1983 :

(i) Mr. 'X', whose remuneration has been raised from Rs. 2,800/- to Rs. 3,200/- per month effective from 1st October 1983.

(ii) Mr. 'T'—who was drawing a monthly remuneration of Rs. 1,000/- sought voluntary retirement on 31st March 1983, and was paid Rs. 15,000/- as leave encashment and ex-gratia compensation.

Hints : Page 343.

Q. 88. (a) As the Secretary of a public limited company, how would you deal with each of the following situations :

(i) All the directors except one are interested in a resolution.

(ii) Due to resignation of one director out of a total of three, the strength of the Board has fallen below the minimum required under law?

(b) At a general meeting :

(i) Only one person, authorised representative of five shareholding companies, is present at the meeting.

(ii) Name of a shareholder is proposed at the meeting for appointment as director, in place of a director retiring by rotation whose resolution for reappointment has not been passed?

Hints : Pages 343-44.

Q. 89. At the forthcoming Annual General Meeting, the directors of PQR Ltd., Mumbai, propose to appoint ABC Ltd., Delhi, as sole selling agent for their company. Draft a complete notice of the Annual General Meeting together with the explanatory statement.

Hints : Pages 203-05.

Q. 90. (a) The tenth Annual General Meeting of a Company covering accounts up to 30th June 1982, was held on 29th September 1982. What are the contraventions under the Companies Act, if the eleventh meeting is held on :

(i) Sunday the 1st January 1984;

(ii) Saturday, the 31st December 1983.

(b) The Annual General Meeting of your Company is scheduled to be held on the 19th January 1984 at Room No. 101 in Hotel Taj? How will you deal with the following situations, assuming that the meeting is automatically adjourned for want of quorum :

(i) Same day in the next week falls on 26th January 1984, a public holiday.

(ii) Room No. 101 in Hotel Taj is not available up to 30th January 1984?

Hints : (a) Refer to Sections 166 and 210. Contraventions of the Act are (1) Time gap between two meetings is more than 15 months; (2) No meeting was held in 1983; and (3) Meeting on Sunday—a public holiday—is a contravention of the Negotiable Instruments Act,

1881. (4) Accounts have not been placed before the annual general meeting within 6 months from 30th June 1983. In case the meeting is held on 31st December 1983, there will not be any contravention regarding time gap of 15 months.

(b) In terms of Section 174, the meeting stands adjourned to next week at the same time and the same place. Therefore,

(i) Adjourned meeting may be held even on a public holiday.

(ii) Meeting can be held at any other room of the hotel or the directors may fix a new venue.

Q. 91. Advise the legal position :

(a) Directors A and B are going abroad :

(i) Mr. A desires that, during his stay abroad, notice of Board Meetings be served on him at his London address.

(ii) Mr. B desires that no notice be sent to him during the next three months.

(b) Previous meeting of the Board of directors was held on 1st October 1983. Due to non-availability of majority of directors in India, the Chairman proposes to hold the next meeting :

(i) On 31st March 1984, in India; or

(ii) On 31st December 1983, in London, where majority of directors may be present.

Hints : (a) (i) In terms of Section 286 of the Companies Act, no notice at the director's London address needs to be served.

(ii) Notice should be sent to the director in spite of his request.

(b) (i) In terms of Section 285, the proposed meeting on 31st March will be in order.

(ii) Meeting may be held in London with the prior permission of the Reserve Bank of India. Please refer to Section 301(5) of the Companies Act also.

Q. 92. Draft the minutes of the first meeting of the Board of Directors of XYZ Ltd., Calcutta.

Ans. : Write on the lines of Ans. to Q. No. 14, pages 189-90.

Q. 93. Write short notes on any THREE of the following :

(a) Resolution by Circulation,

(b) Point of order,

(c) Two-way Proxy Form,

(d) Amendment to a Motion, (e) Class Meetings.

Ans. : (a) Page 186 (b) Page 168 (c) Page 177 (d) Page 153 (e) Page 141.

INDEX

P

UNIVERSITIES' QUESTIONS AND ANSWERS

THE UNIVERSITY OF BURDWAN

SECRETARIAL PRACTICE

GROUP B

1994

Q. 6. (a) Define Secretary.

(b) Name the different types of secretary found in a modern society.

(c) Point out the importance of the Secretary in a modern business.

Ans. : Pages 1-4.

Q. 7. Discuss the usual steps of dealing with the 'Incoming' and 'Outgoing' mails in a big office.

Ans. : Pages 73-76.

Q. 8. Discuss the different kinds of meeting of a company.

Ans. : Pages 140-42.

Q. 9. (a) Define the term 'minutes'.

(b) Draft the minutes of the 10th Board Meeting of Capital Electronics Ltd., Durgapur.

Ans. : Refer to pages 172 and 189-90.

Q. 10. Sarkar Brother of Chinsurah, Hooghly, has received an order placed by Roy Brothers of Burdwan for the supply of 500 tins of mustard oil within one month. Draft a letter on behalf of Sarkar Brothers informing acceptance of the order and seeking the extension of time by one week.

Ans. : Write on the lines of Q/Ans. No. 39, page 291.

1994 (Special)

Q. 6. (a) Who is a Company Secretary?

(b) Is it compulsory for a company to appoint a full-time Company Secretary?

(c) What are the statutory functions of a Company Secretary?

Ans. : Pages 23-24 and 26-28.

Q. 7. (a) What are the requisites of a good filing system? (b) Discuss four labour-saving devices used in a modern office.

Ans. : Page 82.

Q. 8. Discuss the powers and functions of the Chairman of an Annual General Meeting of a Public Limited Company.

Ans. : Pages 150-51.

Q. 9. (a) Distinguish between Motion and Resolution.

(b) Draft a suitable notice for the 10th Annual General Meeting of Alpha Company Ltd., Calcutta.

Ans. : Pages 152 and 203.

Q. 10. Banerjee Brothers of Burdwan desire to place an order with Ghosh Brothers of Bankura for supply of 1,000 reams of writing paper within one month. Draft a letter on behalf of Banerjee Brothers placing the order.

Ans. : Refer to Q/Ans. No. 19, pages 273-74 and write yourself.

1995

Q. 6. (a) What are the different types of secretary found in modern societies? Explain them.

(b) What are the rights of a Company Secretary?

Ans. : Pages 1-4 and Ans. to Q. No. 22 (1st paragraph only).

Q. 7. (a) What are the advantages of decentralised office services?

(b) Explain the important bases of departmentation.

Ans. : Pages 56 and 58.

Q. 8. Explain the requisites of a valid meeting.

Ans. : Page 143.

Q. 9. (a) Define minutes.

(b) State the different methods of recording minutes.

(c) What points should a secretary keep in mind while recording minutes?

Ans. : Q/Ans. No. 50, pages 172-73.

Q. 10. Draft a letter on behalf of Eastern Trading Company, Burdwan, confirming and accepting the order from Anand Brothers, Howrah, for the supply of 1,000 quintals of fine rice within 15 days of receiving the order.

Ans. : Write on the lines of Q/Ans. 20, pages 274-75.

1996

Q. 6. Who is a qualified Company Secretary?

Ans. : Pages 24-25.

Q. 7. State the advantages and disadvantages of centralised office services.

Ans. : Page 56.

Q. 9. (a) What is the Notice of a meeting ?

(b) What are the requisites of a valid Notice?

(c) What is meant by Quorum? What are the provisions of the Companies Act relating to Quorum? What are the provisions of the Companies Act relating to Quorum for different types of company meetings?

Ans. : Pages 145 and 163.

Q. 10. Draft a suitable letter cancelling the order you have placed with your supplier because of his unusual delay in the delivery of goods.

Ans. : Page 279.

1996 (Special)

Q. 6. (a) Define Company Secretary. (b) Discuss the legal and actual position of a Company Secretary.

Ans. : Pages 23 and 32-33.

Q. 7. (a) Define the term 'Indexing'.

(b) Why indexing is so important to filing?

(c) Discuss the different methods of indexing.

Ans. : Pages 88-89.

Q. 8. What are the different methods of voting in the Company Meeting? Discuss briefly.

Ans. : Pages 159-60.

Q. 9. As the Secretary of a Company, draft a report for submission to the Board of Directors analysing the causes of the declining trend of discipline in the office and suggesting remedies.

Ans. : Refer to pages 236-37 and write yourself.

Q. 10. Draft a letter to a supplier cancelling an order for his failure to supply materials within the specified period.

Ans. : Refer to page 279.

VIDYASAGAR UNIVERSITY

1987

Q. 1. Answer any ten questions :

(a) What do you mean by office layout?

(b) What is Vertical Card Index? How does it differ from Visible Card Index?

(c) What do you mean by Alpha-numerical system of filing?

(d) State the difference between Motion and Resolution.

(e) What are the Right Shares?

(f) What do you mean by Guillotine Closure?

(g) What is Proxy in Company Meeting? State his rights in the meeting.

(h) What is a quorum?

(i) State the effect of absence of quorum in a meeting.

(j) Where and on which days can the Annual General Meeting of a Public Company be legally held?

(k) What is the difference between Report and Minutes of meeting?

(l) What is a Poll and how does it differ from Ballot?

(m) What is a Private Limited Company?

(n) What is Continuous Stationery? What are its advantages?

(o) What are the different parts of a commercial letter?

Ans. : (a) Page 52 (b) Page 90 (c) Page 85 (d) Page 152 (e) Page 45 (f) Page 178 (g) Page 165 (h) Page 162 (i) Page 162 (j) Page 140 (k) Pages 228 & 172 (l) Page 160 (m) Page 355 (n) Page 102 (o) Page 261.

Q. 2. Discuss the role of a Secretary as an advisor to the management, as an office executive and a liaison officer.

Ans. : Pages 28-29.

Q. 3. While the Directors are the brains of the Company, the Secretaries are the ears, eyes and hands. Elucidate this statement with reference to the functions of the Company Secretary.

Ans. : Pages 26-28 and 32-33.

Q. 4. Describe the principal departments of a modern business. State the factors which should be borne in mind in planning the layout of an office.

Ans. : Pages 52 and 62-64.

Q. 5. Suggest a suitable procedure for handling incoming mail for a fairly big office, having several departments.

Ans. : Pages 73-74.

Q. 6. Write short notes on any four of the following :

(a) Loose-Leaf Ledger;

(b) Addressing Machine;

(c) PBX and PABX; (d) Cross-Reference;

(e) Centralised Typing Pool;

(f) Office Manual.

Ans. : (a) Page 102 (b) Page 99 (c) Page 104 (d) Page 83 (e) Page 324 (f) Page 65.

Q. 7. (a) What are the different elements necessary for a valid meeting?

(b) Can one man constitute a valid meeting? If so, mention three such cases.

Ans. : (a) Page 143 (b) Page 163.

Q. 8. What do you mean by Privilege in Meeting? State, with suitable illustrations, the difference between Absolute Privilege and Qualified Privilege.

Ans. : Pages 170-71.

Q. 9. How would you ascertain the sense of a meeting?

Ans. : Page 159.

Q. 10. (a) 'A Chairman is born, not made.' Describe some of the inherent and acquired qualifications of a Chairman. (b) How is he appointed?

Ans. : Pages 149-50.

Q. 11. What is a Motion? What are the different kinds of Motion? Distinguish between Motion and Resolution.

Ans. : Page 152. Kinds of Motions—Motions may be of four types, viz. (i) Primary or Original Motion, (ii) Secondary Motion, (iii) Substantive Motion, and (iv) Formal Motion.

Q. 12. Explain any four of the following :

(a) Deliberative Vote and Casting Vote;

(b) Personal Vote and Proxy;

(c) Amendment;(d) Kangaroo and Guillotine Closure;

(e) Minutes of Decision and Minutes of Narration;

(f) Authentication of Proceedigs;

(g) Annual General Meeting of a Limited Company.

Ans. : (a) Page 151 (b) Page 165 (c) Page 154.

(d) Guillotine closure is applied as and when a definite time is fixed for discussion on a motion. On expiry of the stipulated time, discussion on the main motion stops and it (motion) is put to vote. Use of guillotine closure is common in the meetings of the Parliament and Assemblies.

(e) Page 175 (f) Page 174 (g) Page 140.

Q. 13. (a) Draft a suitable notice of the 17th Annual General Meeting of Bikram Industries Limited to be held on 5th April 1987 (with necessary Agenda).

(b) Draft the proceedings of the Meeting of the Board of Directors of a large co-operative credit society.

Ans. : (a) Page 203 (b) Pages 115-18.

Q. 14. As Secretary of an Institution, draft a report to the director, mentioning at least four long-standing grievances of the office staff and suggesting remedial actions.

Ans. : Q/Ans. No. 20, pages 248-49.

Q. 15. (a) You have received an enquiry about the standing of a firm. Draft a favourable reply.

(b) Write an application to the Branch Manager of a nationalised bank of your locality requesting to grant loan of Rs. 20,000/- which you are in need for working capital for your company.

Ans. : (a) Pages 270-71 (b) 295-96.

1988

Q. 1. Answer in brief any ten of the following questions :

(a) What is meant by "Typing Pool"?

(b) A private meeting is going to be held in a public park. Will it be a lawful meeting?

(c) How is a Zilla Parishad formed?

(d) How is a 'Panchayat Pradhan' elected?

(e) Is company secretaryship a 'Profession' in India?

(f) What should be the qualification(s) of a person going to be appointed as secretary of a company having a paid-up share capital of Rs. 50 lakhs?

(g) What is Chairman pro tem?

(h) If a poll is properly demanded, when must the Chairman take the poll?

(i) What do you mean by indexing? What is its utility in filing system?

(j) What is Statutory Report?

(k) What do you mean by Amendment motion? Who can move the Amendment Motion?

(l) What is a point of order in a meeting?

(m) State the maximum and minimum number of shareholders of a private limited company.

(n) Define a substantive motion.

(o) What is Commencement Certificate for a Company? Who issues the Certificate?

Ans. : (a) Page 324 (b) Page 144.

(c) A Zilla Parishad is constituted with the elected members of the constituencies, 'Sabhapatis' of Panchayat Samitis and the Members of Parliament (M. P.s) of the district concerned.

(d) A Panchayat Pradhan is elected by the members of a Gram Panchayat from amongst themselves in their first meeting which is convened by the Block Development Officer.

(e) Page 29 (f) Page 28 (g) Page 326 (h) Page 150 (i) Page 88

(j) Page 194 (k) Page 154 (l) Page 168 (m) Page 13 (n) Page 177.

(o) A Commencement Certificate is issued by the Registrar of Companies to a public limited company on completion of some more formalities after its registration. The certificate entitles the company to start or commence its business.

Q. 2. How is a Company Secretary appointed? What are his rights and liabilities?

Ans. : Pages 25 and 34.

Q. 3. Define a 'Private Secretary'. Discuss the usefulness and functions of a Private Secretary.

Ans. : Pages 4-6.

Q. 4. Describe the various functions of a secretary :

(a) before the meeting;

(b) at the meeting;

(c) after the meeting.

Ans. : Q/Ans. No. 18, pages 30-32.

Q. 5. What are the requisites of a good filing system? State the importance of filing.

Ans. : Pages 81-82.

Q. 6. Write notes on any four of the following :

(a) Centralised Correspondence;

(b) Inward letter register;

(c) Post Box and Post Bag;

(d) Franking Machine;

(e) Dictaphone;

(f) Cash Register;

(g) Business Directory;

(h) Lighting and Ventilation in office.

Ans. : (a) Page 57 (b) Page 76 (c) Page 69 (d) Page 325 (e) Page 75
(f) Page 101 (g) Page 226 (h) Page 54.

Q. 7. What is a 'Notice' of a meeting? What are its requisites? Should a notice contain agenda? Why?

Ans. : Pages 145-46.

Q. 8. What is quorum of a meeting? Should quorum be present throughout the meeting? What is disinterested quorum? What should the Chairman do if the quorum is not present?

Ans. : Pages 162-63.

Q. 9. Write notes on the following explaining their differences in meaning in connection with the joint stock companies :

(a) Ordinary Resolution;

(b) Special Resolution;

(c) Resolution requiring special notice.

Ans. : (a) Page 154 (b) Page 154 (c) Page 157.

Q. 10. What is a Statutory Meeting? What are the main provisions of the Companies Act regarding the Statutory Meeting of a Public Limited Company?

Ans. : Page 140.

Q. 11. Explain any four of the following :

(a) Qualified and Absolute Privilege;

(b) Adjournment and Postponement;

(c) Resolution passed unanimously and Resolution passed without any opposition;

(d) Public and Private Meetings;

(e) Requisition meeting of any association known to you;

(f) Previous Question and Next Business;

(g) Rules regarding quorum of members' meeting and Board's meeting of a Limited Company;

(h) Lawful and unlawful meeting.

Ans. : (a) Page 170 (b) Page 168.

(c) When all the members present at the meeting vote in favour of a motion, it is said to be carried unanimously. When some of the members prefer not to vote in favour of or against a motion, the members are said to abstain from voting.

(d) Page 145 (e) Page 141 (f) Page 168 (g) Page 340 (h) Pages 143-44.

Q. 12. (a) Draft a notice with suitable agenda for the first meeting of the Executive Committee of a club.

(b) Draft the minutes of proceedings of an Annual General Meeting of a Public Limited Company transacting ordinary business.

Ans. : (a) Page 112 (b) Page 209.

Q. 13. The workshop of a manufacturing concern broke down causing serious injury to some workmen resulting in suspension of production by agitated workers. As secretary of the manufacturing firm, write a report to the partners about the incident, suggesting suitable actions.

Ans. : Write on the lines of Q/Ans. No. 28, pages 255-56.

1991

Q. 1. Answer any ten of the following :

(a) A Secretary is a mere servant of the Company. Do you agree?

(b) What is meant by Office Layout?

(c) What is the difference between Post Box and Post Book?

(d) Is Company Secretaryship a 'profession' in India?

(e) What is Statutory Report?

(f) What is a Typing Pool?

(g) What is the use of Franking Machine?

(h) What do you mean by Proper Length of Notice?

(i) What is meant by Continuing Quorum?

(j) State the difference between Motion and Resolution.

(k) What is meant by Pro tem Chairman?

(l) What is the use of Inward Letter Register?

(m) What do you mean be Amendment of a Motion?

(n) What is Continuous Stationery?

(o) What is Office Manual?

Ans. : (a) Page 32 (b) Page 52 (c) Page 69 (d) Page 29 (e) Page 194
(f) Page 324 (g) Page 324 (h) Page 145 (i) Page 162 (j) Page 152
(k) Page 326 (l) Page 76 (m) Page 154 (n) Page 102 (o) Page 65.

Q. 2. (a) State the qualifications that a Private Secretary should possess.

(b) Discuss the rights and liabilities of Private Secretary.

Ans. : Pages 4-6.

Q. 3. (a) What is the position of the Secretary in the administrative set-up of a Company?

(b) Discuss the rights and liabilities of Company Secretary.

Ans. : Pages 32-33 and 34-36.

Q. 4. Mention four types of Labour-Saving Devices usually used by a big mercantile office and also enumerate their uses.

Ans. : Page 92.

Q. 5. Write short notes on any four of the following :

(a) Loose-leaf Ledgers;

(b) Duplicating Machine;

(c) Addressing Machine;

(d) PBX;

(e) Phonogram;

(f) VPP.

Ans. : (a) Page 102 (b) Page 324 (c) Page 99 (d) Page 103 (e) Page 104 (f) Page 67.

Q. 6. (a) Define 'Meeting' and enumerate the points of distinction between a Public Meeting and a Private Meeting.

(b) An insertion has appeared in The Statesman that Prof. Stanley of Oxford University shall deliver a lecture on 'Danger of Air Pollution' at 4 P.M. on 15th May 1991 in the meeting hall at Vidyasagar University. Is it a Public Meeting? Give reasons for your answer.

(c) How will you decide whether a meeting is Lawful or Unlawful?

Ans. : (a) Pages 139 & 145.

(b) Since the meeting is open to all, it is a public meeting.

(c) Pages 143-144.

Q. 7. Enumerate the duties of the Secretary of a Company

(a) Before the meeting;

(b) At the meeting and

(c) After the meeting.

Ans. : Q/Ans. No. 18, pages 30-32.

Q. 8. What is the Notice of a Meeting? What are its requisites? What is the importance of Notice?

Ans. : Pages 145-46.

Q. 9. Write short notes on any four of the following :

(a) Substantive Motion;

(b) Proxy;

(c) Previous Question;

(d) Note of Dissent;

(e) Authentication of Minutes;

(f) Quorum;

(g) Casting Vote.

Ans. : (a) Page 177 (b) Page 165 (c) Page 168.

(d) A motion may be adopted by the meeting unanimously or by the majority votes. Some of the members may not vote and some may vote against the motion. Also, those voting against the motion may request the chairman to incorporate their decision of not supporting the motion noted in the minutes. This is known as note of dissent.

(e) Page 174 (f) Page 162 (g) Page 151.

Q. 10. (a) As a Secretary convene the 14th Annual General Meeting of International Rubber Company Ltd. (10 Russell Street, Calcutta 700016) to be held at 3 P.M. on May 3, 1991 at its registered Office. (Ordinary business only will be transacted.)

(b) POB Co. Ltd. could not pay their creditors XYZ Co. Ltd. Rs. 10,000 on the stipulated date, 14th March 1991. Draft a letter on behalf of POB Co. Ltd. requesting for extension of time by a month.

Ans. : (a) Page 203 (b) Q/Ans. No. 41, pages 292-93.

Q. 11. A fire broke out in the godown of Pax Machinery Co. in the night of 14th April 1991 in which machinery worth Rs. 10,00,000 were destroyed. Draft a letter to the Insurers asking them for inspection on site and requesting for an early settlement of claim for compensation.

Ans. : Pages 301-02.

THE UNIVERSITY OF CALCUTTA

1989

Q. 1. Answer any ten questions :

- **(a) Can a firm be appointed Secretary of a company?**
- **(b) How does a private secretary differ from a 'Personal Assistant'?**
- **(c) The office performs a valuable service function. How?**
- **(d) What is an Office Form?**
- **(e) Name three machines for copying letters without repeating the original process of preparing the letters.**
- **(f) What is the difference between "Post Book" and "Book Post"?**
- **(g) What do you mean by Labour Saving Devices?**
- **(h) When can a member speak twice on the same primary motion?**
- **(i) What is the purpose of moving the "Next Business" motion?**
- **(j) What is meant by qualified privilege?**
- **(k) Mention at least two cases when one-member quorum ensures a legally valid company meeting.**
- **(l) The day fixed for holding the Annual General Meeting of a company is declared as a public holiday subsequent to issue of notice. Can the meeting be held as originally scheduled?**
- **(m) What is a Status Enquiry?**
- **(n) What do you mean be "Quotation" as used in business transactions?**

Ans. : (a) According to Section 2(45) of the Companies (Amendment) Act, 1974, Secretary means any individual and, as such, a firm cannot be a secretary of a company.

(b) Page 7 (c) Page 49 (d) Page 76 (e) Page 94 (f) Pages 69 & 323

(g) Page 92 (h) Page 153 (i) Page 168 (j) Page 170 (k) Page 163

(l) Page 176 (m) Page 332 (n) Page 331.

Q. 2. (a) Define a Secretary.

(b) Discuss in brief the features of Secretary's functions.

(c) Point out the importance of secretaries in modern business world.

Ans. : Pages 23 and 26-28.

Q. 3. (a) State the statutory qualifications of a secretary of a public limited company having a paid-up capital of Rs. 50 lakhs. (b) Discuss the legal and actual position of a company secretary.

Ans. : Pages 24 and 32-33.

Q. 4. (a) Who is a secretary of a Co-operative Society?

(b) Briefly discuss the functions of the Secretary of a Co-operative Society.

(c) Does he participate in the management of the Society?

Ans. : Pages 8-10.

Q. 5. (a) What is Filing?

(b) Discuss the requisites of a good filing system.

Ans. : Pages 82-83.

Q. 6. How do lighting, ventilation and colur-conditioning contribute to the efficiency of office staff?

Ans. : Pages 53-54.

Q. 7. Write short notes on :

(a) Office Manual;

(b) Subscribers Trunk Dialling (STD) Service;

(c) Card Index,

(d) Postal Orders;

(e) Dictaphone.

Ans. : (a) Page 65 (b) Page 106 (c) Page 90 (d) Page 66 (e) Page 75.

Q. 8. Explain the essentials of a valid notice for an Annual General Meeting of a Public Limited Company.

Ans. : Page 145.

Q. 9. "The success or failure of a meeting depends on its Chairman". Discuss in this connection the powers and duties of the Chairman of a meeting of a Company.

Ans. : Pages 150-51.

Q. 10. Write short notes on any three of the following :

(a) Authentication of minutes;

(b) Unlawful meeting;

(c) Statutory Report;

(d) Poll;

(e) Extra-Ordinary General Meeting.

Ans. : (a) Page 174 (b) Page 144 (c) Page 194 (d) Page 160 (e) Page 141.

Q. 11. The Directors of Alpha Limited ask the Secretary to submit a report on the declining trend of sales of the company. Draft a suitable report suggesting remedy.

Ans. : Refer to pages 234-35.

Q. 12. Draft the minutes of proceedings of the Seventeenth Annual General Meeting of New India Limited, Calcutta 42, held on 30th September 1988, in which the items of ordinary business were transacted.

Ans. : Refer to page 209.

Or

Draft the notice of any meeting of the Board of Directors of a Public Limited Company (not being its first Board Meeting).

Ans. : Refer to page 184 and write yourself.

Q. 13. Draft a circular letter notifying increase in selling prices due to rise in cost seeking continued patronage of the customers.

Ans. : Page 253.

Q. 14. Draft a letter to a supplier cancelling an order due to failure to supply within specified period and reserving the right to claim payment of difference in price, if any, arising out of purchase from other sources.

Ans. : Q/Ans. 32, page 286.

1990

Q. 1. Answer any ten questions :

(a) Can a director of a limited company having only two directors be appointed Secretary of that company?

(b) In what respects does a Company Secretary differ from a Private Secretary?

(c) The office is called the hub of the business organisation—Why?

(d) State the significance of the 'straight-line flow' of office work.

(e) What is a Franking Machine?

(f) Mention the advantages of 'Loose-Leaf Index'.

(g) What factors do usually influence the location of the office of a commercial enterprise?

(h) What do you mean by disinterested quorum?

(i) How can a proxy be revoked?

(j) State the difference between a 'Motion' and a 'Resolution.'

(k) What is meant by a meeting?

(l) Indicate the purpose of a Trade Circular.

(m) Mention the chief characteristics of a good business letter.

(n) What is meant by 'Precis'?

(o) What is meant by 'Confirmation of Minutes'? Does it envisage any change or revision of the Minutes?

Ans. : (a) No. (b) Pages 2 & 3 (c) Page 49 (d) Page 58 (e) Page 325 (f) Page 88 (g) Page 52 (h) Page 162 (i) Page 166 (j) Page 152 (k) Page 139 (l) Page 330 (m) Page 351 (n) Page 330 (o) Page 174.

Q. 2. (a) Indicate the purposes for which a Private Secretary is usually appointed. (b) You have been appointed Private Secretary of a business executive. Draw up an outline of the work to be performed by you as his Private Secretary.

Ans. : Pages 4-6.

Q. 3. (a) Classify different types of Secretaries found in a present-day society. (b) Discuss the statutory liabilities of a Company Secretary.

Ans. : (a) Page 1 (b) Page 26-27.

Q. 4. "A modern Company Secretary is an Adviser to the management, an Office Executive and a Liaison Officer." Discuss fully.

Ans. : Pages 28-29.

Q. 5. (a) What do you mean by Office System and Office Procedure?

(b) What are the purposes of such systems and procedures in office work? **(C.U. 1990)**

Ans. : Refer to pages 61-62.

Q. 6. (a) Discuss the usual procedure of handling the outgoing mails in a big mercantile office.

(b) Point out the registers and mechanical devices generally used by such an office.

Ans. : (a) Pages 74-76 (b) Page 76.

Q. 7. Write short notes on any three of the following :

(a) Office Layout

(b) Centralisation of office services

(c) Telegraphic Address

(d) Business Reply Card

(e) Certificate of Posting.

Ans. : (a) Page 52 (b) Page 56 (c) Page 69 (d) Page 70 (e) Page 68.

Q. 9. (a) Discuss the various methods of ascertaining the sense of a meeting. (b) In Annual General Meeting of a Public Limited Company a proxy was present, but the Shareholder who appointed the proxy came to attend the meeting himself. What will happen to the proxy?

Ans. : (a) Page 159 (b) Page 166.

Q. 10. Write short notes on any three of the following :

(a) Point of Order;

(b) Substantive Motion;

(c) Minutes of Narration;

(d) Adjournment of a Meeting;

(e) Agenda.

Ans. : (a) Page 168 (b) Page 177 (c) Page 175 (d) Page 168 (e) Page 148.

Q. 11. The Nova Udyog Ltd., 19 N.S.C. Bose Road, Calcutta 700001, has decided to hold its 8th Annual General Meeting at its registered office. Draft the notice of the said meeting with the usual items of business to be transacted at that meeting (use imaginary but logical dates and particulars).

Or

Messers Galaxy (India) Ltd., 3 Clive Row, Calcutta 700001, held the first meeting of their Board of Directors at their registered office. Draft the Minutes of Proceedings of that meeting (use imaginary but logical particulars).

Ans. : Page 203 or Page 168.

Q. 12. M/s Supernova Printers Ltd. of Calcutta has received a bulk supply of paper from M/s Nova Paper Syndicate of Madhya Pradesh. The paper is of inferior quality. Address a letter to the suppliers requesting them to settle the deal either offering an additional discount on the price charged or arranging for taking the paper back at their own cost.

Ans. : Refer to pages 280-81.

Q. 13. You want to start a small-scale industry in a semi-urban area. Address a letter to a nationalised bank in that area with a request to provide you with a loan of Rs. 20,000/- which you require as your initial capital to start the business. (C.U. 1990)

Ans. : Refer to pages 295-96.

Q. 14. As the secretary of a large manufacturing concern, draft a suitable report for consideration by the Board of Directors on the opening of a stall in the ensuing Calcutta Industrial Fair. (C.U. 1990)

Ans. : Refer to page 248.

Q. 15. The ABC Co. Ltd., B.B.D. Bagh, Calcutta 700001, wants to purchase the following goods : 400 Wilson Dot Pens—ordinary quality, 5 Facit Typewriters—small types of letters — English, and 2 Calculating machines for ordinary use. They want to write a letter to M/s. C.C. Co., B.B.D. Bagh, Calcutta 700001, asking them to quote their prices for the goods. Draft the letter.

Ans. : Refer to pages 268-69 and write yourself.

1991

Q. 1. Answer any ten questions :

(a) **Who is a Secretary?**

(b) **What is meant by a Director-Secretary?**

(c) **Why is office called a service centre?**

(d) **What is meant by Statutory Books? Name three Statutory Books which are required to be maintained by the Secretary of a Company.**

(e) **Should every company have a registered office? If so, why?**

(f) **What are the different methods of dictating letters?**

(g) **What is a Card Index?**

(h) **The notice of an Annual General Meeting of a Public Limited Company is dated the 8th April 1991, while the date of the meeting is 30th April 1991. Comment on the validity of the notice.**

(i) **What is proxy in respect of a company meeting?**

(j) **How can a resolution be passed without holding a meeting?**

(k) **Why is the Chairman of a meeting called 'umpire of debate'?**

(l) **What is a substantive motion?**

(m) **How will you distinguish between 'Book Post' and 'Post Book'?**

(n) **Who is a Del Credere Agent?**

(o) **What is meant by Status Enquiry?**

Ans. : (a) Page 1 (b) Page 322 (c) Page 49 (d) Page 335

(e) Page 350 (f) Page 75 (g) Page 90 (h) Notice is valid

(i) Page 165 (j) Page 186 (k) Pages 151-52 (l) Page 177

(m) Pages 323 & 369 (n) Page 353 (o) Page 332.

Q. 2. (a) How is the Secretary of a Co-operative Society appointed? (b) Discuss the functions of the Secretary of a Co-operative Society.

Ans. : Q/Ans. No. 8, pages 8-10.

Q. 3. (a) Who is a qualified Company Secretary? (b) How is he appointed? (c) Discuss the role of a Company Secretary as an Office Manager.

Ans. : Pages 23-25 and 27.

Q. 4. "Company Secretary is not only a servant of the Company but also a servant of Law"—Examine the statement.

Ans. : Pages 23-28.

Q. 5. (a) What do you mean by office organisation?

(b) What is its importance?

(c) Describe the organisation of a modern office. (C.U. 1991)

Ans. : (a) Henri Fayol in his book "General and Industrial Management" has defined the term 'organisation' as follows : "To organise a business is to provide you with everything useful to its functioning : raw materials, tools, capital, personnel." According to G. E. Milward in his book "Large Scale Organisation", "Organisation is a process of dividing work into convenient tasks or duties, of grouping such duties in the form of posts, of delegating authority to each post and of appointing qualified staff to be responsible that the work is carried out as planned."

The management experts opine that because of great variety of organisation in existence, it is not desirable to standardise the principles of office organisation. They have, nevertheless, designed certain principles which can be used as a guideline depending on the circumstances obtaining in the organisation. The principles can be enumerated as follows :

(i) The objective of the organisation must be clear and means of achieving it must be indicated in sufficient detail.

(ii) The organisation structure must be flexible to take care of the changing circumstances.

(iii) Every employee should be responsible to only one supervisor.

(iv) Authority to be granted to the employees must be commensurate with responsibility.

(v) Every effort should be made for an even distribution of work amongst the employees and maximum utilisation of their abilities.

(vi) There must be effective co-ordination between various units/divisions/sections of the organisation.

(b) Page 50 (c) Page 50.

Q. 6. (a) Why is it necessary to classify files?

(b) What do you mean by modern methods of filing?

(c) Point out the advantages of modern methods of filing.

Ans. : (a) Page 84 (b) Page 86 (c) Pages 86-88.

Q. 7. Write short notes on any three of the following :

(a) Calculating Machine;

(b) Intercom System;

(c) Open-type Layout;

(d) Post Box and Post Bag;

(e) Ready Reckoner.

Ans. : (a) Page 106 (b) Page 104 (c) Page 52 (d) Page 69 (e) Page 105.

Q. 8. (a) What are the requisites of a valid notice of an Annual General Meeting of a Public Limited Company?

(b) Under what circumstances service of a notice is not obligatory?

Ans. : (a) Page 145 (b) Page 147.

Q. 9. (a) Distinguish between Minutes and Proceedings.

(b) Point out the different methods of recording Minutes of Decision.

c) State the provisions of the Companies Act in regard to recording of Minutes.

Ans. : (a) Pages 172, 328 (b) Page 175 (c) Page 172.

Q. 10. Write short notes on any three of the following :

(a) Dilatory Motion,

(b) Agenda Book,

(c) Quorum,

(d) Resolution with Special Notice,

(e) Casting Vote.

Ans. : (a) Page 177 (b) Page 149 (c) Page 162 (d) Page 149 (e) Page 151.

Q. 11. Draft the notice with agenda of a Board Meeting (other than the First Meeting) of Debsons Ltd. of 11 Madan Street, Calcutta, to be held on 24.5.1991 (Use imaginary particulars).

Or

Draft the Minutes of the 7th Annual General Meeting of Deshapran Consumers Cooperative Society Ltd., Calcutta, held on 12th April 1991. Record all the usual items of business transacted at such meeting with imaginary particulars.

Ans. : Pages 189-90.

Q. 12. Draft a report to be submitted to the Board of Directors in the matter of declining trend of sales. Suggest suitable measures (including advertisement campaign) for boosting up sales.

Ans. : Pages 234-45.

Q. 13. Write a letter for Gupta & Sons, Calcutta, to Banarasi Das of Pune requesting them to settle up their account within a month. Point out that the amount has been lying due for a long time and that legal action may be taken in default.

Ans. : Refer to pages 286-87.

Q. 14. Draft a letter to the insurance company notifying them of a fire at your godown. Request the company to arrange for an early inspection and settlement of claim.

Ans. : Pages 301-02.

Q. 15. Address a letter to Messrs. Basu & Bajaj, Cycle Manufacturers, Asansol, requesting them for granting a selling agency to sell their products in your locality.

Ans. : Pages 302-303.

1992

Group A

Q. 1. Answer any ten questions :

(a) What do you mean by 'Visible Card Index'?

(b) When is a letter called a 'circular letter'?

(c) What is a Franking Machine?

(d) What is meant by a "Typists' Pool"?

(e) Discuss the advantages of Addressing Machine.

(f) Is there any difference between an 'occupation' and a 'profession'?

(g) What is a 'Phonogram'?

(h) What is the purpose of moving a 'closure motion'?

(i) When is an extra-ordinary general meeting of a company held?

(j) **What is Continuous Stationery?**

(k) **How does the Chairman of a meeting break a tie on a voting?**

(l) **What is "Proper length of notice"?**

(m) **Explain the term 'Continuing Quorum'?**

(n) **What do you mean by 'confirmation of minutes'?**

Ans. : (a) Page 90 (b) Page 330 (c) Page 325 (d) Page 324 (e) Page 99

(f) Page 29 (g) Page 104 (h) Page 169 (i) Page 141 (j) Page 102

(k) Page 151 (l) Page 145 (m) Page 162 (n) Page 174.

Group B

Answer any one question

Q. 2. 'A secretary is an advisor to Management, an office executive and a liaison officer'. Discuss fully.

Ans. : Pages 27-38.

Q. 3. (a) Who is a Private Secretary? (b) What are the functions of a Private Secretary? (c) Does he require any special qualification?

Ans. : Pages 4-6.

Q. 4. (a) What are the different types of secretaries found in a modern society? (b) Briefly outline the functions of any three types of secretaries.

Ans. : Pages 1-4.

Group C

Answer any one question

Q. 5. (a) What do you mean by layout of an office?

(b) Discuss the factors to be taken into consideration while planning the layout of an office.

Ans. : Pages 49 and 52-53.

Q. 6. Discuss the different steps involved in handling 'incoming' and 'outgoing' mails in a fairly large business undertaking.

Ans. : Pages 73-76.

Q. 7. Write short notes on any three of the following :

(a) Business Reply Card,

(b) Vertical Method of Filing,

(c) **Postal Order,**

(d) **Microfilming,**

(e) **Dictaphone.**

Ans. : (a) Page 68 (b) Page 87 (c) Page 68 (d) Page 85 (e) Page 75.

Group D

Answer any one question

Q. 8. (a) Discuss briefly the requisites of a valid meeting. (b) Distinguish between a public meeting and a private meeting.

Ans. : Pages 143-44 and 145.

Q. 9. (a) Who is a Chairman of a meeting? How is he appointed? (b) Describe the powers and duties of the Chairman at a meeting.

Ans. : Pages 149-50.

Q. 10. Write short notes on any three of the following : (a) Amendment, (b) Statutory Meeting, (c) Special Resolution, (d) Point of Order, (e) 'Clear days' notice.

Ans. : (a) Page 154 (b) Page 140 (c) Page 154 (d) Page 168 (e) Page 176.

Group E

Answer any three questions

Q. 11. Draft the notice convening the 20th Annual General Meeting of Bata India Ltd., Esplanade East, Calcutta, with usual agenda.

Or

Draft the minutes of the First Board Meeting of a Public Limited Company.

Ans. : Page 209 or Page 188.

Q. 12. Draft a Report to be submitted to the Board of Directors about the location of a new show-room proposed to be opened by the company.

Ans. : Q/Ans. No. 18, page 247.

Q. 13. Write a letter to your banker for increasing the overdraft limit to cover the increases in the price of raw materials and labour charges.

Ans. : Pages 296-97.

Q. 14. Write a letter to your supplier complaining about shortage in quantity and inferior quality of materials supplied claiming suitable remedy for the same.

Ans. : Q/Ans. No. 29, pages 281-82.

Q. 15. Draft a letter of enquiry concerning the status of a firm.

Ans. Q/Ans. No. 13 or 14, pages 270 & 271.

1993

Group A

Q. 1. Answer any ten questions :

(a) What is Colour Conditioning?

(b) Mention the advantages of 'Loose-Leaf Index'.

(c) State the difference between a 'Motion' and a 'Resolution'.

(d) Indicate the purpose of a Trade Circular.

(e) What is a Substantive Motion?

(f) How will you distinguish between 'Book Post' and 'Post Book'?

(g) What is a Special Report?

(h) What is meant by 'Status Enquiry'?

(i) Define "Telegraphic Address'.

(j) State the advantages of 'Micro-filming'.

(k) What do you mean by 'Proxy'?

(l) What is meant by 'Point of Order'?

(m) Explain the term 'Poll'.

(n) What do you understand by 'Privilege in Speech'?

(o) What is Dictaphone?

Ans. : (a) Page 54 (b) Page 88 (c) Page 152 (d) Page 330 (e) Page 177
(f) Pages 323 & 71 (g) Page 229 (h) Page 332 (i) Page 69 (j) Page 95
(k) Page 165 (l) Page 168 (m) Page 150 (n) Page 170 (o) Page 75.

Group B

Q. 2. (a) Who is a qualified Company Secretary?

(b) How is he appointed?

(c) Discuss the functions of a Company Secretary.

Ans. : Write Answer to Question No. 14, pages 23-28.

Q. 3. (a) How is the Secretary of a Co-operative Society appointed?

(b) Discuss the functions of a Secretary of a Co-operative Society.

Ans. : Write Answer to Question No. 8, pages 8-10.

Q. 4. Discuss the nature and principal functions of a Secretary of a Club or Association.

Ans. : It is not a legal requirement to appoint a full-time secretary for clubs and associations. However, to perform the day-to-day functions of the clubs and associations, it is the usual practice to appoint a wholetime paid secretary. Generally, clubs and associations which are small in size usually appoint one of their members to do the work without any remuneration. The principal functions of such a secretary can be discussed under three broad groups : viz. (i) As an executive officer; (ii) As an agent; and (iii) As an adviser to the Managing Committee of the Club or the Association.

As an Executive Officer : (a) To supervise the day-to-day routine functions of the office, e.g. correspondence, maintenance of records and managing the staff. (b) To supervise, conduct and control the activities of the organisation bearing in mind the main object of the club or association.

As an Agent : The decisions taken by the Managing Committee at various meetings should be implemented. He has to liaise between his organisation and the outsiders which include various people, press and other organisations.

As an Adviser : Since he remains close to the members, he has the opportunities to ascertain their needs and grievances. He can communicate his opinions and ideas to the Managing Committee to help it take proper decisions for growth and prosperity of the organisation. He has also to advise the Managing Committee about any legal implications in connection with action proposed to be taken by the organisation.

Group C

Q. 5. (a) What is filing?

(b) State the conditions of a good Filing System.

Ans. : Pages 81 and 82-83.

Q. 6. Define office and describe its functions.

Ans. : Write Answer to Question No. 1, pages 49-52.

Q. 7. Write short notes on any three of the following : (a) Centralisation of office services, (b) Post Box and Post Bag, (c) Outward Mail Register, (d) Office Manual, (e) Certificate of Posting.

Ans. : (a) Page 56 (b) Page 69 (c) Page 76 (d) Page 65 (e) Page 68.

Group D

Q. 8. (a) What are the essential requisites of a valid notice of a General Meeting of a Company? (b) What is amendment? How does it change the primary motion?

Ans. : (a) Write Answer to Question No. 8, pages 145-46. (b) Write Answer to Question No. 19, pages 153-54.

Q. 9. Discuss the different ways of voting.

Ans. : Write Answer to Question No. 29, pages 159-60.

Q. 10. Write short notes on any three of the following :

(a) Agenda;

(b) Quorum;

(c) Adjournment;

(d) Minutes;

(e) Closure.

Ans. : (a) Page 148 (b) Page 162 (c) Page 168 (d) Page 172 (e) Page 168.

Group E

Q. 11. Draft the minutes of the 15th Annual General Meeting of the Allied Steel Ltd., 15 Netaji Subhas Road, Calcutta 700001.

Or

Draft the minutes of the 10th Annual General Meeting of the Calcutta Consumer's Co-operative Society, 10 Lake Road, Calcutta 700029.

Ans. : Page 209 or page 112 (Please change the names, addresses etc. as necessary).

Q. 12. Draft a report to be submitted to the Board of Directors in the capacity of secretary of that company suggesting suitable measures for improving the sales performance of the company with particular emphasis for spending more money under advertisement head.

Ans. : Q/Ans. No. 6, pages 234-35.

Q. 13. Write a letter to a bank with a request to provide you with a loan assistance of Rs. 50,000 which you require to meet the working capital need of your growing small scale unit.

Ans. : Q/Ans. No. 48, pages 299-300.

Q. 14. M/s Calcutta Printers Ltd. has received a bulk supply of paper from M/s Gupta & Sons (P) Ltd., Calcutta. The paper is of inferior quality. Address a letter to the supplier requesting them to settle the deal — either offering an additional discount of 20 per cent on the price charged or arranging for taking the paper back at their own cost.

Ans. : Q/Ans. No. 27, pages 280-81.

Q. 15. M/s ABC Ltd., Bangalore, specialised in the manufacture of most durable road building materials, wish to appoint a Sole Agent for their products in West Bengal. On behalf of XYZ Ltd., Calcutta, write a suitable letter expressing their willingness to accept the offer of ABC Ltd.

Ans. : Refer to pages 302-04.

1994

Group A

Q. 1. Answer any ten questions :

(a) Can a director be appointed as the secretary of the company of which he is the director?

(b) Who appoints the secretary of a Zilla Parishad?

(c) How long can the members of Gram Panchayat hold office?

(d) What are the advantages of a 'Franking Machine'?

(e) What is meant by 'Point of order' in a meeting?

(f) What are the advantages of "Loose-Leaf Registers"?

(g) What is a visible card index?

(h) What is meant by a 'Proper length of notice'?

(i) When is a statutory meeting of a company held?

(j) Can a company meeting be held with one-member quorum?

(k) Name two statutory books which a company secretary has to maintain.

(l) What is an 'Annual Return'?

(m) What is meant by 'labour-saving device' in office work?

(n) The day fixed for holding the Annual General Meeting of a company is declared as a public holiday subsequent to the issue of notice. Can the meeting be held as originally scheduled?

(o) Name the characteristics of a good business letter.

Ans. : (a) Page 335 (b) Page 119 (c) Page 120 (d) Page 325 (e) Page 168 (f) Page 102 (g) Page 90 (h) Page 145 (i) Page 140 (j) Page 163 (k) Page 337 (l) Page 200 (m) Page 92 (n) Page 176 (o) Page 351.

Group B

[Answer any one question]

Q. 2. Outline the role of a secretary in a co-operative society.

Ans. : Pages 8-10.

Q. 3. Discuss the functions of a company secretary.

Ans. : Pages 26-28.

Q. 4. (a) Who are required to appoint a private secretary?

(b) Indicate the purpose for which a private secretary is usually appointed.

(c) Outline the usual functions performed by a private secretary.

Ans. : (a) Pages 4-6 (b) Page 5 (c) Pages 5-6.

Q. 5. (a) Why is the service of a secretary necessary for a Panchayat Samiti?

(b) State the duties to be performed by the secretary of a Panchayat Samiti.

Ans. : (a) Page 120 (b) Page 120.

Group C

[Answer any one question]

Q. 6. (a) Discuss the usual procedure of handling outgoing mails in a big mercantile office.

(b) What are the mechanical devices generally used in the process involved?

Ans. : (a) Pages 74-76 (b) Page 74.

Q. 7. (a) What do you mean by "Office Services"?

(b) State the advantages and disadvantages of centralised office services.

Ans. : (a) Pages 74-75 (b) Page 56.

Group D

[Answer any one question]

Q. 8. (a) Who is Pro-tem Chairman?

(b) Discuss the rights and duties of the Chairman of a meeting.

Ans. : (a) Page 326 (b) Page 150.

Q. 9. Write short notes on any three of the following :

(a) Kangaroo Closure;

(b) Qualified Privilege;

(c) Proxy;

(d) Quorum;

(e) Amendment.

Ans. : (a) Page 178 (b) Page 170 (c) Page 165 (d) Page 162 (e) Page 153.

Group E

[Answer Q. No. 13 and any one from the rest]

Q. 10. Draft the minutes of the proceedings of the First Board Meeting of Alpha Company Ltd., B.B.D. Bagh, Calcutta 700001, held on the 24th September 1993.

Ans. : Page 188.

Q. 11. The Managing Director of ABC Company Ltd. asked the Secretary to submit a report on the declining trend of discipline in the office. As the Secretary, draft a suitable report analysing the causes of the decline and suggesting suitable remedies.

Ans. : Please refer to pages 237-38 and try yourself.

Q. 12. Draft the notice of the meeting of a Panchayat Samiti with imaginary but reasonable agenda.

Ans. : Page 134.

Q. 13. Draft a letter to the General Insurance Company reporting damage caused to your factory by fire and requesting for immediate action in respect of survey and settlement of claims.

Ans. : Page 301.

1995

Group A

Q. 1. Answer any ten questions :

(a) Should a Co-operative Society appoint a full-time secretary?

(b) Can a firm be appointed secretary of a company?

(c) Who appoints the first secretary of a company?

(d) Should every company have a Registered Office?

(e) There are four methods of dictating letters. What are those?

(f) What is a "Typing Pool"?

(g) Name three machines of copying letters without repeating the original process of preparing the letters.

(h) A meeting is going to be held in a public park. Will it be a lawful meeting?

(i) What is meant by 'Continuing Quorum'?

(j) Mr. X moves a motion before a meeting and Mr. Y seconds it. Can Mr. X withdraw the motion after seconding?

(k) What is 'Proxy' in respect of a Company Meeting?

(l) What is the time limit for writing the minutes of Board Meeting?

(m) What should be the quorum of a meeting of a Panchayat Samiti?

(n) What should be the time limit for holding an ordinary meeting of a Zilla Parishad?

(o) What is a 'Post Script'?

Ans. : (a) Page 8 (b) No (c) Page 25 (d) Page 350 (e) Page 75

(f) Page 324 (g) Page 94 (h) Page 325 (i) Page 162 (j) Page 326

(k) Page 165 (l) Page 172 (m) Page 131 (n) Page 125 (o) Page 331.

Group B

[Answer two questions]

Q. 2. "A Secretary is an advisor to management, an office executive and a liaison officer." — Discuss.

Ans. : Page 26.

Q. 3. Define Company Secretary. Discuss the position of a Company Secretary in the organisation.

Ans. : Pages 23 and 32.

Q. 4. Who is a Secretary of a Gram Panchayat? State his qualification. Discuss the functions of the Secretary of a Gram Panchayat.

Ans. : Pages 121-22.

Q. 5. What is your idea about the profession of Secretaryship? State the scope of such profession in our country.

Ans. : Page 29.

Group C

[Answer one question]

Q. 6. What is departmentation? Describe the main departments of a modern business.

Ans. : Page 58.

Q. 7. What do you mean by lay-out of an office? Discuss the factors to be taken into consideration while planning the lay-out of an office.

Ans. : Page 52.

Group D

[Answer one question]

Q. 8. (a) State the requisites of a valid meeting.

(b) Distinguish between a lawful meeting and an unlawful meeting.

Ans. : (a) Page 143 (b) Pages 143-44.

Q. 9. Explain any three of the following :

(a) Agenda.

(b) Adjournment of a meeting.

(c) Minutes.

(d) Poll.

(e) Casting vote.

Ans. : (a) Page 148 (b) Page 168 (c) Page 172 (d) Page 150 (e) Page 151.

Group E

[Answer two questions]

Q. 10. Draft the notice of the 12th Annual General Meeting of Ruma Industries Limited with usual agenda.

Ans. : Page 203.

Q. 11. As the Secretary of a company draft a report for submission to the Board of Directors on irregularity in attendance by some of the members of the staff and suggesting suitable measures for stopping this undesirable practice.

Ans. : Refer to page 236.

Q. 12. Draft the minutes of the meeting of a Zilla Parishad.

Ans. : Page 126.

Q. 13. Draft a letter to your customer requesting him to extend time for execution of order stating suitable reasons.

Ans. : Refer to pages 291-92.

1996

Group A

Q. 1. Answer any ten questions :

(a) Who is a Secretary?

(b) A Company has only two directors. Can one of them be appointed Secretary of the Company?

(c) How is the Secretary of a Panchayat Samiti appointed?

(d) What is an office?

(e) What is the difference between 'Post Book' and 'Book Post'?

(f) Mention four advantages of a 'Loose-leaf Register'.

(g) Why office equipments are often termed as labour-saving devices?

(h) What is meant by 'proper length of notice'?

(i) What is 'point of order'?

(j) What is the time limit for holding a Statutory Meeting?

(k) When can a member speak twice on the same primary motion?

(l) How can a resolution be passed without holding a meeting?

(m) Who can convene a meeting of a Zilla Parishad and what should be the quorum of such a meeting?

(n) Distinguish between a 'Circular' and a 'Notice'.

(o) What is a Status Enquiry?

Ans. : (a) Page 1 (b) No (c) Page 120 (d) Page 51 (e) Page 369 & 323

(f) Page 102 (g) Page 92 (h) Page 145 (i) Page 168 (j) Page 140.

(k) When the motion is seconded, it is said to be before the meeting and then the proposer is given an opportunity to fully express his view. This apart, the proposer or mover of the motion may be allowed to speak twice for further clarification of his views.

(l) Under Section 289 of the Companies Act, 1956, a resolution may be passed by the Board of Directors or its committee by circulation without holding any Board/Committee Meeting.

(m) Page 125 (n) Page (o) Pages 330 & 145.

Group B

[Answer any two questions]

Q. 2. Who is a Private Secretary? How does a Private Secretary differ from a Personal Assistant? State briefly the functions of a Private Secretary.

Ans. : Pages 4-6 and 7.

Q. 3. "A Company Secretary has no power of his own, yet he enjoys enough of it." —Discuss.

Ans. : Page 32.

Q. 4. State the functions of a Secretary of a Co-operative Society. Does he take part in the management of the Society?

Ans. : Page 8.

Q. 5. How is the Secretary of a Zilla Parishad appointed? State the duties to be performed by the Secretary of a Zilla Parishad.

Ans. : Page 119.

Group C

[Answer any one question]

Q. 6. Discuss the factors that should be taken into consideration while selecting the location of an office of a big mercantile firm.

Ans. : Page 51.

Q. 7. State the importance of filing. What are the principles of a good filing system?

Ans. : Pages 81 and 82.

Group D

[Answer any one question]

Q. 8. Discuss the various methods for ascertaining the sense of a meeting.

Ans. : Page 159.

Q. 9. Write Short notes on any three of the following :

(a) **Statutory Meeting.**

(b) **Amendment.**

(c) **Motion.**

(d) **Previous Question.**

(e) **Minutes of Narration.**

Ans. : (a) Page 140 (b) Page 154 (c) Page 152 (d) Page 168 (e) Page 175.

Group E

[Answer any two questions]

Q. 10. Draft the minutes of the 10th Annual General Meeting of Roy Industries Ltd., B.B.D. Bag, Calcutta 700001, held on 12.10.95 with usual items of business transacted at the meeting.

Ans. : Refer to page 209.

Q. 11. You have been asked by the Board of Directors of the company where you are working as Secretary to enquire into the causes of the steep fall in production of the Company and to suggest remedial measures.

Ans. : Pages 238-39.

Q. 12. Draft the notice of the first meeting of a Gram Panchayat with agenda.

Ans. : Page 133.

Q. 13. Draft a letter from Messrs. Ghosh Bros., Calcutta, to the Sales Manager, Silk Mills, Mumbai, requesting the latter to appoint them sole selling agent for their silk goods in the state of West Bengal.

Ans. : Refer to Q/Ans. No. 52, page 303 and try yourself.

Q. 14. Write a letter to a supplier cancelling an order due to failure to supply within a specified period and reserving the right to claim payment of difference in price, if any, arising out of purchase from other sources.

Ans. : Refer to Q/Ans. No. 32, page 284.

1997

Group A

Q. 1. Answer any ten questions :

(a) Is secretaryship a profession?

(b) Who is a Private Secretary?

(c) Is it compulsory for a Co-operative Society to appoint a full-time Secretary?

(d) Can a firm be appointed Secretary of a Company?

(e) Who appoints the Secretary of a Zilla Parishad?

(f) State the difference between a 'Motion' and a 'Resolution'.

(g) What is meant by Colour Conditioning?

(h) What is an Extra-ordinary General Meeting?

(i) What is 'Proxy' in respect to a meeting?

(j) What is a 'Personal Computer'?

(k) What is 'Card Index'?

(l) What is meant by 'Continuous Quorum'?

(m) What is a 'Circular Letter'?

(n) What is Panchayat Samiti?

(o) What is a 'Post Script'?

Ans. : (a) Page 29 (b) Page 2 (c) Page 9 (d) Page No. (e) Page 119
(f) Page 152 (g) Page 54 (h) Page 141 (i) Page 165 (j) Page 108
(k) Page 90 (l) Page 162 (m) Page 330 (n) Page 120 (o) Page 333.

Group B

[Answer any two questions]

Q. 2. Who is a Secretary? Discuss the role played by a Secretary as an office manager.

Ans. : Pages 23 and 27.

Q. 3. 'A Company Secretary is an advisor to the management, office executive and a liaison officer'. — Discuss fully.

Ans. : Pages 27-28.

Q. 4. (a) Why is the service of the Secretary necessary for a Gram Panchayat?

(b) State the duties to be performed by the Secretary of a Gram Panchayat.

Ans. : (a) Page 121 (b) Page 122.

Q. 5. (a) Why is a Private Secretary appointed?

(b) State the qualities which a Private Secretary should possess.

(c) Distinguish between a Private Secretary and a Company Secretary.

Ans. : (a) Page 2 (b) Page 4 (c) Pages 2 and 3.

Group C

[Answer any one question]

Q. 6. (a) What do you mean by 'layout' of an office?

(b) Discuss the factors necessary for planning the lay-out of an office.

Ans. : (a) Page 52 (b) Page 52.

Q. 7. (a) What is Indexing? State its importance.

(b) State the advantages and disadvantages of decentralised Filing System.

Ans. : (a) Page 88 (b) Page 83.

Group D

[Answer any one question]

Q. 8. (a) Who is the Chairman of a meeting? How is he appointed?

(b) State the powers of a Chairman in a meeting.

Ans. : (a) Page 149 (b) Page 150.

Q. 9. Write notes on any three of the following :

(a) Notice of a meeting;

(b) Disinterested Quorum;

(c) Pro-tem Chairman;

(d) Qualified Privilege;

(e) Agenda and Minutes.

Ans. : (a) Page 145 (b) Page 162 (c) Page 326 (d) Page 170 (e) Page 148 and172.

Group E

[Answer any two questions]

Q. 10. Draft the notice convening the 2nd Annual General Meeting of 'Zenith Industries Ltd.', Elgin Road, Calcutta 700020, with usual agenda.

Ans. : Page 203.

Q. 11. 'XY Printer' of Calcutta has received a bulk supply of papers from 'R Paper Syndicate' of Madhya Pradesh. The paper is of inferior quality. Write a letter of Complaint to the supplier and ask them to settle the deal by offering 10% discount on the price charged or make arrangement for taking back the papers supplied at their own cost.

Ans. : Refer to Q/Ans. No. 28, pages 280-81 & try yourself.

Q. 12. Draft a circular letter notifying increase in selling prices of 'tea' due to rise in cost and seeking continued patronage of the customers.

Ans. : Refer to Q/Ans. No. 22, page 251.

Q. 13. Draft a letter to the General Insurance Company reporting damage caused to your factory by fire and requesting immediate action for survey and settlement of the claim.

Ans. : Pages 301-302.

Q. 14. Draft a report to be submitted to the Board of Directors about the location of a new showroom proposed to be opened by the Company.

Ans. : Page 247.

1998

Group A

Q. 1. Answer any ten questions :

(a) Explain the significance of the term "Secretary".

(b) Under what circumstances can one person form a quorum?

(c) What is an Organisation Chart?

(d) What do you understand by Statutory Report of a company?

(e) What is "Certificate of Posting"?

(f) What is a Zilla Parishad?

(g) Mention any four of the labour-saving devices used in the office of a large corporate business enterprise.

(h) Name any four of the principal departments of the office of a business firm.

(i) What is a "motion" in relation to a meeting?

(j) How can a proxy be revoked?

(k) Enumerate a few basic rules for holding the meetings of a Gram Panchayat.

(l) What do you understand by Courier Service?

(m) What is meant by Modular Furniture?

(n) What is the significance of "Confirmation of Minutes" of a meeting?

(o) What is an "Annual Return"?

Ans. : (a) Page 1 (b) Page 163 (c) Page 63 (d) Page 194 (e) Page 68 (f) Page 124 (g) Page 92 (h) Page 63 (i) Page 152 (j) Page 165 (k) Page 120 (l) Page 70.

(m) **Modular Furniture :** The dictionary meaning of the term modular is 'constructed with the standardised units or dimensions for flexibility and variety in use'. Conceptually, modular refers to a rational grid system. Modular furniture may be made to have a horizontal as well as vertical grid designed on the basis of anthropometrics, office dynamics and service net-working. There is an option to add on or subtract from the existing furniture — both vertically and horizontally — depending on the actual need of the organisation. Though the initial cost is more than the standard furniture, modular furniture, ultimately, proves cheaper to the fast-growing organisations. (n) Page 174 (o) Page 200.

Group B

Q. 2. Discuss the essential qualifications of a Secretary.

Ans. : Page 24.

Q. 3. What are the different types of Secretary and what is the status of each type of Secretary?

Ans. : Page 1.

Q. 4. Discuss the functions of the Secretary of a Public Limited Company.

Ans. : Pages 26-28.

Q. 5. Discuss the duties and responsibilites of the Secretary of a Zilla Parishad or the Secretary of a Co-operative Society.

Ans. : Pages 118-19 or 8-10.

Group C

Q. 6. What are the advantages and disadvantages of centralisation or decentralisation of office servies?

Ans. : Pages 56-57.

Q. 7. Write short notes on any two of the following :

(a) Nature and importance of office environment;

(b) Factors influencing the choice of location of an office;

(c) Requisites of a good filing system;

(d) Importance of office to a business organisation.

Ans. : (a) Page 52 (b) Page 51 (c) Page 82 (d) Page 50.

Group D

Q. 2. Discuss the points you will take into consideration while drafting the notice of a meeting.

Ans. : Page 145.

Q. 3. Write short notes on any three of the following :

(a) Objects of holding the Annual General Meeting of a Company;

(b) Different kinds of Resolution;

(c) Kangaroo Closure;

(d) Point of order;

(e) Minutes of narration.

Ans. : (a) Page 140 (b) Page 152 (c) Page 178 (d) Page 168 (e) Page 175.

Group E

Q. 4. Draft the notice along with the agenda of the first meeting of the Board of Directors of a public limited company.

Ans. : Page 183.

Q. 5. Draft the Minutes of the tenth Annual General Meeting of a public limited company.

Ans. : Page 209.

Q. 6. Draft a circular letter to the shareholders of a public limited company informing them that the company will issue Bonus shares in the ratio of 2 : 1, and that the shares will be sent to them in due course.

Ans. : Refer to page 40 and write yourself.

Q. 7. As the Secretary of a developing business, draft a report addressed to its Chief Manager stating the advantages of installation of a computerised accounting system in the firm.

Ans. : Refer to Q/Ans. No. 16, page 244 and write yourself.

Q. 8. Draft a business letter to your customer drawing his/her attention to the expiry of the period of credit granted to him/her, and requesting him/her to settle the overdue account at an early date.

Ans. : Page 292.

1999

Group A

Q. 1. Answer any ten questions :

(a) Name the constituents of the three-tier system of panchayat.

(b) Who has the authority to appoint the secretary of the gram panchayat?

(c) When can the secretary of the company be dismissed without notice?

(d) Mention the different types of company meetings.

(e) How is 'office procedure' related to 'secretarial practice'?

(f) What is an office lay-out?

(g) Name four methods used in dictating letters.

(h) What do you mean by alpha-numerical system of filing?

(i) Why is cross-referencing useful?

(j) In what way is the franking machine a labour-saving device?

(k) When can the chairman adjourn a meeting?

(l) There was equality of votes 'in favour' and 'against' a motion. How can a decision be taken in this case?

(m) How can a proxy be revoked?

(n) How can a resolution be passed without holding a meeting?

(o) When is an extra-ordinary general meeting of a company held?

Ans. :	(a) Page 123	(b) Page 121	(c) Page 36	(d) Page 139	(e) Page 61
	(f) Page 52	(g) Page 75	(h) Page 324	(i) Page 83	(j) Page 325
	(k) Page 332	(l) Page 151	(m) Page 165	(n) Page 186	(o) Page 141.

Group B

Q. 2. (a) 'A private secretary is more than a good shorthand typist'—Discuss.

(b) 'A qualified and well-trained secretary is an asset to a limited company.' —Elucidate.

(c) Draft the resolution of the appointment of a secretary of a limited company.

Ans. : (a) Page 7 (b) Page 32 (c) Page 23.

Q. 3. (a) 'The position of the secretary of joint stock company is full of duties and responsibilities and not a sinecure one.' Discuss.

(b) Explain the nature of company secretary's liabilities. How can he be removed?

Ans. : (a) Page 32 (b) Pages 34 and 36.

Q. 4. Describe the various functions of a company secretary (a) before a meeting, (b) during a meeting and (c) after the meeting.

Ans. : Pages 30-31.

Q. 5. (a) What is a 'municipality?'

(b) How does it differ from a 'municipal corporation'?

(c) How is the secretary of a municipality appointed?

(d) What are the duties of the secretary of a municipality?

Ans. :

(a) While municipal corporations are established in big cities, municipalities are found in smaller cities and towns, e.g. Rajpur Municipality, Khardah Municipality, etc. Both the municipal corporations and municipalities are established under specific Acts passed by the State Governments. The members of a municipality are elected by the citizens of the town on the basis of adult franchise and secret ballot.

(b) Municipal corporations are established under the Act passed by the State Governments, viz. Mumbai Municipal Corporation Act, Calcutta Municipal Corporation Act, etc.

(c) Page 117 (d) Page 118.

Group C

Q. 6. (a) Distinguish between 'postponement' and 'adjournment' of a meeting.

(b) Explain the application of a 'closure' motion at a meeting.

(c) Discuss in brief two principal methods of ascertaining the sense of a meeting of a company.

(d) What document is to be consulted to ascertain the number of a valid quorum for a board meeting?

(e) Differentiate between a motion and a resolution.

Ans. : (a) Page 168 (b) Page 169 (c) Page 159 (d) Page 340 (e) Page 152.

Q. 7. Discuss the factors that should be taken into consideratkon while planning the layout of an office. How does an office layout influence the efficiency of office staff?

Ans. : Pages 52-53.

Group D

Q. 8. (a) What is a statutory report? What are its main contents?

(b) Enumerate the major provisions of the Companies Act, 1956, in respect of statutory meeting.

(c) What are the legal consequences if the statutory meeting is not held in time?

Ans. : (a) Page 194 (b) Page 140 (c) Page 140.

Q. 9. (a) State the principal contents of a directors' report.

(b) Discuss the nature of business conducted at a creditors' meeting of a company.

(c) Can an annual general meeting of a company be convened by a shorter notice? If so, when?

(d) What is the time limit for writing the minutes of a board meeting? Who should sign such minutes?

(e) When should the first annual general meeting of a company be held? What are the statutory limits for holding subsequent annual general meeting?

Ans. : (a) Page 242 (b) Page 141 (c) Page 333 (d) Page 172 (e) Page 140.

Group E

Q. 10. Draft the minutes of the 1st Annual General Meeting of J. P. Bagri Industries Ltd., 38 Ezra Street, Calcutta 700001 held on 12.10.98 with usual items of business transacted at the meeting.

Ans. : Write on the basis Q/Ans. No. 14, Pages 208-209.

Q. 11. Draft the notice of the first meeting of a gram panchayat with necessary agenda.

Ans. : Page 133.

Q. 12. Draft a letter to the company's bankers asking them to make enquiries as to the financial standing of a firm with which the company wishes to enter into a business contract.

Ans. : Pages 294-95.

Q. 13. A firm of stationery suppliers submits quotations for stationery articles in reply to an inquiry from a large office. Draft the letter of quotation.

Ans. : Pages 268-69.

Q. 14. Show the organisation structure of local self-government.

Ans. : The organisation chart of local self-government is also known as Panchayati Raj. Refer to page 122

THE UNIVERSITY OF CALCUTTA

B.Com. Examination : (New Syllabus)

2000

Part II

Group A

Q. 9. Answer any five questions :

(a) Who appoints the secretary of Company?

(b) Can a director be appointed as the secretary of a company of which he is the director?

(c) What is an organisation chart?

(d) What is meant by 'Continuing Quorum'?

(e) Can a company meeting be held with one member quorum?

(f) What is 'Point of Order'?

(g) Name four labour-saving machines.

(h) What is Courier Service?

Ans. : (a) Page 25 (b) Page 322 (c) Page 63 (d) Page 162 (e) Page 163 (f) Page 168 (g) Page 92 (h) Page 70.

10. Explain the function of the secretary of a co-operative society.

Ans. : Pages 8-10.

11. What is the usual procedure of handling incoming mails of a big organisation?

Ans. : Pages 73-74.

12. State the rights and duties of the Chairman of a meeting.

Ans. : Page 150.

Group B

[Answer any two questions]

13. Draft the minutes of the 6th Annual General Meeting of the Asian Sky Shop Ltd., Marine Drive, Mumbai.

Ans. : Page 209.

14. Draft the notice along with the agenda of the first Board Meeting of a limited company.

Ans. : Pages 188-89.

15. Draft a letter to your banker requesting them to grant your company a loan of Rs. 5,00,000 for which your company is ready to hypothecate machineries worth Rs. 10,00,000.

Ans. : Pages 299-300.

THE UNIVERSITY OF CALCUTTA

[illegible] Examination [illegible]

[illegible]

Paper [illegible]

Group [illegible]

9. Answer any [illegible] the questions:

(a) [illegible]

(b) [illegible]

(c) [illegible]

(d) Write [illegible]

[illegible]

(f) [illegible] Point of [illegible]

(g) [illegible]

(h) What [illegible]

Ans. [illegible]

10. Explain the function of [illegible]

Ans. [illegible]

11. What is the [illegible]

Ans. [illegible]

12. [illegible]

Ans. [illegible]

Group B

[illegible]

13. [illegible] of the [illegible]

[illegible]

Ans. [illegible]

14. [illegible]

[illegible]

Ans. [illegible]

15. [illegible]

[illegible]

Ans. [illegible]